ROYAL HISTORICAL SOCIETY
STUDIES IN HISTORY
SERIES
No. 39

T.P. O'CONNOR AND THE LIVERPOOL IRISH

Recent volumes published in this series include

For a complete list of the series please see pp. 303-4

T.P. O'Connor at the 1885 election

T.P. O'CONNOR AND THE LIVERPOOL IRISH

L.W. Brady

LONDON: Royal Historical Society
NEW JERSEY: Humanities Press Inc.
1983

The Society records its gratitude to the following,
whose generosity made possible the initiation of this
series: The British Academy; The Pilgrim Trust;
The Twenty-Seven Foundation; The United States
Embassy Bicentennial Funds; The Wolfson Trust;
several private donors.

The publication of this volume has been assisted by a
further grant from The Twenty-Seven Foundation.

British Library Cataloguing in Publication Data

Brady, L.W.
T.P. O'Connor and the Liverpool Irish.
(Royal Historical Society studies in history series; no. 39)
1. O'Connor, T.P.
2. Politicians – Ireland – Biography
3. Journalists – Ireland – Biography
I. Title   II. Series
941.081'092'4   DA958.05

First published in Great Britain in 1983 by Swift Printers (Publishing) Ltd, London EC1
for The Royal Historical Society
and in the U.S.A. by Humanities Press Inc., Atlantic Highlands, NJ 07716

Printed in England by Swift Printers Ltd, London EC1

For my mother and in memory of my father

CONTENTS

MAPS

PLATES

PREFACE

I do not want to present this book as a biography without at least suggesting that more is implied. Some of it derives from a doctoral thesis which I completed more than ten years ago. My aim has been to keep the book short. Lethargy is not the reason, nor even lack of interest, but because I hoped the point would come across more easily in a concentrated account. Perhaps, too, something has been gained in waiting and using some care about an investigation and reconstruction of a man's life. I have managed to retain a sympathy for the subject, but not, I hope, an excessive one, nor one which might prevent my placing T.P. O'Connor in context.

T.P. O'Connor played an important, though neglected, part in the development of Anglo-Irish relations in the late nineteenth and early twentieth centuries (from the rise of Parnell to the Anglo-Irish Treaty), and was during this time the chief spokesman for the Irish in Britain. He was also, and the conjunction is unusual, an entrepreneur who contributed considerably to the evolution of popular journalism; what he wrote was perhaps an encouragement to popular politics, though his example when looked at in detail was less certain in this respect. (As luck would have it, while this book was being prepared for the printer two books appeared which provide further background for O'Connor's life, Stephen Koss's, *The Rise and Fall of the Political Press in Britain, vol. 1, The Nineteenth Century* (1981) and P. J. Waller's *Democracy and Sectarianism: A Political and Social History of Liverpool 1868-1939* (Liverpool, 1981)). How a life could encompass all these things has been what has interested me, how they existed alongside each other in any one span of time. In addition, such a periodic emphasis seems a fair way to represent the lives of Irishmen in the nineteenth century, of T.P. O'Connor specifically. If it is fatalistic, this was the way many Irishmen lived, and such was the attitude and customary mood of O'Connor. But, as it affects the framework which follows, this has also meant that the treatment is sometimes less strictly chronological than might appear at first sight because some overlap, or reference forward or back was necessary for comparison or exposition. The first chapter is introductory, and brings in not only the main character, but also his colleagues and fellow migrants, a chorus; the second sees the politician in action from 1880, the third brings out some themes for the Victorian period. The chapters which remain look at politics (both national and local), letters, and journalism in tandem, or sometimes in *troika* for long periods of O'Connor's lifetime because I hope that by that stage the variety of O'Connor's life has been established. It is a diverse, furiously energetic, and occasionally enigmatic life which is followed here; to parcel it up is not to say that this is exactly how it was lived, but the result may give depth and meaning to the unexpectedness of experience, or the unthinking reaction against experience.

L.W.B.
Liverpool
April 1983

ACKNOWLEDGEMENTS

I would like to thank Professor D.B. Quinn for his guidance and encouragement when he supervised the research work for my thesis, and I am grateful to Professor R. Dudley Edwards for his work as external examiner and for the helpful comments he made. The staffs of many libraries were generous with their assistance and I would also like to acknowledge permission to consult and quote from copyright material held by: the British Library Department of Manuscripts, and Newspaper Library; Professor John Dillon (the Dillon papers); the Sydney Jones Library, University of Liverpool; the National Library of Ireland; the National Library of Scotland; the university library, Trinity College Dublin; the University of Sheffield Library (the Mundella papers); Mr. A.J. P. Taylor on behalf of the Beaverbrook Foundation and the House of Lords Record Office (the Lloyd George papers). Thanks are also due to the Bodleian Library; the library of Unversity College Galway; Professor R. Lawton; the Humanities Library and the Inter-Library Loans Unit of Liverpool Polytechnic; Liverpool Record Office; Father Matthew Hall branch library, Athlone; Manchester Central Library; Mrs. Jameson Parker; the Royal Irish Academy; the State Paper Office, Dublin Castle; and Mr. E.P.M. Wollaston. My apologies must go to any individuals whose help I have overlooked, and to copyright holders who I may have omitted here, or have been unable to trace. In locating genealogical material for the O'Connor and Power families, I received the help of Mrs. E. O'Byrne of Dublin, Canon E.H.L. May of Athlone, the National Army Museum, and the Public Record Office. I am grateful to Mrs. J. Godden of the Royal Historical Society for her painstaking advice, and to Miss S. Watson for the care and patience with which she worked on the final typescript. The maps, and the table on p. 264, were drawn by Mr. A. Hull, Lecturer in Geography at Liverpool Polytechnic. Plate 4 and the *Frontispiece* appear by permission of the BBC Hulton Picture Library and plates 1, 2 and 3, by permission of the British Library. Finally, I would like to thank my colleague Mr. R.E. Morley for his assistance and, not least, the taxpayers for the research grant which began the whole endeavour.

ABBREVIATIONS

B.L.	British Library
B.L.P.	British Library of Political and Economic Science
D.P.	*Liverpool Daily Post*
E.H.R.	*English Historical Review*
F.J.	*Freeman's Journal*
H.L.	House of Lords Record Office
I.H.S.	*Irish Historical Studies*
J.H.R.U.	*Journal of the Home Rule Union*
L.R.O.	Liverpool Record Office
Memoirs	T.P. O'Connor, *Memoirs of an old Parliamentarian* (2 vols., 1929)
M.G.	*Manchester Guardian*
N.L.I.	National Library of Ireland
N.L.S.	National Library of Scotland
P.M.G.	*Pall Mall Gazette*
P.R.O.	Public Record Office
R.N.	*Reynolds's Newspaper*
S.P.O.	State Paper Office, Dublin Castle
T.C.D.	Trinity College Dublin, Library
T.H.S.L.C.	*Transactions of the the Historic Society of Lancashire and Cheshire*

1

STAGE-STRUCK APPRENTICES, 1848-1880

In O'Connor's youth and early manhood there were, alongside the commonplace business of 'getting on', signs of great ability, in scholarship, in a sensitivity towards literature, and in his own creative writing, which might lead him in any one of a variety of directions. The choice of politics was, if only in retrospect, a narrowing, and perhaps an unfortunate one. To some extent in his youth, and increasingly thereafter, O'Connor's life had a theme only in a very general or oblique way. After the striving and the ambitions which he had, or which were set out before him in his young days, his breadth of interest marked him out from the more dedicated or ideological of his colleagues in the Irish parliamentary movement, and they frequently noticed the difference. Politics at Westminster was one life, perhaps the one he enjoyed most (though in later life he often denied this, possibly for effect), and this activity sustained him elsewhere. But his other interests sometimes seemed to create separate lives, in which he was tribune of the people, or a creator of newspapers (a particular puzzle to his political friends). At the other extreme, there were the times when he appeared in the guise of a writer, introspective, finding his material worrisome and elusive, and taking little personal satisfaction in his popular successes. Here he ultimately claimed to regret his lack of concentration, perhaps his loss of vision. Possibly he would have been dismayed at the idea of a search for a theme in his life. His well-developed appreciation of individual psychology, seen especially in his studies of Disraeli and Parnell, involved his reaching out for signs of development or meaning in their lives. But his own life was a different matter, too much was accident. His attempt to put his memories into shape was not successful.[1] On a literary level, it could be that his career as a controversialist destroyed his grasp of the deeper meanings of history, and his memoirs are preoccupied with unrelated surface events. But old age, illness, and perhaps most of all disillusion, played a part. Between the young man and the old there was a long life in politics which had meant adopting a public face, more of a struggle for O'Connor than for most 'born' politicians. While it is remarkable just how little he became hardened, he did sometimes indulge in blandness, and he could be evasive. And he did no more than hint, though very frequently, at his disappointments:

[1] For a list of O'Connor's principal works see the bibliography.

they were too powerful to explore. Looking back, his youth, growing up in the midlands of Ireland, following journalism as a reporter in Dublin, and then more haphazardly in Fleet Street in the 1870s, was something which he found almost impossible to recapture, and some of its optimism had become foreign to his nature. He was also, despite his interest in biography (for that very reason aware of how much the written word could search and test), sensitive about his privacy. This was not overcome in the biography which appeared five years after his death, and in which the interviews he had given conceal as much as they disclose.[2] Not that there was much to hide. His background was modest and he was not ashamed of it; sometimes when the political occasion required it he exaggerated the extent of his deprivation. But this was not something he wanted analysed; just a suggestion of social unease. If the only justification for examining someone's youth is that this is where most of the explanations are found, O'Connor might, perhaps unnecessarily, have feared he would have to go too deep.

Circumstances, or history, mean that O'Connor, like many Irishmen of the middle and later nineteenth century, gives the impression of being acted on, not, for all his initiative, being able to act decisively. Other Irishmen, including those who lived in Britain, would not for their part, have relished being lumped together, with or without O'Connor. To the outsider they were undifferentiated, to themselves they were, obviously, individuals, or at the least strongly marked off into families. Yet O'Connor became the one single parliamentary representative for the Irish in Britain. Though he was first elected to parliament for Galway City in 1880, he then became the M.P. for Liverpool Scotland division in 1885, and he was to remain the M.P. for this constituency for the next forty years, until his death in 1929. Such an enduring relationship was one of the few consistent features in O'Connor's life. Paradoxically, to us now, the fortunes of the migrant community may appear of more interest than the career of one politician, however talented. But the beginnings of an explanation of the psychology of these exiled voters must take into account that they seemed themselves to prefer the particular to the general, the person of O'Connor and the familiar cause he exemplified, rather than a more abstract campaign of social protest, justified as the latter might have been. Whether they were deluded through such an attachment is a matter for some speculation, but O'Connor's hold over his isolated Liverpool constituency demonstrated how Irishmen wanted to share in his reflected ability, and it had the added bonus of asserting their individuality against British party machines. Such

[2]Hamilton Fyfe, *T.P. O'Connor* (1934).

associations have been a widespread feature of popular politics and perhaps it was an old fashioned response even in 1885. So marked was it in O'Connor's case, at least until the turn of the century when complaints and rivals became more noticeable in Liverpool, that one perennial critic claimed that the constituency was more complaisant than a constituency in Ireland would have been.

So confident was O'Connor that he often avoided his constituency and his constituents. Some of this was no doubt due to a generally acceptable social wariness somewhat short of snobbery; his fellow countrymen in Liverpool were usually poor and, apart from their respect for well-expressed extremism in politics, they had a fearsome reputation for unruliness. At the same time, in his public manner, O'Connor did preserve a reputation for approachability, or 'sympathy', and this accounts for much of his popularity. He was not expected to be in constant attendance in Liverpool; matters of great importance to Home Rule could be said to have kept him at a distance. Some such consideration was evident in how O'Connor came to be chosen for Liverpool. He appears to have made his first visit as a politician to Liverpool in August 1882 to attend the annual conference of the Home Rule League organized for Britain. Even then he was a major attraction. By 1885, through hard work, as a result of the radical causes he championed in and out of parliament, and most of all in how he appealed to the imagination through his inspiration, wit, and occasional anger, he was the best choice to lead the political movement in Britain. To look at O'Connor at the outset in relation to his fellow countrymen and future constituents in Liverpool helps to illustrate the conscious choice that was everywhere apparent in late Victorian politics. But it also gives a depth of perspective, their shared experience of their adopted country, imperfectly realised at the time, which was a comparison O'Connor might not have recognized, but which may have turned out to be a major intractable circumstance of his career. It is not merely convenient to claim that O'Connor gained in stature through his, admittedly intermittent, relationship with the poorest of his fellow countrymen, and that they gained their voice through his life.

Early Life and Radicalism, Athlone, Dublin, London

O'Connor and his political contemporaries were often aware of their part in a drama: his background and upbringing contributed to the depth of his sensitivity to social and political nuance. It is difficult to trace Irish family trees with any precision, but O'Connor appears to have come out of what might be called the shopkeeper class. Recent studies of Britain in the mid-Victorian period have paid a great deal of attention to the twin pillars of popular politics, the shopkeepers and the artisans. This needs some modification in the case of Ireland, and perhaps O'Connor's family was slightly out of the ordinary in the considerable emphasis they put on respectability and ambition, helped as it was by their son's early signs of ability. Thomas Power O'Connor was born on 5 October 1848 in the town of Athlone in the midlands of Ireland, baptized plain Thomas. He was the first child of Teresa O'Connor and her husband Thomas who was a shopkeeper, the owner of a billiard saloon, though referred to in a hostile Dublin Castle document as a 'billiard marker'.[3] The family name of O'Connor's mother was Power, hence the middle name he assumed later in life, sometime before he entered university. Not only did his name now sound more impressive, the addition bore witness to his mother's pride of family and to her influence on his early life and ambitions, not an unusual occurrence in an Irish family where an eldest son is concerned (though O'Connor saw the matter differently and tended to point out the family responsibilities he soon had to bear). O'Connor had three younger sisters, Teresa, born in 1850, Eleanor Julia, born in 1852, and Mary (probably baptised Anastasia) born in 1859. In his recollections he mentions only two sisters, and only Mary by name, so one sister may have died in infancy. In addition, he had a younger brother Jack, baptised John Joseph, born in 1854.[4]

There is not a great deal of information about O'Connor's parents, and O'Connor did not add much comment, a reticence which is unremarkable. Perhaps he underestimated his father, portraying him as something of a simple soul and part of the landscape of a vanished Ireland. There was an account, for instance, of his father thinking nothing of walking the distance from Dublin to Athlone in his youth. Perhaps this picture is superficial and merely shows the distance placed by convention between Irish fathers and their children as well as suggesting how far O'Connor travelled from his own origins, coming to regard them as more modest than they were. More was made of his mother's connections, but O'Connor was ambivalent here also, and they are still not completely clear. Teresa Power has been variously described as the daughter of an officer, or a non-commissioned officer in the 88th, the Connaught Rangers. The

---

[3] S.P.O., Police and Crime Records 1850-1920. The report on O'Connor is given in Appendix A.

[4] St. Peter's, Athlone, baptismal record, which also gives the baptism of O'Connor on 7 October 1848.

evidence appears to suggest that her father was Thomas Power, a colour sergeant, originally a weaver from Waterford, discharged from the army in 1830 and probably settling in Athlone, which was a garrison town, although there remains a remote possibility that O'Connor's ancestor was the one officer who fits the bill, which would be all the more remarkable since the officer would probably have been a Protestant. O'Connor was proud of this relationship, or at least listed it in *Dod's Parliamentary Companion*, perhaps sometimes he had, equally, to play it down in his days as a nationalist; but otherwise he made no more reference to his mother than he did to his father.[5] There remains the fact that there was some relationship or influence coming from his father or mother which was to help him in his career, as events were to show.

More obviously such a family background suggests modest means but some social standing and respectability. All O'Connor's family were townspeople and they may have had more in common with the self-improving population of urban Britain than with the less easily defined life of rural Ireland. There were a number of O'Connors recorded as tradespeople in Athlone who may have been relations, and O'Connor's parents appear to have been slightly more prosperous than the average. His parents owned, or more probably rented, a substantial terraced house with out offices and a yard, all rated at £21 a year, well above the average. This was in the centre of Athlone in Castle Street, opposite the army barracks. By 1854 this property also appears to have lodged the billiard saloon (and the entry for the family at this address in the local directory persists up to 1891), although earlier, in 1846 and before O'Connor's birth, the billiard saloon had been located in Market Place. The impression is of hard-working people, frugal with some social aspirations. His father was said to have sometimes found it a struggle to pay for his son's education, but on the other hand he always paid a handsome fee for his children's baptisms (10 shillings, or four times the usual fee), and by 1879, probably with his son's financial assistance, he was listed in the town directory as a billiard table manufacturer as well as a billiard room keeper. His father was also described, by O'Connor, as a teetotaller, a discipline O'Connor himself seems to have acquired. There may have been wilder spirits in the family because his younger brother Jack became a victim of drink and O'Connor attributed it to some hereditary trait.[6]

[5]Fyfe, p. 15; Army Lists 1810-1814 in National Army Museum records and P.R.O.; Soldiers' Documents, Chelsea Hospital Out Pensioners in the Connaught Rangers in the P.R.O; *Who's Who of British Members of Parliament*, vol. III, 1919-1945, ed. M. Stenton, p. 628. For a fuller account of the genealogical material see the bibliography.

[6]Fyfe, p. 324, p. 21.

Earning a living in the town was a difficult business, and a distinction between the town and its far from prosperous hinterland cannot be carried too far. Athlone, situated in the midlands of Ireland, about Ireland's mid point, was the chief border town between the provinces of Leinster to the east and Connaught to the west. It was a small town, by British standards at least, with a population of only 6,400 in 1851 and even this was declining. The town was very much influenced by its rural setting and by an overwhelmingly rural economy. The main business of the town (or the most stable, because politics occasionally brought a windfall) was in the carrying trade between Dublin and the west. There was in addition some consumer manufacturing, and some income was obtained from the army barracks, and a military works near the town. In such an environment a billiard saloon might not have been a particularly lucrative venture. O'Connor must have been thinking of his own family when he wrote of Irish townspeople that they were 'consumed by mean cares, by the bitter struggle to keep up appearances, by climbing up the ever climbing wave of pecuniary embarrassment, in towns where the years bring dwindling population, decreasing trade, more hopeless effort'.[7] Daily life cannot have been continually as solemn as O'Connor recollected it; the family billiard saloon may have been a centre of a kind of urbanity, possibly a haunt of soldiers, and an early glimpse for O'Connor of a more raffish side of life. Because of the very proximity of the countryside, the struggle to keep the town's identity may have been all the more determined. But it was a vocation which did not captivate O'Connor and he did not display much affection for his home town, preferred to be identified as coming from the west of Ireland, and he had a greater fondness for Galway city where his uncle's family lived (though whether they were O'Connors or Powers is not revealed). Midlands towns in Ireland have had a reputation for provincialism and small-mindedness. Whether this is deserved or not, O'Connor did his best to further the impression. 'Who but an Irishman', he asked for instance, 'can know the full hopelessness of a youth born in the lower middle class of an Irish country town?'[8] Such an attitude, an exaggerated one, was a further reason why he might not have wanted to dwell on the details of his upbringing. Nevertheless, one important political consequence of his early experience was that although O'Connor's family was not far removed, in our eyes, from the tenant farming class, and although he championed their cause when duty demanded it, he was never himself closely identified with the 'agrarian' element in the Parnellite struggle. Because of the

---

[7] *The Parnell Movement* (1886), p. 100.
[8] *Ibid.* p. 100.

slightly more diverse prospects of town life, and then an awareness of its restrictions, he was prepared for a wider view. Early in his career he championed the agricultural labourers in Ireland, a group that was otherwise easily overlooked, and he was to have closer contacts with the radicals of London (as well as with the more cosmopolitan aspects of the capital) than any other member of his political party.

Another feature of O'Connor's town, its politics, had some negative though scarcely long-lasting effects on his outlook. In its exposure to politics an upbringing in Athlone in the middle years of the nineteenth century was a dispiriting experience. The borough had returned one M.P. to Westminster since the Act of Union with Britain. If the population of the borough was small, the electorate was tiny and diminishing: it amounted to 243 after the 1832 Reform Act, 181 in 1851, and, in 1868 after the second Reform Act, stood at only 318, the total population of the town then being just over 6,100.[9] As has been indicated, a sizeable income was derived by the townspeople from money that changed hands at elections. While recent investigations have shown that influence, treating, and outright bribery were not uncommon in small boroughs throughout the British Isles, it is possible that a zest for politics which broke the tedium of town life, and the lack of opportunity elsewhere, made this aspect of public affairs more noticeable in Ireland. At any rate, irrespective of party or religious feeling, it was generally acknowledged that the best candidate for Athlone was 'the man that leaves the money in the town'.[10]

What made Athlone all the more notorious was O'Connor's own outraged testimony, which remains one of the main first hand accounts. His distaste was, at least as he recollected it, all the greater because between 1847 and 1856 the seat was held by William Keogh who was accused of destroying the independent Irish party of the 1850s when he accepted office as Solicitor General for Ireland in Aberdeen's coalition government in December 1852. O'Connor devoted a considerable amount of diatribe to Keogh's career and this now seems almost like a family quarrel. When Keogh was raised to the Bench in 1856 Athlone was up for grabs, but then usually returned one of the Ennis family who had gained their wealth locally

[9]*McCalmont's Parliamentary Pollbook*, p. 9; C. R. Dod. *Electoral Facts, 1832-1853*, pp. 10-11.

[10]Athlone was one of the eight Irish boroughs with an electorate of under 500 and these were all abolished in the Redistribution Act of 1885. See also H.J. Hanham, *Elections and Party Management* (1959), pp. 39-67 and C. O'Leary, *The Elimination of Corrupt Practices in British Elections* (1962), pp. 129-30; *Parnell Movement*, p. 90.

8

in trade and who usually described themselves as Liberals.[11] None of this would have pleased an idealist, or even convinced a man of few means that the way into politics was particularly accessible or attractive. At first sight, it is difficult to see how anyone growing up in the Ireland of the 1850s and 1860s, a country recovering from the Famine and uncertain and divided in its politics, could ever be attracted to parliamentary politics. Some did turn instead to Fenianism, but parliamentary politics remained the kind most likely to appeal to self-made men, or those who had risen through education. In addition the unsatisfactory state of Irish politics – corrupt boroughs for instance – could be a convenient target for new and more radical politicians, and the change when it did come attracted the likes of William O'Brien, T.M. Healy and, more latterly, O'Connor, to Parnell. They would accept and implement Parnell's determined control of constituency organization.

But O'Connor's upbringing was not in any specific way a preparation for a political career. His strictures on Athlone were the product of more mature reflection. He may have grown up absorbing an atmosphere of distaste for William Keogh or alternatively he may have felt guilty about his father's preferences, for it is more than possible that O'Connor's family was more closely involved in Athlone politics than he has suggested. O'Connor showed less sign of precocious nationalism than other Parnellites. What his education does reveal is self-sacrifice on his parents part, and determination and ability on his own. Except for when he stayed with his cousins in Galway City (more congenial to him than Athlone), and where he appears to have attended the local National School, O'Connor spent his boyhood and youth in Athlone where he attended the College of the Immaculate Conception. The college was some way outside the town and O'Connor seems to have been a full boarder, thus perhaps not being subject to the full influence of provincial town life. School routine was repressive and emphatically academic, typical of that Irish Catholic puritanism which has frequently been described by emigrés, but which was perhaps not less enlightened than much English schooling of the period. No description of O'Connor as a boy remains, except a stereotype. It is likely that he was observant, sensitive (acutely aware of his relative poverty), but at the same time robust in constitution and outlook, guaranteed the certainties of an eldest son.

---

[11] *Who's Who of British M.P.s*, vol. I, pp. 128-9; for Keogh see O'Connor's *Parnell Movement* under 'The Great Betrayal' and his *Memoirs of an Old Parliamentarian* (1929) where he included an Appendix on 'The Treachery of William Keogh'.

In 1863 he was enrolled at Queen's College, Galway, and was joined for a time by his parents, brother, and sisters. This was an attempt to limit expense and staked a great deal on his future career. Finances may have been eased slightly when he won a scholarship in the Literary Division of the college at the end of his first year (though any financial terms are unclear this could have been the prize of £40 which it is recorded he turned over to his parents). As additional evidence that his early promise was not eclipsed in a more adult atmosphere is the fact that even F.H. O'Donnell, another future Irish parliamentarian who was O'Connor's senior at Galway (and who never distributed praise gladly), remarked on O'Connor's ability, especially in debate. In 1866, when he was eighteen, O'Connor became Senior Scholar in History and Modern Languages at the college, and this was also the year in which he graduated.[12] He was now the chief hope and support of his family, a long-term duty since his father was still alive in 1891 and his mother probably lived even longer into old age, though it is not clear when either of them died. O'Connor did not appear to find this responsibility onerous, or not at first when he still lived in Ireland. But it remained a weight on him at least up to the late 1870s when he began to make some success for himself in England. He always acknowledged his parents' sacrifices, but perhaps failed to realize that he had had a better start than many Englishmen. In his study *The Parnell Movement*, he insisted that poor Irishmen hoping to be able to enter the professions had to have the 'luck to live in a town with a Queen's College'.[13] Yet O'Connor had not originally done so; his family had arranged for him to live in Galway and may have given up their home and business in Athlone, if only temporarily, in order to help him. This again was more assistance than might have been forthcoming from family life in England. Then, although some years of uncertainty followed in Ireland, they were neither so lasting nor so worrisome as O'Connor and his biographer have suggested.

Scholastic ability notwithstanding, the choice of career open to O'Connor was not a wide one. Any young man starting out in the Ireland of the 1860s would have faced a difficult prospect. A career in the Church was not a serous consideration, despite what has been surmised. If such an ambition did occur to O'Connor's parents, they had surprisingly few qualms about sending him to one of the Queen's Colleges, which had been condemned by an episcopal synod at

[12]F.H.O. O'Donnell, *A History of the Irish Parliamentary Party* (1910), i, 319; Calendar of University College, Galway, entries for 1863-4, 1866-7.

[13]*Parnell Movement*, p. 101. There is no record of a will for Thomas O'Connor in the Probate Calendars 1891-1916.

Thurles in 1850, shortly after their foundation, as a danger to faith and morals. In the 1860s they might still have raised a few clerical eyebrows.[14] In short, there is nothing in O'Connor's recollections – in his writings generally or in his life – to suggest that the Church ever figured in his early ambitions. On the contrary, he quickly gained a reputation in his first year in England for anti-clericalism, if not atheism. And this in its turn was no sign of an inverted religiosity, he was no *prêtre manqué*. There was little that was ascetic in O'Connor's character; his radicalism turned him against religion (somewhat in the French manner). Some degree of intellectual detachment from the Church may already have been apparent, open disbelief was for the future. Only in old age and as an elder statesman did he and the clergy allow each other some toleration, and even this may have been entirely a matter of public policy.

O'Connor's first attempt to gain preferment, which came close to home, was not a success. He approached the sometime M.P. for Athlone on his father's advice (which suggests that the family had quickly come back to the midlands after O'Connor's graduation). This was Sir John Ennis the elder of Ballinahoen Court. Ennis had been defeated in the Athlone contest in 1865, and the seat was not regained by his son until 1868. O'Connor and his father thought that Ennis could nominate him for an examination in the civil service (such nomination being the practice both in Britain and in Ireland at that time). Perhaps Ennis had some political favour to return to O'Connor senior. The probability is that he was a voter in Athlone (O'Connor implied as much). The 1832 £10 household franchise was a high one when applied to Ireland, and the household franchise remained more restricted compared to Britain even when it was cut to £8 in 1850, but the family house was rated at £21.[15] Certainly a vote was a qualification worth some sacrifice, and in addition O'Connor's father may have had some minor part to play in the routine of political persuasion as the proprietor of a billiard saloon. Some political or family influence was at work with Ennis, though equally it was not unreasonable to ask for support for a local candidates of outstanding ability. Yet influence also played a part in O'Connor's first regular job, in Dublin, and his first employment in Fleet Street. Lobbying of friends and relatives was usual in Ireland (and is not unknown today everywhere) but the impression remains that more was involved here; perhaps family influence through the Powers, or political influence

[14]Fyfe, p. 25. For the Queen's Colleges see J.C. Beckett, *The Making of Modern Ireland* (1966), p. 331.

[15]*Parnell Movement*, p. 90; *Griffith's Valuation of Co. Westmeath* (1854). There are no pollbooks for Athlone.

through his father. Whatever the influence involved, O'Connor's interview with Ennis was not a success. His excuse for not helping was simply that he was no longer an M.P. It is difficult to believe, as O'Connor's biographer maintains, that O'Connor and his father were so innocent of the ways of the world and of politics that they had not foreseen this objection. This may increase the possibility that they believed Ennis had some special obligation which meant that he would still try to use his good offices. Perhaps O'Connor made a bad impression, and he certainly left with a poor view of Ennis whom he still remembered thirty-five years later as 'the worst type of snob, the Irish snob', a weakness on Ennis's part that may have been encouraged by the fact that he had only come into the baronetcy in 1866.[16]

Nevertheless O'Connor appears to have had an essentially good opinion of himself which caused him to be impatient with the early lack of opportunity. Since he lived in an intensely competitive society such an attitude was necessary for survival, and as it is the other side of ambition it is customarily overlooked. O'Connor had taken some pains to prepare himself beyond the academic training he had received at Galway. In his last year at the college he had learned shorthand and had used this to obtain work as a government note-taker. This work took him from Galway to other unspecified parts of Ireland where, so his biographer claims, he came across religious or political animosities such as he had not encountered either in Athlone or in Galway. O'Connor said that this opened his eyes, but that he never himself shared in this sort of animosity. Once again the suggestion is that O'Connor, at least in his early days, was an innocent in politics. But his later career does tend to indicate that he shared few of the orthodox prejudices of his countrymen, and remarkably few of the prejudices of his age. In escaping from the former, he could more easily criticize the latter. Other Irish exiles, especially those in a literary walk of life, have shown the same ability. What remains slightly unusual is his work as a government note-taker at this time. This meant that he went round the country as a minor agent of the Dublin Castle administration, attending trials and possibly public meetings and making a record. It was out of the ordinary for a future nationalist, but not unprecedented.

Something similar can be said about O'Connor's first regular employment in journalism. This was with the Dublin *Saunders' Newsletter*, and O'Connor must have moved to the city in 1867

---

[16]Fyfe, p. 13; *Who's Who of British M.P.s*, vol. I, p. 129. See also *Parnell Movement*, pp. 100-11. O'Connor gave this description of the interview in about 1902.

because he witnessed the Manchester Martyrs' procession in Dublin which occurred in that year. The time of uncertainty after graduation was therefore not of any great duration and hardly compared to the hardships he had to face in his first years in England. In gaining this employment family influence was at work. His father, so it was said, was acquainted with the family who owned the newspaper. This was curious because the *Saunders' Newsletter* was, as O'Connor admitted 'a good old stout, State and Church full-blown Protestant organ', and had been so since at least the 1820s when it had received a secret service grant from Dublin Castle.[17] Perhaps, once again, his father was not altogether the unsophisticated soul he was made out to be, or the influence may have lain elsewhere in the family.

The job was no sinecure. O'Connor was hired on approval and then given a salary of £2 a week with which to provide for his brother and his two sisters, who had joined him in the city. Yet he recalled that the period he spent in Dublin, between 1867 and 1870, was one of the happiest in his life. A reporter's life was an arduous one, but it was not oppressive. While it did have its sordid side in the reporting of the law courts or domestic tragedies it was a diverse and diverting occupation, replete with temptations (usually summed up by O'Connor and others under 'drink') and, even in Dublin, it was a strongly competitive occupation, and one not sure of its social acceptability. All this O'Connor took in his stride and there was little sign of the sort of introspection he sometimes projected back on his earliest days. Neither is there much evidence of a radical or a nationalist in these early years in Dublin. O'Connor could show sympathy for a condemned Fenian, was impressed by the Manchester Martyrs' demonstration, and angered by a sadistic official he encountered in the Crown Prosecution Office; he was equally annoyed by the spectacle of Judge William Keogh walking abroad in the city. He could add that his work sometimes required him 'to attend meetings where every utterance was opposed to my idea of right and wrong', presumably Unionist meetings which had the sympathy of his employers.[18] But most of his views at this time were still undeveloped, and the occasional ideological difficulty merely illustrates that journalists could be expected to work for a newspaper irrespective of its political opinions.

In 1870 O'Connor left Dublin to try his luck in Fleet Street. He was never again to live permanently in Ireland. This exile of the

[17]Fyfe, p. 30; J.A. Reynolds, *The Catholic Emancipation Crisis in Ireland* (1954), pp. 76-7.

[18]Interview with O'Connor in *P.M.G.*, 16 Jan. 1888.

subsequent leader of the Irish in Britain caused him to be regarded in future years as not typical of Irishmen, and yet not concerned about being accepted as an Englishman. Those he led in Britain tended to share the same characteristics, with an equanimity that was possible so long as Ireland remained part of a larger British identity and while other questions of nationality remained unresolved. Looking back, O'Connor's attitude towards Ireland, for all his protestations of affection and insight, was detached. For instance, in his work, *The Parnell Movement* he gave an account of nationalism which was partly the political history of Ireland in his own life time (since the fall of O'Connell), and partly a collection of short biographies of men similar to himself who had joined Parnell. Like most of O'Connor's work, it still reads well, even though he was arguing a case. This case was that the emergence of Parnellite nationalism could be understood in the language of British politics, and was a natural response to history. His tone was generally a cool one, his portrayal of Ireland objective. Even when referring to the Famine he was detached, though he tried to suggest a close personal involvement, as in the passage, 'In my boyhood there were plenty of middle-aged men who had lived through the Famine and seen it at close hand. From the stories I heard from their lips I was able to get a more vivid picture of what the Famine really meant than in all the hours I spent over the study of events.'[19] Early on, perhaps, O'Connor was aware of the susceptibilities of the British reading public whose views he often shared and from whom he derived his living. He was informative, looking at Ireland from the outside.

O'Connor was not ashamed of his background: frequently in later life he ascribed to the *petit bourgeoisie*, out of which he said he came, the natural genius denied to his political opponents among the aristocracy.[20] But it was all a generalization. He came to regard the Ireland of his boyhood and youth in something of a fixed light, as part of 'an Irish life that was centuries old but which soon after [the 1890s] ceased to exist'.[21] This Ireland was summed up, so O'Connor believed, in the works of Somerville and Ross. O'Connor became more cosmopolitan (as is shown by his liking for these writers who were the bane of sterner Irish nationalists), and by the turn of the century and up to the first world war he became somewhat impatient of Ireland, sceptical, and hard-headed. At the same time the years of

[19] *Memoirs*, i, 79.

[20] See chapter 5, p. 201.

[21] Mark Sullivan, *The Education of an American* (1938), p. 7. He also said that the Irish were 'just God Damn Rotarians now' (*ibid.* pp. 7-8). This passage also indicates that O'Connor had some talent as a mimic and comic performer.

exile meant that, although he never lost touch with political events in Ireland, his familiarity with their resonance or consequences diminished. The final collapse of the Home Rule movement, and the success of republicanism was therefore in many ways a surprise to O'Connor, and part of his personal misfortune. To the failure of his political ideals can be traced the major reason for his cursory treatment of his early years in Ireland.

O'Connor's memoirs begin with his coming to London in 1870 and this is a justified emphasis because it was from then on that he came closer to politics and this was the prelude to his intense political activity during the 1880s. These years made him a radical, something of a break with his conformist background and then, by 1885, brought him firmly within the Parnellite movement, though the latter development was more of an accident than might at first be supposed. Although O'Connor provided enough ambition and enterprise, events appeared to run away with him, and he often seemed to lack foresight. This may be the common fate of men from modest backgrounds who aim high (or of men of ability caught in a subordinated country), but O'Connor did not, at first at least, show even that he was guided by his wits. It could be that this is what led him in his reminiscences to accuse himself of ingenuousness. For instance, in remembering his time on the *Saunders' Newsletter* he said that he failed to see the opportunity to advance himself.[22] Yet after only three years work in Dublin he went to London, with apparently no promise of employment and with hardly any savings. This can be regarded either as foolhardy or as a necessary risk, but it also shows that when the occasion seemed right, or when impatience overcame the immersion in hard work, O'Connor had his sights on more than an influential post in provincial journalism.

There is yet another puzzle associated with family or other influence here. Although O'Connor's search for work in Fleet Street may have been a desperate one, the post that he finally obtained, with the *Daily Telegraph*, was due, in part, to 'some slight influence in Ireland'.[23] He was on the staff of the *Daily Telegraph* for only a brief time and then either resigned or was fired after asking unsuccessfully for a rise, even though his salary had been a comfortable one. This

[22] Fyfe, p. 43.

[23] The fuller context, information which W.T. Stead the interviewer and the editor was quick to note down, was, 'then, no matter how, it was through some slight influence in Ireland, I continued to approach a noble lord who had the ear of Mr. Levy [Lawson] of the *Daily Telegraph.' P.M.G.,* 16 Jan. 1888.

again shows the mixture of diffidence and opportunism in his character, alternating between extremes and not allowing a straight course in his affairs. Within a day he became London correspondent for the *New York Herald*, but this lasted for only a year and a half when the paper faced an economy drive and O'Connor was dismissed.

His luck had run out. For the next seven years, roughly from 1873 to 1879, he was, as he puts it in his *Memoirs*, 'without any regular job or certain income'. These years played a large part in shaping his more enduring attitudes to life and to politics. He began, he said 'to know life's realities in their grimmest form'. He fell in with, and for a time became one of, 'that curious population which dwells in Fleet Street, a population sad and disappointed, often hungry, and often very brilliant, to whom fortune had not yet come, or has already deserted'.[24] He was a young man of the middle classes, accustomed, for all his family's hardships, to a minimum of comfort and security. When this was destroyed he was shocked, his private tendency towards melancholy increased, and his conscience was stirred. In some ways the strain was greater on him than it would have been on an unskilled migrant. He had more to lose; he had been the chief hope of his family, and one of the fears which may have kept him going was the dread of returning to Ireland a failure.

However, O'Connor did become involved in the life of the capital, and then in its radical politics. Soon, he came to regard himself more as a citizen of London than as a native of Athlone, and he appeared to have been too busy to show much regret for Ireland. Unlike some Irish nationalists – Justin McCarthy, Andrew Commins, and Lysaght Finigan in Liverpool, John Barry in Manchester, or T.M. Healy in Newcastle – O'Connor did not consider the possibility of an apprenticeship in the English provinces. London was his capital as it was for all Irishmen, and especially in his case because of the glamour of its literary and political life. By contrast his experience of poverty in the 1870s was real enough. Such an existence had its raffish aspects, and O'Connor as a young man relished them and was always fascinated by low-life (the memory of the tavern life of London remained vivid). But his life in the 1870s was not merely an experiment in bohemianism.

Occasionally, he came close to politics, as in a brief spell with the Central News Agency, when he was a member of the reporter's gallery in the House of Commons. This was to prove useful in familiarizing him with the forms of parliament but, apart from a short

[24] *Memoirs*, i, 3; Fyfe, p. 49, pp. 53-4.

term as a sub-editor on the *Echo*, O'Connor earned his living by writing hack-work for sensational magazines, all of which he later disowned.[25] But his life in London was not all stoic endurance. He was resilient and cheerful, so much so that his friends as well as his enemies often mistook this for total superficiality; possibly these years increased his determination.

Details of his life in the 1870s are hard to come by. His political friends were mainly to be found in the numerous radical associations in London. F.H. O'Donnell said that long years of poverty had turned O'Connor into an 'extreme radical' and 'a delegate to a Bradlaughite convention', and he must have been effective in this area because by 1880 he was vice-president of the Lambeth Radical Association which had gained a reputation for being 'easily the most advanced and aggressive body of the kind'.[26] His friends also included middle class *littérateurs* who had an interest in politics. Throughout his life O'Connor was to have a wide range of friends and acquaintances, because of his interest in literature, and because he was more sociable than most Parnellite M.P.s. Some of his correspondence with Blackwood's, the Edinburgh publishers, survives from the 1870s and reveals that in 1871 he proposed to write an article for *Blackwood's Magazine* on 'the present position of Austria', at first sight an unlikely subject but in fact in response to a controversy in the popular press. *Blackwood's* do not appear to have published this article, but one with almost the same title appeared in the short-lived journal *Dark Blue* the following year. O'Connor's approach in this piece showed signs of his undergraduate studies, pedantic in its exposition of the numerous Austrian nationalities, and tedious (and not very clear) in its rehearsal of the intricacies of the Austrian constitution

> this Parliament selects from its members a certain number of delegates for the Reichsrath, or Central Parliament. Now, as in the greater number of provinces the Slavs form the majority of the population, the Federalist party carries the majority in the provincial parliament. This majority in the provincial Parliament takes care that every delegate shall belong to its party; and thus the minority is left completely unrepresented. Now the Reichsrath. . .

Later, probably when he was forced to rely more and more on his free-lance work in the 1870s, O'Connor quite consciously altered his style to a more popular 'interesting' one. He also obtained his M.A. from

---

[25] *Memoirs*, i, 4-5. See also the bibliography.

[26] O'Donnell, *Irish Parliamentary Party,* i, 393. M. MacDonagh, *The Home Rule Movement* (1920), p. 137.

Galway in 1873, probably by purchase, which would at least give his heavier articles more weight. Even more surprising, O'Connor wrote to Blackwood submitting almost an entire novel, presumably for serialization, in 1875. According to the covering letter which outlined the plot, the work was a 'photographically reliable' picture of Irish life and it was also emphasized that the four leading characters would each represent a 'type', the fanatical Catholic conspirator, the informer, the priest, and the sham patriot; there was also a Fenian jailbreak, and the novel ended on a public hanging. Altogether, it was not a very edifying picture of Ireland, and it does not appear to have been published in *Blackwood's*. Even so, much of O'Connor's true interests are here; a cosmopolitan outlook (though his knowledge of foreign affairs was still largely gathered through bookwork), literature coming before life, and nationalism used merely for local colour.[27]

Other correspondence which survives from the 1870s shows the pleasanter side of O'Connor's life. For example, he made arrangements to go on a walking tour of the 'Tennyson country'. Two particular friends appear to have been S. Bennett of the Lambeth Radical Association, who wrote a life of Gladstone which was published in 1890, and George Barnett Smith, who had written two large works on Gladstone by the early 1880s when Gladstone still had much to do, and who also wrote a life of John Bright.[28] This slightly more serene aspect of O'Connor's life came at around 1875 when he was given a commission to write a book. He was asked by S.O. Beeton, husband of the definitive writer on cookery, to produce a work on 'the great scenes in parliament'. Instead, O'Connor surprised everyone including himself by concentrating on the career of Disraeli; there were after all enough great scenes there to satisfy anyone's taste.

Work on his first published book took him from 1875 to 1878 and was supposed to have involved 'the hardest and most exacting work' that O'Connor ever undertook, though it would be unexceptional to any research student today.[29] The book shows further signs of O'Connor's metamorphosis into a popularizer. Scholarly apparatus was slight, though no less than usual for this type of work. His sources were Disraeli's speeches reported in the press and in *Hansard*. When

[27]'The Present Condition of Austria', *Dark Blue*, 3, no. 13 (1872), 15-23; Calendar of University College, Galway; N.L.S. Blackwood Correspondence, MS 4280, f.178, O'Connor to John Blackwood, 'Monday' (dated 1871); *ibid*. MS 4337, f.61, O'Connor to Blackwood, 11 June 1875.

[28]N.L.I. MS 4360, eleven personal letters of O'Connor to James Hooper, 1877-82. This collection also includes four letters from S. Bennett to O'Connor.

[29]O'Connor went through 200 volumes of *Hansard*; his own career covers 516 volumes.

the narrative turned to the Balkans and Middle East crises of the 1870s, and an indictment of Disraeli's foreign policy, he used the account of J.A. MacGahan of the *Daily News* (who was also a personal friend) of the Bulgarian atrocities, as well as government blue books on the same subject. This slight documentation was, in its turn, relegated to extensive footnotes in order that, as he said in the preface to later editions of the work, the ease and popular nature of the text should not be disturbed. Instead, the emphasis was put on psychological interpretations of Disraeli, what biographers might call an 'intuitive' approach. Great play was made with Disraeli's novels (another major source for the work), especially *Vivian Grey* and to a lesser extent *Lothair*. At every stage these were held to be the essential keys to Disraeli's character, a prologue to or a commentary on his actions. In summary the persona which emerged was that of an actor, concerned with success and power for its own sake, unscrupulous, essentially immoral, and unpatriotic in appealing to the base instincts of English xenophobia or 'jingoism' (the latter being, according to O'Connor 'the gospel of the English people'). Such a catalogue appears far-fetched, but during the Bulgarian crisis Gladstone had used similar language to denounce Disraeli. At the same time much of the comment was justified; there are many parallels between Disraeli's novels and his political postures, and he was an actor, fond of the astonishing gesture and pleased to remain enigmatic.

O'Connor's emphasis on Disraeli's Jewishness has also been remarked on. But while this was an important theme, for example Disraeli viewing the Eastern Question in particular 'from the standpoint of the Jew', attacks on Jewishness did not then receive the opprobrium they have later attracted. O'Connor was not alone in drawing a parallel between Disraeli's Jewishness and his recent foreign policy, could point, with perhaps too much emphasis, to the importance which Disraeli attached to the Jewish purpose in history and, although anti-semitism was far from absent from radical or Irish Catholic circles, could still claim his own freedom 'from any vulgar bigotry'. O'Connor also apologized for the detail given to the Bulgarian atrocities in the work but this remains perhaps a greater blemish and suggests sensationalism with more than a hint of the prurient.

Despite its faults the book was in the best tradition of political vituperation, more usual in an earlier century and a minor indication of how O'Connor could approach matters with clarity if not without preconceptions. The book certainly fitted the popular mood when it was first published, after a false start, in 1878 at the height of the great debate on Disraeli's foreign policy. Both O'Connor's biographer, and to a lesser extent O'Connor, were inclined to play down the work as a youthful *tour de force*, but it would not have survived if it had not shown some insight, capturing the core mystery of Disraeli, an ability O'Connor was later to show in his short biography of Parnell; it went into at least eight editions, the last probably being issued in 1905.[30]

The biography also showed that O'Connor knew, or had come to realize, a few important things about the real world of politics, that, for instance, 'self complacency is almost the greatest of political talents', and that there was a 'spirit of elastic self-confidence' which might by itself bring success. Neither of these observations were intended to be complimentary, but they might stand him in good stead in future years. Neither was there much in the book on Ireland, apart from praise for Disraeli's sympathetic speech on Ireland of 1844, and condemnation of the equally notorious attack on Ireland in Disraeli's election letter of 1880. More specifically, such was the success of the biography that it directly provided O'Connor with the opportunity to stand as a member of parliament; it was his breakthrough.

O'Connor's recollections as to how this parliamentary opportunity came about were simpler. He gave the impression that he woke up famous and that the invitation to stand for an Irish constituency came while he was sitting in his garret in Holborn. But his book had first been published, albeit annoymously, in 1878, and was then re-published in a revised form in 1879 when it gained more publicity through being used as ammunition by Liberal candidates in the election which followed.[31] Certainly O'Connor might have entertained the grand ambition of becoming a member of parliament from his first days in London, it may have been there from his earliest days. To be an M.P. could be an aspiration for any successful man, including a man of letters. When O'Connor had received his first royalties he had sent them home, and the prosperity of his family, his father's venture as a small manufacturer, appears to date from 1879. Then he began to consider standing for parliament. But his first instinct was to stand as a radical. Most of his political experience so far had been in radical circles in London. He had received some notice from a prominent provincial radical, A.J. Mundella, who as early as January 1878 recommended him as a possible London correspondent to Robert Leader, the editor of the *Sheffield Independent*. O'Connor himself had also written to

[30]*Lord Beaconsfield: A Biography* (1879), pp. 27-42, 6, 7, 26, 601-4.

[31] The British Library lists the biography for 1878 as by 'T.P. O'C' and describes it as a different work from the one published in 1879. There is a suggestion that the 1878 work was first published in monthly parts (*Annual Register* for 1929, p. 132) but though such a plan is mentioned by O'Connor, he implied that it did not come about (*Memoirs*, i, 10).

Sir Charles Dilke in February 1879 saying that he had tried to get the revised biography of Disraeli ready before parliament met, which may indicate that O'Connor had some sort of acquaintanceship with Dilke, but at any rate shows where his first allegiance lay. Furthermore, it was for a radical seat at Dewsbury, near Sheffield, that O'Connor first tried to gain nomination, standing as a radical and with Dilke's assistance.[32]

Radicals such as Dilke and Mundella, who were not easily impressed, saw O'Connor as a man of promise for their cause, but O'Connor ended up standing as a Home Ruler and a supporter of Parnell, and for a different constituency, Galway City. This was no sudden conversion. What happened was that F.H. O'Donnell, the secretary of the Home Rule Confederation of Great Britain, heard of the Dewsbury negotiations when O'Connor asked for the support of the Irish vote in Dewsbury. Since all Irish voters were in any case instructed to vote Liberal in 1880, this may have been an impetuous move on O'Connor's part. The Dewsbury negotiations then fell through either because of O'Donnell's intervention or of their own accord. In the meantime O'Connor obtained an invitation to stand as a Liberal for Londonderry City and for this seat would undoubtedly require the assistance of the Irish organization and, again, he asked for Parnell's blessing. According to O'Connor's testimony, he had met Parnell twice before, probably when reporting on parliament for the Central News Agency. On the first occasion Parnell made little impression; on the second, which occurred during Parnell's campaign of obstruction, Parnell took him down to the terrace of the House and O'Connor was struck most of all by Parnell's loneliness, his 'air of a man who had no other place to go'. Parnell did quite possibly, as O'Donnell records, ask the latter for advice about O'Connor and the Londonderry contest though this was possibly intended to find out O'Connor's political loyalties and this is when O'Donnell, just to be helpful, described O'Connor as an advanced radical and a Bradlaughite.[33] Parnell was on the look out for pledged candidates who could pay their own expenses. A Liberal stood the best chance of election in the barely marginal areas of Ulster such as Londonderry but on past experience Liberals were often not enthusiastic about Home Rule. Parnell therefore agreed to support this promising

[32]University of Sheffield, Mundella Papers, box 1874-9, A.J. Mundella to Robert Leader, 14 Jan. 1878; B.L. Dilke Papers, Add. MS 3910, f.252, O'Connor to Dilke, 'February' 1879. For background on radical hopes in Dewsbury see H.J. Hanham, *Elections and Party Management*, pp. 95-6 and T.M. Healy, *Letters and Leaders of my Day* (1928), i, 76.

[33]O'Connor, *Charles Stewart Parnell, A Memory* (1891), pp. 51-2; O'Donnell, *Irish Parliamentary Party*, i, 393.

candidate but only as a pledged Home Ruler in a nationalist constituency, and this was Galway City, O'Connor's old university town.

O'Connor fell in with Parnell's offer but in retrospect he appears to have received the worst of the bargain. In recollecting his introduction to nationalist politics O'Connor also suggested that he had some forebodings because he had, so he said, 'read much and seen much of the misery which pursued with unerring regularity those who tried to serve Ireland. I had seen too many, even in my own time, go down in poverty or despair and sometimes in dishonour, to have any illusions as to what the position of a member of parliament involved.'[34] This comment was articulated with such directness because it came at a time in O'Connor's life which followed the failure of Home Rule and while a savage public battle with republicanism was still fresh in his mind. But he may have had his doubts as early as 1880. There had been the example of Wiliam Keogh to jaundice him with politics and there was the more recent example of the rejection and death of Isaac Butt. Irishmen could take a more realistic and more cautious view of nationalism than Englishmen sometimes realized. To Irishmen nationalism was one of the large facts of life and in such a case they were able to discriminate all the more subtly among its various manifestations. Irishmen like O'Connor, long resident in Britain, or those who had made a name for themselves outside politics, such as Andrew Commins, Justin McCarthy, or A.M. Sullivan, did not wish to be associated with the jobbery of Irish Liberalism, neither did they want to have anything to do with physical force Fenianism. These men, precisely because of their success, were worth attracting to nationalist politics. But, unlike the full-time nationalists such as William O'Brien, John Dillon, or T.M. Healy, the likes of O'Connor needed more convincing. O'Connor knew of the dangers but he was persuaded by Parnell and attracted to him personally.

While O'Connor may have believed that there was something new in Parnell's type of nationalism, he needed a sense of realism to tackle the election in Galway. Much proved similar to elections for Athlone in the mid-century. O'Connor's radical reputation was sufficient to precede him, as was the infamy attached to anyone who lived in London. His youth, tall stature, and brooding good looks could almost have been the creation of a romantic novelist, if the sketch of him drawn at the time of the Galway contest is anything to go by. So, not unnaturally, he was accused by the Galway clergy during the election campaign of living off the immoral earnings of two ladies in St. John's

[34]Fyfe, pp. 68-9. He says much the same in his *Memoirs* (i, 35).

Wood, a charge which, as O'Connor said, was 'more flattering to my charm than my morality'. Dublin Castle informers added to this by saying that he had taken a Fenian oath during the campaign which had further annoyed 'the priests of Galway'. The slightly snobbish voice of established nationalism, the *Freeman's Journal*, said that they had no knowledge of O'Connor and he was, lastly, informed that he had just managed to scrape home with the help of dead men's votes.

He was returned for the borough behind J.O. Lever, a Lancashire mill owner, and a carpetbagger if ever there was one, who nevertheless had previously sat for Galway between 1859 and 1865; O'Connor defeated a Dublin publican into third place by only six votes.[35]

O'Connor's first taste of electioneering might have been personally exciting, more so than elections in later life. But, apart from the shock of being the focus of attention, when he may have been more nervous than he appeared, the style of Galway politics must have seemed depressingly familiar to him, and not so much of a surprise as his recollections suggest. The real contrast here is, nevertheless, not between Galway and the rest of the British Isles, but between Galway as it still was in 1880 and Galway and other British boroughs as they were to become under Parnell's influence as his parliamentary and constituency machine developed. In these crucial years it was not through the Galway connection that O'Connor's career developed but, aside from the plans that Parnell might have had in store for him, because of events at Westminster, and because of events in the Irish movement at large. O'Connor's approach to the Irish in Britain was detached, possibly because the prospect of being too closely involved in the affairs of a migrant community bored him. There was much about the Irish in his future constituency in Liverpool that he did not appreciate. But as this was where his future lay, and in order to see what O'Connor might have had in common with his future exiles, it is necessary to turn to the experience of Irishmen in Liverpool and elsewhere in Britain, in these same years in which O'Connor grew to maturity.

---

[35] *Memoirs*, i, 39; Police and Crime Records, report on O'Connor. There is little evidence that O'Connor ever shared Fenian sympathies, apart from one wrong-headed description by Bernard Shaw (see Chapter 3, p. 115). Compare this with the statement of Sir Charles Russell for the defence in the Pigott forgeries case where he denied that O'Connor was ever a member of the Fenian movement (*Speech before the Parnell Commission* (1899), p. 487); 'Mr. T.P. O'Connor we know nothing of. He is said to be a journalist.' *F.J.*, 29 Mar. 1880. O'Donnell was pleased to record this also (*Irish Parliamentary Party*, i, 394); McCalmont, pp. 117-18, *Who's Who of British M.P.s*, vol. I, p. 236. The result was, Lever (Conservative Home Ruler) 503, O'Connor (H.R.) 487, Alderman Tarpey (H.R.) 481.

Liverpool; Politics as a Stoic Comedy

O'Connor's constituency of Liverpool Scotland division (so named after Scotland Road, a notorious highway which ran through the constituency) was created by the Redistribution Act of 1885; its attitude to politics had grown up over a period of forty years – longer than O'Connor's lifetime at that juncture. Antagonism to conventional British politics had become so ingrained that it was no great surprise when O'Connor was returned for the division as an Irish Nationalist M.P. in the election of 1885. Much of British opinion might have thought this an example of nationalist or separatist disloyalty, peculiar at first sight, squalid and mindless on closer investigation. But then, for all the time that O'Connor was an M.P. for this northern English constituency, the matter was usually passed over with a shrug, except by the local Unionist press who often complained about O'Connor in some detail.

It was not just the Unionists who might have found O'Connor and the Nationalists tiresome and opportunist. These reactions were understandable since little occurred to improve the condition of O'Connor's constituents during most of his lifetime. He complained about this himself in the Commons in his later years, leaving most M.P.s bored and exasperated; he had not helped appearances by his own frequent absences from the constituency. Looking forward and looking back, the constituency seemed marked by despair, futility, and stalemate. But this leaves aside too much explanation and comment. Although it was not until the 1870s that the Irish of Liverpool became vocal about their own politics, articulate in a way that approaches evidence, this somewhat narrow and self-righteous expression, the not very widespread prerogative of local politicians, was not merely the opportunism of a few, it was itself based on a variety of opinions, moods, and conclusions among thousands of individuals.

Without doubt the political problem began with, or was traced back to, the Famine. Attitudes appeared to have become fixed, automatic, but this was because they were a summary of grievances where nationalism approximated most closely to perhaps deeper feelings, a reaction to greatly altered lives, which had sometimes been improved, at least materially, more often wrecked. The Irish presence in Liverpool was, in fact, one of some antiquity, hardly surprising in what might be regarded as a 'border' area. By the sixteenth century there were 2,000 Irish labourers in Liverpool, as well as a merchant colony.[36] Later, Irish migration to Britain began to increase appreciably,

[36]D.B. Quinn, *The Elizabethans and the Irish* (1966); C.F. Routledge, 'Liverpool and Irish Politics in the Sixteenth Century', in *Miscellany Presented to John Mackay* ed. O. Elton (1914), pp. 142-56.

and it ran at a high level from the end of the eighteenth century to the 1840s. Yet all of this was eclipsed by the influx at the time of the Famine. This can be illustrated for Liverpool by two sets of figures. In 1846 280,000 Irish entered the city; in 1847 a further 300,000, the latter by itself more than the permanent population of the city in 1841 (when it stood at 286,000). Just under half of the migrants moved overseas (106,000 in 1846 and 130,000 in 1847) and others travelled inland to the industrial areas of Lancashire, Yorkshire, and the midlands. Those who stayed in the Merseyside area, particularly those in Liverpool's dockland, were usually the least fortunate. This dispirited pattern, with Liverpool at its focus and deriving least benefit, continued to be the rule for at least twenty years after the Famine crisis.[37]

What this led to was a concentration of Irish-born in Merseyside for much of the remaining century, from a total close to 50,000 in 1841, to almost 84,000 for Liverpool in 1861 (the peak year which gave a total for Merseyside of one sixth of the migrant population). In 1861 almost a quarter of the population of Liverpool was Irish-born. From 1861 down to 1931 there was a decline in the absolute total of Irish in Britain, and, less obviously, the total relative to the British population; the proportion of Irish-born in Liverpool also declined, though Liverpool remained a major area of Irish concentration. To some extent the figures were less dramatic than they now appear. The Irish quarters of Britain in Liverpool and elsewhere, though given an inter-mittent amount of dismal publicity, were not altogether isolated from their British neighbours. There was, for instance, some inter-marriage, perhaps marginally more common with English and Welsh partners than with the Scots. Similarly, the diminution of the Irish-born population meant that those recognized in politics as 'Irish', were increasingly second generation Irish-English. This was clearly the case by 1911, though it is probable that those of Irish descent out-numbered the Irish-born in the total population sometime in the 1890s; residence and householding restrictions meant that the number of voters of Irish descent did not become a majority until 1918.[38]

[37] For a more detailed account see Arthur Redford, *Labour Migration in England* (1926, rev. ed., 1976), pp. 150-65, R. Lawton, 'Irish Immigration to England and Wales in the Mid Nineteenth Century', *Irish Geography* 4 (1959), 35-54, and W. Smith, *A Scientific Survey of Merseyside* (1953), pp. 115-28.

[38] Smith, *Scientific Survey*, p. 131. See Appendix F. A fuller account of the changes in the Liverpool population is given in R. Lawton and C.G. Pooley, 'The Social Geography of Merseyside in the Nineteenth Century', final report to S.S.R.C., July 1976.

Political loyalties from the time between the 1867 Reform Act, which effectively gave Irish migrants the vote, and 1918 when their descendants were enfranchised, remained unchanged, threatened but not altered by social radicalism, perhaps mellowed into a convention. Those of Irish extraction were encouraged by precept, example, and circumstance to follow their parents. By 1916 one estimate, given by O'Connor, put the figure for the Irish community in Britain as high as 2.5 million, clearly including those of Irish descent; this was by that date an optimistic estimate because the children of the migrants were starting to have second thoughts about Ireland, or at least about the Irish Nationalist party. But such claims were a habit O'Connor had acquired after a lifetime as a spokesman. His appeal to this community had also sometimes become cliché-ridden. For instance, in 1911, in a speech he made as president of the United Irish League of Great Britain when it met for its conference that year in Cork city, he said that 'he spoke in the presence of Liverpool men whose fathers had told them that their people died like flies in the hospitals of Liverpool, Manchester, and Glasgow'.[39] O'Connor and, it is not unfair to say, the Liverpool men distanced themselves from these recollections (just as O'Connor had done in the passage previously quoted on the Famine). No more convincing was O'Connor's assertion that the position of Irishmen in Britain had improved out of all recognition. In retrospect the impression might be, on the contrary, one of stultification.

Formal descriptions of Liverpool politics up to the second Reform Act are usually free from any description of the Irish. No itemization either by nationality or, as might have been expected, by religion occurs in the Liverpool pollbooks which exist for every election and by-election between 1830 and 1857. This does not mean that political organizers were unaware of the Irish, or of Roman Catholics in general, it does mean that there were relatively few such voters (estimated for the 1830s at about 1,000 Catholic voters out of a total of just over 11,000 voters for the city), that in the unenfranchised mass they were no more expert in parliamentary politics than were the English poor, the Irish perhaps having a slight edge because of the influence of Daniel O'Connell. Nor was there any point in promoting an exotic or disruptive influence such as the Irish; there might have already been an awareness of the Irish as a factor to be outmanoeuvred. What remains obvious is the Conservative domination of the city, a

[39] R.N., 26 June 1916; D.P., 5 June 1911.

brief Whig reformist honeymoon after the 1832 Reform Act giving way, from 1835 in municipal elections, and from 1837 in national elections, to a virtual Conservative monopoly, a hold on the city's politics which was to remain undisturbed for most of the nineteenth century and last well into the twentieth century, except for one short period of control by the Liberals in alliance with the Irish in 1892.

The negative part played by the Irish in this Conservative success was a large one, though it was not openly acknowledged (and the worst excesses of bigotry did not reach the press), and was not so marked in the early part of the century as it was to become later. What can be seen as early as the 1830s, setting the pattern for O'Connor's day, was the first reaction against the Irish, together with some attempts by the Irish and other Catholics to organize themselves in politics. Given the circumstances, the moves towards organization were remarkable although this did not disturb what appears to have been the resolve to exclude Catholics from a wider share of the franchise. Perhaps the crucial, symbolic, issue here was concern with municipal schooling which the reformed Council of 1835 had thrown open to all schoolchildren, including Catholics. A furious reaction came from Conservatives, Anglicans, and Irish Protestant sentiment in the city, particularly in the person of the Revd. Hugh McNeile, an Ulsterman by origin, first of a long line of popular Protestant leaders in the city. This squabble, and the Protestant campaign, was sufficient to have the Council's decision reversed and, more than anything else, gave Conservatism in the city a new lease of life. Conservatism, or its earlier version of old toryism, did not originate through anti-Irish sentiment, nor from anti-popery (though there was obviously an element of this in its former guise). Toryism had previously owed more to a maritime connection, with its military and protectionist overtones. Some of this old tory politics persisted in the persons of the freemen voters who also continued to have a deserved reputation for corruption, but the new Conservatism was based on the recently enfranchised £10 householders (the freemen amounting to only 2,000 out of the electorate of 11,000). Neither was the electorate particularly democratic, the parliamentary commissioners estimating in 1865 that 13 per cent came from the working classes.[40]

What this also points to is a remarkable record of Conservative organization in Liverpool, a Tradesman's Conservative Association

[40] J.R. Murphy, *The Religious Problem in English Education* (1959), *passim*; J.R. Vincent, *Pollbooks, How Victorians Voted* (1967), p. 16; H.M. Walmsley. *The Life of Sir Joshua Walmsley*, (1879), p. 161; Derek Fraser, *Urban Politics in Victorian England* (1976), pp. 220-2; *Borough Electors (Working Classes), Return* P.P. 1866, lviii, pp. 47 ff; E.M. Menzies, 'The Freeman Voter in Liverpool, 1802-1835', *T.H.S.L.C.* 124 (1973), 85-107.

being founded as early as 1836, followed tardily (reversing the usual national pattern) by the Liberals. Some of this facility in popular organization was probably a hangover from the experience of dealing with the freeman vote, but it was to remain a feature of Liverpool Conservatism, giving 'tory democracy' more of a reality in the city than elsewhere in Britain. Liverpool Liberals were less enthusiastic but in contrast to the Liberals, with whom they were usually in uneasy alliance, the Catholics and the Irish among them showed an energetic attitude to popular politics. Any Irish vote operated first through Catholic auspices, English Catholicism being particularly strong in Lancashire where two-thirds of its English congregation had lived even before the coming of the Irish. In July 1839 a Protector Society was established in Liverpool to organize the Catholic vote led by John Rosson, who had played a large part in the agitation for Catholic Emancipation, assisted by Richard Sheil (cousin of the Irish Liberal M.P. of the same name), an Irishman, a merchant, and a councillor for Scotland Ward on the local Council. Although, as the title of the Society suggests, the Catholics were on the defensive and intent on safe-guarding the political rights so recently won, rights perhaps threatened by the municipal dispute, the importance given to politics, the ability of the Society was apparent at an early stage. The main aim of the Society was to register more Catholic voters. It was quite soon after the Society was founded, in 1841, that Sir Joshua Walmsley, one of the Liberal candidates in the general election, and in alliance with the Catholics, claimed that only 1,000 Catholics had the vote whereas, so he claimed, there were 100,000 Catholics in a Liverpool population of 300,000 (the 1841 census figure for Liverpool was 286,000). This was electioneering by round figures but it might indicate the proportion of Irish to English Catholics (just over half at this date, the Irish population of Liverpool being 57,000 in 1841). More importantly, it does suggest that more Catholics were qualified to register than had done so, and that some effort was expended to keep them off the electoral roll. The Protector Society had brought in a scheme to enable Catholics to pay rates by instalments thereby qualifying, and perhaps 300 new voters had been enfranchised this way. They were struck off again however when the instalment scheme was declared invalid by the registration revising court.[41] The suspicion arises that for all the blandness of items such as pollbooks, the analysis of voters

[41] J.R. Vincent, *The Formation of the British Liberal Party* (1966), p. 296; for the Protector Society see T. Burke, *A Catholic History of Liverpool* (1910), pp. 58-9; the organization of the Liberals and their attitudes are described in C.D. Watkinson, 'The Liberal Party on Merseyside in the Nineteenth Century' (unpublished Ph.D thesis, University of Liverpool, 1968), pp. 208-10. This work also identifies many of the political clubs which emerged before the 1860s.

by religion and nationality was an object of legitimate and perhaps even accurate speculation: the Liberals hoping to bring the Catholics in, the Conservatives usually succeeding in keeping them out.

Walmsley's hopes were not realized in 1841, but the pattern of Liberal-Catholic co-operation seen here persisted up to the 1870s. Catholics still found it necessary to form their own political associations, the Liberals never being easy to work with or enthusiastic about popular, let alone specifically Catholic issues. In 1844 the Catholic Club was founded as a successor to the Protector Society. This was augmented in turn by the Irish Catholic Club founded in 1851 which seems to have been a more radical and aggressive body, having as one of its aims the return of a Catholic M. P. for the city within twenty years by organization and registration.

Co-operation between the Liberals and the Catholics was damaged by Lord John Russell's Ecclesiastical Titles Act of 1851 which prohibited the establishment of a Catholic hierarchy in England and Wales, and by the considerable anti-Catholic hysteria and violence which this Act provoked. Although the Liberals had succeeded with the help of the Catholics in returning one M. P. in 1847, in the election of 1852 both Conservatives were returned. Some of this success was due to the Conservatives in their turn exploiting the anti-Catholic feeling whipped up by the Liberal prime minister, though they also relied on the old standby of gross bribery. But Liberal failure also owed something to lack of enthusiasm among the Catholics. Richard Sheil, for example, who had been active in the Catholic Club and who had then formed a Catholic Registration Committee, urged Catholic voters to pledge themselves to no candidate in 1852. From then on, through the 1850s, and up to and including the election of 1865, the Conservatives continued to dominate the politics of the city. Irish Catholicism had set this Conservative success in train, but another major contributory factor was that this challenge was not met by the patrician and priggish Liberals of Liverpool. The result was to prevent the development in Liverpool of a popular Liberalism similar to that developing elsewhere in the north of England between 1857 and 1868.[42] In this case the 1867 Reform Act, which enfranchised large numbers of Irish voters, would make the value of co-operation more apparent to the Liberals but would not substantially decrease the difficulties in fighting the Conservatives.

[42]Burke, *Catholic History,* p. 80; Liverpool *Mercury,* 25 Mar. 1851; *Mercury,* 30 July 1847; *Report from the Select Committee on the Liverpool Election Petition* H.C. 1852-3, xv, *passim;* Vincent, *Liberal Party,* pp. 293-298. See also P. Joyce *Work, Society and Politics* (1980), pp. 251-3.

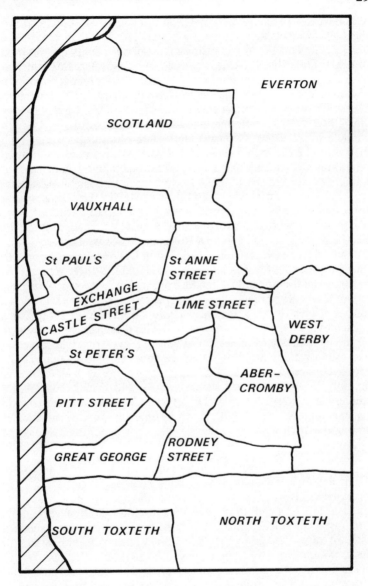

MAP 1

LIVERPOOL: *Municipal Wards*
1835 - 1895

When we turn to those Irish voters some of whom, like a proportion of their fellow townsmen in Liverpool, had their first chance to vote in 1867, their concern for constitutional politics seems anything but obvious. This attitude perhaps derived from a social reality which, to us at least, may appear far removed from the major preoccupations of Victorian politics; in the case of the Irish the disparity is particularly acute. The world in which the majority of the Irish of Liverpool lived was a horrific one, suffering, like the Irish communities in London, Manchester, western Scotland, and south Wales, the worst social distress to be found in Victorian Britain.[43] In Liverpool the Famine migration had exacerbated a near disastrous public health problem though the city had already begun to tackle this through the pioneering work of Britain's first Medical Officer of Health, Dr. Duncan. The Irish had settled in the centre of the city and northwards through dockland, the wards of Exchange, St. Paul's, Vauxhall, and the two Scotland wards astride Scotland Road (the wards which were to form the bulk of Scotland division), while a smaller concentration could be found to the south of the city centre at Toxteth. In 1846-7, at the height of the Famine influx, deaths from typhus in Liverpool reached 7,000. The worst threat to health had passed by 1850, but there was a further epidemic in 1854, and a cholera epidemic in 1866 which caused over 2,000 deaths. Associated with these raw statistics were all the circumstances of neglect in housing, overcrowding, violence, and crime which can be more easily itemized than imagined (and which continued to give O'Connor's constituency a notoriety as possibly the most poverty-stricken in Britain) even though recent studies have suggested that the very worst period for the Irish in Lancashire was over by 1870, by which time economic circumstances among the Irish were indistinguishable from conditions among the unskilled English.

Occupation and wages also became slightly more regularized. After playing a large part in dock construction, the vast majority of Irishmen in Liverpool were employed in the dock estate as was most English labour (and there was, again, little in their economic circumstances at least to distinguish the two), as stevedores on board ship, or quay porters, although another large category, among a cosmopolitan work force, became sailors and ship's firemen. Wages in the docks were, nominally, relatively high, enough to continue to attract new labour, an incursion sometimes resented by Irish labour. In practice however, not only was there considerable and crucial variation in types of labour and rates of pay but the casual hiring

---

[43]For works on the Irish in Britain as a whole see the bibliography, section F.

system and trade fluctuations depressed the level of actual earnings. As one historian of the Liverpool dock labour force has remarked, the persistence of low wage rates was remarkable; the basic rate which emerged in 1870 was five shillings a day for stevedores and four shillings and sixpence for quay porters, rates which remained unchanged down to 1915. Such a stultified pattern of work, still however leaving many circumstances which were precarious, fitted the Irish into their neighbourhoods, but this was a further factor which encouraged a lack of change in attitude.[44]

In such circumstances, it is hardly surprising that the Irish showed little concern for the 'wider' political issues of the city, or for the politics oi Britain in general. What was from the Irish point of view a struggle for existence, seemed merely a struggle to keep the peace, a sort of anarchistic side-show so far as the Liverpool authorities and townspeople were concerned. It is no longer possible so readily to imagine that the Irish immediately blamed Britain for the Famine, even though this became a lynchpin of nationalist sentiment by the 1860s. Nevertheless, the Irish response to the catastrophe was confused – passive and fatalistic, or rhetorical and violent, and with the latter came an added ingredient in politics. Perhaps it is the case that the Famine influx, unlike even the crisis migrations which followed in the 1850s and 1860s, contained a lawless element which had proved troublesome in Ireland itself, and this may have been a legacy which was particularly bequeathed to Liverpool by those Irish who stayed in the city (though contemporaries made no such fine distinctions).[45] The raconteur (it is hardly possible to sing) of 'The Rocky Road to Dublin' was a countryman, but his sentiments have been representative enough for the song to prosper;

> The boys of Liverpool when we safely landed
> Thought meself a fool, I could no longer stand it
> Blood began to boil, temper I was losing,
> Dear old Erin's Isle they began abusing.
> 'Hurray my soul', says I, my shillelagh I let fly. . . .

As well as the undoubted horror of the Famine years (not enlarged upon even long afterwards by the Irish, hardly mentioned by the

---

[44] *Medical Officer of Health*, reports, 1841, 1847, 1866; W.J. Lowe, 'The Irish in Lancashire, 1846-71; a social history' (unpublished Ph.D. thesis, University of Dublin, Trinity College, 1974), *passim;* E.L. Taplin, 'Dock Labour at Liverpool: Occupational Structure and Working Conditions in the Late Nineteenth Century', *T.H.S.L.C.,* 127, (1977), 145-6. For further background see E.L. Taplin, *Liverpool Dockers and Seamen* (1974).

[45] Patrick O'Farrell, *Ireland's English Question* (1971), p. 112; Patrick O'Farrell, *England and Ireland Since 1800* (1975), p. 77 citing an argument on the nature of the Famine emigration put forward by Emmet Larkin.

British), there was a well-attested humour running the gamut from brutality to whimsy. Some of this was no doubt over-emphasized by British commentators of whom Carlyle, though, was not best pleased by the reaction. But the humour derived from something in the Irish spirit, ignoring reality. Details of Irish life in Liverpool in the 1840s and 1850s are difficult to come by, but one practice was reported to be 'storming the Peelers'. There was a similar edge, almost a zaniness found in politics. They carried their politics with them from Ireland. Daniel O'Connell was followed rather than the Chartists, the Young Irelanders were given support and attempts were made to organize mass meetings for Michael Doheny and John Mitchel, and in 1848 one Dr. Lawrence Reynolds opened an ironmongers shop in Scotland Road to sell arms (cutlasses 6½d and blunderbusses 12/6d).[46]

Something similar can be said about the involvement of Irishmen from Liverpool and elsewhere in Lancashire in the Fenian movement in the 1860s. Liverpool was an important centre for the movement, and continued to be so into the 1880s, because the port was a crossroads in travel to and from Ireland and to and from the United States, a place of concealment, (though not as it turned out a very effective one) for the Irish American Fenian officers. Contemporary estimates about the number of Fenians in Lancashire were alarmist but one recent commentator has put the total for the county at 5,000. In Liverpool, Fenian activity was particularly prevalent in the Scotland Road area, especially in its public houses, the movement's weakest point. Probably the Fenians were no great threat to the peace of the city, or this at least is how a much criticized local police force, which called in the expertise of the Royal Irish Constabulary to keep a watch on suspects, made the matter appear.[47]

Yet the local press, admittedly inclined to panic, was not convinced. Perhaps it had the imagination to see the consequences of any large scale Fenian action, whether successful, partially successfull, or even a failure which would create martyrs. Any such initiative could well have led to widespread unrest among Irish communities in the cities of Britain. As it was, the Fenians were able to plan a large scale raid on Chester Castle in February 1867, and made a rescue of prisoners from a prison van in Manchester in September. The latter led to the trial and execution of Allen, Larkin, and O'Brien, the

[46] Colin O Lochlainn (ed.), *Irish Street Ballads* (1965), p. 103; Liverpool *Porcupine*, 21 Nov. 1879, 'Recollections of an old Liverpudlian'; John Denvir, *The Irish in Britain* (1892), p. 139. Reynolds had to flee the country.

[47] Hanham, *Elections and Party Management*, p. 304; John Denvir, *Life Story of an Old Rebel* (1910), p. 131: W.J. Lowe, 'Lancashire Fenianism, 1864-71', *T.H.S.L.C.*, 126 (1976), 158.

Manchester Martyrs, in November 1867. This in turn led to protest processions in Manchester and in Dublin (the procession witnessed by O'Connor), and similar marches were planned by the Irish in Leeds, Glasgow and Liverpool, though these were all banned. O'Connor, sensitive to popular moods, was possibly correct in seeing in this activity a new awakening of interest by the Irish populace in their politics, an idealism which turned away from the whig jobbery and clerical influence of the 1850s.

There were immediate consequences in places like Liverpool. British, and specifically, Liberal opinion when contemplating its supposed allies, woke up in alarm to the reminder of a large and not all that well-disposed or well-behaved Irish population. Irishmen appear to have sensed this reaction, even if they did not go so far as to read Liberal newspapers, but remained unalarmed by Fenianism and unconcerned even if it was thought to be disreputable. Although there appeared to be much good sense in the urgings of the press that the peace must be kept where 'thousands of Irishmen have found employment and a home', there was also more latent sympathy for Fenianism and for the protest processions than might have been anticipated. The way in which advice and warnings were joined cannot have helped matters. The Liverpool *Porcupine*, a satirical weekly founded in 1858 in imitation of *Punch*, suggested in a way that was not unrepresentative of local opinion when the procession scare was at its height at the end of 1867 that such activities would provoke the city's Orangemen and would have a bad effect on charitable effort. 'Think', Irishmen were urged, 'what sort of winter we have coming on. Think how hard the times will be with many of your countrymen . . . requiring the combined energy [and] earnestness [of] the benevolent individuals and charitable authorities of Liverpool to take the poor population over the coming winter. . . '[48] These phrases illustrate in miniature why the Liberals and the Irish did not always hit it off; Irishmen were unlikely to be impressed by appeals to their good sense as paupers. Otherwise the upsetting of the Liberals, and the rest of the townspeople of Liverpool was all to the good; the Irish response to the Fenians was also their first delayed reaction to their years of migration, intended to be provocative and bloody-minded.

It is probably not being too critical to believe that the exchange (column after column in the press, taciturnity from the Irish side) was given extra point, that the attitude of the Irish was all the more alarming to the Liberals, because at this very juncture, late in 1867, the second Reform Act was about to enfranchise large numbers of

[48]*Mercury,* 14 Dec. 1867; Liverpool *Porcupine,* 14 Dec. 1867.

34

Irish householders. Conservative organizers needed no prompting, were not prepared to be charitable, in the registration court they objected to street after street of householders in the dockland area, using the psephological formula of identifying Irish names and therefore Liberal voters. They claimed, with little evidence except free association, that these householders had been on poor relief and were therefore disqualified. In a bout of even rarer frankness one Conservative said that there was a difference between working men (presumably Conservative), and those objected to, whom he called 'the lowest scum of the earth'.[49] These objections were dismissed as vexatious, but this verdict appears to owe more to the impatience of the judge and the numbers involved rather than to any advocacy by the Liberals. Grateful for Irish votes, but even more squeamish the more popular and seamier politics became, the Liberals, the great whig Liverpool merchant families of Outrams, Gaskells, Mellys, Ewarts, and Rathbones (known collectively for some reason as 'red currant jelly', perhaps because the taste was an affected one), retained their distaste for and neglect of politics. Perhaps it was for this reason more than any other that the Liberals lost the chance to rob the Conservatives of their hold on the city for otherwise, as one account of Liverpool Liberalism has suggested, the Conservative majority over the Liberals was never a massive one.[50]

Conservatism showed no such inhibition. As early as May 1867 the Liverpool Conservative Workingmen's Association was formed, successor to other popular Conservative clubs, but even more active, especially when under the control of such a formidable political organizer as A.B. Forwood, or later, in 1892, the more popular Archibald Salvidge. It was precisely the sort of metropolitan Conservatism to be found on Merseyside that gave the party its pattern for national organization and its most progressive M.P.s, two of whom, Samuel Graves of Liverpool and John Laird of Birkenhead, worked particularly hard to help Disraeli persuade Conservative back-benchers to accept the Reform Act of 1867.[51] In the election of 1868 Graves and Viscount Sandon were returned for the Conservatives, and the Liberals were pleased to return the third minority member, William Rathbone. During the years which followed down to the first

[49] Report from the Select Committee on the Registration of Voters in Boroughs H.C. 1868-9, vii, p. 354, p. 443; D.P., 24 Sept. 1868.

[50] M. Ostrogorski, Democracy and the Organization of Political Parties (1902), i, 279 for the whig nickname; Watkinson, 'Liberal Party', p. 486.

[51] William Forwood, Recollections of a Busy Life (1910) and S. Salvidge, Salvidge of Liverpool (1934) are two accounts of popular Conservatism in the city; F.B. Smith, The Making of the Second Reform Bill (1966), pp. 158-60.

world war the Liberals were fortunate if they returned one M.P., even after the Act of 1885 had created nine divisions for the city. This is another way of saying that most of the old features of Liverpool politics survived reform, indeed became intensified when politics became slightly more popular. The only major difference after 1867 was that, after the first shock of Fenian activity, and after a more thorough-going if unproductive attempt to work with the Liberals, the Irish became more articulate and more critical, this in turn putting Orangemen and others within the Conservative camp more on their guard.

The reason for such a quick response by the Conservatives seems blatantly obvious. One Liberal journal in 1881 put the explanation into A.B. Forwood's mouth, that Conservative success was due to

> The presence of a large Irish population; that enables us to get a hold of a large number of working men who hate the Irish for coming to this country and lowering the rate of wages. In addition to this there is the question of religion. People are still afraid of Popery and in a place where there is a large number of Roman Catholics any party which allies itself with Popery will meet with strong opposition. We get in Liverpool what our party receives in no other town in the kingdom – a large proportion of the non-conformist vote.[52]

This fiction was thought adequate enough to bear repetition, justifying Liberal lack of success, and it was reprinted in full seventeen years later in 1898. Yet the indirect form of attack indicated that the Conservatives did not even have to mention the Irish in the latter part of the nineteenth century. The response had become traditional, taken for granted, so much so that Conservatives were embarrassed when Orangeism revived in the early twentieth century as a result of the activities of Pastor George Wise and the Revd. H.D. Longbottom, though it had become acceptable again by the time of the elections of 1910.

By comparison the Irish still had difficulty in translating their presence into a voice in parliamentary politics. The Irish had formed one-fifth of the population of Liverpool in 1841, a quarter by 1861, and about one-sixth by 1871. By the 1870s the number of Irish voters was thought to be around 9-11,000 out of a total electorate of about 58,000 (slightly under their percentage of the population, but not remarkably so).[53] For a short while, the Irish did not appear to want an

[52]Liverpool *Review*, 1 Oct. 1898, reprinted from 8 Mar. 1881. Compare Forwood's own account of the local party which, hardly surprisingly, nowhere mentions the Irish or religion, 'Democratic Toryism', *Contemporary Review* 43 (1883), 294-304.

[53]Eleanor Rathbone, *William Rathbone, A Memoir* (1905), p. 296; *McCalmont*.

independent presence in British politics, they were divided among themselves, and the Roman Catholic church in particular did not favour separate nationalistic ventures. Yet perhaps this is best seen as a period in which the Irish did not realize their strength, and the fact that they did then come out for their own candidates, against all the pressures that were merging them into their new home in Britain, is an indication of the determination in the vote, at least in its earliest decades, a sign of some political sophistication and not, at least for the remainder of the ninetenth century, an imposed alternative to more radical or class politics.

The Catholic Church, as an international and missionary body, and one concerned for the pastoral care of the Irish, would not want any unnecessary barrier placed between Irish and British parishioners, or between Irish communities and their British setting. Added to which although the Catholic Church in Britain became, for a while, increasingly Irish, its clergy and the leaders of the Church (especially in Lancashire) often stressed their Englishness and, on the score of education if nothing else, became increasingly Conservative in their politics. In 1867 the Church was still to a large extent the holding power where migrant politics were concerned. Prior to Fenianism the Church, in the person of the local priest, was frequently the only authority on which they could rely (and perhaps the only authority they recognized). In their new communities it is likely that the priest had more influence than in the rural areas of Ireland. As late as the election of 1868 (or then given their opportunity on a large scale), the clergy were said to have organized the Irish voters in Liverpool, gathering Catholic electors together in church schools before marching them off to the poll.[54] The Liberal was to be supported in national contests, at least until disputes on education became more evident. The candidates for whom they voted in local politics, in the central wards of Exchange and St. Pauls, and in the northern wards of Vauxhall and Scotland, were usually Catholic Liberals. The latter might have been a rare breed elsewhere in Britain but in Liverpool (and in Manchester) they often had an Irish connection and, unfortunately, often bore a resemblance to the Irish whigs O'Connor had found so unsatisfactory in Athlone. However exasperating a state of affairs this was for the more determined nationalists, it was a difficult pattern to break and proved unchallengeable in the honeymoon period of co-operation between the Irish and the Liberals when Gladstone, from 1868 to 1872, introduced reforms in church and state in Ireland. The Church also remained implacably opposed to the

[54]*Report of the Select Committee on Parliamentary and Municipal Elections* H.C. 1868-9, viii, p. 133 evidence of A.B. Forwood.

Fenians, when it was ex-Fenians who provided the driving force behind the new Home Rule movement, at least as it applied to the Irish communities in Britain.

Nevertheless, the Church's aim of reconciliation, though laudable, was often an exercise in optimism and assertion, more constructive, and, as it turned out, more durable; nationalism was more realistic, recognized and defended differences. In retrospect, even Catholic spokesmen admitted that the Irish had often been driven in on themselves in the nineteenth century.[55] Home Rule councillors were first returned for the local Council in Liverpool in the mid-1870s, Lawrence Connolly in 1875, joined by Charles McArdle, Dr. A.M. Bligh, and Andrew Commins the following year. The Home Rulers concentrated on the Vauxhall and Scotland wards, where six seats were at stake, and by 1877 all these seats had been won and the Catholic Liberal element defeated. The new representatives were men of some ability. Lawrence Connolly, born in Dublin in 1834, had come to Liverpool as a young man to manage the family firm of fruit merchants. Commins was an even more impressive figure, from Ballybeg, Co. Carlow, of farming stock, educated at Carlow College, Queen's College, Cork, and London University; he was one of the first leaders of nationalism in Liverpool, where he had settled in 1860. He was a barrister with a prosperous practice and later went on to become an M.P. while still remaining leader of the Home Rulers in Liverpool. Another example from among local Irish councillors, and one of the nine Irishmen who lived in Liverpool who were to become Nationalist M.P.s for Irish constituencies, was James Lysaght Finegan who was, in turn, a Liverpool journalist, a notorious radical and, briefly, an M.P. for Ennis. A final example is that of Justin McCarthy, the popular novelist and historian who, while coming later and not enthusiastic about politics, had lived in Liverpool in his younger days ('a stepping stone on my way to London', just as O'Connor saw Dublin perhaps). He had played a part in the Liverpool Parliamentary Debating Society, and had been active in setting up the Liverpool *Northern Daily Times* in 1853, one of the first provincial daily newspapers, coming before the Liberal Liverpool *Daily Post* which was founded in 1855. There were men here who could rival O'Connor, and Commins at least had a more intellectually distinguished career even if he was not as well known.[56] What this illustrates is not

[55] Burke, *Catholic History, passim;* K.S. Inglis, *Churches and the Working Classes in Victorian England* (1963), pp. 119-42; Liverpool *Catholic Herald,* 23 Apr. 1910.

[56] For Commins, see the description in the *Porcupine,* 29 July 1893 in the series 'Local Celebrities'; Justin McCarthy, *Story of an Irishman* (1904), p. 102; A.J. Lee, *The Origins of the Popular Press* (1976), pp. 67, 140. McCarthy said that most of the

so much the truism that the migrant community contained men of ability, but that this had become more evident by the 1870s, and that once given the chance, they rivalled and then overtook the political influence of the Church remarkably quickly; that, under greater pressure, this took place much more quickly in Britain than in Ireland itself.

Not that the Liberals were convinced; their response was to move into a cautious phase of the love-hate relationship with the Irish. Slightly more interest had been taken in the Irish in the early 1870s, due perhaps to their exercise of the vote, and also possibly resulting from surprise and outrage in the national press (as shown by *The Times*) at the health and crime statistics for the city published in 1874. This led to more reports by the Medical Officer to supplement his annual report, specifically where the worst fever district 'inhabited by the lowest of the Irish population', was concerned.[57] Such reports were not uncommon in Victorian England, a cathartic process. Much the same might be said of more literary ventures into the Scotland Road area. Irish quarters were never wholly free of voyeurism, often the impression is given that this is where the apprentice journalist tried out some purple prose. 'I find', said 'A Stroller' on 'A Sunday evening in Scotland Road',

> that there is in this space twenty four public houses, all of which seem to be doing a roaring trade . . . [there is] a restless stand at ease from end to end of the street, knots of young fellows, some of whom receive a passing notice which they seem to know . . . something up . . . at the end of the passage are knots of women, whom the voice of my friend [his guide for the night] is sufficient to send like frightened deer to their lairs.[58]

Liberals could not square what they knew of the Irish, their social appearance or place, with the ambition of Irish politics, and affected not to take the Irish seriously, at least not at first. Once Home Rule councillors were returned, it was then merely suggested that faction resulted and that the development was absurd, In 1876, for instance, a literary journal proposed that 'only Home Rule Councillors be allowed to rise three at once and become seriously alarmed at a

staff of the *Northern Daily Times* were Irish. Irish M.P.s who lived in Liverpool are listed in Denvir, *Life Story*, p. 230. One of these was William O'Malley who became T.P. O'Connor's brother in law and who wrote an autobiography, *Glancing Back* (1933).

[57] *The Times*, 26 Dec. 1874; *Council Proceedings 1874-5*, pp. 142-3 and 'Medical Officer of Health's Report as to the Area, Population, and Death Rate of Two Districts of the Borough', also in *Council Proceedings 1874-5*, pp. 647-661.

[58] *Porcupine*, 16 May 1874. For something similar see the Liverpool *Wasp*, 30 Apr. 1880.

harmless joke' (a suggestion put under the heading 'Town Council Standing Orders').[59] Hostility could not become too clear, given the reality of the Irish vote, so instead there was much pained and confused advice. This ran to the oddity of a criticism of those who had deserted Catholic politicians because 'your bishops and priests who, if theological [sic], are at least educated and in accord with the ablest laymen you have'. Comparisons were also drawn with the U.S.A., never far away when Englishmen wanted to express their fear of democracy in the nineteenth century, and Irishmen were accused of creating something like a 'Tammany ring'. At the same time such critics were ready to assume an air of bored detachment when their advice was ignored, then suggest that there was very little difference between local candidates and that it was foolish to believe that elections in Liverpool had any bearing on Home Rule for Ireland.[60]

Apart from their own special interest, the Liberal attitude might appear sensible but, like Liberal distaste for organization, the advice was inapplicable in failing to take into account what the Irish wanted. By contrast, and bearing in mind that the Conservatives did not set up their central organization, the National Union, until 1867, and this was not effective until the 1880s, while the Liberals did not come together in the National Liberal Federation until 1877, the Irish grasp on organization throughout the British Isles was both sudden and far-reaching. In the first place they realized that local politics were a training ground for national politics. Then the somewhat conservative organization founded by Isaac Butt in Dublin in 1870, the Home Government Association, was seized on, particularly by the Irishmen of Britain, who turned it into a radical movement thereby giving their more local efforts a national framework and effect. Irishmen from Liverpool had attended the inaugural Dublin meeting of the H.G.A. in 1870, John Denvir is an example about whom there will be more to say. A Liverpool branch of Butt's movement was formed in January 1872 by Commins, Bligh, and McArdle, with the help of Denvir. In February 1873, owing largely to the initiative of Fenians and ex-Fenians in Manchester and Liverpool, John Barry and the ubiquitous Denvir, the Home Rule Confederation of Great Britain was founded, and then grew to have a total of 116 branches in Britain by 1875. This

---

[59] Liverpool *Critic*, 25 Nov. 1876.

[60] Descriptions of local contests are complicated by the fact that not all municipal seats were contested every year. The elections and disputes between Liberal Catholic and Home Rulers can be followed most clearly in the Liverpool Liberal *Journal*, 16 Oct. 1875, 2, 16, 23 Sept. 1876, 31 Jan. 1877. A fuller description from the Liberal point of view is given in Watkinson, 'Liberal Party', pp. 406-11; Liverpool *Critic*, 4, 21 Oct. 1876.

development among the Irish in Britain predated the reconstruction of the H.G.A. as the more popular and more nationalist Home Rule League, which occurred in Dublin in November 1873.[61] So radical and active an influence were the Irish in Britain that although the headquarters of the H.R.C. were located in Liverpool in 1875, to be near the chief centre of Irish population, the following year they were moved to London, in order to be nearer Irish M.P.s and, so one commentator has suggested, because it was feared that the influence of the Irish working classes in Liverpool, and in Lancashire generally, might make the organization too extreme.[62] Despite this, the H.R.C. proved too much for Butt to handle. Irishmen in Britain supported the obstructionist tactics used by Joseph Biggar, F.H. O'Donnell (the secretary of the H.R.C.), and Parnell. When the annual conference of the H.R.C. met in Liverpool in 1877, Butt was replaced as president by Parnell, the latter's first victory in his task of gaining control of the Home Rule Movement.

Home Rule aspirations in Liverpool did not stop short at municipal politics and support for the H.R.C. There was also more of a possibility in Liverpool than in any other part of Britain, that a Home Ruler could be elected for parliament. While it was difficult enough for Liberals to win a seat in Liverpool, they could not, for that reason, afford to antagonize the Irish, who could muster over 9,000 votes. Andrew Cummins allowed his name to go forward as a Home Rule candidate in a by-election in 1873. This may have been a coat-trailing venture, but in the more celebrated Liverpool by-election of February 1880, the possibility that the Irish might put up the veteran nationalist A.M. Sullivan was enough to cause the Liberal to make promises that if he were elected he would call for an enquiry into the government of Ireland. This promise seriously embarassed the Liberal leadership at Westminster and both angered and cheered the Conservatives. Although the result was another Conservative win, it was not such a success either in the number of votes cast for their candidate, or if, as is sometimes suggested, the by-election victory caused Beaconsfield to go to the country in 1880 over Home Rule.[63]

[61] *Critic*, 21 Oct. 1876; Fraser, *Urban Politics*, pp. 9-22; Denvir, *Irish in Britain*, pp. 265 ff.

[62] Denvir, *Irish in Britain*, p. 267, Lawrence J. McCaffrey, *Irish Federalism in the 1870s* (1962), p. 37 citing John Goulding to Butt, 3 Dec. 1875 (N.L.I. Butt Papers, MS 6897).

[63] *Mercury*, 30 Jan. 1873, *D.P.*, 28 Jan., 1, 3, Feb. 1873. See also John Patrick Rossi, 'Home Rule and the Liverpool By-Election of 1880', *I.H.S.*, 19 (1974), 156-69; Conservative and Anglican celebrations can be found in the *Christian Herald*, 18 Feb. 1880. For the by-election and national politics see Trevor Lloyd, *The General Election of 1880* (1968), pp. 16-17.

By contrast, the Irish had at least shown that their tactical skill had developed, alongside a flair for advertising Home Rule.

Other kinds of obstruction and advertisement, those practised in parliament by Biggar, O'Donnell, and Parnell, appealed to the Irishmen of Britain (and popular Irish opinion generally) because of a supremely ironic twist, that they were articulate, and turned the accusations and pretensions of British society inside out. Not only did the Irish parliamentarians stop a wide range of business and draw attention to Irish matters, but they did so by speaking interminably, by practising rules of procedure, by steadily making fun of Westminster. Some of this technique, and the reason for its popularity can be gained from F. H. O'Donnell's comment at the 1877 H.R.C. conference at Liverpool. 'The Irish', he said, 'did not appear on the scene with a small pipe in their mouth and twirling a shilelagh, saying, "hello Pat, Who is afraid?" They were quite up to the civilization of the age.' O'Donnell himself was a special case and something of a social climber, but what he said mirrored what John Denvir had been saying in Liverpool for some time past. Denvir provides the chief sources which break the illusory silence on the Irish side, the monopoly of comment coming from outside. He founded various newspapers, such as the *United Irishman* in September 1876 and the Irish *Programme* which became the *Nationalist* in 1883 and 1884. There were other publishing ventures in which he was involved, and he wrote a history of the Irish in Britain and a fragment of autobiography which amounts to another history. He had been a Fenian, was active, as has been indicated, in the forming of the H.G.A. and the H.R.C., and went on to become a national organizer of the Irish vote. Whether his campaign, or even all his comments, were typical is as questionable for him as for any propagandist or man of letters. He was out of the ordinary, perhaps too bitter, self-righteous, and more determined than most but this, coupled with ability, could mean that he often hit the nail on the head. For instance, in 1876, he protested against the spectacle of Irishmen breaking up a meeting of Joseph Biggar's in Manchester (for the transition from Fenianism to constitutional politics was not accepted easily), and he did so by showing that one consequence would be a strengthening of English prejudices, that this would be seen as another example of

> The Rowdy Irish, the Riotous Irish, the Disorderly Irish, Irish Ruffians, Irish Blackguards, Miserable Irish Factions, another Irish Row, the Savage Temper of these Low Irish, Irish Savagery, Irish Scum, a nice people to govern themselves,

another Donneybrook Fair, Irish in all their Glory, [and] the
Kilkenny Cats in Manchester.[64]

This was a satire of everyone involved. Pride was also at stake as it
was again the following month when Denvir claimed that the Irish in
Britain 'were driven . . . to seek the means of subsistence in the lowest
paths of life and forced to mingle with the poorest – which is in Great
Britain what it is not in Ireland – the worst class of society'.[65] This sort
of claim raised a lot of questions. Was the comparison between
Ireland and Britain justified, even in response to criticism? Was it
necessary to remember quite such an ideal picture of Ireland? In the
struggle to earn a living was nationalism worth the effort? The curious
fact is that most Irishmen answered these questions positively.
Undoubtedly, there was a wide range of attitudes to politics, with
some Irishmen in Liverpool and elsewhere being uninterested, some
being convinced Liberals, or later a few might become socialist,
almost none it seems safe to say, Conservative. To many, especially
local politicians and organizers, the campaign for nationality was a
serious business, though still treated with scepticism by observers.
Here is a more than usually affectionate and perceptive description of
O'Connor in Liverpool Scotland division in 1901. He spoke to

a bowler hatted audience of some two hundred Irishmen,
liberally perspiring sons of toil, with dented and furrowed faces
eloquent of hard couches and rough experience. They sat
inelegantly, with determined faces [and when O'Connor entered]
haloed by local Irish leaders, the audience stood up as one man,
doffed hats and let go a ragged hoarse throated cheer . . . . For
about three quarters of an hour he spoke, upon the ever fresh and
fruitful Irish Question, spoke learnedly, smoothly and eloquently,
bringing to bear upon the subject all the power and fervour
begotten by a lifetime's unrivalled political experience. To say
he moved and delighted his audience is to describe the effect of
his eloquence tamely; he thrilled them and held them as it were
in the palm of his hand.[66]

In fact, the occasion was not a matter of routine, since it was rare to
have O'Connor in his constituency, and he was there at this particular
time to consolidate his position after heading off a local rebellion in
the election of 1900. His electorate were not totally uncritical,
especially not by 1900, but they did approve of how he retained his
capacity for being critical or awkward, his radicalism. Sometimes,

64 *D.P.*, 28 Aug. 1877; Liverpool *United Irishman*, 23 Sept. 1876.

65 *United Irishman*, 7 Oct. 1876.

66 'At the Feet of T.P.' by 'Brother Sam', Liverpool *Review*, 12 Oct. 1901.

apart from the more humorous descriptions of O'Connor, the local Irish electorate were portrayed in a less flattering light, usually when they saw off the victorious O'Connor, as they did in 1906,

> a tumultuous crowd of unwashed women and fierce looking males in mad Gaelic effervescence, screeching, singing, yelling like maniacs, the pandemonium intensified by a distant band, a tall dark featured, haggard faced man [O'Connor] in an open carriage wildly waving a glossly silk hat to the deluge of sansculottes.[67]

These scenes were the partisan, pavlovian response which existed here as in all other varieties of politics. A response like this was not always typical of Irishmen in the city, especially not those who lived some distance, both physically and mentally, from Scotland division (as did most political organizers). In between the obvious importance of the issues and the banal partisanship of elections, there is no reason to exclude the possibility that because of the dislocations of their past, politics among the migrants, and especially in Liverpool where they had some effectiveness, were made to carry a considerable burden of symbolism, not only of protest, but of the awkwardness and obstruction first seen in the 1870s. 'Stoic comedians' is a phrase that has been used to describe James Joyce and Samuel Beckett, and, in a city known for its comedians, the educative process of comedy had to begin somewhere, in the surprises between Lancashire and Ireland, and in politics as much as anywhere.[68] Politics in Liverpool was never as bland, eventless, or monolithic as the record might suggest, though the vitality given by comedy will have to be inferred in what follows, in between the large events. It was a provincial performance that O'Connor approached with some coldness and exasperation but to which he finally had to become resigned.

[67] *Porcupine,* 20 Jan. 1906, 'T.P. as King Mob'.
[68] Hugh Kenner, *The Stoic Comedians* (1964).

2

FOLLOWING PARNELL, AN M.P. FOR LIVERPOOL, 1885

'Where is Dandy Pat now?'[1]

Between his election for Galway in 1880 and the two elections in 1885 and 1886 O'Connor's life was busier, more testing, and more complicated than it was ever to be again. This mirrored the considerable changes of fortune which took place in the Irish parliamentary movement in these years, changes which nave come in for considerable scrutiny by historians. O'Connor moved from being a relatively unknown journalist to a position where he was responsible for much of Irish strategy in elections. On the way, he was chief parliamentary spokesman for the Irish in the debates on coercion in 1881, an emissary to the Irish Americans in 1882, and acknowleged leader of the Irish in Britain by 1883 – all duties delegated to him by Parnell. So various was his life during these years that it is difficult to pin him down – and not only geographically because his ideas suffered something of a change. From the radical, reluctant, and perhaps opportunist recruit, he became a fully fledged nationalist prepared, however momentarily, to bargain with the Irish vote and, if necessary, to use it against the Liberals.

O'Connor took to this tide in his affairs with what appears, for all his disclaimers about his reluctance and shyness, to have been a great deal of ease. His energy, ability in debate, and intelligence in planning are equally remarkable. But perhaps, too, something was lost: he made a choice between radicalism and nationalism without fully realizing that he had done so. As the relation between these two forces is one of the most difficult aspects of Anglo-Irish relations, the need to decide between them, as well as the reluctance to see that a decision had been made, can be readily appreciated. Added to which the compensatory benefit to O'Connor and to the Irish movement appeared to be considerable. It was a time for high hopes: in many ways, politically at least, it was the high point in O'Connor's career.

---

[1] A shout from the stalls when O'Connor was nominated, *D.P.,* 11 Nov. 1885. 'Dandy Pat', or Patrick Byrne, was a local councillor who had fished for support. He was something of a dresser. He may at this time have become the proprietor of the 'Morning Star' public house (the 'blood pub') which was later to be used as committee rooms for the Irish party.

An optimism had developed in a few short years as the cohesion and effectiveness of the Parnellite machine increased. O'Connor suggested as much in his first speech at Liverpool which he made after a League conference in 1882, when he thought the time had come to compare the Irish in Britain with the Irish in the United States, and then to describe their common movement as an international one.[2] Too much conscious purpose can be read into how the vociferous constituents and the celebrated politician came together, but when the audience came to cheer O'Connor at his nomination speech in the League Hall in Liverpool in November 1885, they knew they had chosen, or had been given (it was good luck either way), a spokesman with an international reputation rather than a merely local celebrity. That in itself was a sign of confidence, and of their importance. O'Connor's own moves, as impresario of the migrants in the elections of 1885 and 1886 when the Irish vote was put in the balance between the Conservatives and the Liberals, could also be seen as one of the more important elements in the larger struggle. On the debit side for O'Connor, intense activity in politics from day to day, while it did not completely exhaust his interests, could come to be a fascination in itself, especially when augmented by new gifts of authority and command. For a time O'Connor gives the possibly deceptive impression of being fascinated by power, losing sight of, or toning down, his principles, and forgetting the stubborn persistence of ideas and conviction in explaining how men act. Perhaps too it was a necessary journey, from youthful idealism to political practicality (though it was concentrated into a few years), or a momentary aberration, or simply a matter of priorities while supporting Parnell's unique enterprise. Out of internal rancour, feuding, and social ostracism there now seemed to have succeeded, as far as the Irish in Britain could see, real hope that Home Rule would come quickly, that a change was imminent and that they were a party to that change.

In the House of Commons, 1880-1

How O'Connor first acted in the arena of parliament in 1880 and first impressions of him are not only of intrinsic biographical interest (such as the appreciation by John Bright, still the figurehead of radicalism in the Commons, that here was a new member of some charm of delivery) but it also shows a combination of qualities which is unusual, the arrival of a politician of subtlety, at least in expression,

---

[2] See below p. 63.

and impact. Such was the crush of events which occurred in his first year at Westminister that it would be deceptive to dwell on what O'Connor thought of the House in his more reflective moments, and it is doubtful whether he had many such moments in 1880 and 1881 outside the hurried, summary descriptions called for by his journalism. This, the lifetime of themes which he drew from parliament, is returned to later. His early vivacity and good looks when he first entered parliament at the age of thirty-two were long remembered, if only by way of an unflattering comparison to his maturity. Even so, whether in substantial middle age or in his later senatorial years he always cut an impressive figure, acquiring though a slight trace of Disraelian artifice (perhaps a necessary ingredient in the lives of many M.P.s). O'Connor put his arrival in a low key stressing his nervousness ('my awe of the House was immense').[3] This was an appropriate recollection, in keeping with the inauspicious beginning of the Parnellite party at that time. O'Connor was present at the party meeting in Dublin in May 1880 which, somewhat fortuitously, elected Parnell chairman by twenty-three votes to eighteen. It was from this meeting that O'Connor dated his own prominence in the party, at least when his impact here was augmented by speeches he made in the new parliament. In Dublin O'Connor made one of the first speeches in favour of Parnell, implied in his recollections that many of the other Parnellite supporters were more inexperienced than he, suggested that Parnell was unwilling to stand against the existing chairman William Shaw, and went so far as to suggest that he, O'Connor, had first had the idea of proposing Parnell.[4] Certainly O'Connor made his impression quickly, and was already, at least, an acquaintance of T.M. Healy, who was also at the Dublin meeting but who had not yet been elected to parliament. But the progression of events described or casually let slip by O'Connor is a partial account, and probably stresses his nationalism and his links with other members of the party too strongly. It would seem an unusual circumstance, for instance, for a candidate who had been almost press-ganged by Parnell after the intercession of F.H. O'Donnell, to then to be able to nominate Parnell as party leader. Instead the record suggests that to begin with O'Connor appeared in the guise of a radical. At the same time he did not abate his activities as a journalist and did not appear so single-minded as other followers of Parnell, as the other followers, and particularly the lieutenants around Parnell, were quick to point out. In other words, O'Connor started his career as an ambiguous figure, ill-

[3] *Memoirs*, i, 42.
[4] *Ibid.* i, 45, 48.

defined politically, idealistic in supposing that definition was unnecessary. One consequence was that adjustment to his own party and to nationalism added to O'Connor's difficulties, especially in the first year or two in parliament.

First of all it is necessary to see what O'Connor attempted in the way of radicalism which succeeded in upsetting probably the more conservative of his colleagues, what they and Parnell made of this, and how, principally over the issue of coercion, O'Connor was then persuaded to turn his attention to matters which, as far as Parnell was concerned, were more pressing.

O'Connor's maiden speech, which so impressed John Bright, was given on 20 May 1880 in the debate in answer to the address. He had also attended at least one Irish political meeting in the capital at this time, at the Temperance Hall, Blackfriars Road, in May, but he had taken a back seat to Arthur O'Connor and Justin McCarthy, and did not appear to make a speech. Certainly his first speech in parliament had an Irish colouring, it would be unusual if this were not so given the new acquaintances and new responsibilities he had taken up. But his starting point was foreign affairs, and O'Connor half acknowledged that Gladstone had come back into politics as a protest against tory policies in the Balkans. This was, after all, an area of policy where O'Connor had recently made his name, with his biographical study of Disraeli, and it might be that he was still more at home discussing such matters, inclined still to resort to generalities when talking of Ireland. Even so, attention was turned to Ireland despite Gladstone's extraordinary, and unusual lack of preparation for the crisis breaking over Irish agriculture and landholding. 'It was', said O'Connor 'the fortunate fate of the peasants of Bulgaria and Roumelia that their country formed the battleground of great nations [while] the Irish peasants were left to perish', a type of irony which contained some contrast to his treatment of the Balkans previously.[5] O'Connor went on from this to be one of the main movers in a moderate Irish Bill intended to limit the number of evictions for non-payment of rent, the Compensation for Disturbance Bill (or as O'Connor was blunt or optimistic enough to call it, the 'Fixity of Tenure Bill'). This bill was so moderate it was accepted by the government, including W.E. Forster the Irish Secretary, but it was then rejected contemptuously by the Lords in August.

It is what occurred then, and over matters which seemed far removed from Ireland, which marked O'Connor off from his colleagues.

[5]*The Times*, 11 May 1880; *Hansard, 3,* 252 col. 154, 20 May 1880.

48

He launched what was virtually a one-man campaign against the Lords. Whatever his professed nervousness on first entering the Commons, it was well hidden. He was no stranger to the procedure of parliament, a familiarity which came from his time in the press gallery when he worked for the Central News Agency. He was so familiar with parliamentary forms that he was inclined to ignore ancient usage when it suited him. He did not hesitate to sponsor petitions which came from the many radical clubs of London on 27 and 31 August and which attacked the very function and existence of the Lords. He was unimpressed by the procedural objections of the Speaker on the first occasion and by similar objections which came from Lord Hartington, the deputy leader of the Liberals, on the second.[6] It was something of an achievement, no sooner elected for one House than demanding the abolition of the other. Some of it was tongue in cheek, but it also marked the beginning of a life-long emnity between O'Connor and 'another place'. His friends in the radical clubs had no doubt that they had found a champion, and by comparison to the suspicion, almost isolation, he had so far met with in the Irish party, the South Lambeth Radical Association were the only body to congratulate him on his election. The radicals from Lambeth appeared to be in little doubt that he had been elected as a radical. Shortly after his tussle with the Lords, at the end of the same week, O'Connor and two other radical spirits in the Irish party, J.J. O'Kelly and John Barry, led a demonstration in Hyde Park against the Lords which was intended to rouse both radical and Irish support. Impressions of O'Connor as a radical might have been confirmed by a detailed and perceptive article which he published in the Contemporary Review in June 1880, and with only a few passing references to Ireland, which investigated the power still exercised by money ('the purse') in the British electoral system, and which made a plea for intelligence, represented by littérateurs and journalists.[7] Apart from the one abortive draft of a novel, O'Connor had yet to write at any length on Ireland.

There was the distinct danger that O'Connor would quite quickly cut himself off from even the more progressive spirits in the Parnellite section of the nationalists when he turned to champion the claim of Charles Bradlaugh, the atheist, to affirm and take his seat in the Commons. Here, to his credit, O'Connor showed little caution (at

[6]Ibid. 255 cols 653-4, 27 Aug. ibid. 256 col. 946, 31 Aug.

[7]N.L.I. MS 43460, four letters of S. Bennett of the South Lambeth Radical Association acknowledging invitations to celebrate O'Connor's election; The Times, 6 Sept. This demonstration was a precursor of the foundation of the Social Democratic Federation: 'The Rule of the Purse', Contemporary Review (June 1880). In Dod for 1880 O'Connor described himself as an 'Advanced Radical'.

least this was so in the earlier years of this controversy, which dragged on throughout the second Gladstone administration). He antagonized the 'clerical' section of his own party, and then protested that his opponents were attempting to 'draw me into a profession of belief'. His retort was that 'the part of champion of the faith has been played out in Ireland. . . . I have been sent [to parliament] on political grounds and on those only'. The 'priests of Galway' might have had their worst fears confirmed; so, at least, did Philip Callan of the Parnellite party, whose differences with O'Connor led to a fist fight in the same debate. O'Connor was to learn that Irishmen had long memories where religious matters were concerned. Although he remained contemptuous of the opposition to Bradlaugh, he did change his own view to the extent that he saw the disadvantage of dividing the Irish party on the issue, and was later even ready to see a large Irish vote against Bradlaugh, which occurred in 1883 and 1884, as evidence of party discipline.[8]

But before O'Connor could become reconciled with the rank and file of the party, he had to overcome the suspicions of the lieutenants around Parnell. Objections to O'Connor arose precisely because of his ability and breadth of interest. The election of 1880 was remarkable for returning in the Irish ranks many new recruits touched by youth, individualism, and ability; it was a landmark in Irish politics, and perhaps in the politics of the British Isles. The trouble with O'Connor, sensed by the more lukewarm electors in Galway, was that here was a swashbuckler, likely to carry his individualism too far, too ready to believe that his interests could be added to the Parnellite programme.[9] For a start, O'Connor was always reluctant to rely on politics for a livelihood, even if funds for this purpose could be obtained from the Irish in America, which in 1880 seemed unlikely, and even though in a larger perspective all of O'Connor's writing, such as the books derived from journalism which he produced in this Gladstonian parliament, were to be heavily dependant on what he experienced in politics. His captivation by politics was, however, still far from complete. Something of the nationalist, but, as before, far more of the broad-minded man of letters was to be seen in his editing of the final volume of *The Cabinet of Irish Literature*. This is a type of collection which has since fallen into disrepute, where what was Irish

---

[8]*Hansard, 3,* 252, col. 412, 24 May 1880; *Gladstone's House of Commons* (1885), p. 335.

[9]On the election of 1880 and the intake of new members see O'Connor's *Memoirs,* i, 147 and William O'Brien, *Recollections* (1905), pp. 243-4. See also C.C. O'Brien, *Parnell and his Party,* (1957, rev. ed. 1964), pp. 26-7 and Alan O'Day, *The English Face of Irish Nationalism* (1977), p. 17.

might be extended to cover a long forgotten place of birth, or an attenuated descent. Yet it was a more substantial work than might be supposed, and O'Connor was responsible for writing short, sympathetic biographical pieces for each contributor, which covered figures as diverse as W.H. Lecky, Sir Garnet Wolseley, Isaac Butt, Justin McCarthy, Dion Boucicault, and Lady Wilde, to name only a few.[10] After this literature had to take a rest until a period of greater calm and prosperity came back into O'Connor's life, after 1886.

He could not however afford to neglect his career as a journalist. His election as a Home Ruler had cost him a job with the conservative *Scotsman*, but his newly won reputation then secured for him the coveted position of parliamentary correspondent with the *Pall Mall Gazette* which since the election had come under the editorship of John Morley. This was not O'Connor's only journalistic work: he informed T.M. Healy that he had earned £1,200 for various journalistic ventures in the first year of Gladstone's parliament and, although this was not an extravagant figure for the world of journalism, it was not entirely welcome among a spartan political party. Similarly, while it was no handicap for Healy, William O'Brien, or John Dillon to obey Parnell's precept and example and have little to do with London society, it was a galling obligation to place on the infinitely sociable O'Connor. O'Connor still did not quite fit the bill: the first impressions of his contemporaries show their doubts clearly. Healy, who was acting as Parnell's secretary at this time and who, even at this early stage, regarded himself as Parnell's *alter ego*, found O'Connor likeable but, Healy thought, 'he is more of an English radical and only stood for an Irish constituency because he could not get elected for an English one'. William O'Brien said much the same, that 'all that was known, or indeed asked, about [O'Connor's] politics was that he had lived a long time among English radical associates and was supposed to be one of the rising hopes of that party'.[11] F.H. O'Donnell, most unfairly of all considering the part he had played in recruiting O'Connor, criticized him continually, or at least saved up his criticisms for inclusion in his history of the Irish parliamentary party. The impact O'Connor was beginning to make was seen here; but these

---

[10] *The Cabinet of Irish Literature* (1879), vol. iv. For a further discussion of O'Connor's attitude to literature in this period see chapter 3 below.

[11] Healy to his brother Maurice, *Letters and Leaders of my Day*, i, 98; O'Brien, *Recollections*, pp. 244-5. Healy had worked as a clerk in Newcastle and moved to London in 1878 as parliamentary correspondent of the *Nation*; he first entered parliament after a by-election in November 1880 as M.P. for Wexford. O'Brien was one of the most brilliant journalists in the Parnellite party. He had had some association with the Fenians but broke with them in the mid-1870s. In 1881 he founded *United Ireland* which became the most influential Parnellite newspaper.

were not just first reactions, and they were correct in sensing that
O'Connor was not a single-minded nationalist. Whether O'Connor
was aware of this mood of caution and reserve and was thereby
confirmed in his view that Irish politics was a difficult and sometimes
ungrateful business is not recorded, but he soon came to be slightly
more defensive towards the British radicals and began to justify an
increased concentration on Irish matters.

Parnell's attitude here appeared to be crucial. He was attracted to
O'Connor personally because they were so dissimilar in temperament.
But it is unlikely that O'Connor had much influence over Parnell's
strategy. Some of the waspish comments of Irish M.P.s suggested
otherwise. Over the Bradlaugh incident, for example, Healy warned
Parnell not to give O'Connor so much support and claimed 'He is
using you'.[12] Parnell said that the opposite was true, and although he
merely meant that O'Connor was being kept from his newspaper
work, this is also an indication of how O'Connor was being restricted.
It was to Parnell's advantage that some of his followers had the air of
desperate men and acted more like European romantic nationalists
than British parliamentarians (none more so than O'Connor, and to
be a minority member of a minority party could also suit his outlook).
Such an incursion would help to placate and then devalue the physical
force nationalism still to be found in Ireland, and even more so in the
United States. But this use of resources was only part of Parnell's
strategy, his populist phase when he was 'widening the area of the
agitation' – a phrase he first used early in 1881. During this time he
could look benevolently on the Bradlaugh campaign, and on contacts
O'Connor made with radicalism. O'Connor was, it has been suggested
elsewhere, the chief agent of this policy at Westminister, and Michael
Davitt the chief instrument outside parliament.[13]

To O'Connor there never had been, and sometime in the future
there was not to be, any contradiction between nationalism and
radicalism. In practice, and especially in the early 1880s, it was not so
easy to equate the two, and O'Connor moved away from the radicals
and some of his former friends so that by 1882 if not earlier it was clear
in his parliamentary speeches that some alteration had taken place.
Otherwise, the move is difficult to detect, especially as it was neither
sudden nor final, and O'Connor's motives are difficult to pin down
because he was torn between old and new loyalties. Of considerable
importance in this change was the advice, or direction, of Parnell.
Through Parnell O'Connor was introduced to the world of political

[12]Healy to his brother, 'August' 1880, *Letters*, i, 98, Fyfe, p. 102.
[13]O'Brien, *Parnell*, p. 62.

organization and, in the same way, he was made to see the necessities and dangers of high policy, an area which he might not hitherto have been aware of. As a matter of duty O'Connor attended the yearly conferences of the various leagues in Britain; in 1880 at Newcastle, in 1882 at Liverpool, and in 1883 at Leeds (where he was created president of the Irish National League of Great Britain). Much of his attention was therefore directed away from populism, or at least that aspect which emphasized links with British radicals, and by 1884 the Irish were left free to decide their own tactics in the run up to the election. Parnell had seen the necessity to choose and had turned O'Connor's attention away from social radicalism for a while: to be part of this unprecedented and fascinating enterprise was worth a concentration of effort.

Partly too O'Connor's shift of emphasis was due to what came across in the Commons as an impatience with the gradualism of British radicalism. This evidence has to be treated with caution considering how far his own colleagues had typified O'Connor as a British radical, William O'Brien and others comparing him to Chamberlain and pointing out how much the radicals had lost by not recruiting O'Connor.[14] Furthermore, O'Connor's complaints that the radicals were not helping the Irish came quite early on. In the debate on the Irish constabulary estimates in August 1880, for instance, O'Connor professed his own radicalism, admitted it had caused some difficulties with his colleagues and his constituents, and confessed his disappointment with the silence from the radical benches.[15] Much of this was tactical however, a species of obstruction. To attack radicals from a more radical position was an enviable posture for a young parliamentarian, and appealed on occasions to O'Connor's sense of humour. Sometimes, too, O'Connor was inclined to protest too much in chastising the radicals, perhaps to justify himself in his own eyes. Nevertheless, there was one area of policy where the issues were so serious that some real change in conviction could well have occurred. This was in the Liberal government's coercion policy towards Ireland. Here, Parnell gave O'Connor the principal role in attacking the policy in parliament, believing perhaps that he had already shown the right blend of qualities to be effective in debate, and this was a task which created O'Connor's political reputation more than anything else. Yet even at his most dismissive O'Connor still remained a parliamentarian, determined to settle by discussion: even when tempers were at their highest he still retained a more sympathetic

[14]*Recollections*, p. 245.
[15]*Hansard, 3*, 256 cols. 127-222, 26 Aug.

attitude towards British public opinion than was the case in much of the Irish party.

The battle over coercion lasted for much of 1881, and although the opposition to Forster and Gladstone was often furious (and sometimes savage), the yard-stick by which the Irish judged this Liberal legislation was the normal rule of law, and O'Connor more than any other Irish M.P. drew frequent analogies with British experience.[16] O'Connor seems to have been given the task of leading opposition to coercive legislation. This may have been because he had the right blend of qualities to be effective in debate in parliament while others were more active elsewhere. Parnell's initial policy, evident in the first session of Gladstone's parliament in the autumn of 1880, had been to work fully within parliament and merely press for compensation for disturbance for evicted tenants. When this failed with the Lords' rejection of the Compensation Bill the dispute intensified almost beyond recognition. It was in the recess before the first session of 1881 that Parnell advocated what was soon to be known as 'boycotting' in his Ennis speech. He and the Irish party were anticipating the customary dilemma of British governments which felt obliged to apply a coercion Act in order to make 'normal' law effective in Ireland.

O'Connor, like many of his colleagues, was active in Land League agitation in Ireland at this time and was supposed to have received some payment from Land League funds as late as the end of 1882; one of his meetings, in Drogheda, was proscribed.[17] Much of this has remained obscure; more obvious was his work in Britain aimed at public opinion. He wrote an article for the *Contemporary Review* at the end of 1880 in which he anticipated the introduction of coercion by the Liberals and criticized it precisely because coercion could more properly be described as a weapon of the tories, an instinctive reaction of the tory mentality. Accordingly he claimed that the British public's view of affairs in Ireland had been distorted by the testimony of Irish Conservatives and especially their mouthpiece the Dublin *Daily Express*, whose editor was also Dublin correspondent of *The Times* and who was to remain one of O'Connor's main political and journalistic enemies. On the one hand O'Connor stressed, paralleling what Parnell had said at Ennis that coercion would not be

---

[16] For a fuller description of obstruction see D. Thornley, 'The Irish Home Rule Party and Parliamentary Obstruction, 1847-1887', *I.H.S.*, 12 (1960), 38-57.

[17] This was O'Connor's claim (*Hansard, 3,* 257, col. 1052, 20 Jan. 1881). The claim that O'Connor received money from Land League funds, presumably for loss of earnings, is in the police report reproduced in the Appendix.

accepted easily that, in O'Connor's words, 'the lessons of 1847 and 1848 [had] taught the legislators of 1879 and 1880' but, on the other, this was because Irishmen had become 'defiant freemen' organized in the Land League. The analogy was with an Englishman's defence of his rights and the appeal was to common liberal principles. O'Connor here tried, as on many occasions to come, to break the stale habit of mind whereby Ireland was either ignored or treated with sensationalism. How news from Ireland reached England was therefore of great importance and it could be assumed that O'Connor knew something about this. It was reasonably to try and convert the problem into something more familiar, a political problem where something constructive ought to be done, and done by the Liberals.[18]

The appeal to the British audience was obvious and it was to continue. When the Irish party moved more openly into the offensive, attacking the references to coercion in the Address, O'Connor throughout emphasized that what was involved was a fundamental issue of respect for the ordinary processes of law and continually drew comparisons with Britain. He could variously suggest that the Liberals ought to hand over the government of Ireland 'to those who really exercised it', namely the Land League, that boycotting was similar to the practices of trade unions, and that the Irish had followed the 'English masters' of the art. He brought the paradox home: 'every day that I live in England, breathing a free atmosphere, I become more and more indignant at the manner in which my country has been treated by the English government.'[19] None of this did much to overcome the scepticism of the government and the Conservative benches and Gladstone complained that the debate on the Address had led nowhere. Debate and the logic of a case did not settle the political difficulty but there is no denying the good sense of O'Connor's arguments and how well they still read. If the House remained unimpressed and comparisons with trade union rights fell particularly flat that apparently was all the more reason for the Irish party, including one of its most recent recruits, to be confirmed in its self-confidence and not treat the House with too much awe.

Paradoxically, O'Connor's attachment to parliament and to the ideals of Liberalism also emerged when Forster introduced the Coercion Bill itself, the Protection of Persons and Property (Ireland) Bill on 24 January 1881. This was a mere four days after the end of the debate on the Address and the House could only be aware that it faced more wearisome debate. This was the nub of O'Connor's criticism of

[18]'The Land League and Its Work', *Contemporary Review*, 38 (Dec. 1880), 981-99.

[19]*Hansard, 3*, 257, cols. 122 and 127, 6 Jan. 1881; *ibid.* col. 1053, 20 Jan.

the government. Accepting that some Irish M.P.s did resort to blatant obstruction, this was the manifestation of a deeper grievance which O'Connor emphasized. T.M. Healy and A.M. Sullivan were among the few to use obstructive tactics with any skill. O'Connor found procedural devices irksome and his interventions here did not go beyond repeating motions that 'the Speaker leave the chair', or reading at length from Blue Books in the manner first pioneered by Biggar in the 1870s. He was unenthusiastic. Instead, his criticism went back to first principles: if the House were weary of the issue O'Connor could claim that, legally, the Irish were still entitled to a full debate when the government introduced its Bill and developed the evidence for the need for coercion. More simply he could demonstrate that the way the debate had emerged confirmed his fears that fundamental rights were being taken away from the Irish with insufficient discussion. He further drove the point home by suggesting that coercion was unpopular with radicals in England, 'condemned by large and enthusiastic meetings in Birmingham and Newcastle-on-Tyne [and by] a large number of Clubs and Associations' and he asked for discussion to be postponed until the working classes of England had given their verdict, a suggestion which was dismissed by the Speaker because of its irregularity but which might have stirred a few consciences and prolonged Chamberlain's and Gladstone's uneasiness about coercive legislation. A party in power had great advantages in defining what was or was not a nuisance but O'Connor's arguments help to show, in perspective, that the charge of obstruction was often a majority verdict. O'Connor realised this at the time, having failed to convince the government that the House of Lords had obstructed radical proposals in 1880. In our eyes, the way the forms of the House were used by the government came close to showing the inability of parliament to deal with extraordinary grievances.

Obstruction was a last resort, as it always had been, and when it resulted in the infamous forty-one hour sitting of 31 January, the introduction, whether legal or not, of the closure on 2 February and the suspension of thirty-six Irish M.P.s the following day for disrespect to the chair, this could have led, under one of the possibilities first aired when Parnell negotiated the 'New Departure', to a rejection of parliament: if such a policy were to be followed this was an ideal time. But it is unlikely that the majority of even those thirty-six M.P.s who had been suspended would have approved of an abstentionist policy. It is certainly unlikely that O'Connor, who had been among the thirty-six, would have approved. He was one of the most determined of politicians and still refused to believe that the resources of parliament had been exhausted. Parnell perhaps realized this in delegating the further campaign against coercion to O'Connor. This operated in two areas. O'Connor and Thomas Sexton kept up the parliamentary battle, making Forster's life a misery, while the other Irish leaders were imprisoned or in exile in France. In addition extra-parliamentary activity was intended to frighten yet another political generation and put pressure on parliament. O'Connor, possibly more than any other Irish M.P., and probably more than Parnell himself, agreed with Parnell's announcement from Paris in an open letter to the Land League in February 1881 that their policy must now be to 'go on widening the area of the agitation. . . to include the English masses'; it was the theme he had tried to give to his own opposition to coercion. Much of the wider agitation was left to Michael Davitt but O'Connor played his part here too, so that in February O'Connor's collaboration with his radical allies led to the formation of the Anti-Coercion Association with H.M. Hyndman, the immediate forerunner of the Social Democratic Federation. This is some indication of the extent of O'Connor's friendships, or at least acquaintanceships, his early familiarity with the most extreme politics Britain could produce and perhaps where he could be placed early in life in relation to official Liberalism.[20]

For all Sexton's and O'Connor's efforts, the analogies with England, or the ridicule heaped on Forster, the Coercion Bill could now only be delayed. It was passed on 28 February and quickly augmented by the Peace Preservation (Ireland) Bill, passed by 11 March. Ameliorating legislation was due to follow. After the alarums and excursions over coercion the Irish could be forgiven for not thinking much of the chances of a good Land Bill. O'Connor, once his and the Irish party's advice to introduce reform first had been ignored, offered to see some method in it. 'Land reform, which according to popular rumour had been developing in the revolutionary mind of the prime minister' would, according to O'Connor, come when 'the two parties [English and Irish] were ready, like stage lovers, to fall into each others' arms and commence the comedy of profession their mutual affection and cordial agreement in principle'.[21]

---

[20]*Ibid.* cols 1903, 1747-8, 31 Jan.-1 Feb. 1881; O'Brien, *Parnell*, pp. 59-62; Healy, *Letters,* i, 107; Henry Pelling, *Origins of the Labour party* (1954), p. 15. O'Connor claimed that he saw the 'inherent weakness' of the obstructionist policy (*Parnell*, p. 109). It was at about this time (or perhaps even earlier, in his more footloose days in London), that O'Connor met Karl Marx at his home in Chalk Farm. In recollection at least, it was hardly a high point in O'Connor's intellectual development. He recalled Marx benevolently, and mischievously as 'a typical German bourgeois [with] a quiet and emotional middle class nature', (*R.N.,* 18 Jan. 1914).

[21]*Hansard, 3,* 258, col. 2005, 1 Mar.

Gladstone's Land Bill, his second and most revolutionary piece of land legislation, was introduced on 7 April 1881 and showed once again how he was prepared to break with most assumptions about property. It allowed the right of tenants in Ireland to a free sale of their interest in a farm, fixity of tenure while rents were paid and, most important of all, a fair rent to be arrived at by a decision of the courts in disputed cases. While the development of the land agitation since 1879 and the fight over coercion meant that it was difficult for the Irish to accept the Bill without a murmur, these proposals were so far-reaching that they threatened to split the movement on its agrarian side into moderate and extremist factions and to split both from the parliamentary party. Parnell hoped to extricate himself from these difficulties by putting the onus upon the Liberals to prove their good intentions. Most of the parliamentary party at once feared that such opposition might lose the Bill for Ireland but in the new session when the debate on the Bill continued Parnell had to make a gesture which would preserve his independence and that of his party. He made abstention on the bill's second reading a matter of confidence in his leadership; it is probable that this was the only way to enforce abstention. O'Connor was surprised at Parnell's sudden announcement and those whom O'Connor called the 'old parliamentarians', such as John O'Connor Power, were even more dismayed.[22] O'Connor thought Parnell's action unwise, and Sexton thought it a mistake, but they were both among those who agreed to abstain. The oracular way in which Parnell had announced his policy was an early sign of the distress he could cause his party and distinguishes him from parliamentarians such as O'Connor who looked to the legislation itself but were aware of the wider context. O'Connor could also, in his first parliament, be distinguished from more ardent nationalists such as John Dillon whom O'Connor on at least two occasions had to defend in the House for speeches made in Ireland.[23] When parliament worked properly, when the Liberals listened, it needed little defence against those who advocated abstention and O'Connor might feel his part was equally justified by the detailed work he did for his Galway constituency. In later life he was more impatient but these moods were temporary and from the first he had a realistic horror of violence and extremism. His favourable verdict on land reform, by June, was that it 'would do more for Ireland than half a dozen Coercion Acts and 50,000 soldiers'. Although O'Connor could not resist guying Gladstone's notorious cost-consciousness and what he regarded as an English trait

---

[22]*Memoirs*, i, 177; *Parnell Movement*, p. 231.
[23]*Hansard, 3*, 255, col. 1374, 17 Aug. 1880 and *ibid.* 259, col. 168, 2 Mar. 1881.

of 'admiration at their own generosity with other people's property', [24] Gladstone had gone as far, if not further, than O'Connor would have expected. Perhaps understandably the liberal benches were not won over by these wry expressions of gratification and it was at this late juncture that Sir William Harcourt, the Home Secretary, praised Forster for jailing Dillon and Sexton but regretted that he had missed Healy and O'Connor whom he described as 'the noisiest of them all'. [25] This was not an unbiased opinion and it is a testament to O'Connor's determination, free of any misplaced reverence. In parliament O'Connor was the Irish party's greatest asset, asserting liberal principles and finding them lacking in the government.

On Tour in the U.S.A. and Britain, 1882-5

There remained a larger theatre than parliament: the Irish in America, the Irish in Britain, the little world of political organization, the hurried but hypnotic activity of electioneering. Outside parliament O'Connor developed most. Perhaps both parliament and the discipline of politics were to prove confining to a journalist as diverse in his accomplishments as O'Connor and there had already been, for instance, more experience to be gained in 'widening the area of the agitation'; though it is not evident what he made of Hyndman. O'Connor's journalism since the beginning of Gladstone's parliament had been primarily concerned with parliamentary reporting and had caused something of a stir, either of jealously or anger, in his own party and even more so among opponents because of what he wrote and because it allowed him an independence or objectivity and a jauntiness of manner. Yet O'Connor's preoccupation with Ireland in 1880 and 1881 and the depth of his involvement in parliamentary debate was not so characteristic of his later career despite his parliamentary proficiency. At the end of the 1881 session O'Connor might well have thought that he must look to his finances and take more care of his journalistic affairs and he planned to deal with both by making a lecture tour of the United States.

This venture, once again, showed O'Connor's enterprise and ambition. Again it was interrupted by Parnell who would rather

---

[24] *Ibid.* 262, col. 925, 20 June; *ibid.* 263, col. 323, 7 July. O'Connor also attempted to demonstrate some moderation; he 'could not admit the principle that wages and the relations between employers and labour could be regulated by the direct intervention of the state' (*ibid.* 262, col. 1164, 23 June). This serves to indicate O'Connor's very real attachment to laisser faire, even though such conviction is no longer a useful guide to a politician's place in the spectrum of left and right.

[25] A.G. Gardiner, *Sir William Harcourt* (1923), i, 431.

O'Connor had visited the U.S.A. on behalf of the Irish party. Concern about the American end of the movement had been felt by Parnell during the Land League conference which had met in Dublin on 10 September; it was occasioned by the telegrams of protest received from Irish Americans who opposed the new Land Act. Parnell's policy of 'testing the Act' in the courts could only have a stop-gap effect and it was therefore highly convenient to have O'Connor as an intermediary with the Americans, the chief financial backers of the movement. Perhaps O'Connor could ensure their continued support, if not their obedience, on a more stable basis than the American interpretation of the New Departure. O'Connor, agreeable as always, accepted this extra burden, even though a prolonged absence for political reasons might disturb his newspaper contacts in London. It was because he was amenable, had the journalistic quality of being a non-committal listener, that he could deal with the Americans. Parnell, in writing a letter of introduction to Patrick Ford, the powerful Fenian leader in New York, said that O'Connor 'Would represent my views and those of the Irish organization'.[26] Parnell did this in the midst of a campaign of provocative speeches which were almost certainly designed to ensure his own arrest, out of the way of responsibility for agrarian agitation. O'Connor, as Harcourt had remarked, was one of the few Irish parliamentarians left at liberty or not in exile from the law. In his variety of exile he represented the trust that Parnell could safely place in him and in his abilities.

O'Connor's tour of the U.S.A. was to last six months, up to May 1882, and was to prove an unqualified success. American ways in politics took some getting used to, especially the silences of audiences who had come to listen to lectures rather than agree or disagree with speeches. It was all certainly less disrespectful than the House of Commons had been in the previous year. Despite the hectic timetable of a journey which took him, as so many lecturers before and since, from coast to coast, it was something of an orator's holiday because he was enthralled at the more obvious demonstrativeness of American politics and he proved popular with Americans.[27] His own early interest in the theatrical parts of politics meant that he found Americans an agreeable surprise, though in all his new experiences he did not lose sight of the practicalities of his mission. According to Healy, who joined him in the U.S.A. in November, O'Connor was an accomplished fund raiser, 'adept at laying siege to the pockets of our

---

[26] Parnell to Ford, 1 Oct. 1881, quoted in O'Donnell, *Irish Parliamentary Party*, ii, 154.

[27] Fyfe *O'Connor*, p. 97.

exiles'.[28] This talent may also have been something which O'Connor discovered in the United States where he may have been a slight relief from the harsher realities of Irish politics brought to America by Davitt and Parnell.

The American Fenians and the branches of the American Land League were a more difficult prospect but here too O'Connor achieved a modest success. To some extent O'Connor's task was aided by the continuing seriousness of Irish affairs, the arrest of Parnell and yet more Irish M.P.s for instance, which would make it difficult to criticize the parliamentary movement for being too moderate. At the same time O'Connor may have had to go some way towards meeting Irish American susceptibilities. What O'Connor may have said or appeared to promise (for show or when it did not matter) remains unclear. Critics of these expeditions to foreign countries, many Englishmen or envious Irishmen like F.H. O'Donnell, maintained that O'Connor was more exteme when speaking to American audiences and one Irish Conservative body claimed to have picked up a speech in which O'Connor declared himself dissatisfied with rent reduction and demanded 'absolute independence of landlordism and the restoration of Irish national independence'.[29] O'Connor may have said something like this on isolated occasions or when an awkward moment demanded it: the distinction between what was or was not 'for the record', was not finely drawn. But O'Connor, unlike Davitt or Ford, was not an advocate of land nationalization. His chief task while he was in the U.S.A. was to follow the pattern of negotiation set by Parnell, of appearing to promise infinitely, giving away little in practice, all the while keeping American backing for the constitutional movement. Hence it was on his initiative that a convention of all American branches of the Land League was summoned and met in Chicago from 20 November to 2 December, 1881. Finally, O'Connor was able against formidable and persistent negotiators such as Ford, to obtain a stalemate. At the end of the convention there were expressions of continued support for the parliamentarians rather than any commitment to expropriation, or readiness to risk the sort of violence which the extreme nationalists had in mind.[30]

---

[28] Healy, *Letters*, i, 39.

[29] According to O'Donnell, the 'Ribbon Fenians in America wanted their Irish news hot and strong' (*Irish Parliamentary Party*, ii, 48). O'Connor's speech was first reported in Ford's *Irish World*, an account then appeared in the Dublin *Irishman* (14 Jan. 1882); it was later included in a piece of Irish Conservative propaganda, *A Guide to the '86, Chiefly Contributed by Themselves* (1886).

[30] O'Connor's attendance at the Chicago convention nevertheless incriminated him in the minds of many British M.P.s, especially with Conservatives; the matter was

Healy, by contrast, was not very much impressed by the United States and somewhat sardonic in his memoirs about O'Connor's reaction. He believed, for instance, that O'Connor was fascinated by 'the American method of railroading conventions without debate'. Healy echoed a British suspicion of the American example in politics which dated at least from the 1860s and which received added impetus in the 1870s and 1880s with fears of 'caucus' politics.[31] To O'Connor, however, America offered an example of greater freedom and wider possibilities and this visit in particular may have been decisive in opening his eyes to opportunities for innovation in journalism. Whatever the doubts of Healy, O'Donnell, or indeed most British M.P.s, it gave O'Connor an added perspective on politics which helped to sustain his enthusiasm and optimism and the belief that he could well have felt, at least up to 1890 and the Parnell divorce crisis, that real change was imminent. It was the first of six tours of north America which O'Connor conducted in his parliamentary career each one, apart from one made during the first world war, playing some part in strengthening his belief that although parliament was the only way to affect change, its frame of reference was often parochial and unimaginative.

When O'Connor returned to England via Cork and Dublin in May 1882 some of this rapid assimilation of experience can be discerned at work in the tasks he now faced. Immediately it seemed that relations with the Liberal government had deteriorated once more on account of the Phoenix Park murders. Yet although this involved more coercion and another round of intense parliamentary opposition, the disagreement was more apparent than real. At the same time O'Connor was now able to deal with organization among the Irish in Britain with greater confidence, almost as an acknowledged expert.

The situation which faced O'Connor when he arrived back in England was in marked contrast to the confidence of his American tour (a circumstance which was going to be repeated when he returned from the United States after the break-up of the party over the divorce crisis). His youngest sister Mary had been imprisoned as a result of her work for the Ladies' Land League. O'Connor himself had offered to return and be arrested along with other Irish leaders but Parnell had thought him too useful to be sacrificed.[32] The assassination of Lord

brought up during the Parnell commission (see the *Report* pp. 106-7) and, prior to that, was mentioned when O'Connor was in correspondence with *The Times* (see chapter 3, p. 94); it also caused O'Connor's quarrel with John Bright which is referred to below.

[31] Healy, *Letters*, i, 139; Hanham, *Elections*, pp. 125-154.

[32] As reported in *The Times*, 4 Apr 1882.

Frederick Cavendish and T.H. Burke in the Phoenix Park in Dublin had exacerbated relations between British and Irish possibly more than the battle over coercion in 1881 had done, but its paradoxical consequence was to make things easier for Parnell and the Irish party. It was recognized, at least for the time being, that Irish M.P.s were not implicated in the atrocity. Parnell was as horrified as British ministers; but he could demonstrate the bankruptcy of extremism; attention was directed away from the controversial Kilmainham 'treaty' which Parnell had negotiated with Gladstone which had brought tenants in arrears within the Land Act but which had been criticised as a sacrifice of the land agitation; the prestige of the Irish party with the public in Ireland was augmented when it fought the coercion which followed.

O'Connor was again in the forefront of the parliamentary battle when the Crimes Bill was introduced by G.O. Trevelyan, the successor to Cavendish as Irish Secretary. Henry Labouchere, a journalistic and political friend of O'Connor's, had warned Healy on coercion and had indicated that the government was compelled to legislate. Yet even more than in 1881, O'Connor warned that the Bill would harm 'constitutional agitators'.[33] This was at the end of the session in July 1882 when twenty-five Irish M.P.s, including O'Connor, were again suspended. This was rehabilitation to the Irish, to the English it ought to have suggested that to remove M.P.s solved a temporary difficulty but left the state clear for violence.

O'Connor moved among his countrymen in Britain with a greater, almost an imperial, confidence. Just how specific his interest in the Irish in Britain had been prior to 1883 is problematic. In his memoirs he associated it with the election of 1885, saying that by then he had 'become to some extent identified more prominently than my colleagues with the Irish in Great Britain'.[34] Signs of this interest, or a closely related one, were apparent in a concern O'Connor showed for the condition of emigrants and in particular the suspect condition of emigrant ships bound for the U.S.A. In the summer of 1881 he had launched a one-man campaign in parliament, when parliament and the Irish were equally busy with coercion. He cross-questioned Joseph Chamberlain, the then President of the Board of Trade and was not satisfied with Chamberlain's answers. Perhaps it was from here that a noticeable coolness between the two radicals began. After his return from the U.S.A., almost exactly a year later, O'Connor returned to the

---

[33]Labouchere to Chamberlain, 17 May 1882, quoted in A.L. Thorold, *The Life of Henry Labouchere* (1913), p. 162; *Hansard, 3, 271*, col. 1118.

[34]*Memoirs*, ii, 6.

attack, criticising Chamberlain's permissive emigration schemes which had been developed in 1882 and characterising the schemes as 'the emigration of the peasantry in Ireland in order to become bondsmen in America'. At the same time he took the opportunity to demand a fuller inquiry than was usual into anti-Irish riots which had taken place in Tredegar in south Wales in July 1882.[35]

O'Connor's American experiences were translated into the words of optimism and encouragement with which he addressed the League conference in Liverpool in August 1882. Here he was given a far more prominent place than when he had attended the Newcastle conference the previous year. In the public meeting on 13 August, after the conference (from which the press, as was often the case with Irish nationalist meetings, had been excluded) he made the major speech and spoke of 'the great scenes he had witnessed in America' and concluded that their struggle 'was no longer a conflict about land... it was the battle of a great race'. Privately O'Connor's attitude was not so clear-cut; on returning from America he had, so he said later, compared its 'high and proud hope' with the 'limited' conditions of Ireland. His public criticism of the emigrant traffic showed also how sensitive the issue could be among Irishmen. Healy had put the matter of the Irish 'diaspora' another way when describing the Irish Americans. His opinion, which was common among nationalists, was that 'American politics, like English politics, are a source of division among our countrymen'.[36] This was typical of Healy's *realpolitik*, on a par with his contempt for the Liberals. O'Connor was more subtle, sensitive, and less calculating. It was true that O'Connor gave Irish audiences in Liverpool and other parts of Britain a sense of loyalty beyond their own parish or their own local politicians, and it may have appeared more obvious to many of them that they belonged to a world-wide movement. Yet whereas the Irish Americans found this no disadvantage, the Irish in Britain, contrary to what Healy may have thought proper, did experience difficulties over loyalty. Perhaps this can be seen in the concern shown for the needs of labour at both the Newcastle and the Liverpool conferences. This had fitted in with 'widening the area of the agitation', but it had also been what O'Connor and the Irish in Britain wanted. O'Connor's attacks on emigrant conditions were further proof of substance behind his oratory.

[35] *Hansard, 3,* 260, col. 1554, 2 May; *ibid.* col. 1660, 30 May, 262, col. 1104, 23 June, 264, col. 1381, 9 Aug. 1881; 272, cols. 1228-33, *ibid.* 442-3, 31 July 1881.

[36] *D.P.* 14 Aug. Fyfe, p. 100; Healy to his brother, 13 Nov. 1881, *Letters,* i, 141. In one rare instance, O'Connor affected to believe that the Irish in Britain were 'far more extreme' than the Irish in America (*Parnell Movement,* p. 162) but this was possibly designed for its tonic effect.

So was the work he did the following year in 1883 in piloting through the Commons a Bill, which was in essence an extension of Disraeli's Artisans Dwellings Act, for the better housing of labourers in Ireland, a group with, as yet, no political power, no franchise and of whom O'Connor said there was 'general agreement with regard to their unhappy condition'.[37] As with emigrants, they had been largely overlooked until O'Connor championed their case. This sort of unprejudiced and persistent intelligence in radicalism was characteristic of O'Connor, as was his sincerity. Radicalism was always liable to re-emerge if the nationalist aim appeared remote or not worth fighting for; from 1883 onwards nationalism was given priority and this appeared to be satisfactory to the Irish in Britain.

The League conference which set up the Irish National League of Great Britain (or I.N.L.G.B.) met in Leeds at the end of September 1883. It was a pragmatic affair with no reference to the larger developments which had taken place since the previous year's conference; there was, for instance, no mention of the Kilmainham treaty despite its earlier unpopularity. Parnell appears to have been turning away from the wider agitation, with O'Connor following his lead, partly no doubt because of his own impatience with the Liberals. The emphasis was on the practical and what could be immediately achieved. O'Connor, coming from his work in parliament on the Labourer's Bill, was made president of the new League, a position he was to hold until 1918 and even after that in various guises. He was as yet untested in an executive capacity but Parnell was to prove as justified here as when he gave O'Connor a free hand in the expedition to the United States. Further than this a new executive was established composed of members of the parliamentary party. In all, Parnell's control was increased and these changes looked forward to what might be achieved in the next election.

Organization and control of this kind, although apparently routine, was both essential for the Irish movement and a sign of growing confidence. For a number of years after 1883 the crucial and in many ways novel role of the League was to drill the Irish vote in Britain to such an extent that it could be used as a fine tuning device to regulate the response of the two British parties to Home Rule. This began to appear more noticeable because of the opportunities which might be given to the Irish by parliamentary reform and because of the approach of an election. A change in emphasis whereby what mattered was political effectiveness had become discernible in

[37]*Hansard, 3,* 279, col. 1240, 30 May 1883.

O'Connor's attitude at Westminister and could also be seen among Irish organizers throughout Britain.

O'Connor's concern for Irish matters continued, and these were of the sort which might also interest the Irish in Britain. He returned to the issue of emigration in a debate in July 1883 where he claimed that 'feeling against emigration. . . was becoming more intense every day', which may have been the case or may have reflected nationalist sentiment.[38] More generally, in the same debate, he attacked the government for its handling of Poor Law relief in Ireland. Perhaps closer to his heart were his complaints about education. Here, O'Connor's attitude was markedly different from the policy urged on the Irish party by the Catholic hierarchy, namely to emphasize the right to denominational education. Instead, in a witty speech much appreciated by the Irish secretary Trevelyan, he attacked the content of secondary education in Ireland. He ridiculed textbooks used in secondary schools which claimed, for example, that 'the people of Ireland are a clever lively people, formerly very much given to drink; but now it is believed they are one of the soberest nations in Europe'. The attack was that of an intelligent, literate critic but some of the pride that had been hurt in his childhood and youth showed through. The Irish, he said, 'should not be asked to read books insulting to their own nationality'.[39]

For the complaints there was however a remedy; to use political leverage at Westminster more effectively. By the summer of 1883 O'Connor was prepared to be enthusiastic about the use of the Irish vote in the Commons itself. He had been a champion of Bradlaugh but in May 1883 celebrated the defeat of the Affirmation Bill which would have allowed Bradlaugh to take his seat. On this occasion it was seen as an indication of how the Irish held the balance in the Commons and could give victory to the Conservatives – perhaps the earliest indication of how O'Connor might have seen a general election contest developing.[40] More directly, the following month in a speech in parliament replying to an attack made by John Bright in Birmingham on O'Connor's conduct at Chicago, which itself raised the question of whether Bright had infringed on parliamentary privilege, O'Connor returned the compliment. Possibly his attack on Bright here was the most bitter criticism of any individual which he was ever to make (and it was a speech which caused great hostility in

---

[38] *Ibid*. 281, col. 909, 9 July.

[39] *Ibid*. 283, col. 1047, 17 Aug.

[40] *Gladstone's House of Commons*, p. 335. The debate was on 3 and 4 May.

the Commons). On the same occasion he claimed that 'both the great political parties at times evinced a strong anxiety to disavow anything like alliance with the Irish. . . party' but that the Parnellites were 'equally conscious that anything like an alliance with the English parties was regarded by [Irish] constituents with dislike and suspicion'.[41]

This was a large and possibly disingenous claim. Both British parties had at times denied Irish influence, the tories with little need to do so strenuously, the Liberals with more apprehension because it was common knowledge that they and the Irish had often agreed to differ. Some sort of alliance with the Liberals had been the only practical policy hitherto; not very productive but the only one which, for the most part, might have occurred to Irish voters. What is more important is that the claim was made, the matter brought out into the open; it advertised to British parties and Irish voters alike that the Irish parliamentarians were now able to make greater demands.[42]

This was the accompaniment to the League conference of 1883 and the change of mood among the Irish parliamentarians, the Irish organizers, and possibly the Irish voters is exemplified by the case of John Denvir in Liverpool. Just at this juncture, in January 1884, Denvir founded the *Irish Programme*, a newspaper for the Irish in Britain in which he not only attacked the discrimination Irishmen faced, in being stereotyped and in being denied education – the very areas which O'Connor had touched on in emigration or education debates – but went on to single out the existing friendship with the Liberal party as the cause of neglect. The very title of Denvir's newspaper, by comparison, suggested a political alternative.[43] Perhaps the stage had been set by Parnell as early as the end of 1883 when, speaking at the Rotunda in Dublin, he had said that 'it will be for the Irish people in England – separated, isolated as they are – and for your independent Irish members, to determine at the next general election whether a tory or a Liberal English ministry shall rule England'.[44]

This foresight derived principally from the possibilities presented to the Irish by parliamentary reform. A long-awaited Franchise Bill was introduced in February 1884 at the beginning of the new session. Parliamentary Reform Bills were, and still are, regarded as the great

---

[41] *Hansard, 3,* 280, cols. 816-17, 18 June.

[42] For the previous political alignment of the Irish in Britain see Vincent, *Liberal Party,* pp. 293-9.

[43] *Irish Programme,* 16 Feb., 10 May, 27 Sept. 1884.

[44] Speech of 11 Dec. 1883, quoted in John Morley, *The Life of William Ewart Gladstone* (1903), iii, 143.

landmarks in nineteenth-century politics, whether or not they changed the anatomy of power. February 1884 marks the beginning of a period of fluidity within and across party lines which lasted until the summer of 1886.[45] In all these complicated circumstances the Irish could hope for immediate benefits from franchise reforms and then some advantage from redistribution of seats and, partly using these expectations, could take advantage of uncertainties in the Liberal and Conservative camps. In all this, both in debate and in the implementation of tactics, O'Connor was a key figure; he may even have had some inkling of Parnell's overall strategy though Parnell was never generous with his confidences. The stakes here were so high that O'Connor's radicalism was forgotten until he carefully picked up the pieces after the election of 1886.

Gladstone's franchise proposals were simply to extend the borough franchise created in 1867 into the counties; he wanted to keep it simple and he largely succeeded. But such a straightforward reform could have wide implications for Irish representation; it would mean that in the boroughs the vote would at last be extended to householders, thus bringing it in line with the franchise in Britain, and in the counties the result would be that to the tenant farmers would be added many of the agricultural labourers. Largely as a result of intensive organization Parnell was expected greatly to improve his position in Ireland at the next election. Chamberlain, in a private calculation, did not expect franchise reform so much as the work of the Parnellite organizers to improve Parnell's prospects. There has even been the suggestion more recently that the new labourers' vote was an unknown, radical, quantity which caused the Parnellites some apprehension since it would upset the support which they had carefully built up since 1879.[46] Yet the advantages were more obvious. They certainly were to O'Connor. It was he who, in the Commons, had to deal with the protests of both Conservatives and Liberals who were both more obviously fearful of the change than were the Parnellites. Conservative objections were blunt; that on the basis of a strict comparison of population, Ireland's representation ought to be reduced (an argument that was to become more strident after the turn of the century). Lord Randolph Churchill and his 'fourth

---

[45] Political manoeuvre in this period has been examined in great detail, see especially, Andrew Jones, *The Politics of Reform, 1884* (1972) and A.B. Cooke and John Vincent, *The Governing Passion* (1974).

[46] This view is in Jones, *Politics of Reform*, pp. 91-4 and in F.S.L. Lyons, *Charles Stewart Parnell* (1977), p. 267. O'Connor's verdict later was that the 'franchise had been reduced and it was clear that we were going to sweep the country' (*Parnell*, p. 154). In his memoirs he was even more positive that the reforms would increase Parnellite strength (*Memoirs*, i, 337 and 341).

party' for their own reasons did not support these objections, helped to have them withdrawn or defeated and so began their peculiar though short-lived friendship with the Irish. Liberal, or rather whig, objections over Ireland were aired less frequently in public but were more dangerous since they had a spokesman in Lord Hartington, the presumed heir apparent to the Liberal leadership, who might have been supposed to have some influence with Gladstone. The whigs in Ireland, even more than in Britain, had more to lose in any democratisation of the franchise; it could mean the end of the Irish whigs. O'Connor met the objections of Conservative back-benchers in the debate in May 1884 and when he reported the debate for the *Freeman's Journal* departed from journalistic neutrality by presenting the matter as a victory for the Irish. Henry Chaplin's motion for the reduction of Irish representation was withdrawn despite the protests of E.R. King-Harman, the Irish Conservative, and Lord Claud Hamilton, the Anglo-Irish member for Liverpool, though the matter was raised again at the end of the month by other Conservatives and then defeated with the help of Randolph Churchill and his followers. As for the whigs, for all their apparent power Gladstone ignored them and in the following election they were wiped off the electoral map in Ireland. To O'Connor 'the great central Historic fact [was that] the right of Ireland to absolute equality with England was not questioned by a divison in the Imperial parliament of Great Britain' at least not when the matter was first raised, and it marked also 'the birth of another epoch'.[47] It would be too easy to say that this concern for a demonstration of justice was meant for popular consumption only; it was a surprisingly rare occasion in O'Connor's long career when he would make a distinction between politics and what it was fit to tell the public. Yet the removal of the amendments was important because securing of the franchise must have been seen as an important step in the Irish bid for greater influence.

Confidence that the Irish were increasing their strength was observable at that year's I.N.L.G.B. conference which, as if in celebration, met in Dublin in September. In his usual public speech, O'Connor promised the full allegiance of the vote in Britain to Parnell and called for 'the organization of our strength in England and Scotland, so as to make the Irish vote a controlling force in English electoral contests'.[48] There was no suggestion that O'Connor was apprehensive about any category of voters introduced by the new

[47]Gladstone's *House of Commons*, pp. 402, 404, 406, reporting the debate of 1 May. For the debate of 20-1 May, see *Hansard, 3*, 288, cols. 853-913.

[48]*Irish Nationalist*, 13 Sept. The *Programme* became the *Nationalist* in August.

franchise. On the contrary, he both shared in their demands and helped to define them: as late as August 1885 he was still piloting his Labourers Bill through the Commons when he attempted, unsuccessfully, to have unemployed labourers brought within the scope of the Bill.[49] If, as may possibly have been the case, it was believed that the new franchise would be a great advantage among the Irish in Britain, then here is where O'Connor's interest lay and he had closer ties with the more popular elements in nationalism than most other Irish M.P.s. It is merely difficult, going by the record of nationalist preponderance in the affairs of the most radical of Irishmen, namely, the Irish in Britain, and given the success of Parnellism by 1884, to see how, even if Gladstone intended it, the extension of the franchise was regarded as, or could prove to be, a threat to the parliamentary position of Parnell.

Yet if, as was recognised, O'Connor was the ideal choice to confirm the nationalism of the voters behind Parnell, it remains true that Parnell made a decisive break with radicalism just at this juncture and O'Connor said nothing. This was in April 1884, one month before O'Connor and other Parnellites defended the franchise in the Commons. Parnell attacked Michael Davitt's attachment to 'English' radicalism and to land nationalization.[50] O'Connor had never had any enthusiasm for the latter but links with English radicalism had been what marked him out in the ranks of the Irish party. This was the culmination of a change which had been taking place since 1882 in Parnell's policy and in O'Connor's whose consequences had also included the Irish opposition to Bradlaugh in February 1884. There is no evidence that Parnell consulted O'Connor over the attack on Davitt; it would have been difficult for O'Connor by that time to protest in any case and he was kept occupied with strictly Parnellite matters. Even so, in none of O'Connor's dealings with the I.N.L.G.B. from here until the election of 1886 was there any reference to friendship with the radicals or the working classes of Britain and this was in marked contrast to the record of that organization and its immediate predecessors. There must have been at least a tacit agreement that O'Connor could keep quiet about radicalism.

Attitudes of the Irish to Chamberlain, that is to a force nominally associated with radicalism within parliament, were a more difficult business and mistakes here were not to prove so easily rectified. Why the Irish should prove so remarkably unfriendly towards Chamberlain,

---

[49] *Hansard, 3,* 300, col. 1013, 3 Aug. 1885.
[50] The breach here is particularly highlighted by O'Brien (*Parnell,* p. 88).

and to a lesser extent Dilke, while at the same time showing
themselves prepared to entertain Randolph Churchill, even when it
became more obvious that he could secure little advantage for the
Parnellites, has been speculated on to some effect elsewhere.[51] There
were good tactical reasons; Chamberlain's and Dilke's overtures to the
Parnellites came at the end of 1884 and negotiations here, sometimes
through the less than adequate medium of Captain and Mrs. O'Shea,
lasted until the end of 1885 when, as Chamberlain's biographer
indicates, Chamberlain washed his hands of Parnell and his party.[52]
If, as much of the evidence appears to indicate, the parliamentary
leaders of radicalism were looking forward as a matter of course to an
alliance with the Irish then they left it a little late, just to the time the
Irish were intent on demonstrating their independence. Furthermore,
Chamberlain's local government proposals for Ireland and his views
on education were dangerous to the Irish party. Unconsciously
perhaps, they attacked the Parnellite alliance at its weakest points,
where short term and long term objectives met. The Catholic church
might favour Chamberlain's local government proposals in order to
gain control of education and save it from radicalism, while to the Irish
leadership the government proposals might initially appear an instalment on Home Rule but then might appear a pretext to bar the way to a
fuller settlement; such a fear would have accurately gauged the
development of Chamberlain's thinking. There is also the suggestion
that the Irish, for their part, believed that Chamberlain's support
could be picked up whenever they chose. In the meantime, first
Cardinal Manning, and then Archbishop Walsh of Dublin for the
church, and then all of the nationalist press condemned Chamberlain
and Dilke for proposing to make a fact finding tour of Ireland and by the
end of the year relations with Chamberlain had broken down
irretrievably. It remains curious that the Irish, who more than any
other Victorians set great store by personality in politics (and this was
almost a theme of O'Connor's) should so ignore it in this case.

O'Connor neglected and underestimated Chamberlain and the
parliamentary radicals more than most – or his neglect appears the
more obvious because of the emphasis he had once placed on these
allies. As if in compensation, to make up for his lack of perception, his
hatred of Chamberlain after the Home Rule split was all the
greater.[53] At one time Chamberlain's local government schemes, and
even more so his proposals in favour of secular education, would

[51] *Ibid.* p. 115.

[52] J.L. Garvin, *Joseph Chamberlain* (1932), ii, 12.

[53] See chapter 3, p. 113 and chapter 4, p. 128.

have appealed strongly to O'Connor. Perhaps, all other things being equal, they still did. Furthermore Dilke had once looked on O'Connor's career with favour and in some sense O'Connor had looked on him as his natural leader. After this O'Connor showed considerable disillusion with the parliamentary radicals, though some of his distaste was feigned. He pointed out, or hastened, the decline of the onetime radical Forster; he made personal attacks on John Bright and Dilke, as though he saw hypocrisy at its most intense in those who could not make the small leap he had made towards Home Rule; and he abandoned Bradlaugh while celebrating political tactics. From the first there was, too, a lack of any obvious cordiality between O'Connor and Chamberlain. There is no recorded correspondence between the two; unlike Dilke, Chamberlain was not in any case very sociable at this stage in his career and he left social engineering to Dilke. On at least two notable occasions O'Connor had attacked Chamberlain in his office of President of the Board of Trade for his handling of emigration. From then until 1886 O'Connor made remarkably few references to Chamberlain, even during the election campaign of 1885. There was in no sense an antipathy of similar characters; no two politicians could have been personally so dissimilar. But on O'Connor's part there may have been a rivalry over issues and prestige. He did not abandon radicalism but it was for a few years subsumed in furious activity. A line was kept open to the radicals through Henry Labouchere, whom O'Connor had first befriended in the journalistic world, and through him to Chamberlain and Gladstone, but Parnell made sure this was largely ineffective and relied more on the O'Sheas; once again Parnell kept his subordinates' attention fixed on an immediate set of problems.

Immediate and expanding prospects appeared to offer more than a tired and customary bondage to the Liberals. Cabinet disagreements over Chamberlain's local government proposals and the government's intention to introduce a new Crimes Bill for Ireland, almost as a rehearsal of the Home Rule split, caused seventy Liberals to abstain on a routine budget division and caused the defeat and resignation of the government in June 1885. But what caught attention was the new factor of Parnellite-Conservative co-operation. Decisive action appeared to be the best way of exploiting the uncertainties of parliament and the potential in a new electoral system. O'Connor had detailed, novel, and important work to do here both in urging on organization in the provinces and in arguing a case for a share of the new constituencies under the Redistribution Bill, introduced in December 1884, and barely passed before the Liberal government fell in the following summer.

Immediately after the I.N.L.G.B. conference at Dublin, O'Connor set out on a grand tour, investigating constituencies in Ireland and in Britain. He addressed his constituents in Galway in September and spoke at Athlone, his birthplace, in October. But, probably because it was apparent that the south and west of Ireland were safe for Parnell, O'Connor appears to have concentrated his attention on the more marginal areas of Ulster (which might, incidentally, be more likely prizes for the Parnellites because of the extension of the franchise), and then turned his attention to the Irish communities of Britain, areas which he still might not have known very well. In both cases there could be an absolute gain in seats or in organization. At Dungannon he met with a counter-demonstration from Orangemen. In Belfast, his claim that Ireland had succeeded in returning the same number of seats whatever the Redistribution Bill proposals, may have proved equally provocative.[54]

When O'Connor turned his attention to the Irish in Britain it was Denvir who described it as a tour of inspection of the organization. One speech of O'Connor's that survives from this period, made in Birkenhead on 7 December and fully reported in Denvir's newspaper, gives some indication of O'Connor's task. Priority was given to a statement of political independence, that Liberals and Conservatives 'had made Ireland their battleground' and they ought not to complain if the compliment was returned. Making such a policy effective was more difficult. Particularly in the Liverpool area, the Irish organization had been driven by disputes which arose because Charles McArdle and Patrick Byrne, who could read the signs as well as anyone, were clearly vying for support as local candidates for parliament. Denvir had called for an Irish M.P. for Liverpool as early as May 1884 as well as attacking those who lapsed back into Liberalism, but he savaged McArdle for his presumption and praised by comparison 'the magnificent group of young Irishmen upon whom, in our day, the mantle of Irish oratory has fallen'. O'Connor had to tread carefully. The new executive created by the 1883 conference was intended to cut out internal squabbles in the League but he could not trespass too far into the province of local officers. He was, equally, totally lacking in interest in local affairs, a characteristic which stayed with him for much of the rest of his career, and he often thought them divisive. In his Birkenhead speech O'Connor did allude to 'painful differences which existed between their countrymen in this district' but claimed that, as

[54] Healy, *Letters*, i, 197; *Irish Nationalist*, 3 Jan. 1885. See also O'Connor, *Parnell*, which refers to a tour of Ulster with Parnell. The description of O'Connor in Ulster in Thomas Macknight, *Ulster as it is* (1896), ii, 39, may refer to this campaign and not, as Macknight suggested, a campaign in 1883.

president of the League 'it is my duty to maintain an impartial and judicious position. I can only lay down the policy. How this [is] carried out is a matter over which I can have little control.' This was ingenious and disingenuous; he asserted his authority, administered a reproof, sided with no one but made it clear that central policy was to be obeyed. In this new territory his grasp of affairs was quick and his confidence was unshakeable (until Parnell intervened). As Denvir indicated and as others grudgingly admitted, Parnell's young lieutenants had flourished mightily since 1880.[55]

O'Connor's tour had been a reminder of the demands of the executive and this and similar preparations were to prove adequate by the time the election came at the end of 1885. Parnell's and O'Connor's interventions in the Redistribution Bill debate were not to prove so successful. Again the concentration was on the Ulster seats and then on constituencies in Britain. Single member constituencies were to be created by the Bill, which was steered through its parliamentary stages by Dilke as President of the Local Government Board. It seems probable that Parnell did hope to use the Irish vote in Britain as the specific bargaining factor between the Liberals and the Conservatives and the Irish may have hoped for much here because Dilke, Chamberlain (at one remove), and the Conservatives were all at this stage in the market for Irish support. O'Connor first raised the matter in the debate on 10 March, asking what provision had been made for the 'Irish minority' in England and Scotland which he numbered at two million and making a somewhat simplistic comparison with what he sarcastically called the 'loyal minority' in Ireland which he said had been given between 17 and 27 seats, the uncertainty of forecasting constituency loyalities being allowed even in accusations. Once the claim had been made however, the difficulties emerged. This ought perhaps to have been an object lesson to the Irish on the difficulty of making pressure work. British M.P.s were not likely to openly antagonise the Irish, especially if they were M.P.s who had Irish communities in the new constituencies they hoped to inherit, but this was no reason for automatically giving the Irish the opportunity to express their power by handing constituencies to them. Put more simply, constituencies were nearest to British M.P.s' hearts. More generally Dilke, and then the Conservatives, did not wish to antagonise possible allies but they tacitly agreed not to make those allies stronger and more demanding.

[55]*Irish Programme* and *Irish Nationalist*, 13 Dec., 10 May, 1 Nov., 1884. O'Donnell *Irish Parliamentary Party*, ii, 298-9. See also O'Brien, *Parnell*, p. 153.

There were also technical difficulties. The new Act was replacing 'interests' to some extent by a more individualistic type of voter set in a national and more uniform electoral system. The Irish welcomed the greater democratization of the franchise but wanted to preserve an 'interest'. Irish representation had been dealt with generously, except for the Irish Liberals, though this did not stop O'Connor attacking the supposedly over-generous treatment of the loyalists. But, later, there was disagreement about the number of Irish in Britain; figures for migrants could be almost as contentious then as they have become more recently. O'Connor used the good round figure of two million which was that of the whole community including, when they mattered, those of Irish descent. Shaw-Lefevre from the Liberal benches, who took an interest in these things, produced the equally convenient figure from the census returns of half a million Irish-born, from which he calculated 150,000 Irish voters. These figures were not to change appreciably up to the first world war except that the number of those of Irish descent increased to give a total community figure of two million and an Irish vote of 200,000 by 1911. It was, however, not a negligible total whichever criterion was used and it was commonly believed that 20 to 40 seats might be involved. Argument over numbers was augmented by difficulties over the location of the migrant population. There could be no exception taken to the general need for Irish representation, merely doubts when it came to discussion on particular constituencies.[56]

As a result of these difficulties O'Connor and Parnell achieved very little in these debates, with the added difficulty that because the Irish were holding out the possibility of being someone's ally, they could not become too argumentative. To O'Connor it might have been the institution of parliament at its most bland and obstructive. Dilke answered O'Connor's query about representation by 19 March and said that there would be provision for the Irish but he could not say what. In the debate on the London constituencies in March Dilke referred the Irish to those who knew most about local conditions and also to the impartiality of the boundary commissioners. In the debate on the main prize, Liverpool, on 10 and 29 April O'Connor fared little better. Parnell helped O'Connor considerably in the later debates and hoped that the case would be met 'in a fair spirit' but in the debate both Edward Whitley, the junior Conservative member, and Lord

[56] *Hansard, 3,* 295, col. 1695, 19 Mar; *ibid.* 297, col. 1077, and see Shaw-Lefevre, *Gladstone and Ireland* (1912), p. 284. Figures on the Irish-born population and those of Irish descent are given in Appendix E.

Claud Hamilton, the senior M.P. for the city, prevented any alteration to the Abercromby or Exchange division boundaries and both protested, with some imagination, that they looked on the citizens of Liverpool as one people and trusted that the days of sectarianism had passed. The Irish and, even more so, the Catholic interests in Britain could not argue against this, however little resemblance it bore to reality or to what was to occur in Liverpool in the next half century and more. T.M. Healy did intervene at this stage to note that Claude Hamilton's leaders were 'conveniently absent' and O'Donnell made a bitter attack on English attitudes in the debate on 29 April. But neither O'Connor nor Parnell could afford to make these sort of comments and run the risk of antagonizing the holding power in Liverpool, and it is possible that even at this early stage Parnell was on the lookout for a constituency in England, such as Liverpool Exchange, to hand over to Captain O'Shea. As for the Liberals their minority member for the city, Samuel Smith, had most to lose. Concessions to the Irish might make Liberalism a forlorn hope anywhere in Liverpool. On 29 April O'Connor made his last bid with what looked like some desperation, 'in a perfectly candid spirit', in order to have 'a better chance of carrying another division of the city'.[57] This was unexceptional; it was what redistribution debates were for, to press special claims. But at the end of the debate it looked very much as though Liverpool Scotland division were all that the Irish were certain of. O'Connor had reason to feel exasperated and discontented because it looked possible that he, as president of the I.N.L.G.B., and with prior claims to any seat in Britain, would be the only Irish nationalist M.P. returned for a British constituency. Yet the strength of the Irish in the new constituencies was still left open after debate and through the period of the caretaker Conservative administration. The disadvantage of being a minority party had been demonstrated in the Redistribution Bill debates. A balance of advantages and disadvantages in the Irish position was now to be put to further proof in two general elections and it was largely up to O'Connor to make the Irish vote in Britain decisive.

[57] *Hansard, 3*, 295, col. 1695, 19 Mar; *ibid.* 296, cols. 1364, 1369, 1368, 10 Apr.; *ibid.* 297, col. 1073, 29 Apr. For an example of the frequently expressed Catholic view that English and Irish ought not to be separated out politically, see the editorial in the *Tablet*, 31 Oct. 1885.

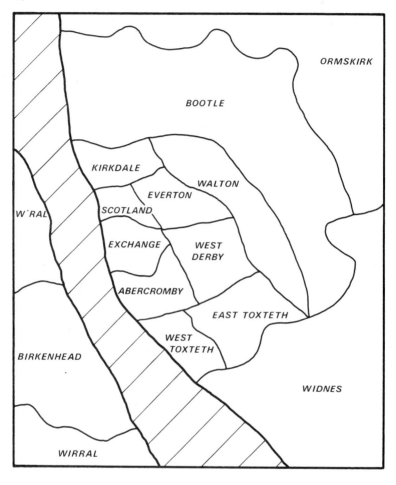

MAP 2

LIVERPOOL: Parliamentary Divisions after 1885

Two Elections, 1885-6

In his handling of the campaigns in Britain in 1885 and 1886, O'Connor occasionally showed a lack of control and a lack of insight which was particularly inappropriate when most of the intention in the Irish camp was to influence one party or another. So many factors were at work that it is difficult now to say categorically whether the notorious decision, announced finally in O'Connor's manifesto of 21 November, that the Irish in Britain should vote tory, was a successful or a disadvantageous policy. On balance, the 'vote tory' manoeuvre can be said to have justified itself. O'Connor emerges with credit though perhaps not so much as he might have hoped for, especially in view of the difficulties he had to face, not least from Parnell himself.[58] To concentrate on O'Connor's difficulties might at least show what O'Connor hoped to achieve and explain more adequately what at first sight appears an aberration both in O'Connor's career and in the record of Irish nationalism.

The first problem was that although the Irish vote had been advertised as a new force and bargaining counter as early as 1883, and had to be if the Irish voters were to be given a motive for more intensive organization, there was then a long wait until it was announced, by manifesto and a few days before the election, that the vote would be swung behind the Conservatives. It may well be that O'Connor had decided in his own mind that the Conservatives would be the best bet for the Irish as early as 1883. This would partly explain his attacks on the radicals, his desertion of Bradlaugh and his friendship with Churchill. By the summer of 1885 O'Connor appeared to be particularly inclined towards the Conservatives; it was as late as July, when the Conservatives were in office, that O'Connor again attacked Bright in the further debate on Bright's alleged breach of parliamentary privilege, and especially for a supposed lack of sympathy towards Ireland. In the same debate he emphasised that many liberals owed their seats to Irish votes and went so far as to invite the Irish to vote against the Liberals in the next election. By the end of the year Labouchere could still report to Chamberlain that O'Connor favoured the Conservatives, or, as Labouchere put it with journalistic exaggeration, had been 'bought' by them.[59] Yet personal

---

[58] There has been a sizeable debate on the 1885 election; for the Irish part in the election see C.H.D. Howard, 'The Parnell Manifesto of 21 November and the Schools Question', *E.H.R.* 65 (Jan. 1947), and O'Brien, *Parnell*, pp. 104-8 and p. 116.

[59] Labouchere to Herbert Gladstone, 9 and 10 Dec. 1885, quoted in R.J. Hind, *Henry Labouchere and the Empire* (1972), p. 114. For the further attack on Bright see *Hansard*, 3, 300, col. 279, 28 July.

inclination on particular occasions has to be treated with some care. If O'Connor had wanted to convince the Liberals that the Irish were independent, the only way to do it, clearly enough to convince any Liberals who regarded the Irish vote as traditionally theirs, was a strident flirtation with the Conservatives. An overture to bargaining, from both Liberals and Conservatives, must have been intended in statements like the one made in the Bright debate; otherwise the commitment of the vote would not have been left so late. At the I.N.L.G.B. conference for 1885, which met at Glasgow in October immediately preceding the election, there was an ideal forum for announcing the use of the vote, when provincial organizers were assembled, and one local Irish newspaper was convinced that there would be an announcement at the conference on the 'policy which our party is to adopt at the forthcoming election'. Perhaps this does indicate a miscalculation, that the Parnellites had hoped to achieve their ends by this date. All that happened instead was something approaching a holding operation, with officers appointed for the election. John Redmond was made responsible for voters in Scotland, John Barry, the ex-Fenian from Manchester, given responsibility for London, and O'Connor himself concentrated on Lancashire where the Irish were thought to be strongest. At the beginning of November the League was still instructed merely to 'hold aloof' from all British parties and wait for the advice of the executive. Throughout November the local branches were busy declaring their independence of British parties. It may have been essential that the use of the vote be kept secret until the last minute, both to increase the tension between parties and in order to assist the League organizers in convincing the Irish voters that there was some urgency in doing something as unnatural as voting tory; but this obviously also indicates no immediate benefit for the Irish from the Liberals. It was not until 18 November, less than a week before the election, that Parnell wrote to O'Connor and, among other things and with a marked lack of enthusiasm, advised him that 'it appears to me almost certain that we shall have to vote for the tories at the next election'.[60] Even here the options were left open, but Parnell's late forecast was to prove correct.

What this points to was a second difficulty, that the use of the vote was at the mercy of the demands of high policy as Parnell interpreted them. Parnell for much of the period from June was involved in negotiations with the Conservatives. The Salisbury administration

---

[60] *Liverpool Irish Herald,* 31 Oct; *F.J.,* 2 Nov.; *Liverpool Irish Herald,* 31 Oct; *D.P.,* reports of branch meetings, 1-11 Nov; N.L.I., MS 15735, Parnell to O'Connor, '16-18' Nov. Compare O'Connor, *Parnell,* p. 159, where he said that he and his colleagues had decided for the Conservatives, but also complained about Parnell's procrastination.

offered some short term benefits to Ireland; the Crimes Act was not renewed and Lord Carnarvon, the new Lord Lieutenant, appeared to offer a more conciliatory regime than that of his predecessor Lord Spencer. Any long term benefits were more dubious but to Parnell it could serve to keep the pot boiling. Parnell, perhaps with some justice, told his lieutenants little. But the trouble in this case was that the conduct of the election in Britain depended upon what Parnell could obtain from Gladstone. Here little was achieved before the election. Gladstone's Midlothian speech of 18 September 1885, Parnell's speech at Liverpool on 10 November offering the vote in return for some commitment to Home Rule and Gladstone's rejoinder on 19 November, clarified only the point that Gladstone, believing the electoral settlement for Ireland had been generous, now expected that the Irish electorate would be able to give their clear verdict on Home Rule before parliament went any further; to the Irish it was hardly distinguishable from delaying tactics. Parnell could hardly base his calculations on the assumption that Gladstone would pledge himself to Home Rule after the election. Neither could he or O'Connor afford to be impressed by Labouchere's warnings concerning the Conservatives nor Labouchere's comment, made as early as 26 November, that the Irish ought to have given Gladstone a sufficiently large majority to prove he was not acting under Irish dictation. All that they could see was that Gladstone remained impervious. A similar impression was given by Chamberlain, and in fact he was now more hostile than the Irish realized. Other Liberals, and especially Herbert Gladstone, made some attempts to find a formula on Home Rule which would restore the friendship with the Irish, and other candidates were often effusive and insistent in their expressions of goodwill and in their 'guarantees' over religious education.[61] Nevertheless the Irish had to fulfill their threat and vote Conservative.

Parnell's interference in the campaign in Britain also proved a hindrance to O'Connor. Parnell had first spoken in Liverpool in the speech aimed at Gladstone of 10 November. At the same time he also acknowledged that Liverpool was the area of Britain where the Irish were strongest electorally (which was true so far as numbers went though perhaps they did not have the leverage in Liverpool that they were to prove to have in other parts of the country). O'Connor was nominated for Scotland division and Irish plans for four other Liverpool seats, Exchange, Abercromby, West Toxteth and Kirkdale, were hinted at.

[61] *D.P.*, 11 Nov; *Truth*, 26 Nov; Labouchere to Chamberlain, 20 Oct., quoted in Thorold, *Labouchere*, p. 240. For an example of Liberal M.P.s' assurances on religion see the speech of Samuel Smith, the former minority member for Liverpool, who stood for Liverpool Abercromby division, report in *D.P.*, 13 Nov.

The occasion of Parnell's support of O'Connor was in many ways the highest point reached by Irish nationalism in the city. Parnell's visit provoked Orange antagonism and some violence, whatever the understandings were at Westminister. At the St. Anne Street meeting, where the League Hall was full to overflowing, the secrecy and the drama had been well stage-managed. Parnell rose to this occasion and his praise for O'Connor was generous to the point, for Parnell, of profligacy. O'Connor's part in parliament was emphasized, any question about his radical antecedents forgotten. His special ability was recognised especially when

> in sending him over from Ireland to you, we regret his loss but recognize that you in England contend under difficulties superior to those which we now have to face in Ireland (hear, hear) [and we] offer the ablest and best man we can find in the country for [this] special service.[62]

It was appropriate that O'Connor be given the one safe Irish seat in Britain, it was popular among an audience that had long wanted their own Irish M.P. and it was now clearly a mark of the importance given to the British campaign that someone of O'Connor's eminence be given the nomination and that Parnell should be there to announce it. As the quotation at the head of this chapter suggests, local candidates could now, perhaps with some relief among their peers, be laughed out of consideration.

But Parnell might also have been impelled by a well-merited sense of guilt. At the 10 November meeting the candidature of Justin McCarthy for Liverpool Exchange, the next most favourable seat to Scotland division from the Irish point of view, was withdrawn. McCarthy, instead, was to go on and fight Londonderry City. On 15 November Captain O'Shea's candidature for Exchange was announced and he stood as a Liberal. Parnell also stood for the division, then withdrew on nomination day, 24 November, and worked vigorously for O'Shea. Parnell's return to Liverpool on 22 November, and the O'Shea candidature, were astonishing, irksome and embarrassing to O'Connor and he said as much when he came to write his biography of Parnell, though all he would permit himself to say when he came to write his memoirs was, 'I was quite in a position to deal with the situation [in Liverpool] and in Great Britain generally, and Parnell's presence for that purpose was quite unnecessary'; nothing about O'Shea.[63] O'Connor had enough difficulties as he ran the campaign

[62] *D.P.*, 11 Nov.

[63] *Parnell*, pp. 160-3; *Memoirs*, ii, 7.

from Liverpool – the complaints of Liberals, the 'rebellion' of Irish League branches in Gorton and Hyde and, to a lesser extent, those in Widnes, St. Helens and some London seats. To add to these, O'Shea now had to be made an exception in the manifesto, whereas the only other exceptions, S. Storey of Sunderland, Joseph Cowen of Newcastle, and Labouchere, who sat for one of the Northampton seats, had all been outstanding allies of the Parnellite party. This was more than could be said of O'Shea, who was noticeably unwelcome both to Irish and Liberal voters in Liverpool. In addition, Parnell announced Redmond's candidacy for Kirkdale which, as O'Connor recognized, was a forlorn hope and once again O'Connor was not consulted. In Liverpool, O'Connor, as expected, was elected by a wide margin, O'Shea was narrowly defeated, where a victory, to do Parnell some sort of justice, would have avoided considerable future difficulty and, would have ended O'Connor's embarrassment because, as it was, he had to hand over his Galway seat to O'Shea the following year. Redmond came bottom of the poll in Kirkdale.[64]

There are some reservations which could be held against O'Connor in the election result and in the verdict, open or otherwise, on how he had organized the campaign in Britain. Although neither O'Connor nor the party generally could afford to recognize that there had been a setback, there was much to be said both for and against O'Connor's tactics. The Liberals had gained a victory of a sort with 334 seats, though this was a decline from their 1880 total of 354. The Irish vote had been effective, though to what degree is still arguable. It has generally been accepted that it caused the Liberals to lose from 25 to 40 seats, though Parnell had claimed more power than this for the vote hitherto and the figures are made more uncertain by the new constituency system and must include seats the Liberals had hoped to gain as well as areas they definitely lost compared to the 1880 result. So far as the position of the parties in the Commons was concerned, Ensor said that Parnell had realized his object with 'fantastic precision' even though the Irish could now keep either British party out but only keep the Liberals in. It is also suggested that the 'vote tory' policy had proved a mistake by the time the Liberals had become converted to Home Rule and when every vote in support of Gladstone was crucial. This has been answered by C.C. O'Brien who has pointed out, as has been suggested above in relation to Gladstone and Labouchere, that the Irish did not know Gladstone's intentions and

---

[64]The figures were, Scotland, O'Connor 2,824, Woodard 1,474; Exchange, Baily (C) 2,964, O'Shea 2,900; Kirkdale, Baden-Powell (C) 3,301, Samuelson (Lib-Lab) 1,981, Redmond 765. Redmond's intervention caused some ill-feeling among trade unionists.

had to believe that they were exerting pressure in a more conventional way. Neither is it true that the Conservatives could not be kept in power. Mathematically, it was just possible that the Irish could keep the Conservatives in office and, further, Gladstone was anxious that Salisbury should continue; both factors together kept the Conservatives in power until January of the new year.[65]

But the result was not so dramatic as O'Connor, for one, might have anticipated. The Irish vote was quickly criticized on the score of effectiveness by the Conservative Dublin *Daily Express*, which clearly had an axe to grind and wanted not even the suggestion of an alliance between Conservatives and 'separatists'. The Liberal *Pall Mall Gazette*, which had employed O'Connor for a few years after 1880 as a parliamentary correspondent, criticized O'Connor's record in Liverpool. O'Connor could fairly have blamed any confusion there on Parnell. Elsewhere, however, he did lay himself open to the charge of over-enthusiasm. The manifesto of 21 November, for a start, was criticized at the time, and has been criticized subsequently, for being too emotive.[66] So partisan was O'Connor at some stages during the election that it was possible, for the one and only time in his career, to mistake him for a champion of the Catholic church. The Liberal record on coercion and the supposed radical threat to Catholic schooling were the two main reasons, given at length in the manifesto, for voting against the Liberals. To many Liberals at least the campaign must have appeared like a Catholic crusade, whereas to the Irish the issue of the schools was a coincidental and subordinate one.[67]

O'Connor remained unrepentant, a political virtue that O'Connor had recognized in his descriptions of other politicians. But he had miscalculated and continued to miscalculate. There was admittedly no victory celebration in the Irish camp in Britain, which may have been an indication of disappointment. However it has been borne in mind that, even among the Irish, a comparison might have been made with the runaway Irish success in Ireland itself, which was bound to be more dramatic and which would eclipse any real merits in the harder campaign in Britain. Moreover, now that the election was concluded, a concern for Liberal susceptibilities could be resurrected. The

---

[65] The Irish total was eighty-six, the difference between the two British parties eighty-four; Ensor, *England, 1870-1914* (rev. ed., 1966), p. 94 gives the difference as eighty-six. Minority parties have stayed in power on less.

[66] Dublin *Daily Express*, 26 Nov; *P.M.G.* 12 Dec; Healy, *Letters*, i, 231, where he called the manifesto 'flaming verbiage'. See also O'Brien, *Parnell*, p. 116. Part of the text of the manifesto is in Appendix B.

[67] The religious issue is emphasized in Howard, 'Parnell Manifesto' *passim*.

Liberals, for their part, Gladstone, Chamberlain and some back-benchers, did emphasize the Irish part in the election in Britain, whether this was partly as an excuse or not. Yet O'Connor, in many ways at the height of his political influence, announced his own victory in Liverpool almost in a swaggering way, defending his record in, of all places, *The Times* correspondence column and advertising that he had been returned for 'a constituency Irish and Catholic in Liverpool'.[68] All that can be admired here, possibly, is what O'Connor might have called his 'cheek'. It persisted up to the debate on the first Home Rule Bill and O'Connor's intervention in June 1886 when it had mellowed into a tongue in cheek irony. In such a way he was able to defend the language of the manifesto, by saying that the Irish had been under the spell of Randolph Churchill and his 'Byzantine' style. He also played down the Irish attachment to the Conservatives. Co-operation between the Conservatives and the Irish had appeared to be one of the most obvious things about the election, and the manifesto, while not specifically urgeing support for the Conservatives, left Irish voters with no alternative and, after the manifesto, instructions to the Irish voters did name the Conservatives. But O'Connor, by 1886, was ready to claim that he and Parnell could have reversed their policy during the election and were consciously aiming at a small Conservative majority, difficult enough to believe on the grounds of organization alone, but an indication, especially because of the number of times he reverted to this theme, that O'Connor retained some sense of disturbance about the policy for the rest of his career.[69] For most practical purposes this apology after the event was sufficient, especially as O'Connor could question the motives of the Conservatives at the same time. But, as in the case of his and the Irish party's treatment of Chamberlain before the election, O'Connor ignored the possibility of making permanent enemies, overlooked the political convictions in the Liberal camp. As the first Home Rule debate showed, the Liberals could also indulge in long memories; neither did they regard the dictates of tactics as sufficient justification for inconsistency. Chamberlain had perhaps been finally antagonized as early as July 1885; many more among his followers and elsewhere were antagonized during the election. It was a difficult lesson to learn: the Irish vote was not, as O'Connor appeared to imagine, a finely honed blade, it was a blunt instrument.

---

[68] *The Times* 19 Dec. It was here that other correspondents raked up the issue of O'Connor's part in the Chicago convention.

[69] *Hansard, 3,* 306, cols. 848, 868, 3 June 1886. The claim about the Conservative majority also occurs in O'Connor's *Parnell Movement,* p. 272, and he repeated the claim in the 1900 election.

There were further hard knocks for O'Connor to take after the election. He might have imagined, after the onerous work he had undertaken and the not discreditable result, that he was now in a position to have some say on policy or at least some influence in negotiations in the period of suspense following the election, a time of uncertainty which lasted until Gladstone replaced the Conservatives in February 1886 and then introduced his Home Rule Bill in April. O'Connor was quickly disillusioned by Parnell's fierce monopoly of all direct negotiations with British parties; in retrospect, what is surprising is that he even tried to begin some sort of discussion. As early as December 1885, on writing to *The Times*, O'Connor had called for a Home Rule settlement on the lines of the Canadian federal system, which he distinguished, not very clearly, from Isaac Butt's federal plan. This, and other less radical plans made public by Justin McCarthy and Michael Davitt, were condemned as 'mischievous' by Parnell when writing to E. Dwyer Gray, the editor of the *Freeman's Journal*. There was much sense in Parnell's argument that it was pointless to announce differences of opinion and that the initiative ought to be left to Gladstone (the initiative was, after all, what Gladstone always wanted). But O'Connor's political sense told him to keep options open and he could still be found discussing the matter with Labouchere, a Liberal friendship fortunately left undisturbed, who reported to Herbert Gladstone. This was an initiative similar to Healy's prior to the election. O'Connor and the other leading Irish politicians might justifiably complain that, by comparison, Parnell could not be found to discuss policy matters. Perhaps, too, as early as this, O'Connor realized what Healy had suggested to Labouchere, and as O'Connor wrote in his memoir of Parnell, that Parnell even at the best of times would not consult his colleagues 'except individually'.[70]

Parnell imposed upon O'Connor further, and to an incredible extent. As if O'Connor had not had to bear with enough at Liverpool during the election, Parnell now insisted on imposing O'Shea on O'Connor's vacated Galway constituency. In England, and during a general election, O'Shea might scrape by, but now O'Connor was personally involved in having to break a moral debt to his constituents, all in the glare of publicity. O'Connor went so far as to suggest that he and Healy should resign. Parnell, in a rehearsal of the 1890 divorce crisis, then made O'Shea's election a matter of confidence and threatened his own resignation if O'Shea were not supported. This forced O'Connor to withdraw his threat, as Healy sardonically

---

[70]Parnell to E. Dwyer Grey, 24 Dec. quoted in T.W. Moody, 'Parnell and the Galway Election of 1886', *I.H.S.*, 9 (Mar. 1955), 323.

reported. Healy and Biggar persisted in their opposition and Parnell's relations with Mrs. O'Shea were revealed by Biggar, who remained O'Shea's most vehement opponent. O'Connor, obviously torn between duty to his cause and loyalty to Parnell, campaigned in Dublin for Parnell's candidate from February and then went to Galway with Parnell for a mercifully short time during the same month to speak to a murderously hostile electorate. O'Shea was elected against a Nationalist opponent. O'Connor put his doubts on one side, just as he had restrained himself and his own ideas on a Home Rule settlement.[71]

Gladstone's Home Rule proposals appeared to justify the uncertainty and the demands of party discipline. The Bill was introduced in that very spring of 1886, on 8 April, one of the most dramatic scenes in parliamentary history. O'Connor had to a large extent gone along with the need for caution. Speaking to Irish voters in Kennington in London just before this, he had emphasized the 'extraordinary delicacy' of the Irish position and his hopes for 'permanent friendship with England', a marked contrast to his public attitude since 1882.[72] Differences on the Home Rule proposals led to an adjournment debate in June, held to decide whether to proceed with the second reading. This was the debate where O'Connor spoke at length, put up by the Parnellites to secure the attachment of parliament to at least the principle of Home Rule and trying to prevent the adjournment and the dissolution of parliament which would follow. Here was where he half explained and half defended Irish tactics during the election and kept it all in a light key. His speech was a masterly piece of rhetoric. Even Chamberlain got off with an affectionate rebuke. Chamberlain's alternative to Home Rule was, presumably, some sort of local government scheme or as O'Connor put it, 'if we rose to the heights of our sires, if we were but equal to the great arguments, if we revolted against the Prime Minister's offer, what would be our reward?' 'Enquiries', said the right honourable and reverend gentleman [Chamberlain] 'as to railway and canal bills and gas water bills ought to be conducted in Ireland by Irish tribunals'.[73]

Chamberlain was not diverted; he and his followers and Hartington and his right wing support were convinced that they had been

---

[71] For a full account see Moody, *loc. cit.* and O'Brien, *Parnell*, pp. 164-84.

[72] *The Times*, 5 Apr.

[73] *Hansard, 3,* 306, col. 857, 3 June. O'Connor's speech was thought sufficiently impressive for it to be printed separately and an excerpt is given in Appendix C. O'Connor was also more conciliatory towards the Liberals, and more in favour of compromise in debating the principle of the Bill than was Parnell; see Healy, *Letters,* i, 254, and O'Connor, *Parnell,* p. 183.

consistent. They voted for the adjournment and there were sufficient of them to carry the motion. The hurt so casually done to Chamberlain was repaid almost exactly one year later. Parliament was dissolved on 25 June 1886.

O'Connor had to some extent anticipated the possibility of an election when speaking to Irish voters in Kennington and had warned Irish voters in general to be ready, though if an election could have been avoided the wounds in the Liberal camp would have been given a chance to heal. The 1886 campaign was a more straightforward one for O'Connor. He spent most of it in London where he was active in supporting Liberal candidates and did not reach Liverpool until 27 June. The League executive had delegated organizers to the regions of Britain on 17 June, John Redmond was to look after Liverpool and John Barry to supervise in Manchester. John Dillon spoke widely in Britain and Liberal-Irish co-operation was cemented by the Home Rule Association formed by the Liberals. O'Connor was not assigned to any particular part of Britain; he probably thought it would be invidious to campaign in Lancashire so recently after supporting Conservative candidates there. The general instructions of the League executive were also, in comparison to 1885, terse and reticent in supporting the Liberals, to the point of saying 'it is deemed unnecessary to point out to you the considerations which have impelled the executive in this decision'. This was a contrast that was seized upon by the Conservative Irish Loyal and Patriotic Union in one of their pamphlets. Support for the Liberals was easier for O'Connor though he could not be too demonstrative. An exception was his admiration for Gladstone, one which not all Irishmen shared, and he and the 'grand old Liverpudlian' exchanged compliments, Gladstone's coming in a speech he made at Liverpool on June 28.[74]

The election, for the Irish, could only be something of an anti-climax both to the previous election and to the Home Rule debate, though the campaign in Britain and in Belfast was a noisy and sometimes a violent one. The results were a further disappointment. A Liberal, D. Duncan, was returned for Exchange division and O'Connor won comfortably in Scotland division, demonstrating that 1885 had not been a freak result. But the hold of the Conservatives on Liverpool and Lancashire was not broken. The Conservatives won the election, increasing their numbers to 316 with a still uncertain additional support of seventy-nine Liberal opponents of Home Rule. The Irish

[74]*D.P.*, 18 June; *Parnell Manifesto to the Irish Electors in Great Britain, Then and Now* (1886); *Porcupine*, 26 June; B.L., W.E. Gladstone Papers, Add. MS 44498, f. 68, O'Connor to Gladstone, 27 June; *Porcupine*, 3 July.

vote, though not O'Connor in particular, came in for some antagonism although it is arguable whether, as has sometimes been maintained, this election saw the emergence of an 'anti-Irish' vote in Britain.[75]

O'Connor was now more cautious and the Irish vote was to be used more circumspectly and probably more effectively in the years which followed up to 1914. O'Connor had emerged from obscurity to being, in 1885 and 1886, something like Parnell's second in command. He had been too enthusiastic and too insensitive. From about 1883 when he was given the direction of the Irish vote he seemed for a time to think of politics as the abstract operation of a skill divorced from ideas, a matter of fine implacable calculations, a delusion usually restricted to teachers of political science. He and Parnell had obtained their primary object; Home Rule was taken up by one of the British parties. O'Connor had retrieved the Irish position after 1885 by his own brand of wit and he had assumed the thick skin of a politician which served him for most routine controversies though it was not to prove effective in the larger crises of his life. He had also perhaps been warned about Parnell, who had treated him badly, been checked more than once in his own political ventures, seen some of the ruthlessness of high politics and the enormous threats it posed to self-esteem. Perhaps by 1886, with Home Rule a possibility, with an alliance with the Liberals in operation, O'Connor felt that he could now gain the fruits of experience and these were not to be found in action, but as a commentator.

[75] Criticism of the vote can be found, for instance, in the *Porcupine,* 10 July, or in the *Daily Telegraph,* 1 July. The possibility of an anti-Irish vote is put forward by C.C. O'Brien (*Parnell,* p. 194), and is at least implied in other studies of the period after 1886, such as in Henry Pelling's, *Social Geography of British Elections* (1967) and P.F. Clarke's *Lancashire and the New Liberalism* (1971).

3

NEW JOURNALISM, PARLIAMENT AS AN ART-FORM 1887-90

> The recollection of this splendid pride of his, now, as I write, makes me think of him with a passion of regret that dims my eyes.[1]

Busy politicians often highlight a problem in interpretation, of what matters most, ideas or action. O'Connor's writings show a strong sense of personality but also a reminder of the depth and seriousness of the politics of his age. He was guileless and sincere in his political writings and in his set speeches: there was so much that he wanted them to get across. He wanted, like any radical, to convince. No distinction was allowed here between ideals and their implementation, at least not until his later years. Time deals harshly with such hopes: activity itself is taken more and more to be part of character, and what ideas remain appear superficial because they themselves are usually designed to influence immediate circumstances. But, for a moment in the years after the 1886 election and down to the Parnellite split of 1890, O'Connor had the chance, or rather created the opportunity, to bring the central interests of his life together. There was a range of responses in politics, the immediate seizing of opportunities in debate, some enlargement on events in oratory, and a commentary in political reporting that was almost as rapid, and this for a cause that appeared to need only a brief respite before its realization. Then, in journalism, he had the creative insight and the persuasiveness to found probably the most impressive radical newspaper Britain has ever seen, the *Star*. This newspaper for a few years, from its inception in 1888 until his resignation as editor in 1890, monopolized his attention. Nevertheless, it did not cut him off from politics, rather the *Star* provided the finest instrument possible for converting ideas into practical politics.[2] It was as the creator of ideas made real that O'Connor possibly saw himself – something more than a journalist and more than a man of letters. A failure to achieve recognition here was to lead to some recrimination and complaint. O'Connor had some grounds for blaming other men's lack of vision and, if he had cared to, he could

---

[1] O'Connor, *Parnell*, p. 95.

[2] Cf. Fyfe, *O'Connor*, p. 101 for the view that O'Connor was commonly regarded as a celebrated journalist who had not been particularly active in parliament.

have blamed fate which dealt him two bitter blows, first in his own ventures and then, through Parnell's fall, in his political hopes. Perhaps the latter shock, in the unifying drama of political life, was the more grievous though a defensive taciturnity intervened and it was more hidden and long lasting.

Liberal Alliance, Marriage, Letters

For what remained of 1886 and for much of 1887 O'Connor could afford to turn his attention away from the organizational and electoral matters which had lately taken up so much of his time. He could justifiably claim that the task of organizing the vote in Britain had largely been accomplished and, the implication was, he was far better employed as a leader of the Irish movement in turning his attention to championing the larger ideas which would finally secure Home Rule. Some such suggestion, and a certain amont of impatience, appeared to lie behind the proposal coming from the platform at the 1886 I.N.L.G.B. conference, which met in Liverpool in November, that League branches ought not to concern themselves with local British politics. Certainly there was much to recommend such a policy of abstention. Leading M.P.s like Healy, or O'Connor himself when he first looked closely into League affairs in 1885, could regard local politics as divisive. Added to this but not so clearly stated was the danger that attachments formed in the localities might prove an embarrassment if the vote had to be switched from one party to another. However, as O'Connor may have appreciated, local officers of the League were also interested in politics closer to their new homes. O'Connor's proposal was strongly opposed from the body of the conference in 1886, especially by two Liverpool Irish who as it happened had both recently contested the Liverpool Scotland wards, E. Purcell and P.E. O'Hare. If the matter had been put to the vote O'Connor might well have been defeated; probably to avoid this it was referred back to the executive. The following year participation in local affairs was permitted and the subject was never raised again at a conference. O'Connor accepted the opinion of the Liverpool conference with a good grace and also turned attention away from 'that vehemence and force which occasionally distinguishes minorities, especially if they are Irish (laughter) –' and instead pointed to 'that spirit of temperance and fair play which I am glad to say are the modern characteristics of all Irish deliberative assemblies'.[3]

[3]*D.P.*, 8 Nov. 1886.

There was reason for confidence. The election result was a disappointment but not regarded by the Irish as a shattering blow against Home Rule. They had come a long way since 1880. In the November conference O'Connor had treated the occurrence lightly saying that 'in one election our strength was more apparent than in the other'. He did not specify but also did not doubt the influence of the vote. Similarly, in his study *The Parnell Movement*, written and published just at this juncture, he took the total Liberal and Unionist votes for 1886, found only a slight difference, remarked on the evident Liberal abstentions in 1886 which he chiefly blamed for the defeat, and concluded that the outcome was 'much better than might have been expected'.[4] The problem now was merely to convince the British electorate more completely, a minor matter compared to what the Irish constitutional movement had been through.

Allied to this essay in education there was the need to cement the alliance with the Liberals. At first this presented some difficulty because of the renewed land agitation which threatened to revive all the animosities of the first land war. In anticipation of such difficulties Parnell attempted to disassociate the Irish movement from agrarian violence. In Dublin in August the parliamentary party, in its first meeting after the election, put the emphasis on the political demand, which was for Home Rule as defined by Gladstone. Parnell also despatched Michael Davitt and William O'Brien to the United States, as he had once sent O'Connor, and in the same month as the Parliamentary meeting the envoys succeeded in keeping Irish American support behind Parnell. As C.C. O'Brien has suggested, this marked a new susceptibility to British public opinion.[5] Certainly, to begin with, caution was necessary because the Liberal party for all its brave public face was understandably nervous of the Irish party. O'Connor was at the receiving end of some of this nervousness and suspicion. John Morley, who was most apprehensive about a new blaze of agrarian discontent and atrocity, also had his doubts about O'Connor. In April Morley had written to his constituency chairman in Newcastle protesting that O'Connor 'ought not to have been asked' to a Liberal meeting and that there should be 'no Irishmen present'. O'Connor's potential for mischief-making was recognized elsewhere among the Liberals. Early in the new year Trevelyan, who was still at this time estranged from Gladstone, could be found writing to Chamberlain that O'Connor in his press reports, in this case a 'clever and amusing letter, full of literary gossip which the correspondent

[4]*Ibid.; Parnell Movement,* p. 287.
[5]O'Brien, *Parnell,* p. 165, pp. 197-9.

of the *Northern Echo* writes daily', was attempting to discredit the Leeds conference of the National Liberal Federation, presumably where it might involve reunion with Liberal Unionists; the recent division in the party was a further reason for disquiet.[6]

O'Connor was close to the Liberals and yet all too recently had led a campaign against them. He made considerable amends both in private and in public to conciliate the Liberals which, as something of a reversal, could be regarded as a calculated move. Yet it more accurately indicates where his own sympathies lay. As early as August 1886 he can be found writing to his Liberal go-between Labouchere suggesting a ploy in the Commons whereby O'Connor would propose an amendment, probably to the Address, on land purchase, hoping in this way to disturb relations between the Conservatives and the Liberal Unionists.[7] Unlike the Liberals, O'Connor was prepared to harry the Liberal Unionist section and although he had a vested interest here in Home Rule it is also a sign of his conviction that Liberalism ought to be more clearly identified and stick to its principles.

Publicly, too, O'Connor's support for the Liberals was enthusiastic and did much to establish that co-operation between the two allies, after a faltering start, was a matter of conviction and a new force in British politics. Liberals were genuinely outraged by the turn of events in Ireland and by what was revealed of Conservative policy at Westminster. Parnell's moderate Tenant Relief Bill, intended to halt evictions, was rejected in September as was a more general Bill he introduced in January 1887 which advocated reform rather than coercion. On the surface it was a replay of 1879-80 except that now the Liberals were on the Irish side in wanting to avoid a repeat performance of the land war. By comparison, the land agitation in Ireland, based on the 'Plan of Campaign' was both more effectively organized than the previous agitation and was, above all, peaceful, relying on passive resistance and co-operation among tenants. It was the government, and especially its new and surprisingly aggressive Irish Secretary Arthur Balfour, which was made to appear provocative. O'Connor, with some justice, could convince himself that this polarization and clarification was something he had hoped to achieve since he had first entered politics. The theme of his speeches and

---

[6] Morley to Spence Watson, 17 Feb. 1887, quoted in Cooke and Vincent, *Governing Passion*, p. 54; Trevelyan to Chamberlain, 17 Feb. 1887, quoted in M. Hurst, *Joseph Chamberlain and Liberal Reunion* (1967), p. 281.

[7] B.L., Viscount Gladstone Papers, Add. MS 46011, f. 121, O'Connor to Labouchere, 21 Aug. 1886. For the background see O'Brien, *Parnell*, p. 200 and L.P. Curtis, *Coercion and Conciliation in Ireland* (1963), pp. 335-50.

writings was now the alliance between the British democracy and Irish Home Rulers. He said as much in a speech at Shoreditch in September 1886 after the rejection of Parnell's Bill, admitting that the Irish had been forced to fight for Home Rule hitherto 'on national lines' but now acknowledging 'a debt of gratitude to the working classes of the rest of the country'. This was to some extent thanking the British working classes in anticipation. But in the meantime such support could be encouraged and perhaps O'Connor's attempt to remove the Irish League from local politics was intended to lessen the possibility of friction and improve Liberal electoral chances. By the time of the League conference of October 1887, which met in Cardiff, involvement in local politics was approved. But it was clear that such intervention would be in the Gladstonian interest and this support was to last until the turn of the century when Unionist legislation on education began to cause difficulties with local Catholic interests.[8] Support for the Liberals in national by-elections was actively pursued by O'Connor personally throughout 1887 in contests at Liverpool Exchange, Burnley, and Northwich, in all of which Gladstonian Liberals were successful, and against Liberal Unionists. This was a considerable setback for the latter's hopes and a good indication that the Liberals and the Irish could reverse the decision of 1886.[9] These were the first encouraging signs of the 'flowing tide' of support for the Liberals and the Irish; the Unionist alliance, for its part, was never as secure as the electoral victory of 1886 might suggest.

But what was more important than immediate electoral help was what could be described as propaganda, what the Irish, O'Connor included, termed 'education', an advocacy which was neither so narrow nor so prejudiced as such activities are commonly supposed to be. One example of this was O'Connor's study *The Parnell Movement* which was first published in 1886. This traced the origins of the Anglo-Irish conflict back to O'Connell's day and was clearly intended to enlighten British and other opinion in the English-speaking world as well as to serve as a reminder to Irishmen. It was welcomed by the Liberal press, much as his biography of Disraeli had been welcomed, and O'Connor sent a copy to Gladstone. Such

---

[8]*The Times,* 30 Sept. 1886; *D.P.,* 31 Oct. 1887.

[9]By-elections took place in Liverpool Exchange in February and in Northwich in August. In Exchange G.J. Goschen, one of the leading Liberal Unionists, failed to win the seat and this was regarded as a great setback. For the Unionists see Hurst, *Joseph Chamberlain,* p. 246 and p. 346. O'Connor is supposed to have claimed to one Conservative backbencher, Sir Richard Temple, that 700 removals, 'all Irish', had been brought back by the 'Gladstonians' to vote in Exchange. (R.C. Temple, (ed.), *Letters and Character Sketches from the House of Commons* (1912), p. 199). But O'Connor might have been trying to take a rise out of Temple. See below p. 99.

works provided fuel for an antagonism between the Home Rule and Unionist camps observable perhaps even more in parliament than in the country at large. Whatever the more ruthless and selfish demands of politics which some commentators have seen at work in the middle 1880s, a battle over principles was obvious in parliament in the years 1886-90.[10] To the Liberals, what had begun as a somewhat abstract attachment to a new cause had turned into a crusade, chiefly because of Conservative aggression. Contrary to what Morley and Parnell had feared, Irish agrarian agitation did not at this juncture antagonize English opinion. Liberals in the meantime supported Parnell's Land Bill in its second reading in February 1887 and they, and the Liberal Unionists, were all the more scathing in their attitude to Balfour when his much-vaunted Land Bill of 1887 ended up following the suggestions put forward in Parnell's Tenant Relief Bill which the government had rejected the previous year. Once again the land legislation was preceded by coercive legislation which was introduced in March and passed by April 1887 and which was closely followed by the arrest of Dillon and William O'Brien. Gladstone's government had followed a similar pattern but experience was supposed to count for something in politics.

O'Connor was particularly virulent against the Conservatives because he had the pledges of Conservatives against such a policy to use against them. Most of these pledges dated, it is true, from 1885 when it was easy to condemn coercion and therefore not have to say anything about Home Rule, but some of the pledges were given in the election of 1886. A correspondence about this matter broke out in *The Times* late in 1887. It was begun by O'Connor who wrote to protest against a speech of Randolph Churchill's in which Churchill had attacked Gladstone and had insisted that the Conservatives had never given pledges against coercion. O'Connor began with Churchill's record and then took on all-comers, citing instances of Conservative assurances and rejecting counter-charges about his own, possibly less serious, inconsistency. Although he may not have convinced *The Times* readership, it does look as though O'Connor's charge was securely based that, as he described it, 'when you denounce coercion or any other doctrine you are to be understood not as denouncing that which your readers understand by these words, but something altogether different which... you keep... in perpetuation locked up in your own heart'. O'Connor was not allowed to have the last word, no

---

[10]Reviews of *The Parnell Movement* in *Truth*, 11 Feb. 1886, *Liberal Home Ruler*, 21 Aug. 1886; B.L., W.E. Gladstone Papers, Add. MS 44499, f.294, O'Connor to Gladstone, 28 Dec. 1886.

well run newspaper would allow that to a political opponent and the final comment was given to a 'Cynic' who resurrected O'Connor's never to be forgotten Chicago meeting with Fenians and enlarged on the immorality of Liberal ex-ministers now receiving his support. A similar accusation implicating O'Connor in Fenianism had been made by Hartington during the debate on the Coercion Bill in April and Hartington had then had to withdraw his remarks and apologize.[11] There was a peculiarly ruthless and deceitful character to Unionism on occasions, a *realpolitik* which O'Connor genuinely detested. It was remarkable how much of this conflict in attitudes was carried by the press. On 18 April *The Times* had published the facsimile letter which was said to implicate Parnell in the Phoenix Park murders and it was to take almost two years, down to February 1889, for Parnell to clear his name. Although in the meantime sympathy from the Liberals was gratifying and shown at its clearest in the great banquet for Liberals and Parnellites held in July 1887 in the National Liberal Club, more had to be done. A considerable advantage could be gained through the press, especially a newspaper which could be relied upon. O'Connor had concentrated his chief attention on this problem throughout 1887 and he approached the task with an enthusiasm and imagination which had perhaps been starved of expression since O'Connor had accepted the Parnellite whip.

O'Connor's personal circumstances had altered considerably since the days when he was a struggling journalist barely surviving from one commission to another. O'Connor himself was never ready to admit that struggle was lacking, early hardships were a theme in his reminiscences and further disappointments in courtship and marriage caused him to be continually preoccupied with his health and his finances, a worrier a little way under the *bonhomie*. But this was a highly competitive age and it was as well to be careful. O'Connor might have reflected, but did not, that his troubles had come when he had been too adventurous and he was more obviously optimistic and ambitious in the years immediately after the publication of his life of Disraeli. By the time he entered parliament in 1880 he was comfortably situated though still dependent on a furious energy in planning and following up his freelance journalism and although he

---

[11] *The Times*, 25, 27, 31 Oct., 1, 8 Nov. 1887. O'Connor's final letter was on 31 October. He was also involved with the League conference which met just at this time, on 29 October. At the conference O'Connor made an attack on the entire Conservative party, 'three hundred men in the House of Commons at the present time who had given an open and most shameless lie to their most solemn pledges in the last election'. (*D.P.*, 31 Oct)

was disparaged for his supposed wealth by some of his colleagues his earnings were probably still below average for a successful journalist.[12] Despite such disadvantages and restraints, an M.P. was in one of the best situations possible for publicising the views and the authority of a man of ideas. Because of this, commissions from the *Pall Mall Gazette,* the *Freeman's Journal* and American newspapers, including the *New York Sun,* had followed, and his books, *Gladstone's House of Commons* and the *Parnell Movement,* had been collected from this journalism.[13]

For all the personal references and recollection in his journalism, O'Connor remained elusive. Often in reminiscence he gave the impression of melancholy or introspection, qualities which certainly existed in his make-up and were bound to be admired by a born extrovert with a romantic temperament. Similarly, he, or his biographer, continually suggested a volatility between cynicism and idealism, some acknowledgement of the part played by reflection. It was also appropriate to be reticent about women, though O'Connor was less inhibited or reserved than some of his colleagues. He remained a bachelor through the early 1880s, living a no doubt disorderly but comfortable life, furiously busy with his political duties and journalistic strategies. He had a taste for good living which was by no means inappropriate in a radical: Dilke and Randolph Churchill fit in the same radical-dandy tradition, indeed radicalism all but monopolized the intellectual and creative life of that century.[14] O'Connor enjoyed the company of women. In his youth he had courted a girl in Galway whose memory stayed with him for the rest of his life and who, with good reason, he sometimes regretted not having married. In London, during the difficult early years, he fell in love with a barmaid and, according to Fyfe's account, would have married her but for his lack of means.[15] There may have been some hankering after domesticity and there are some indications of this in the few of his letters which have survived from this period. Writing to James Hooper in May 1878 he mentioned meeting 'two not bad looking girls' and how he

[12] Healy's report that O'Connor earned £1,200 in 1880 compares with the average for a journalist on a London morning newspaper of £1,000 for the 1870s (Lee, *Origins of the Popular Press,* p. 108).

[13] Preface to *Gladstone's House of Commons.* O'Connor's tour of the United States in 1881-2 probably resulted in articles for the *American Catholic Quarterly.* These appeared between 1883 and 1886 (see bibliography). O'Connor was to write a considerable amount of syndicated material for American newspapers (some of it deriving from articles written for the *Freeman's Journal*). This was all helped by his future tours of the United States and only partially disrupted during the first world war.

[14] George Watson, *The English Ideology* (1973), pp. 110-1.

[15] Fyfe, p. 121.

'arranged to meet them again tomorrow', which is open, almost guileless. A few years later in 1882, writing again to Hooper from Paris (which next to London was O'Connor's spiritual home) he complained of the *Hotel du Quai Voltaire*, being 'rather British' adding ruefully that he was in the company of 'Arnold and Wright and you know what that means' (which may have meant nothing more than something out of Jerome K. Jerome) and concluding 'the only chance of being moderately happy is to have a companion and home one likes ... *mais cherchez la femme*'.[16] Sometime in the middle of the decade he met May Carroll, an Irish American actress but she left him and returned to the United States. Shortly afterwards, perhaps on the rebound, O'Connor married Elizabeth Howard, in June 1885.[17]

There was nothing unusual in any of this except perhaps the marriage. O'Connor had not always thought that he wanted marriage but he had then married impetuously. Elizabeth Howard was not an ideal choice, at least not for domestic bliss. There is considerable mystery, which still causes literary historians some doubts, about her origins and early life. Howard was her married name, perhaps assumed, and she may have been married, as she claimed, twice before. Her maiden name was Paschal; she was an American, a Texan, and the daughter of a lawyer who became a Supreme Court justice for Arkansas, who had in his time also been a political journalist. From her first or second marriage Elizabeth Howard had a ten year old son, Francis Howard, and neither he nor his son was to prove much consolation to O'Connor in his old age. Elizabeth Howard was a journalist of a kind, gathering engagements in Europe and Britain when O'Connor first encountered and pursued her, and to do her justice she does not appear, at least from her memoirs, to have encouraged the match. She was anxious to achieve literary and social fame, an eccentric egoist, above all independent. O'Connor wanted, and his biographer said he needed, a willing supporter and listener and yet it is possible to surmise that it was Elizabeth Howard's individuality and push that attracted him in the first place; perhaps, too, it was her Americanism. O'Connor's fascination with America fitted the curious pattern, not entirely a matter of money, which saw Parnell enamoured of an American girl before he met Mrs. O'Shea, Randolph Churchill's marriage, and the marriage of many another leading politician and socialite. O'Connor's marriage did not prove a success but it is hard to believe with Fyfe that this was owing to a clash of national characteristics. Many American husbands would not have tolerated

---

[16] N.L.I., MS 3460, O'Connor to Hooper, 15 May 1878; *ibid.* 28 Sept. 1882.
[17] Fyfe, p. 122.

Elizabeth Howard and many American women were sufficiently fascinated by British society to find creative outlets behind the scenes.[18] Moreover O'Connor lived with Elizabeth for longer than has been supposed, a complete separation probably did not come until the first world war. In the meantime, whatever clashes of temperament there may have been, Elizabeth provided a spur to O'Connor's advancement. For a start he moved into a grander house; the married couple lived for a time in O'Connor's flat in Parliament Mansions in Victoria Street, the latest of O'Connor's bachelor establishments and near to the Houses of Parliament, and then in a house in Grosvenor Road, also in Westminster near the Thames. Shortly afterwards they set themselves up in a flat above the *Star*'s offices in Stonecutter Street and then, sometime in 1890, they moved to a more luxurious address in Upper Cheyne Row in Chelsea, still convenient for Westminster and chosen in preference to a house in Hampstead. This was to be the couple's town house for most of their married life. Whether marriage introduced O'Connor to a more distinguished social life is debatable. Elizabeth in her autobiography was careful to mention celebrated guests entertained in Chelsea – George Moore, Conan Doyle, Cardinal Manning, Henry James, and George Meredith. The latter was a particular friend whom O'Connor kept and admired for the rest of his life.[19] Probably from here on O'Connor's acquaintances did become even less severely political. He might, at least to begin with, have had some reservations about indulging in London social life, which could later be an embarrassment in his political life and which may also have caused his radicalism to mellow, though the political disasters he was to experience were far more effective in this respect. He may have regretted the simple life but Elizabeth was an asset to a successful man; her vivacity and her natural instincts as a hostess promised greater things to come and it is little wonder that O'Connor moved on from the detailed work of organization after 1885 and demanded more of life.

[18] For Elizabeth Howard, see her autobiography, *I, Myself* (1910) in which she describes O'Connor's courtship (p. 141). For her other work (which included a book on touring in Ireland published in 1917) see the bibliography. She was an occasional journalist and for a time president of the League of Women Journalists. Francis Howard regarded himself as a painter and was something of a financial and amatory adventurer. His son, Brian Howard, was the notorious dilettante of the 1920s and 1930s. See also Martin Green, *Children of the Sun* (1977), pp. 136, 140-1 (where there is an entertaining description of O'Connor) and M.J. Lancaster, *Brian Howard* (1968), pp. 6-9. Fyfe gives a long description of the differences between O'Connor and his wife (pp. 122-36).

[19] The choice of a house in Chelsea is referred to in O'Connor's correspondence with the Holidays, sometime after 20 May 1889, letter dated 'Wednesday' N.L.I., Holiday Papers, MS 19581; *I, Myself*, p. 236; Fyfe, p. 135; Siegfried Sassoon, *Meredith* (1959), p. 300.

There is widespread testimony to suggest that O'Connor entered into the life of parliament with great enthusiasm. Much of his effectiveness in oratory, whether in parliament or on the public platform, as well as the most persuasive parts of his writing, depended on the projection of his personality. Informality, an engaging friendliness, and a concern for detail on a human scale won over most of those with whom he came in contact. More was involved here than the traditional attributes of a party 'boss' though his enemies sometimes made the disparaging comparison and the description of popularity suffers from being a commonplace of twentieth century politics. O'Connor was more original, had much that was worth saying, and genuinely wanted to change things.

His colleagues in the Irish party regarded his social and journalistic concerns with a mixture of astonishment, gratification and irony (or, in the case of O'Donnell and, sometimes, Healy, malice) and often the distortion that crept in as a result was because they only recollected the easy-going, superficial journalist. Healy, for instance, remarked on one occasion how O'Connor joined the company of himself and Biggar, 'avid for "copy"', and an aside such as this can quickly assume an air of finality. An engaging nature meant that O'Connor, along with William O'Brien, was one of the few close personal friends of Parnell, making a habit of dining with Parnell in the House, at least until Parnell's increasingly long absences from parliament. This sociability and high level of interest in all parliament's affairs, necessary for a political journalist, impressed itself on other M.P.s. Harcourt, as well as complaining about O'Connor's noisiness could also say that, of the Irish party, 'only T.P. O'Connor is in rude health and he is not a patriot'. Sir Patrick O'Brien, the Irish whig who sat for King's county and who had a deadly tongue, characterized O'Connor as 'the modern Plutarch at £10 a week'.[20] There were many more such brief descriptions or epithets declaring for or against O'Connor. Their cacophony suggests that here was a remarkably active politician with an uncommonly large number of friends and acquaintances. There was sometimes a danger to O'Connor that politics could be taken to mean only the higher gossip and that only the 'character' would remain.

Oratory, either in parliament or on the platform, is difficult to recapture. One of the minor reasons for this is technical: reports either for *Hansard* or by the press cannot always be relied upon because in

---

[20] Healy, *Letters and Leaders*, i, 43; O'Donnell, *Irish Parliamentary Party*, i, 457; O'Connor, *Parnell*, pp. 52-3, 93, 132; Gardiner, *Harcourt*, ii, 49; Viscount Gladstone, *After Thirty Years* (1928), p. 186.

the former case politicans were entitled to polish up the printed version and in the latter reporting was often incompetent. Politicians' concern for what they had said (or perhaps what they had meant to say much better) and, authorial vanity apart, the demand among the reading public for collections of speeches testify perhaps to a facility among the Victorians in connecting the printed page with experience, but more than this it demonstrates how important and how effective the spoken word was thought to be.

Difficulties over the correct text would only be crucial to the weaker brethren. Yet even in the case of a master of rhetoric such as Gladstone it is only now clear as a matter of record that he could keep massed audiences spellbound. Otherwise his extended subordinate clauses and antitheses, circumlocutions and rarified language, read coldly on the page and need to be fleshed out with the sense of place and the theatrics of a great political set-piece. O'Connor may have added to the veneration of Gladstone but he did not follow his example and he commented upon Gladstone's complexity, correctly prophesying that Gladstone's speeches would not 'live': he could be forgiven for not anticipating that the taste for speeches would see a more general eclipse. O'Connor was always more direct and, even in his attacks, more entertaining. Like most good speakers he had had to overcome an initial nervousness. But his experience before entering parliament as an impromptu debater and amateur radical politician stood him in good stead so that many of his colleagues and opponents could have believed, by the 1880s, that his fluency and ease were entirely natural. He soon learnt to adapt a set speech to suit the more practical taste of parliament and acquired a facility in the cut and thrust of debate; he became a 'ready' man and quickly expert in the strategems of the Commons (so that by comparison it was a lack of disputatiousness in public speeches that he noticed when he first toured the United States). Even in a party renowned for its debating talent he could be given pride of place, and even by O'Donnell. In his own works he paid frequent attention to the debating skills of parliamentarians and listed the attributes of other Irishmen in debate in *The Parnell Movement.* He also pointed to the apparent paradox of someone so tongue-tied as Parnell being able to lead the Irish party. O'Connor's English critics fully recognized his abilities though sometimes obliged to suspect the technique itself. To the political commentator Sir Henry Lucy O'Connor displayed a 'thin polish of London manners' and it was Lucy who pointed to O'Connor's neglect of parliament in later life. From the Conservative side a valuable, because perhaps typical, reaction was that of Sir Richard Temple (who was so typical a Conservative backbencher that O'Connor scrutinized him with great relish). Temple found that O'Connor gesticulated too much ('his tall, rather stout figure, his round face and somewhat rollicking gesticulation') embodied 'Hibernian fluency', and was imagined to be 'an inferior copy of O'Connell, and to speak and look somewhat as that famous personage.'[21]

Perhaps this is reminiscent of nothing more than actors waiting for the curtain and quizzing each other for signs of wear and tear and to prove any one politician's contribution by a conclusive quotation is, as has been implied, virtually impossible. As an example of a set-piece O'Connor's introduction to his speech in the Home Rule debate in June 1886 has been included in the appendix to this study; like many best efforts it was published separately. An instance of O'Connor's diatribe gives a clearer picture of the politician in action. One celebrated example was his attack on Forster after Forster had left office and, at the end of February 1883, had himself accused Parnell of being implicated in Fenianism and crime. The cold and dismissive rebuttal by Parnell may, as O'Connor suggests, have turned out to be the most effective response possible here. But O'Connor also attacked Forster and while his speech, relying for much of its point on allusions to Forster's shambling appearance, had its brighter moments, it was not so light-hearted as Fyfe suggested and Forster's compatriots were not spared:

> There are times when the English are seized with a spirit of blood frenzy (Oh! Oh!) . . . Now there is a blood frenzy against the Irish people (Oh! Oh!). I know very well what I am saying is true and you know it too. It is when the tide runs high, especially if it is a foul tide, that political tricksters trim their sails. Political adventurers are always able to gain advantage in crises such as this, especially if their malignant passions are concealed with an unctuous exterior and under a tongue so boorish that good manners suggests them to be artificial.[22]

The conventionalized indications of dismay and anger in the *Hansard* report, even so, do not do justice to the effect of the speech. Not to be outdone by convention, descriptions of the scene in parliament, of Forster and the same idea of a 'blood frenzy' also occur however,

---

[21] For a general discussion see Watson, *English Ideology;* pp. 112-32; *Memoirs,* i, 9; *Parnell Movement,* pp. 180-211, 253-6, descriptions of Thomas Sexton, Arthur O'Connor, J.J. O'Kelly, John Dillon, T.M. Healy, and William O'Brien; *Parnell,* pp. 173-4; Fyfe, pp. 93, 158, 117-18, Temple, *Letters and Character Sketches,* p. 97, pp. 128-9.

[22] *Hansard, 3,* 276, col. 659, 22 Feb. 1883; Fyfe also suggested that O'Connor had been 'put up' to answer Forster (p. 100). Forster's appearance and the exchange with Parnell is in *Gladstone's House of Commons,* pp. 293-9, and the 'blood frenzy' charge, *ibid.* p. 289. Much of the phraseology is similar to O'Connor's parliamentary speech.

written shortly afterwards, in O'Connor's *Gladstone's House of Commons.* These instances in O'Connor's writings show that there is a difficulty of thinness or repetition of material, even for his fertile pen. H.W. Massingham, shortly to be an editorial colleague on the *Star,* regarded him as 'the fastest descriptive writer I ever knew'. The danger here was that the often implied comment which accompanied the description would prove facile; the intention, in making the style reflect the spoken word, was to come as close as possible to the truth or inwardness of an incident. This may appear a truism about journalism, and parliamentary reporting too, had a long history, being revived in the form of parliamentary sketches in the 1850s. At the same time the importance of ideas and men of letters in politics had been a persistent feature of the higher journalism (whether it had been appreciated by all the newspaper reading public is debatable). The unity had been emphasized, particularly on the Liberal side since the foundation of the political quarterlies during the early years of the century and in O'Connor's day found its chief representative in the austere, severely cautious person of John Morley.[23]

Despite all this, the fact that changes in journalism turn out on closer examination to be matters of degree, O'Connor was one of the first of a new breed of journalist to create his own market and put his personal stamp on his material. In the preface to *Gladstone's House of Commons* he made an apology for the haste and inaccuracies of his reports, though still hoping that he had achieved some impartiality. He thought them justified because they were immediate whereas memory, he claimed, was fickle. This did not stop him resorting to memory and in one case, in his study of Parnell, it resulted in perhaps his most impressive book. Similarly, whether it was salutary or harmful to put such an emphasis on the personalities of politics was, according to O'Connor 'a large question' which he left open – and a recent commentator has suggested with some perception that essays such as this were regrettable precisely because they attacked the formality in public affairs which made good government possible.[24] There remained little doubt where O'Connor's interest lay and few signs of disbelief that he was doing something new. He was convinced that 'the reporting columns of newspapers do not give an accurate and rarely a vivid picture of what takes place in a legislative body' and

[23] H.W. Massingham, *The London Daily Press* (1892), p. 181; Lee, *Popular Press,* p. 121; John Gross, *The Rise and Fall of the Man of Letters* (1969), pp. 113-47, for Liberal politicians, especially Morley. Gross does not discuss O'Connor. See also bibliography.

[24] Richard Sennett, *The Fall of Public Man* (1977), *passim.* What remains remarkable is the extent to which this has been resisted in Britain (cf. Maurice Cowling, *The Impact of Labour* (1971), pp. 6-11).

short of being 'vulgarly personal' he intended to give 'some idea of the man who makes [a speech], his manner of speaking, his character, his career'. Ultimately, and apart from the larger questions, it came down to ability or descriptive power and what resulted did have some novelty, especially in giving the sense of place and actuality otherwise so curiously lacking in occasional and biographical writing in English. His style emphasised feeling and emotion and, although O'Connor never claimed this, followed the Swiftian example that if the sense was clear the syntax could take care of itself. In his college days and for some short time afterwards he had, so he confessed, modelled himself on what was as dry and inhuman as possible, the approach of an historian, in this case Robertson (presumably William Robertson, the eighteenth-century historian of the Americas) but had then forsaken this excessive scholarly discipline for what was 'interesting', this being 'the first thing the professional journalist had to learn'.[25] This approach is best judged as journalism, resembling the ephemeral but still leaving the works which O'Connor collected and published in the 1880s, *Gladstone's House of Commons, The Parnell Movement,* and even his too easily dismissed *Lord Beaconsfield,* full of particular insights and well able to capture the reader's attention. One of the essential features of the New Journalism O'Connor was to apply in the *Star* was the accumulation of telling detail, an approach which he believed had been pioneered in historical writing by Carlyle, Macaulay, and J.R. Green. He aimed to destroy the 'dignity' of history. He was rarely colourless; in the Gladstone parliament he could be perceptive and cruel about character and, apart from his early attachment to Bradlaugh's cause, it was also the battle of personalities and ideas here which caught his attention and meant that he was not uninvolved in his reporting, and where even some of his own colleagues could be put in an unfavourable light. An example is the end of one crucial division where

> the two Mr Sullivans, Mr O'Donnell and Mr Daly and several others sprang to their feet and with triumphant looks waved their hats wildly and cheered loudly while Mr Barry, Mr Finegan, Mr Biggar and some of the other Parnellites who had supported Mr Bradlaugh sat in their places with knit brows and vehemently exclaimed 'Shame! Shame!'. . . . . Mr Sullivan dashing in excitedly to his place on the opposition side exclaimed to the bunch of Conservative 'Guerrillas' on the front bench before the gangway 'We have won'.[26]

[25] Ashley Gibson, 'T.P. O'Connor as Author and Journalist', *The Bookman,* Feb. 1910. For Robertson see J.R. Hale, *The Evolution of British Historiography* (1967), pp. 156-66.

[26] O'Connor on 'History' in his article, 'The New Journalism', *New Review,* Oct. 1889; *Gladstone's House of Commons,* pp. 22-3.

Politics then intervened. Bradlaugh was of no importance to the Irish party as such, merely a source of division. Such a contrast between convictions and necessities was less likely after 1886. O'Connor might be pushing things too far; he might not have the scholarly apparatus to fall back on if there were not enough sheer success in parliament, the fountainhead of all his creative work. In the meantime his person, his presence and effectiveness, his readiness with ideas and his ability to seize the moment, made him the popularizer of the Irish party, certainly the most articulate. He was the one best equipped to take on the task of leading both Liberals and Irish in an attack on what was seen as the Unionist's misuse of power.[27]

The 'Star', 1887-90

O'Connor's originality and enthusiasm were the chief forces behind the founding of the *Star* in January 1888, less so his determination. In this variety of qualities it is possible to see why the *Star* was such a remarkable newspaper and why, even so, O'Connor had to relinquish the editorship after a few short hectic years. A newspaper would allow O'Connor to put into effect all the new ideas on journalistic practice which he had absorbed in his work for the *Daily Telegraph* and as sub-editor of the *Echo* both of which had reputations for innovation, added to which was his exposure to the American press in the early 1880s. He had, too, a reputation for ability and controversy which could fit him for a post as editor. He promised a new voice or style and this was imposed on the newspaper. There was to be no hard and fast line between the aims of journalism and of politics; it was this which made the newspaper unique and this is why the *Star* had been remembered. To O'Connor it offered a unity of thought and action. As a radical he could be given something like the leadership of metropolitan radicalism (and by now he was even more of a Londoner by adoption). As a nationalist he saw the pressing need to guarantee the alliance with the Liberals and publicize the cause of Home Rule. For a journalist the advantages in prestige and money scarcely needed mentioning. O'Connor tended to overlook them: they paled beside the chance to create a more decisive role for the journalist in politics.

[27] O'Connor was in this case, just as in oratory, *primus inter pares* in the Irish party because, as must be apparent, many of his colleagues, and many Irishmen, were journalists. See O'Brien, *Parnell*, p. 19, O'Day, *English Face of Irish Nationalism*, p. 20, F.S.L. Lyons, *The Irish Parliamentary Party* (1951), p. 174, and Lee, *Popular Press*, pp. 113-15, who remarks on the ubiquitous Irish journalist in the writings of Thackeray, Trollope, Dickens, Gissing, and C.E. Montague.

After 1886, and especially in London where the Liberals had fared badly in the election, the need for a new Liberal daily newspaper was obvious. The Liberal cause was helped by journals such as the *Pall Mall Gazette* and Labouchere's *Truth*, but this sort of effort was intermittent and possibly too highbrow, both journals had a limited circulation and neither was consistently 'loyal' to the Liberal party. W.T. Stead of the *Pall Mall Gazette* was particularly suspect because of his sensationalism. His agitation against juvenile prostitution in the 'Maiden Tribute' articles had taken place as recently as 1885 and his more recent hounding of Dilke did much to wreck the latter's career.[28] John Morley, recognizing the need for a newspaper, was negotiating with Andrew Carnegie although the initiative in this case appeared to come from Carnegie. Apparently Morley knew nothing of O'Connor's plans, though O'Connor must have been involved in negotiations throughout 1887 since the choice of a staff alone took some months. Although O'Connor's scheme was well advanced and money had been invested he all but withdrew on hearing of Morley's intentions and it was only through the greater determination of O'Connor's wife that Morley was informed of the plans for the *Star* and dropped his own preparations.[29] The desire for a newspaper was evident but O'Connor did have further difficulties, this time with financial backers. Negotiations here have remained obscure and have been given an extended treatment in recent studies of Sir John Brunner, one of the principal backers, and H.W. Massingham, who turned out to be O'Connor's arch-rival for editorial control of the newspaper. Broadly, what appears to have happened is that Brunner and James Williamson, the future Lord Ashton, each agreed to put up £10,000 to total half the amount needed. According to O'Connor's memoirs, one of them then withdrew. This appears to have been Williamson who is identified as wanting to impose an incredible amount of restriction on O'Connor's editorial freedom and who may have broken off negotiations when he failed to have these controls accepted. Of the other backer, presumably still Brunner, O'Connor says that he then agreed to provide half the amount he had originally promised. The bulk of the finance required was then it seems provided by J.J. Colman the mustard manufacturer and prominent East Anglian M.P. Other backers were Thomas Lough, a Liberal M.P., Sir James Whitehead, the Lord Mayor of London who was on the board of directors and may also have been a prominent shareholder, and

---

[28] See J.O. Baylen, 'The New Journalism in Late Victorian Britain', *Australian Journal of Politics and History* 18 (1972), 367-85, 367. This concentrates on Stead. There is no mention of O'Connor.

[29] Fyfe, p. 143.

Wilfred Blunt who was another director, whose progressive views were not much in evidence to help O'Connor when the crisis arose over policy. O'Connor received a salary of £1,200 a year, still not very high and no higher than he had earned in 1880. This, however, was to be topped up by one quarter of the profits after a dividend of 5 per cent had been paid to shareholders, a device intended to ensure O'Connor's loyalty to the paper particularly during the risky initial period. O'Connor could only be removed by a three-quarters (later two-thirds) majority of the shareholders. Healy, no lover of Liberals, stigmatized the backers as 'pharisees' who would cause the ruin of anyone foolish enough to take their principles seriously and he appears to have been more or less correct. Much of this ought to have been more of a warning to O'Connor than it was; it also indicates the extent to which O'Connor put finance second and was perhaps naive over money matters, as he claims in his memoirs. But it was also a sign of something to become more pronounced in O'Connor's later life – that he could be a difficult business partner.[30]

After all this trouble behind the scenes the *Star* finally emerged, a halfpenny evening newspaper, the first issue coming out on 16 January 1888. As in the case of oratory or political journalism, it is difficult to sum up in what way the *Star* was new. None of the techniques used in the *Star* was an innovation (apart from the use of the stop press). Cross headlines covering two columns, the interview (an American development regarded with great suspicion) and sports news all had longer pedigrees.[31] Not even the informal style or the attention paid to gossip or sensation was particularly a product of O'Connor's pen; human interest stories were strong in the eighteenth century press so in a way O'Connor was helping to revive a more popular type. Yet O'Connor managed to orchestrate all these techniques to great effect. One of the difficulties of journalistic history is precisely that even more than oratory or political controversy it depends on a fashion, a receptivity, and a surprise that has passed and its products now seem uniformly unremarkable (a page in the

[30] *Memoirs,* ii, 254; Healy, *Letters,* i, 276; Fyfe, pp. 143, 145, 152; S.E. Koss, *Sir John Brunner* (1930), pp. 157-8, where Brunner is exonerated from blame in O'Connor's difficulties; A.F. Havighurst, *Radical Journalist: H.W. Massingham* (1974), p. 21. See also Lee, *Popular Press,* p. 83 where it is revealed that the nominal capital was put at £100,000, but only £6,000 was called immediately; Wilson Pope, *The Story of the Star* (1938), pp. 12-15; Healy quoted in H. Fyfe, *Sixty Years of Fleet Street* (1949), p. 45.

[31] O'Connor's attitude towards innovation can be found in the interview with Stead, (*P.M.G.,* 18 Jan. 1888) in which he said that he would follow the American model in many ways, though expressing some reservations about banner headlines; he also discussed interviews. American practice was more fully followed from June onwards (Stanley Morrison, *The English Newspaper* (1932), p. 291).

sensational *Star* being reminiscent of *The Times* in the twentieth century before it was brightened up in the 1960s). Characteristically, too, accounts of the press have remained inward-looking, written by journalists with an emphasis upon personalities. The latter pre-occupation helps to explain much of O'Connor's work (although many journalistic accounts appear to be unaware that O'Connor was a politician) but it remains superficial. More recent analyses, especially Alan J. Lee's innovative studies, have suggested that journalism does not escape a common historiographical problem where what is involved is not only what happened but in additon what it was believed was happening. This duality could be taken further because the whole business of journalism is involved with appearances, and newspapermen are perhaps more fascinated than most with what is ephemeral and may mistake it for the truth. In perspective it is possible to see that there was some illusion involved in O'Connor's founding of the *Star*. But he could see the difficulties. Illusion or vision is also the business of journalists and necessary to bring about change. Too much hindsight leads to an underestimation of the work O'Connor put into his new venture.

O'Connor's place in the founding of the New Journalism, given to him by the advent of the *Star*, has always been allowed and is what usually gives him his footnote in history texts. But, given the lack of perspective frequently shown in journalistic histories, there is room for an interpretation which might rate O'Connor's contribution more highly. By comparison, W.T. Stead's role as an innovator has rightly been given prominence by his biographer, but it may be the case that O'Connor did more to change journalistic practice. Stead made great claims for the new type of light or investigative journalism even going so far in one article published in 1886 and entitled 'Government by Journalism' as to claim that the editor was set fair to replace the politician, and it could also be said that this was the first clear statement of a new force in British public affairs.[32] Yet to concentrate too much on Stead here is something of a distortion. Precisely because the newer type of journalism was regarded with some apprehension, it can also be inferred that it was not an isolated phenomenon. Moreover it was equated with that more open threat to parliamentary govern-ment that was supposedly causing some politicians to become nervous in the 1880s, the growth of the 'caucus' system in political organization. Matthew Arnold's celebrated attack on the journalistic front which was published in the *Nineteenth Century* in May 1887,

---

[32] Bahlen, *loc. cit, passim;* Stead, 'Government by Journalism', *Contemporary Review,* 49, May (1886), 53-74, and 'The Future of Journalism', *Contemporary Review,* 50, Nov. (1886), 663-79.

and which first publicized the term 'the New Journalism', was not only a response to Stead's individual example (though that helped) it was a warning, somewhat shrill and exaggerated as such warnings tend to be, of a change in mood or style affecting a large part of the press which would go on to endanger society. The new approach, appealing to the 'democracy' (which did not exist even formally in Britain until 1918, or perhaps 1928), full of novelty and generous impulses and prosecuted with ability was, according to Arnold, essentially 'featherbrained' and unable and unwilling to deal with the unpleasant realities of public life. One recent cultural history has therefore probably been correct in seeing Arnold's attack as a reaction against developments which had taken place since the 1860s and if in response to any one newspaper that would be the *Daily Telegraph*, first founded in the 1860s (and a newspaper on which O'Connor had worked). As for chronology, Stead's article, and another example along the same lines preceded O'Connor's newspaper, but by little more than a year, during which time O'Connor was involved in complicated preparations and Stead's declarations were themselves preceded by articles written by Labouchere in his journal *Truth* which specifically dismissed the pretensions of London editors. Labouchere had about as good a claim to be the originator of New Journalism as Stead. As a politician Labouchere was more dubious about the political role of the press and in comparison to Arnold, had a politician's sense of reality.[33] The same could be said of O'Connor who was aiming at some sort of intermediary's role. O'Connor was to prove less dogmatic and less self-righteous than Stead, more genuinely ready to entertain as well as to instruct, but also more realistic and more responsible than critics such as Arnold supposed possible. O'Connor was practical and effective. He operated through a daily newspaper and let the new style speak for itself for the most part. Perhaps this explains why almost all accounts of contemporaries and near-contemporaries, even when they were those of political opponents, tended to give O'Connor the credit for the change that took place in the 1880s; because he was more completely a working journalist.[34]

The *Star*'s impact and the practical effectiveness of O'Connor comes across nowhere more strongly than in the staff he had carefully

[33] Matthew Arnold, 'Up to Easter', *Nineteenth Century* 123, May (1887), 638-9; Raymond Williams, *The Long Revolution* (1961), p. 218; Labouchere in *Truth*, 5, 26, Nov. 1885. Williams sees the whole period 1855-96 as the second phase of the development of the popular press among the middle classes (*ibid.* p. 201), so diminishing the New Journalism, or placing it in the 1860s, but this is perhaps too undifferentiated.

[34] For histories of journalism, which invariably give descriptions of the founding of the *Star* and its staff, see the bibliography. It is astonishing how derivative these works are.

chosen for the newspaper. He chose them for their promise rather than for their reputation and there were also those, probably the more talented group, to whom he gave their first chance. In the first category were H. W. Massingham as assistant editor and one of the most gifted and wily of radical journalists, Ernest Parke as sub editor, Richard Le Gallienne as chief reviewer, with Clement Shorter and A. B. Walkley as drama and literary critics; all of these were to go on to even more distinguished careers in Fleet Street. Among those who began with the *Star* was a young clerk from the Colonial Office, Sidney Webb, who because of his background was told by O'Connor (so the story goes) not to antagonize any socialist readers the *Star* might have, whereas history shows that some socialists always did agree with Webb. Then there was a young, flamboyant and penniless Irishman (straight out of the pages of a mid-Victorian novel), George Bernard Shaw. It was not clear what he would do.[35] This staff has often been listed, and deservedly; it was probably the most talented newspaper staff ever assembled and much of the credit must go to O'Connor, assisted by Massingham. The enthusiasm this created is now difficult to recapture although journalists remembered it. Even without a larger policy men as gifted as these would have produced something unusual. O'Connor gave them their head, editorial control was slight and this, which became a source of criticism, was possibly a conscious intention on O'Connor's part as such as a sin of omission. He was a hard-working professional and he often left them to get on with their own work. His own experience of lack of opportunity for talent in Fleet Street may have been fresh in his mind.

But O'Connor did lay down a policy in the first issue of the newspaper, 'Our Confession of Faith', which, as the slight irony in the title suggests (itself perhaps a dig at Stead who interviewed O'Connor on the day before publication and the day after) was light without being frivolous.[36] This statement of policy has also become one of the sacred texts of journalistic history, perhaps because it put the case for the new mood in journalism so well, more sympathetically than Stead had ever done. A liveliness of approach was promised, an end to 'the verbose and prolix articles to which most of our contemporaries still adhere'. The poor were championed in probably the most celebrated passage in the Confession, a concern for 'the charwoman that stands in St. Giles, the seamstress that is sweated in

[35] Fyfe, pp. 143-4; Havighurst, *Massingham*, p. 21; B.L.P., Diary of G.B. Shaw, entry for 30 Dec. 1887; *Memoirs*, p. 256.

[36] *P.M.G.*, 16 Jan. 1888; *Star*, 17 Jan. 1888; *Memoirs*, ii, 255, where he said that the article had 'passed into history'. The ideas in the 'Confession of Faith' were more fully developed in his article 'The New Journalism'.

Whitechapel, the labourer that stands begging for work outside the dockyard gate in St Georges in the East'. There would, and this seems to be an unusual statement for O'Connor, be less emphasis on politics. But what he meant by this was that there would be room for other news and in many ways the *Star* turned out to be more overtly political than other popular newspapers. From the start it was declared that the newspaper intended to champion the Liberal-radical cause which had been so weakened by defection since 1886 and there was a practical political attitude put forward, which developed into a programme, of antagonism towards an aggressive foreign policy and the 'racial hatreds' seen in Irish policy. War was declared on 'the House of Lords, the property vote [and] the monopoly of parliamentary rule by the rich'[37] and, nearer home, there was a target to attack in the misgovernment of London, 'ruled by one of the worst and most corrupt oligarchies that ever disgraced and robbed a city'. Some of these issues had concerned O'Connor in his 'Power of the Purse' article in 1880 and little had happened to make him change his mind; he returned to them with a new zest. Politics, without being trivialized, was made anyone's concern. Elsewhere, outside the leader column, O'Connor contributed his own gossip column 'Mainly about People' which, as in his earlier works, was preoccupied with the personalities of politics. It was as though the dam had burst. O'Connor had been given the chance to articulate his own deepest convictions; he remarked of the Confession that no article had ever come more readily or caused him so much satisfaction. What it showed was the enthusiasm of one who knew that much good might well result. He was aware of earlier failures in the realm of campaigning journalism and also of Fleet Street's perennial scepticism but such minor disadvantages were hardly likely to deter him.

Given the opportunity O'Connor now had, it is hardly surprising that for 1888 and up to his resignation from the editorship in the summer of 1890 O'Connor put most of his energy into the *Star*, accepting that this was a major political venture in itself.[38] Back copies of the *Star*, especially its innovative lighter items (which through the callousness of time now includes coverage of the Jack the Ripper murders) still make good reading, but the impact of the newspaper can also be seen by concentrating on its serious side and three major concerns, domestic issues including the government of London, Ireland, and progressive politics.

In all these areas events were to prove that the *Star* was too successful and the Liberals were too timorous. However there was a

[37] *Star,* 17 Jan. 1888.
[38] *Memoirs,* ii, 255.

clear gain in the case of domestic politics and especially in the narrow area of London affairs. Here the effect of the *Star* could be seen clearly. As the historian of London popular politics has suggested, the effect could be quantified. Here, in the reform of London government and in the swing of voters to (or back to) the radicals, the enemy was clear, the issues were comparatively simple, and Liberals and radicals were ready to sink their differences. O'Connor's newspaper, which was after all a London newspaper, might have been thought most likely to appeal to the skilled artisans, those whom O'Connor had first encountered and shown signs of leading in the later 1870s. Certainly it had been Labouchere's view that these were the readership of the radical press, though more recent commentators are not so convinced and it is not clear that in this case O'Connor was greatly expanding the numbers of radicals, though perhaps he did give them renewed confidence.[39] In other words, it was clear even at the time that O'Connor was not founding a mass circulation newspaper and more than a minimum level of literacy was still assumed where the readers were concerned.

The *Star's* foundation coincided with the 'Bloody Sunday' demonstrations in Trafalgar Square and the ensuing trial of John Burns and R.B. Cunninghame Graham. The demonstrators and the accused were given vigorous support while the city authorities, particularly the Commissioner of Police Sir Charles Warren, 'the self-conceited bully who had introduced martial law into London' were just as readily attacked, and in a manner that might have become rare in a large circulation newspaper. As promised, a 'war' on the 'corrupt oligarchy' governing London was pursued throughout 1888. Particular concern for the government of London had been aired in parliament shortly before the *Star* came on the scene. The need for reform in this area, which had long been a demand of the radicals, was now made more urgent because of the changes in London parliamentary representation allowed by the Reform and Redistribution Acts of 1884 and 1885, and the latest agitation was also an accompaniment to one of the Unionist government's rare domestic reforms, the Local Government Act of 1888 which, among other things, set up the first representative council for the capital, the London County Council. A campaign on this issue was well chosen though it is too easy now to say that it was bound to succeed and it took effort and conviction to try and make the reform as thorough-going as possible. The *Star's*

---

[39] Paul Thompson, *Socialists, Liberals and Labour* (1963), pp. 97-8; *Truth,* 9 Jan. 1888. Lee points to the difficulty that, for all the Victorian Liberal's emphasis on the educative power of the press, recent studies have suggested that a readership selects the newspaper nearest to its own views. (Lee, *Popular Press,* p. 18).

campaign reached a peak in the first election for the new council in January 1889 which was won by the Progressive party, a combination of Liberals, radicals and socialists. So much active help was given that one future editor of the *Star* could claim that the council was 'largely nominated in the offices of the *Star*'. This development together with successes in the following general election in London constituencies seemed an unqualified benefit to the Liberals.[40]

But even here there could be doubts. Sir James Whitehead, the Lord Mayor of London and one of the *Star's* backers or directors, could hardly have been at ease with attacks on London government and it was disturbing that after helping to elect London councillors the *Star* had published a 'socialist manifesto' for their future guidance. Over Ireland there was less contention, paradoxically considering the disruptive effect this had had on the Liberal party and was to have again. O'Connor in later life said that he had thought of founding the paper largely to fill a gap, especially in the London press, where Ireland was concerned (although this was in 1912 when Ireland was once again the issue of the day: ultimately, in his memoirs when Ireland had receded into the shadows, he was to put the emphasis on his radicalism). A newspaper for the Liberals and for Home Rule had clearly become necessary by the second half of the 1880s if only to mitigate the alarm raised by Balfour's Irish policy. What followed from the latter's coercionist measures was also an unprecedented interest in Irish affairs by the British public. This involved more than the advocacy of what might be regarded as specialist newspapers like the *Journal of the Home Rule Union* which claimed, for instance, that northern factory workers were 'never weary of receiving information about Ireland', it was, as far as such popular moods can be judged, a widespread genuine, and unusual sympathy. The *Star* for its part linked Irish grievances with all other popular radical causes and this occasioned least disagreement with the backers, allies, and directors of the paper. Although, according to his biographer, Massingham was involved with the Mandeville case in Ireland which arose out of coercion and which the *Star*, risking prosecution, described as 'judicial murder', it is reasonable to assume that the emphasis placed on Ireland was O'Connor's work and that he was responsible for most of the major items on Ireland in the *Star*.[41]

[40] *Star*, 19 Jan.; *Hansard, 3,* 313, col. 913, 1 Mar.; Pope, *Story of the Star,* p. 19; *Memoirs,* ii, 267, where O'Connor said, however, that he had 'little personally to do with it'.

[41] *Star*, 31 Jan. 1889; Pope, *Story of the Star,* p. 12; *Memoirs,* ii, 255; O'Brien, *Parnell,* pp. 211-13; *J.H.R.U.,* June 1888; Havighurst, *Massingham,* p. 27.

This preoccupation was furthered by the dispute between Parnell and *The Times*, or rather the battle in which the whole of Nationalist Ireland appeared to be fighting *The Times*, which was itself being aided by the government. In reply to accusations that the Irish party had been associated with Fenianism and violence, actions for libel were begun. F.H. O'Donnell, although he had severed his connection with Parnell, brought an action in July 1888 and in the following month both John Redmond and O'Connor entered actions in the Queen's Bench division. Throughout 1888 discussion on Parnell's case proceeded in parliament and in the Special Commission of investigation appointed by the government. Parnell had denounced the Pigott letters as forgeries on 19 April 1887 and did so again on 6 July 1888; but the high point was reached when Pigott was discredited under cross-examination in February 1889 and the scenes before the Commission were reported at length by O'Connor in the *Star*. O'Connor himself was examined by the Commission in June and this was reported, the ultimate coincidence in O'Connor's interests, in the *Star* on 20 June. This was the cross-examination which finally tried to establish the truth about the Chicago meeting of 1881 and O'Connor's embassy to the United States. Valuable help for the Irish cause was also given by using the *Star* to attack what was seen as papal interference aimed against the Plan of Campaign. The Persico mission of 1887-8 which condemned the Plan was dismissed by the *Star* with the comment that 'they [the Irish] take their religion from Rome but they take their politics from Ireland'.[42]

These statements may have gone a long way towards reassuring the more sensitive Liberals, the vindication of Parnell before the Commission even more so, and in general the concentration on Ireland appeared to be justified by the extraordinary coming together of politics and journalism. Some of Stead's prognostication about 'government by journalism' appeared to be coming true. Added to this, O'Connor continued to support 'Progressive', that is Liberal or radical, parliamentary candidates in the *Star* in a way that he was to continue to do for the rest of his career. This helped along the 'flowing-tide' of by-election victories. O'Connor also still found time to intervene personally in by-election contests, as he did in Colchester in December 1888 and Govan in January 1889. Furthermore, perhaps something of an innovation in politics, the *Star* financed travelling political (or 'Home Rule') vans from which O'Connor spoke at Reading and Leominster in October 1888, and Kennington in March 1889. The *Star* leaders and political columns continually advocated

[42]*J.H.R.U.*, 13 Aug. 1888; *Star,* 7 July, 20 June 1889; *ibid.* 28 Apr. 1888.

alliance between radicals, Irish, and socialists, all behind progressive Liberalism.[43] A similar pattern was seen in the affairs of the I.N.L.G.B. except that here the emphasis was even more on the benefits to the Irish of support for the Liberals. In particular at the League conference at Birmingham in September 1888, O'Connor in his presidential address maintained that there was a new Irish interest in British elections, a greater difference than formerly between the two British parties, and that the Irish were a 'power in this country'. By the time of the next conference, however, more attention had to be paid to labour. A conference of London Irishmen meeting in April 1888 was advised to vote solidly Liberal. Also in April a manifesto, issued by the League executive during the celebrated Mid Lanark by-election in which Keir Hardie stood as an independent labour candidate, advised support for the Liberal. Hardie received support form Davitt but otherwise his distrust of the Irish League probably began here.[44]

Yet even in this broad area of co-operation, the Liberals were disquieted by O'Connor and by the *Star*. O'Connor's language, or some of the descriptions used in the *Star* which had, correctly, been attibuted to him, left much to be desired. Hartington had been mercilessly attacked from the outset for his 'dull, stupid mind. . . his faith in brutal methods', Chamberlain was a 'glass-eyed Kaffir', and the machine politics of Birmingham were denounced in even stronger terms. O'Connor took his dislike into the Commons where on 30 July 1888 he caused a sensation by calling Chamberlain 'Judas', apologized, and then all but spelt out the name again in the *Star*. This was faintly disparaged even in radical newspapers; to the more sedate Liberals such attacks were aimed at respectable men who happened to be ex-Liberals and none of it would help unity. In style, it was reminiscent of O'Connor's early disagreements with the Speaker. What was vulgarity to some, was to O'Connor and his newspaper forthrightness and plain-speaking. This sort of incident was also a sign of O'Connor's self confidence. Certainly the quarrel in parliament did not diminish the political and social triumph he was enjoying. From the first the *Star* had sold about 140,000 copies daily; O'Connor had expected at the

---

[43] *J.H.R.U.*, Oct. 1888, Mar. 1889. See also O'Brien, *Parnell*, p. 275; *Star*, 'The New labour Party', 7 May 1888, 'The Labour Party and the Elections', 7 June, 1888. The first article referred to Richard McGhee of the Glasgow I.N.L. supporting Labour, the second to John Wilson's support for Labour in the north east. In both cases the *Star* advocated co-operation with the Liberals. The Labour party discussed here appears to be H.H. Champion's Labour Electoral Association.

[44] *D.P.*, 1 Oct. 1888; *Star*, 5 Apr. 1888. See also Pelling, *Origins of the Labour Party* pp. 65-9.

[45] *Star*, 18 Jan. 1888; Fyfe, *Sixty Years of Fleet Street*, p. 45; *Hansard, 3,* 329, cols. 884-5, 30 July; *Star, 3* Aug., 'We leave our readers to guess what 'J. . . ' would spell'.

most a circulation of 40,000. In their flat above the *Star* offices in Stonecutter Street he and his wife gave receptions or 'at homes', characterized according to Labouchere by 'a great crush of British and Irish M.P.s, and representatives of science, art, journalism and beauty', the soul of progressive society. O'Connor in the guise of president of the I.N.L.G.B., was given a complimentary banquet at about the same time. For the most part Ireland, and the concentration on Ireland in the *Star* ended up by giving the Liberals little cause for anxiety.[46]

What was a cause for deep concern, however, was what was associated with the Irish cause, namely the mixture of all progressive politics in the late 1880s and the lengths to which some ardent spirits were prepared to go. Even in the *Star* it was suggested by the spring of 1889 that the paper was 'not for Home Rule alone'; the radicals and socialists on the paper, particularly Massingham and to a lesser extent Shaw (mainly because he articulated the difficulty, with some exaggeration) wanted to achieve far more than Home Rule and general support for the Liberal party conference proposals of 1888. Much of the advanced political thinking was provided by Massingham while Shaw contributed some political notes for about two months, most of which were rejected by O'Connor. Yet O'Connor, to his credit, could see no difficulty in supporting the cause of labour and the *Star* helped greatly in the growth of New Unionism. The affairs of labour both in the provinces and in London were reported in more detail than had been usual and particular help was given in the match girls' strike of July 1888 and in the London dock strike of 1889. O'Connor's view, however, was that labour's interest was best served within the Liberal (or Progressive) fold. This did cause some strain when it came down to details, even in cases where O'Connor was directly involved, in Irish politics. When he spoke at the League conference at Manchester in September 1889 he showed that he had, perhaps belatedly, realised that many of the dockers on strike were London Irish, or, 'exiled sons of Erin', and concluded that 'in working for the rights of labour in Great Britain' they were also working 'largely for the masses of the Irish race', which was not the order in which he usually put these causes. All this was after the dock workers had been helped by Cardinal Manning but not by the Irish organization. Yet O'Connor's attitude, most clearly seen in his article on the New Journalism written at about this time for the *New Review*, was at least practical. He said that a separate Labour party would be justified if the two British parties 'were as united against labour as they were [once]

---

[46] *Truth*, 4 July; diary of G.B. Shaw, entry for 27 June 1888; *J.H.R.U.*, 11 July.

against Ireland'. Similarly in the *Star* the leader writer had replied to the criticisms of H.M. Hyndman and asked what was 'the special form of socialism with which the radical can have nothing in common'.[47]

Radicals such as Massingham and socialists such as Shaw and his Fabian friends, though, were not to be appeased. It is, and must have appeared to O'Connor, a disheartening spectacle that something as original and creative as the *Star* could attract such carping, impatient, and destructive criticism. Of Shaw it can be said that his comments on politics and personalities, though superficially modern, were lacking in an appreciation of what politics are about (perhaps that is the nub of Shaw's complaint). In his memoirs Shaw was given full rein to describe how he was moved from politics to musical criticism (he stayed with the *Star* until the spring of 1890). Yet, despite the impression he gives, it does not appear that he was hired to write political notes. O'Connor's criticism that, as Shaw remembered it, 'man alive, it would be five hundred years before such stuff became practical political journalism' was essentially correct, and Shaw prided himself on not dealing in political realities. Similarly, Shaw's criticism of Morley, taken to be representative of the Liberal intellect, for his 'eighteenth century Rip Van Winkelism', was no doubt appreciated by O'Connor who privately had a more sombre opinion of his Liberal ally – that he had 'a frozen soul'. O'Connor co-operated with Morley because it was a political necessity. Shaw's estimate of O'Connor, that his politics had 'never advanced beyond the year 1865', had a grain of truth: this is an indication of the slowness of political change. But his view that O'Connor had 'a hearty detestation' of the English and held 'Fenian sympathies' was little more than the forensic effects of an elderly dramatist. O'Connor, with his advantage in experience, was far more perceptive about Shaw's brand of humanitarianism.[48] Shaw's colleagues, the Fabians, were also far too impractical. Their belief that they had greatly influenced or 'permeated' the *Star* have been shown to be something of a delusion. Shaw in later years said that plans had been made, presumably by Massingham or O'Connor to ward off the Fabian influence but this too may have been

[47] *Star*, 12 Apr. 1889; *D.P.*, 30 Sept. 1889; 'The New Journalism', *New Review*, Oct. 1889; *Star*, 17 Jan. 1888, 12 Apr. 1889.

[48] G.B. Shaw, *Sixteen Self Sketches* (1949), p. 40 asserted that he had been hired to join the *Star's* political staff but Dan H. Laurence (*The Unrepentant Pilgrim* (1966), p. 78) has indicated that this was a fabrication; G.B. Shaw, *London Music in 1888-9, v;* Shaw to O'Connor, quoted in St. John Ervine, *Bernard Shaw*, p. 187; Phillip Gibbs, *The Journalist's London*, p. 94; Shaw, *London Music*, p. 5; B.L., Shaw Papers, Add. MS 50512 (provisional), O'Connor to Shaw, 5 May 1890, where O'Connor said he would 'make large allowance for the latitude in their private relations of those who preach the fraternity of all mankind'.

wisdom after the non-event. Even Massingham, the arch-radical concentrating on social reform, was wary of a whole range of influences, the Fabians, the S.D.F., and, even more so, the type of European socialist influence represented in Britain by Engels and Eleanor Marx.[49]

Yet it was Massingham who proved O'Connor's undoing. The disagreement on policy which arose between the two at the turn of 1889-90 and which lasted until June 1890 is, like the founding of the *Star* itself, one which figures largely in journalistic histories, though here again the details are still not clear. Massingham's persistent advocacy of a more radical programme concentrating on labour and in particular his championing of the miner's eight-hour-day caused the Liberals great embarrassment, especially during their opposition to the Miner's Bill in parliament. It was O'Connor here who had to deal with Morley and backers of the *Star* (especially Colman) who were increasingly perturbed by the 'vulgarity' of the paper. O'Connor had the policy of support for the miners reversed but then Massingham appealed to the directors and presented evidence to show that O'Connor had not been devoting enough time to the newspaper. This document is something which O'Connor could not easily forgive. Writing to Dilke in April he said that Massingham had 'treated me so badly I could not sit at the same table as him'. It is true that O'Connor had not exercised editorial dictatorship over the paper (and this, after all, is what gave Massingham his opportunity). During the Parnell Commission his absorption in reporting had meant that Ernest Parke, the sub-editor and Massingham's assistant, had largely been responsible for getting the paper to press. At this juncture, to add to the interpretations that O'Connor was too much of a writer to make a good editor, he is described as spending too much time in the Commons and neglecting his journalism.[50] An accusation of neglect was perhaps something that the Liberal backers could understand and the result was that Massingham won them over. It was a great and sudden shock, so much so that it was kept hidden from the public. O'Connor was voted out by the necessary two thirds majority and then bought out for £15,000, being replaced by Massingham and Professor James Stuart as joint editors, an incompatible partnership that lasted only until January 1891 when Massingham too resigned.[51] O'Connor's

[49] Thompson, *Socialists, Liberals, and Labour*, pp. 97-8; for the European socialists see Havighurst, *Massingham*, pp. 35-6.

[50] B.L. Dilke Papers, Add. MS 43914, f.229, O'Connor to Dilke, 1 Apr. 1890; Pope, *Story of the Star*, p. 25; J.W. Robinson-Scott, *"We" and Me* (1956), p. 139.

[51] *Memoirs*, ii, 269-70; Fyfe, p. 153.

sense of dismay and grievance over his own failure in what remained the largest enterprise in his life was something which persisted for many years. From a conventional point of view (that which had voted him out) he had been trying to do too much, be both journalist and politician, but there is no reason why this could not have succeeded. Similarly, although O'Connor was fallible in business matters and possibly too trusting on occasions, newspapers generally in the 1880s were lacking in business efficiency.[52] Liberal backers had been hypercritical as well as not being very clear what they wanted a newspaper for, had not solved the problem of how to regain popularity without giving away influence. Radicals and socialists had been narrow, naive and short-sighted. Perhaps it could even be argued that O'Connor was attempting to put the clock back and resurrect a more gentlemanly and prestigious attitude towards letters, comment, and politics but that he was met with pressures which were tending to make all of the press less literary and less independent in the late 1880s. More simply, O'Connor failed to impress his ideas on the venture, a political failing. Perhaps it was all the more of a blow to O'Connor when he realized that ruthlessness was even more necessary in journalistic and literary matters than it was in politics. A unity between the two worlds had been broken.

'Charles Stewart Parnell, A Memory', 1890-1

Late in 1890 an even greater disaster than his troubles with the *Star*, broke in O'Connor's political life. The Parnell divorce crisis persisted for longer and was conducted in the full glare of publicity. If anything, the effect of the divorce crisis on O'Connor's life was more long-lasting, largely because more was involved than the political issue of who should lead the parliamentary party. Parnell was close to O'Connor and this gave O'Connor's political decisions a particular anguish. Because of his interest in personality and the drama of politics, O'Connor also saw the tragedy of Parnell more vividly and was more prescient than most in suspecting the effect on the imagination and on the future history of Ireland. The outcome of the crisis is well known and has been well detailed elsewhere.[53] What remains astonishing is how unprepared Parnell's lieutenants were, how much of him they had taken on trust. Parnell's affair with Mrs

[52] Lee, *Popular Press*, p. 85.

[53] The divorce crisis is given in detail in F.S.L. Lyons, *The Fall of Parnell* (1960) and O'Brien, *Parnell*, pp. 277-346. The most recent account is in F.S.L. Lyons, *Charles Stewart Parnell*, pp. 453-626.

O'Shea was known by the Liberal leaders as early as May 1882. O'Connor later suggested that the Irish party knew in the same year that Parnell was conducting some sort of affair and that he, O'Connor, was alarmed at the political dangers of Parnell's secret life, and more so by Parnell's lack of concern. O'Connor and his colleagues had heard rumours, at least, concerning Mrs O'Shea by the time of the Galway by-election in 1886, though it still remains unclear whether Biggar then announced this publicly. Parnell's leadership was not one which his lieutenants wished to question, if for no other reason than that doubts here might jeopardize Home Rule, and by the end of the eighties Parnell seemed unassailable. O'Shea's divorce petition, filled on 24 December 1889 and naming Parnell, predated the final verdict of the Commission on *The Times* allegations. These had been dragged out to examine all aspects of the Irish party's connections with extremism, although much of this was of little interest to the British public once the letters implicating Parnell were found to be forgeries. O'Connor, still at this time editor of the *Star*, took the usual view in linking the O'Shea case with the Pigott allegations and the particular common denominator he found was a mendacious Conservative press. Following on from the exoneration of Parnell it was easiest to accept his (somewhat ambiguous) assurance; the alternatives were too appalling to contemplate and, in the circumstances, hardly credible. This was also the view of the I.N.L.G.B. though there had been signs of disquiet. At the League conference at Edinburgh in September 1890 the strongest note of criticism was merely that Irishmen in Britain would wait to see how the petition was met; in the meantime it was more apparent that they joined the rest of the Irish movement in rallying round Parnell.[54]

One further indication of the party's confidence in Parnell was the decision taken in October 1890 to send a delegation to the United States on another fund raising tour. O'Connor, who took his wife with him on the tour, joined other Irish leaders in this delegation, William O'Brien and John Dillon (the other members being T.P. Gill, Timothy Harrington and T.D. Sullivan). At the end of October O'Connor left Liverpool for New York. On the eve of his departure he spoke to the Junior Reform Club in Liverpool (of which he was by now vice-president) and appeared full of confidence. It was appropriate that the most popular member of the Irish party should help to raise money in the U.S.A. and for a time he experienced a personal

[54]S. Gwynn and G. Tuckwell, *Sir Charles Dilke* (1917), i, 445; O'Connor, *Parnell*, p. 133, p. 156; *Memoirs*, ii, 101 and Lyons, *Parnell*, p. 325; *Star*, 8 Jan. 1890, which attacked the 'rumours and suggestions' and 'the irresponsible twaddle', of the *Yorkshire Post*; *D.P.*, 29 Sept. 1890.

triumph, a greater success even than his tour of 1882; after the *Star* business it was a welcome break for him and his wife.

Scarcely more than a fortnight later, on 15 and 17 November, the verdict in the divorce case was announced and found for Captain O'Shea. The result appeared all the more damaging because Parnell gave no evidence in his own defence. Even then the break did not come. The tour was turned into a near rout with American pressmen besieging the delegates in their hotel rooms but initially, with the exception of T.D. Sullivan, they all expressed support for Parnell. A telegram of support, drafted by O'Connor, was sent to Ireland and this was influential in swinging the Leinster Hall meeting of 20 November behind Parnell and helped to have him re-elected chairman on 25 November.[55] A complicated struggle then ensued, as a consequence of Gladstone's doubts on Home Rule if Parnell remained chairman, together with Parnell's manifesto addressed to the Irish people of 30 November in which he revealed the details of his Hawarden conversations with Gladstone and in the process attacked the Liberal alliance. The choice now appeared to be either to support Parnell or to support Home Rule and the Liberal alliance. To the politicians in the United States this choice expressed the worst of all possible outcomes but there was little doubt that they would prefer Home Rule to Parnell and by 30 November they all, with the exception this time of Timothy Harrington, repudiated Parnell and called on the party to follow their lead.

None of the delegates was forthcoming about his personal reactions to the crisis. Their reticence was justified while they were so far distant from the scene of the struggle, and especially from the debate on the leadership which was conducted in the Irish committee room in the Commons at the beginning of December. They had, too, been caught out by their first, impulsive, expression of support for Parnell. Even so, it is possible to discern that O'Connor was more disoriented than the other delegates. This can perhaps be seen in O'Connor's lack of energy in the negotiations which followed, and the other delegates, especially Dillon and O'Brien, could justifiably regard this as a lack of determination. O'Connor thought that Dillon's fears about Fenian influence were exaggerated and he also, though with less cause, shared a general suspicion of Dillon which had arisen because the latter was the natural successor to Parnell. Another indication of O'Connor's distaste for what had occurred, amounting almost to despair, was that he continued in the United States when the

[55] *The Times*, 30 Oct.; detail on the delegates' reactions can be found in F.S.L. Lyons, *John Dillon*, pp. 113-43.

other delegates had returned. By the middle of December only Dillon and O'Connor were left of the delegates and they together issued a manifesto in favour of the anti-Parnellite candidate, Sir John Pope-Hennessy, in the North Kilkenny by-election. Dillon left for France on 10 January and O'Connor stayed in America until the following spring.[56] There was still a desperate need for funds – now more than ever because the majority against Parnell had to be consolidated and its right to control the finances of the party affirmed. The loyalty of the American League also needed to be re-emphasized. O'Connor was the best person for this task but it would also allow him some respite and at least the appearance of a possibility that he could delay making a final decision.

This was an impossible decision for O'Connor to reach with total conviction. All the practical arguments were on the anti-Parnellite side. O'Connor had signed the manifesto of 30 November. He had been co-opted in his absence onto the anti-Parnellite committee of the party and, at the same time as he denied fears of Fenianism he also, as one who was regarded as an expert on the opinions of the Irish in Britain, said that from their point of view Parnell's continued leadership would be a disaster. Strictly speaking, the attitude of the Irish in Britain, and O'Connor's reputation as their spokesman, still had to be put to the test. The key to O'Connor's attitude here and the deciding factor in his opposition to Parnell had been the attack Parnell had launched against Gladstone. This reversed all that O'Connor had worked for since 1886. It is true that he had once implemented a policy that emphasized independence of British parties, but too much had happened since then. By the middle of January he had reached some sort of resolution and in writing a long letter of explanation, timed to reach Dillon shortly after the latter arrived in Boulogne, O'Connor may have been moderating or going along with Dillon's preoccupations, particularly the need to secure 'the detachment of the more reasonable of his followers from Parnell'. Even more, he stressed the needs of the Liberal alliance and in particular the debt owed to Gladstone, 'all the affectionate devotion to him which was so strong a factor in gaining the success of our cause'. Despite this determined attempt to draw on his reserves of common sense, there still remained the friendship with Parnell and a reluctance to face the new situation. According to Healy's testimony this went as far as O'Connor, on his return, suggesting that he still had the opportunity to make up his mind, and remarking on 'the cheerfulness of you fellows'. Of course, the options were closed. Yet O'Connor, before he returned

[56] O'Connor to W. O'Brien, 19 Dec. 1890, cited in Lyons, *Fall of Parnell*, p. 191; *Memoirs*, ii, 294-5; Lyons, *Fall of Parnell*, p. 188.

to Britain, might well have remembered how Parnell had been able to turn defeats into victories and had been the first to introduce O'Connor to the large possibilities of politics. O'Connor was, characteristically, much more generous in his verdict on Healy shortly afterwards, remarking on his 'moral and physical courage' at a time when Healy was by no means popular even with the anti-Parnellites as a result of his attacks on Parnell.[57] Perhaps, too, this was guilt for his own, understandable, lack of decision.

O'Connor probably returned to Britain late in February and he spoke to his constituents in Liverpool at the end of March. It was Healy, once again, who said that O'Connor had avoided his constituency by returning via Southampton. O'Connor may have been nervous of the prospect but much here is speculation, including the contrary view given by O'Donnell and Fyfe, that Liverpool Scotland was an easier division to represent than an Irish constituency would have been. There would be times at the turn of the century and after when O'Connor would have reason to doubt the latter, whatever impression he may have given to his biographer. O'Connor's opinion, that the Irish in Britain would oppose Parnell's continued leadership, was probably correct but it remained an agonizing business to put this to the test. This was especially true if O'Connor had in mind the opinion of the organizers of the League. They had been busy co-operating with the Liberals in the localities (to such good effect that in one instance, in Liverpool by 1892, the Liberals and the Irish Home Rulers briefly won control of the Council). Many of these organizers, such as G.J. Lynskey who had replaced Commins at the head of the League in Liverpool by 1890, had begun by supporting Parnell strongly. Their opposition then arose when they realized, as O'Connor had done, the consequences for the Liberal alliance. Apart from the organizers the tide of opinion might have seemed less clear, more dangerous. The most radical of the rank and file might well have become opposed to Parnell, sharing the view taken by Michael Davitt, who had called for Parnell's resignation in November 1890, even before the full political implications of the divorce were known. There were also signs, more noticeable in retrospect, that living in Britain had made the Irish communities more sensitive to British politics and at one with O'Connor in their belief in the value of the Liberal alliance. The more radical were beginning to turn to trade union activities or to Labour

[57] O'Connor to O'Brien, Dec. 19; T.C.D. Dillon Papers, MS 6740-4/f.3, O'Connor to Dillon, 14 Jan. 1890; O'Connor quoted in Healy, *Letters*, ii, 359; Dillon Papers, MS/6740-4/f.4, O'Connor to Dillon, 30 July 1891. Dillon shared the dislike of Healy but O'Connor's opinion was that 'his method, though rough, was made necessary by the action of Parnell, and that judging his conduct as a whole we owe him a debt of gratitude for the extraordinary moral and physical courage he displayed in the struggle'.

politics. During 1890 James Sexton launched the 'Bootle rebellion' against the local Irish party machine, though to little affect. To Sexton, Parnell apeared divisive and right wing in his social attitudes but this is recollection in his memoirs. As it happened none of the press reports of League branches in the Merseyside area from December 1890 to February 1891 did show a decision in favour of Parnell. By the time Justin McCarthy, the new majority chairman, spoke to the Reform Clubs of Manchester and Liverpool in February, he was presented in return with extravagant addresses of loyalty from local Irish worthies, even though in the case of the Liverpool delegation they had to wait in the lobby of the club.[58] None of this detracts from the probability that for O'Connor, so long Parnell's champion, going back to Liverpool to face his electorate was an ordeal, perhaps a greater test than facing the enraged voters of Galway in 1886, and possibly the gravest strain on his nerve and on his beliefs in all his long career.

O'Connor's speech at Liverpool in March still reads convincingly and is full of moderate, if somewhat defeated, good sense. He admitted to his good luck (though it had not been all a matter of chance) in being out of the British Isles when the main argument had raged. He deplored the language used on both sides. British moralists he denounced as 'ranting and calumnious pharisees. . .shamsters and camp followers'. His main objections were, by contrast, political. Parnell's manifesto had, he said, 'brok [en] down the whole course in which we have been working for Home Rule. It was an appeal to racial hatred and mistrust. . . If we receive Home Rule from England because we hate England and want to use Home Rule for the purpose of injuring England [we ought to accept] "the policy of men with arms in their hands".'

Parnell, he said in conclusion, had shown 'a worse vice than political credulity, namely political ingratitude'.[59] It was a strong, reasoned and restrained defence of the anti-Parnellite cause and O'Connor further assured the branches of the League on Merseyside that he visited in the following days that they could put their trust in the Liberal alliance. Yet O'Connor did not attend the I.N.L.G.B.

[58] Healy, *Letters,* ii, 360. Healy also mentioned at the same point that O'Connor in his study of Parnell (p. 206) had claimed to be a constant opponent of Parnell; O'Donnell, *Irish Parliamentary Party,* i, 394; Fyfe, pp. 108-9; James Sexton, *Sir James Sexton* (1934), pp. 83-4. A cutting of an article in the *Empire News* on which this book was based gives the date for the 'Bootle Rebellion' as 1890. Cutting on file in L.R.O.; *D.P.,* 3 Feb. 1891.

[59] *The Times,* 26 Mar. 1891. For Liberal attitudes see J.F. Glaser, 'Parnell's Fall and the Nonconformist Conscience', *I.H.S.,* (Sept. 1960), 119-38.

conference that year. The meeting was in May 1891 in Newcastle and, predictably, resolutions against Parnell (moved by F.L. Crilly and John Denvir, both of Liverpool) were overwhelmingly endorsed, and a campaign against suspected Parnellites remaining in the League organization was begun. O'Connor probably thought he had done enough; he was fully occupied in that month founding his newspaper the *Sunday Sun;* he sent a letter instead.

Parnell's death in October 1891 added a detailed postscript on O'Connor's attitude towards Parnell. Possibly within a week O'Connor had published *Charles Stewart Parnell, A Memory,* an achievement, if that is what it was, which appears to have been widely known afterwards. It needs to be asked why he felt the need to write this study and write it so quickly. In retrospect there may appear something indecent in such haste and something morbid in probing so recent a wound. On the charge of doubtful taste O'Connor's defence of public interest had not always been convincing, and morbidness can be found in his study of Disraeli and in his history of the Parnell movement. There could have been an element of opportunism, journalistic enterprise, in the biography. The case cannot be proved. It is at least equally possible that O'Connor wrote the book out of a sense of guilt, recalling his friendship with Parnell, and out of a need to comprehend the events of the previous year. A mark of this in the work is, as Healy noted, how O'Connor asserted the consistency of his position towards Parnell; this may have been to hide his doubts. Despite O'Connor's reputation as a rapid descriptive writer, the book may have been written so quickly because the ideas, curiosity, justification and perplexity needed urgently to be expressed.[60]

Because of what was contributed by circumstance, it is fair to say that *Parnell* was O'Connor's best piece of work. The book is reasonably long, more than an essay, though not so extensive as his earlier works: beside it, the biography of Disraeli is monumental. Compression and a subject in which O'Connor was passionately involved were both beneficial. Of all O'Connor's works, that is the one that has lasted; the *Parnell Movement* may be cited more frequently because it provides the sort of local colour O'Connor intended, and his memoirs might be quarried by those who happen to be interested in O'Connor himself, but for historians particularly, apart from any considerations of style, it is this study that is of most

---

[60] On the final page of the book O'Connor wrote of Parnell's funeral 'last Sunday'. See also L. R. O., 'Brother Sam', 'At the Feet of T. P.', Liverpool *Review*, 12 Oct. 1901, and 'T. P. in a Nutshell', *ibid.* 4 Jan. 1902, which accept that the book was published very shortly after Parnell's death.

interest. There are two reasons for this. Since O'Connor was a friend of Parnell, he could recollect personal details and place them in context. He described, for instance, his two visits to Parnell's home at Avondale and Parnell's domestic circumstances, his appearance and his presence, his difficult way of speaking – a 'dreary monotone. He barely looked at the person to whom he was speaking' – his calmness under attack when he appeared as 'in some respects a man slow to resent'. All these details are memorable and valuable because they are so rarely come by and they have proved of importance in a recent study of Parnell and his family background. O'Connor had attempted on one occasion to anticipate what would be of interest to 'the historian of our times at the end of the twentieth century' but his guess proved incorrect.[61] It was not so much the description of Parnell speaking in parliament that mattered, it was what he was like in private. Here, O'Connor elaborated sufficiently to identify the essential historical problem that, paradoxically, Parnell 'lived and to some extend died, in mystery', and his perception of this is the second reason why the book has lasted. By comparison, some of O'Connor's other judgements are perhaps questionable, such as blaming the imprisonment in Kilmainham for a deterioration in Parnell's health and also perhaps a change in his character, questioning the wisdom of obstruction, and decrying Parnell's attention to the details of hand-writing in the Pigott case. In all these instances hindsight allows the comment that Parnell was more realistic than O'Connor. O'Connor's comparison of Parnell before and after 1886 whereby before he was 'more simple, less pretentious, humbler in his estimate of himself, more generous in his treatment of others' and then came a 'terrible change' is too simplistic, but it might well have looked so to a contemporary, remembering the successes and the failures. O'Connor's criticisms of Parnell were also to some extent self-justificatory. O'Connor did have justified grievances which he referred to, such as the handling of the vote Tory campaign and the neglect of parliamentary business and leadership by Parnell. But what is more important is that O'Connor sustained a sense of an enigmatic personality from first to last. There were no easy answers. He said that Parnell was no intellectual and that that was what made his command of men who were his intellectual superiors all the more remarkable, and that Parnell was 'narrow' and that this was what made him so effective. It is this identification, made apparent, which makes this the first serious study of Parnell. Clearly, it lacked the depth which time has allowed but no biographer since has been able to go beyond that mystery which

[61]*Parnell*, pp. 104, 52, 88; R.F. Foster, *Charles Stewart Parnell, The Man and his Family,* (1976) *passim;* 'The New Journalism', *New Review,* Oct. 1889.

O'Connor expressed. Above all, the book was generous in its estimate of Parnell and sensitive in its treatment of Mrs. O'Shea and full of a sense of loss such as that shown in the description which heads this chapter. The power of Parnell was evident still and O'Connor paid tribute to it in closing, in talking of the scenes at Parnell's funeral. Someone else who, like O'Connor, was not present at the funeral but realized its importance and resonance, was the young W.B. Yeats. Poets, and a new generation in Ireland, might begin to look forward with a harsher attitude.[62] O'Connor had warned of the dangers of violent alternatives in his speech at Liverpool. He, along with Healy, might fear the change that could be beginning. O'Connor, as a literary man, realized the power of symbol and myth more than others. In the years which followed perhaps he pushed this knowledge to the back of his mind. As a man of affairs he could always find that there was practical and urgent work to be done.

---

[62]*Parnell*, pp. 11, 127, 109, 145, 85, 159-62, 140-2, 38, 109, 11, 133; See Joseph Hone, *W.B. Yeats* (1971 ed.), pp. 90-1 for the effect of Parnell's funeral on Yeats and his poem 'Mourn – and then Onward'.

4

SOCIAL REALITIES AND NEW ROUTINES, 1891-1905

During the long period of Unionist domination in politics and society which lasted until 1905, O'Connor's convictions and patience were sorely tried. Elements of disillusionment, cynicism, and hypocrisy may have been part of O'Connor's make-up (and a part of which he was aware earlier than the 1890s) but if so he kept it much to himself: there is little trace of it in even his most private correspondence. There would have been every justification for a more calculated outlook during years in which every idealistic cause seemed futile and Conservative hegemony almost a fact of nature. As a popularizing journalist O'Connor was continually, despite the experience of the *Star*, put at a disadvantage by commercial pressures, and as a populist politician he had then to turn to face the realities of power. Ageing, too, is a factor easily overlooked in the fine cut and thrust of personality and abstract ideas in political history. In the struggle over the *Star* it is easy to receive the impression that O'Connor was an ancient monument; perhaps this was suggested convincingly by Shaw. Yet when the *Star* was founded in 1888 O'Connor was only thirty-nine, Shaw was thirty-two, and Massingham was the youngest of the trio at twenty-eight. Besides which, the age looked for maturity. In its politicians, at least if they were of cabinet rank, it was the sphinx-like, or gnarled, wisdom of Disraeli, Gladstone, or more latterly Salisbury, which commanded silence. A man in his forties or fifties could, at a stretch, be regarded as an impudent young pup. Yet perhaps O'Connor had appeared as an impudent juvenile and just as suddenly he may have given the impression of having aged quickly. In the 1890s, during his forties and fifties he became more preoccupied with his own health, suffered from many minor illnesses, put on weight (something which American journalists had pointed out as early as 1882), and in the early years of the new century he was struck down with a major illness. The fret of constant deadlines, the obligations to politics, and the tension between the two, may have taken a toll on his system and his energy (for he was always intensely active without necessarily giving the impression of being so). On top of all this his marriage foundered; it was no dramatic break-up but it was clear by the end of the nineties that he and his wife were not suited and a more formal separation occurred by about 1905. All this, put briefly, would be enough to jaundice any idealist and it was supposed at the time that it had, the historian's assumptions being added to by those of contemporaries (though usually his political opponents). Perhaps there was a fateful revenge here. O'Connor had projected himself and the whole business of personality so much into the public eye that in his middle age the contrast was drawn; he was described, his hypocrisy was assumed, his private life was mulled over. In a period in which the emphasis in the government was on authority, which in turn became the prevailing public mood, it was the radical who was accused of hypocrisy, the radical's concern for the hypocrisies of power itself now dismissed as unrealistic. O'Connor had to bear with this and had to put up with being made, to some extent, a Character, a fate peculiar perhaps to England, and he did compromise, mature, or become less concerned. Then his circumstances began to improve slightly from the turn of the century, partly through his being content with less. But the compression of events or misfortune is also a distortion because it was the everyday duty of politicians (and wage-earners) to remain active and optimistic. By the severe, knowledgeable, standards of one recent school of interpretation, O'Connor may appear uncalculating. But, equally, what remains when comment is replaced by what O'Connor said or what he wrote in these years and later, is the good sense and the integrity.

Failure of the 'Sun', 1891-1900

To begin with, in journalism (as to a large extent in politics) O'Connor's prospects appeared to be undimmed and the decade was full of his ventures even though it was not until the Edwardian years that he regained a public more to his taste. The retirement from the *Star* had been an undoubted blow but he may have immediately realized how much of a setback it was and the biography of Parnell had shown his powers of recuperation. Even before this he began to try and make good his losses. In May 1891 he had founded the *Sunday Sun* using some of the £15,000 capital he had obtained for his shares in the *Star*. In his letter to Dillon in July about Parnell in which he also gave his opinion of Healy, he is found explaining as a preliminary that his newspaper 'tied him down to a certain number of days' and that 'the whole burden . . . is on my shoulders'.[1] What his colleagues thought of such a distraction at such a time is not evident. What does seem slightly clearer from here on is that in journalism O'Connor was now in a more distinctly different world from politics,

---

[1] *Memoirs*, ii, 270; Dillon Papers, MS 6740-4, f.4, O'Connor to Dillon, 30 July, 1891.

an impression no doubt heightened by the bewildering variety of newspaper letterheads on which his correspondence to other Irish politicians is written. Whatever unity there had been between politics and journalism had been severely disturbed. The *Sunday Sun* had been founded in the Liberal interest and in support of Home Rule, assistance particularly crucial just after the divorce crisis. With a famous editor as its chief asset it achieved a respectable success especially when, in 1893, it was changed into the *Weekly Sun* and published on both Saturday and Sunday, an unusual procedure, and the circulation increased from 20,000 to 100,000. O'Connor's receptivity could still be seen, in the features for women (which were an innovation) and in the emphasis on literature, both of which he was warned against but which proved successful up to a point. Literature meant most noticeably his review, the 'Book of the Week'. It was in many ways the forerunner of that type of literary criticism that is so personalized that it has very little to say about the book in question. For its day, and in the popular press, it was an innovation and O'Connor was always a genuine believer in 'democracy' in literature, just as in 'history' or politics. Whatever doubts others might have had this was a tendency he later developed more fully in *T.P.'s Weekly* where it was probably seen to better effect. In politics there was less impact, there was less explanation to be done and O'Connor could justly claim in the first number of the *Sunday Sun* that 'our convictions on most public subjects are pretty well known', and, as a weekly the paper was not a political rival to the Conservative press in the way that the *Star* had been.[2] Material was also lacking in politics. Salisbury's government remained, above all, dull.

To some extent matters improved with the return of Gladstone's government and especially when the second Home Rule Bill was debated in 1893. From his reports here ('At the bar of the House' which appeared in the *Weekly Sun*) O'Connor published *Sketches in the House: the Story of a Memorable Session* and said that this was issued after 'repeated requests of many readers'. This was more in the pattern of his descriptive work of the early 1880s, particularly where it singled out the spectacle of Gladstone fighting through the Home Rule Bill. Apart from such high points as a description of O'Connor once more calling Chamberlain 'Judas', for which, once again, he had to apologize to the House, there was praise for Gladstone's remarkable

---

[2] See the description of typical material from the *Sunday Sun* in Fyfe, *O'Connor*, pp. 163-71; for criticism of his reviewing method see Fyfe, *Sixty Years of Fleet Street*, p.47 ('Skilful gutting') and Russell Stannard, *With the Dictators of Fleet Street* (1934), p. 168; Fyfe, *Sixty Years*, p. 47; a decline in Liberal-radical hopes in the 1890s is described in Lee, *Popular Press*, pp. 311-12.

persistence and, an unusual subject for O'Connor, an account of the final debates in the Lords which gives a good sense of atmosphere. His more conservative readers might have regarded his condemnation of Conservative obstruction with some irony; Liberal politicians might have been made uncomfortable by his talk of the next election and the need to avoid any charge of 'lack of will, competence and energy'. Yet it was a slighter book than *Gladstone's House of Commons*, O'Connor had less to lose, it was more conventional, written with less care, more partisan and more opinionated.[3]

Despite the difficulties, O'Connor founded an evening newspaper in 1893. This was the *Sun*, first published in June 1893 (the *Weekly Sun* continuing separately under his control until early in 1898). O'Connor had come to an agreement with the *Star* proprietors that he would not be associated with an evening newspaper for three years and the new paper appeared on the day the agreement expired. In his memoirs he admitted that one of his main motives was revenge. He was also confident to the point of foolhardiness: it would have been better for him to have been more modest or cautious on this occasion. Although his own maxim was that to be too self-effacing was an error, he himself never quite reached a balance here. If anything, the *Sun* was even more personal that the *Weekly Sun* and he must have believed, with some reason, that his name would prove a great asset. To some extent he kept to the formula he had used in the *Star*, but the platform was more personal. As was now becoming usual, the paper began with a declaration of intent, the 'Gospel according to the *Sun*' (more directly than in the *Star* a quotation of Stead's 'Gospel according to the *Pall Mall Gazette*'). Its politics were progressive but put in a negative way. By now O'Connor argued that it was 'absurd to claim support for any newspaper on the ground of its political aspirations alone'. Their aspirations remained progressive but with limitations. He insisted in the first issue of the paper on drawing attention to the demands of labour for representation, but within the Liberal party. A 'certain capitalistic section' of that party, possibly not dissimilar to the backers of the *Star*, was attacked, and he also urged that 'predominantly working-class constituencies [should] go to working-class members'.[4] Other radicals, such as Labouchere in his newspaper, were taking a similar line and refusing to believe that there was any inherent difference between labour and the Liberal party. It would have been well for the Liberals had they followed such advice.

[3] *Sketches in the House* (1893), pp. 242-51; see also *Hansard, 4*, 15 col. 724, 23 July 1893; *Sketches in the House,* pp. 269-78, 258, 257.

[4] *Memoirs,* ii, 270; 'Gospel According to the *Sun*', *Sun,* 27 June 1893.

But these comments also showed that an issue first aired in the *Star* had still not been resolved and reflect O'Connor's difficulties with nationalistic politics, and his uncertainties about labour. He was inclined in the *Sun* to regard what he called the 'social question' as of great importance but 'standing to some extent beyond and outside the conflicts of the two great parties'; perhaps it was too dangerous. All in all, politically at any rate, the *Sun* appeared to be less genuinely challenging. There was more emphasis on news and on literature. As O'Connor said, 'in the forefront I put my purpose as that of producing a good newspaper' and this has a curious hint of lack of purpose.[5]

A good beginning was made with a staff that was almost equal in ability to that which he had gathered in the *Star*. Two especially valuable recruits were Louis Tracy as assistant editor, a Liverpudlian with experience of provincial journalism and of newspapers in India, and William Kennedy Jones as chief sub-editor, a Glasgow Irishman, determined and ambitious. Nevertheless the *Sun* ran into difficulties. Even its politics were unsteady, beginning as a labour paper (with a small *l*) and then, when it was still under O'Connor's control, being issued under the banner 'For the People of the Empire on which the Sun never sets'. The two attributes were not incompatible, the Liberal Imperialists for instance hoped to join the two, but it is doubtful whether O'Connor thought the matter out. In politics, in any case, the radical position had been pre-empted by the *Star*. Politics was still one of O'Connor's chief interests, whatever statements of intent he made, perhaps to disarm criticism, but the circulation figures showed that a large readership was no longer prepared to follow him. By the end of 1894 the paper was in difficulties and by one estimate losing £30,000 a year.[6] Although in many ways the newest experiment in Fleet Street and attracting the most able new blood, the *Sun* did not make the most of its chances and the fault may have been O'Connor's. He was accused once again of paying too much attention to his own writing. Bringing the paper out was left to Tracy and Jones, who felt uncertain of their future however agreeable they found O'Connor. As before, O'Connor could have been expecting too much or, this time, it could be argued that he was out of date and that commercialism had taken over, all the more so because O'Connor had within his grasp the ingredients of a new type of journalism. First Tracy and then Jones saw the opportunity of developing the *Evening News*, Jones being unsuccessful in his attempt to persuade O'Connor to buy the paper.

[5]*Truth,* 14 July 1892; *Sun,* 27 June 1893. According to Fyfe, the *Sunday Sun* became the *Weekly Sun* in 1893 and then 'passed out of T.P.'s hands at the beginning of 1898' (Fyfe, pp. 171, 191).

[6]R. Pound and G. Harmsworth, *Northcliffe* (1959), pp. 168-71.

The suggestion was then put to Alfred Harmsworth (whose office was on the opposite side of Tudor Street), probably by Tracy. This purchase became the first of Harmsworth's successful ventures in the field of popular dailies although it was William Kennedy Jones who was installed as editor and developed the paper; Tracy also left to find his opportunity with Harmsworth. There was also a suggestion that Harmsworth and O'Connor might combine their interests. Just how enthusiastic Harmsworth had been about this, it is impossible to say; there is no reason to suppose that he had any sympathy for the political content of O'Connor's papers. The *Sun* went into a decline and O'Connor described his continued association with the paper as something of a nightmare. He was vague about when he finally managed to sell off the newspaper (no easy task) and talked of 'three years of abject misery' though this may not have meant that the break came in 1896 but may refer to the three years up to 1900 when the newspaper is recorded as moving into the possession of Horatio Bottomley (itself an indication of a decline in esteem) and it was sold again in 1904 and survived until 1906, or 1910 at the latest. By comparison, it was Harmsworth who now made the major innovation in journalism.[7] O'Connor could not easily have produced the sort of mass circulation daily that is associated with Harmsworth, such as the *Daily Mail* which was founded in 1896. O'Connor had set his sights higher and then found no support but he could still find much to admire in Harmsworth's enterprises, purely as journalistic successes. Writing to Harmsworth in May 1898 he expressed regret that he had not been associated with him. Shortly afterwards he began to write a parliamentary sketch for the *Daily Mail* and contributed other articles, something of a comedown but paralleled in the careers of other radical journalists in a less hospitable age.[8]

O'Connor was still in comfortable circumstances despite the difficulties over the *Sun*. His home in Chelsea, Oakley Lodge in Upper Cheyne Row, was still likely to be a centre for fashionable, radical and bohemian society, and from about 1895 O'Connor and his wife also had a house in Brighton, first of all in Medina Terrace and then in Lansdowne Place, replaced by a more permanent retreat in

---

[7] H. Simonis, *The Street of Ink* (1917), p. 63; *Memoirs*, ii, 270; David Butler and Anne Sloman, *British Political Facts, 1900-1975* (1975), p. 385 which gives the date for the demise of the *Sun* as 1906, whereas Derek Hudson in Simon Nowell-Smith (ed.), *Edwardian England* (1964), p. 322 says that this occurred in 1910.

[8] W. Kennedy Jones, *Fleet Street and Downing Street* (1920), p. 118, who dated the beginning of O'Connor's writing for the *Daily Mail* in 1899 and also said that O'Connor was the first to introduce the typewriter into the House of Commons.

The Drive, Blackrock, in Brighton from about 1903.[9] Many would
have regarded him as a rich man and his income was variously
described by political enemies as either £6,000 or £10,000 a year,
though this is probably an exaggeration, especially as it occurred in
the Liverpool Conservative press which often liked to put O'Connor
in a lurid light. Some of his income would derive from the material he
had syndicated in the United States. This remains unknown in
quantity but it is possible to identify, among what was probably a
much larger body of work, articles on parliament for *Harper's
Magazine* and for the *North American Review*.[10] Later there was also
syndicated material from his magazines *M.A.P.*, and *P.T.O.* In 1895
and 1896 he published two books, both, it is fair to say, pot-boilers;
Napoleon, published in 1896, which was a long book of over 400
pages, and *Some Old Love Stories*, published in 1895 and describing
Lincoln, Mirabeau, Carlyle, Lassalle and their respective partners.
These two books are clearly collections of long reviews, indicating to
some extent O'Connor's passion for foreign, particularly French,
literature, and probably derived from the *Weekly Sun*. The collection
of love stories is the less involved of the two works and went into a
popular edition in 1912 and, apart from showing O'Connor's
appreciation of what sold well, also suggested that O'Connor still
harboured a romantic streak. His own marriage had not yet lost its
glamour, or at least its convenience. In 1891 he had written of
Parnell's belief that marriage 'makes a man too comfortable' and
gives him a distaste for politics. There was something in this view so
far as the Irish party was concerned and O'Connor would perhaps not
have recorded it if his own marriage had not put him at ease. By the
end of the decade however there were strains observable and a
realization that the marriage was no longer a success came, so Fyfe
says, when O'Connor was approaching fifty, in about 1898.[11]

For all this apparent good fortune, in other words, the disappointment and the worry cannot be overlooked. In many ways the second
part of the 1890s was the most difficult time of O'Connor's life. He
suffered less physical hardship than he had done in Grub Street in the
1870s but youth's versatile optimism was gone. His health too gave
more concern. He had always been inclined to melancholy and many
descriptions of him at this time remark on the serious set of his
features, but put it down to minor cares rather than to great
introspection. He was also something of a hypochondriac. He
claimed to have been abstemious in his early years in Fleet Street and

[9] Dates of addresses from catalogue description of O'Connor-Dillon correspondence
T.C.D. and collected from O'Connor-Keary correspondence, N.L.I.
[10] For O'Connor's American articles see the bibliography.
[11] *Parnell*, p. 30; Fyfe, p. 199. For *M.A.P.* and *P.T.O.* see below pp. 155, 187.

by the mid 1890s was, or made great efforts to be, teetotal (following in his father's footsteps). But his irregular life in journalism and politics in the 1880s took its toll and, despite his reputation for robust good health, ruined his digestion. Some degree of recovery was effected by visits to the fashionable spas on the continent. From about 1895 onwards, and before a particularly severe attack of influenza in 1895, his correspondence reveals his presence in places such as Marienbad, Karlsbad, Kissingen or Vichy, interspersed with letters from Paris, Monte Carlo or the French channel resorts. His travels could prove irksome to political colleagues and subordinates, who might have preferred him closer at hand, although the impression that he was continually on holiday in Europe in these years is undoubtedly due to historical compression.

Even so, mentally as well as physically he was in danger of stretching himself too far. And there were sharper critics than his colleagues ready now to point up some of the contradictions in the spectacle he offered to the world. Perhaps the longest piece of sustained criticism was that of Arthur Lynch, a future Nationalist M.P., which was all the more telling because it did not concern itself principally with politics. In a collection published in 1896, Lynch concentrated on O'Connor's style and ideas, though also remarking on his appearance, now 'not in the least like Apollo'. Lynch's criticism was that O'Connor indulged in *schwarmerii*, 'a thousand restless but not unpleasant little devils of bees in the brain that completely buzz away the judgment'. This was fair comment, as was his general debunking of the pretensions of London editors (although he had left that too late, their heyday was past). O'Connor's Irish 'afflatus' and his occasional howlers when he indulged in purple prose were also acceptable targets. O'Connor had laid himself open to attack in his concentration on emotion and, in being himself no respecter of persons, he could hardly complain. Nevertheless some of Lynch's description was malicious. Lynch emphasised O'Connor's continued innocence when he remarked on how listeners could be amused even though O'Connor had not intended to be entertaining. Whatever Lynch made of this, it could be said that it revealed O'Connor's earnestness, willingness to take risks even with his dignity and ignore the superciliousness of the age and its literary critics.[12] On a par with this was the nickname 'Tay Pay' referred to by Lynch and supposedly capturing O'Connor's brogue. As is usual with nicknames, the origins of this are unclear, but it is certain that O'Connor detested it and that he had more sense than to protest. He

[12] Arthur Lynch, *Human Documents, Character Sketches of Representative Men and Women of the Time* (1896). pp. 156-89, 176, 162.

was shrewd enough to see that the name was sometimes not very affectionate (social psychologists might regard such labelling as a form of control; it often came into political attacks). The ultimate in futility came when Lord Curzon referred to 'the one and only Tay Pay' and the phrase stuck as though it were an epigram. O'Connor made the mistake of not being too solemn and then had also to pay the price when his past caught up with him.[13]

There was every reason for increasing dissatisfaction and apprehension as the 1890s progressed. O'Connor may have felt that his life-work had come to nothing. From here on the regrets appear to have multiplied, especially, it seems, the regret that he did not try and fulfil himself as a novelist rather than dissipate his ability and his power of concentration in journalism. He wrote of Morley that 'the inner conflict between the man of letters and the man of politics... pursued and paralysed him all through his life'[14] but that may also have been a danger ever-present in his own life. A disillusionment and impatience with the House of Commons was also particularly noticeable during the middle and late years of the decade, as was his own lack of effective criticism of the Liberals. But before any of this could drive him from politics or before criticism of his neglect of politics for journalism had reached a head, he had made his life simpler. This was achieved by his apparent decision, after the experience of the *Sun*, never again to take on much in the way of editorial responsibility. His editorship of the various journals which followed, *M.A.P.*, *P.T.O.*, and *T.P.'s Weekly*, was nowhere near so onerous. If anything, therefore, he became more rather than less of a full time politician in the new century.

Faction, 1891-1900

In the years from 1891 to 1900 attention to politics was doubly necessary, but at the same time there were many circumstantial reasons why O'Connor was less effective. At first, just as in journalism, O'Connor saw no reason for any lack of confidence. A crisis such as the split in the Irish party was a test to overcome and there was all the more reason to put trust in the Liberals since the break with Parnell had been for the benefit of their friendship. The

---

[13] According to Shaw, O'Connor's nickname was the invention of Edmund Yates, the editor of the *World* (Robertson-Scott, *"We" and Me*, p. 166). Another explanation is that it came in a shout of approval from an Irishwoman in the gallery of the Commons when O'Connor was speaking (*The Times*, 19 Nov. 1929).

[14] Fyfe, pp. 123, 127, *Memoirs*, i, 294.

I.N.L.G.B. had improved its position dramatically. Since 1884 membership had increased tenfold and income had doubled so that by 1890, before the Parnellite split (and that could be a crucial qualification), there were almost 41,000 in the League and it was receiving almost £4,000 a year in funds. Added to which, the by-election successes of the Liberals continued up to the general election of 1892 with no signs of government recovery.[15] O'Connor had to believe both in the coming success at the general election and in the Liberal's determination over Home Rule. Similarly, and for the time being, the Parnellites under John Redmond were ignored; it was partly a case of not wanting to meet trouble half way.

O'Connor made remarkable efforts in the run up to the election of 1892, making up for the indecision in politics which had haunted him throughout 1891. He spoke in his constituency at the beginning of April, well before the election campaign, where he promised that Gladstone would bring in a 'large, generous and final measure' but that even in the remote case of Liberal reluctance, the Irish had the power to 'bring even a powerful Liberal administration to its senses'. The 'honour' of the Liberals was pledged but it was also a 'political necessity' for them to introduce Home Rule and prevent a wider split in the alliance. A week later he was to be found speaking in support of Lloyd George in Caernarvon (a sign of the changing times, at least so far as radicalism was concerned). He welcomed the new radical star with enthusiasm although it is noticeable that Lloyd George confined his own speech severely to Wales and Disestablishment.[16] During May and up to the beginning of June O'Connor joined Dillon in Dublin in an attempt to reach agreement with the Parnellites over the contesting of seats in Ireland. These talks largely failed and there was some division in the contest in Ireland though not enough to let in Conservative candidates. Shortly afterwards the I.N.L.G.B. had its annual conference, held in Bradford on 5 June, at which O'Connor again stressed that the Liberal party was the only choice for the Irish. More than that, he said that the

[15] Reports of the conferences in *F.J.*, 27 Aug. 1888, 18 Sept. 1890, cited in O'Brien, *Parnell*, p. 274. The post of General Secretary had become a contentious one. John Brady was suspected of being a Parnellite but was not replaced until 1894 when J.F.X. O'Brien, the M.P. who had been treasurer of the party was appointed to the post; C. Cook and B. Keith, *British Historical Facts 1830-1900*, p. 146.

[16] *D.P.*, 6 Apr. 1892; *Carnarvon Herald*, 15 Apr. Lloyd George kept a cutting of this newspaper's account of the meeting in his papers. O'Connor kept on good terms with Lloyd George and this was to be of some value in Liberal-Irish negotiations in the future. Denvir claimed that Lloyd George owed his first, narrow, victory in Carnarvon Boroughs in the by-election of 1890 to the Irish vote and also described him as a 'thorough-going Home Ruler'. The first was more likely than the second (Denvir, *Life Story*, pp. 236-7).

Irish must be prepared for a long struggle against the House of Lords, his old enemy, whom it might take two elections to subdue.[17] Probably the conference was held at this time in order to invigorate the League for the task ahead; the initial preparations of O'Connor might have been a sign of nervousness but even more they show an appreciation of an urgent and worthwhile struggle.

During the 1892 campaign proper O'Connor's energy was reminiscent of his efforts in 1885. He spoke at Sheffield in the middle of June where he attacked Salisbury's opinions on Ulster. This was a theme he took up when speaking in Liverpool on 19 June where he compared 'Mr. Gladstone with perpetual freedom for Ireland' and 'the Conservatives with perpetual slavery' and refuted the suggestion that the Nationalists would show religious intolerance in Ulster, saying that such an accusation was 'gross' and that 'of all the dark and truculent bigots in the world, none were darker or more truculent than the bigots of Belfast'. It was a hard-hitting campaign; he did not spare either the Conservative leadership or the Liberal Unionists and this was appropriate because it had been in Liverpool in November 1891 that Chamberlain in company with Salisbury had made the speech which had ended hopes of Liberal reunion. By comparison, the Parnellites were blamed for the split in Irish ranks but O'Connor did not pay them much attention. This aggressiveness went down well, nationalist sentiment showed no sign of diminishing and, on the same night as O'Connor made his major speech in Liverpool, he and Davitt, who had reluctantly agreed to become a parliamentarian, were besieged by crowds of supporters at the Adelphi Hotel. No sooner was O'Connor elected than, as the Liberal press remarked with gratification, he was off to north Wales and Lancashire, speaking at Wrexham and Ince and then Flint, Wigan, Widnes and Runcorn shortly afterwards on 8 July. The following day he spoke at Stretford and Sale, and the day after, on the 10th, he spoke at North Lonsdale before moving south to address meetings of agricultural labourers in Essex, Norfolk and Suffolk, probably in each place driving home the same attack on Salisbury, Chamberlain and the Ulster connection. He may have found electioneering in the 'English midlands' factory areas 'appalling and saddening' but these reflections came later in the decade; there was no time for second thoughts in 1892.[18]

O'Connor's instinct, to concentrate on the Liberal alliance, seemed to be justified by the election result when it was revealed that the Liberals needed all the support they could get. Irish Nationalist

[17] For the negotiations with the Parnellites see Lyons, *Dillon*, pp. 146-7; *D.P.*, 6 June.
[18] *The Times*, 17 June; Mr. Davitt's Cab Home, *Porcupine*, 25 June; *D.P.*, 9 July; Fyfe, p. 184.

numbers remained steady at 81 seats and although this figure included the Parnellites they were reduced to nine M.P.s, thus removing the danger of a major split. Liberal candidates did not fare so well and the Liberal total of 270 seats was less than the Conservatives and Liberal Unionists combined. Unfortunately, Irish support, which gave the Liberals a majority of forty, did not prove sufficient. Spencer and Morley advised against trying to form a government and Gladstone initially was of the same mind. But with some Irish encouragement Gladstone's determination was re-awakened and a Home Rule Bill was made the principal piece of government legislation, to be introduced in the 1893 session. In the meantime discussions between Morley and Gladstone on the one hand and, for the Irish, Dillon, Sexton and Edward Blake (a new Irish Canadian recruit to the majority party), produced a scheme for a Bill even more detailed than that of 1886, providing for a bicameral legislature in Ireland and the retention of 80 Irish M.P.s at Westminster (the major departure from the previous Bill). This Bill was introduced in February 1893 and passed its second reading in April and its third reading by September, in both cases with small majorities. Gladstone's tenacity in these marathon sessions would have been enough to satisfy the most sceptical Irishman and it was the centre piece of O'Connor's *Sketches in the House.*

Opinion in the majority party was that this was a better Bill than that of 1886 (more detailed; the rest may have been wishful thinking), and a meeting of the leaders of the party, including O'Connor, on first hearing Gladstone's proposals, agreed not to be too critical of the Bill. Such self-denial was obvious in O'Connor's case from the few and brief interjections he made in debate. One minor comment of his which is worth noting occurred during the third reading on the question of the retained M.P.s when he said that they would not be, for instance, Irishmen from London (or presumably from any part of Britain) because 'Ireland would be foolish to send . . . a lower or meaner class of representative than she sent to College Green, and she would send to London men having their roots in Ireland'.[19] Considering O'Connor's domicile, this may have been intended as a joke (nothing is harder to distinguish than the everyday humour of the past), or it may be a revelation of his real opinion. In any case an awareness of the difficulty shows the lengths to which he would go to try and cultivate support and gain something tangible in the way of Home Rule legislation. Redmond and his small band of followers, by

[19] Irish party meeting attended by Blake, Healy, Dillon and O'Connor, 13 Feb. 1893, detailed in M.A. Banks, *Edward Blake, Irish Nationalist* (1957), p. 52; *Hansard, 4,* col. 1808, 1 Sept. 1893.

comparison, showed no reluctance to criticize the Bill and did show what could still be achieved by independent opposition. Irrespective of all this, the automatic response of the Lords was to reject the Bill by an overwhelming majority and what followed showed that the Liberals had insufficient determination to pursue the Bill if it meant a constitutional crisis; the conflict was deferred for another fifteen years.

Hopes so resolutely maintained in the 1892 campaign (and, in essence, since the Parnellite split) were now dashed, and precisely on the point of policy asserted by O'Connor. At Bradford he had advertised the fact that the Lords would have to be outfaced and in his *Sketches in the House* he had warned the Liberals against lack of resolution. Yet when Gladstone proposed a dissolution on the issue of the Lords his colleagues refused to support him and he resigned and was replaced by Rosebery in March 1894. Irish reaction when it came to the point was muted. Even though at the League conference preceding the third reading (that held in London at Westminster in May 1893), O'Connor had expressed confidence in victory and an admiration for Gladstone, there was perhaps an air of defensiveness in his speech. His reference to their being able 'to resist all the forces employed against them in the past'[20] anticipated further difficulties, though not ones as great as then did arise. Proof that the Liberal leadership would not automatically follow Gladstone or take Home Rule further during that parliament stunned the Irish party. They had fought this battle since 1890 and were left with nothing but exhaustion, so much so that there is hardly any sign of outrage or resolve even in the private papers of Irish M.P.s. O'Connor can merely be found, in March, writing to Herbert Gladstone hoping that he (Herbert Gladstone) would replace Morley as Irish Secretary if Morley were to be sent to the Lords,[21] and then a few months later passing on a celebratory present from the American League to Herbert's father. A limit was reached when Rosebery declared in March 1894 that England, as the dominant party to the Union, would have to declare for Home Rule before the Liberals could take it up again. The furious reaction to this meant that it had to be explained away. Apart from this outburst of the old spirit, the Irish party was submerged in the general tedium of Rosebery's government as it hung on for the next year up to the summer of 1895. O'Connor had nothing better to offer. Perhaps he could have criticized the Liberals more effectively but he had

[20]*D.P.*, 22 May 1893.

[21]Viscount Gladstone Papers, Add. MS 46054, f. 225, O'Connor to Herbert Gladstone, 1 Mar. 1894; *ibid.* 3 June 1895.

identified himself so closely with them that it was difficult to retrace his steps. Over high policy all he could say at the two following League conferences (those at Liverpool in May 1894 and at Leeds in 1895) was either that the cause of the Irish party was 'indissolubly bound up with the Liberal party' and that it was 'impossible that [Home Rule] should fail' or, in 1895 just before the election, that 'though other parts of the country might waver, the sturdy Liberalism of the north of England would lend them assistance'.[22] But this was whistling in the dark. O'Connor's political fortunes could not improve until the Liberals returned in greater heart; such a prospect was remote.

Not only did O'Connor's larger hopes suffer but from 1894 onwards he had to face quarrels nearer home, within the I.N.L.G.B. where his ascendancy came into question, and within the parliamentary party where the whole movement was threatened, and all this occurred just at the time when his newspaper, the *Sun*, began to run into difficulties. One continuing source of dispute within the League was over the cause of labour. Palliatives had been offered when the possibility of support for labour arose in 1889. Since then the Irish had been too concerned with their own affairs. Nevertheless the matter had been raised in O'Connor's absence, at the 1891 conference. The mover here was J.C. Taggart, a dock labourer from Liverpool, who was active in local politics; his resolution at the conference was rejected.[23] Then during the euphoria of the election and the Home Rule Bill debate labour had been forgotten except that even in the 1893 conference, supposedly concerned with the imminence of Home Rule, O'Connor paid considerable attention to labour issues. This may have been on his own initiative, anticipating an Irish organization in Britain once Home Rule was obtained, and also following the line laid down in the *Sun* where the 'social question' was seen in non-party terms; it may also have been a direct response to the Independent Labour Party which was founded in January 1893. He still gave priority to Home Rule however and hardly clarified the position of the I.N.L.G.B. by claiming that 'they were an Irish National organization, but they were essentially a labour organization'. At the conference which met the following year in 1894 in Liverpool at a time of great social distress, it was laid down that the membership should join no other organization – most probably a reference to the I.L.P. which

[22]*D.P.*, 14 May 1894; *ibid.* 3 June 1895.

[23]*Ibid.* 18 May 1891. Taggart came from Co. Tyrone, was first elected to the Liverpool council in 1892 and was especially active over housing. He has been regarded as Liverpool's first 'unequivocally working class' councillor (B.D. White, *Corporation of Liverpool*, pp. 188, 134).

was mentioned as a possible disruptor of the League by the Liverpool *Daily Post*. The threat was greater than that posed earlier by Champion's Labour Electoral Association.[24] O'Connor's sympathy for labour was genuine but what had served as a reasonable policy in the 1880s was now beginning to look worn. Criticism of O'Connor in this respect was here to stay and it is a matter of opinion how far in the next two decades he resolved the issue in his own mind and also how far the separation of the I.N.L.G.B. from labour was to the benefit of Ireland. O'Connor's reservations here might indicate that he was, or had become, a Liberal by conviction because, for one thing, he approved of the economic assumptions of Liberalism.

But this sort of idealistic competition with Labour did not cause as much trouble as disillusion and dissension within the Nationalist ranks. Here the trouble arose from a variety of areas and was not entirely to disappear in the League until the party was re-united at the turn of the century. Disagreements with Parnellites were the least of these troubles. John Brady, suspected of being a Parnellite, was replaced as General Secretary by J.F.X. O'Brien, probably at the 1894 conference, although effective control possibly went to him somewhat earlier. Lack of difficulty here is a final strong indication that Parnellites were not very numerous in the British League. Far more serious for morale were disputes and weaknesses revealed within the majority party. Where it can be said that O'Connor and other leaders of the party aggravated the problem was in their bad management of the problem of finances. Both the I.N.L.G.B. and the movement generally, after the success of the late 1880s, were in difficulty over funds.[25] Disillusion with the party in Ireland, Britain and, most of all in the United States, had had this direct effect. This gave rise to two near scandals which were not cleared up until after the 1895 election. In the first, an offer of financial support from the Liberals, prominent among them Lord Tweedmouth (an ex whip) and Gladstone, was made in May 1894. O'Connor had drawn attention to the need for funds at the 1893 I.N.L.G.B. conference and then at a meeting in August 1894 an appeal was launched for support from Home Rulers in Britain. At first the Liberal offer had been turned down in the, correct, belief that it would call Irish Independence into question. But then, after the 1894 conference, the donation was accepted, some sign of the extremity of the need, but certainly an unwise move. When Tweedmouth's and Gladstone's names were published in a list of donations in the *Freeman's Journal*, the storm

[24]*D.P.*, 22 May 1893; *ibid.* 3 June 1894.

[25]N.L.I., J.F.X. O'Brien Papers, MS 13432 (8), O'Connor to O'Brien, 27 Nov. 1892; Dillon Papers, MS 67404-4, f. 16, Davitt to O'Connor, 17 Sept. 1894.

which had been feared then broke. It was even suggested that O'Connor and the I.N.L.G.B. executive had instructed Edward Blake to 'sell' seats in the north of England (that is to say, the Irish vote) at £200 a seat. There is little evidence for this but it does at least suggest that the vote was taken seriously by politicians. A similar crisis, in which O'Connor was less directly involved, arose in July 1895 with the apparent abdication of Irish parliamentary responsibility for seats in the marginal areas of south Ulster which, with accompanying accusations from Healy, was so badly handled that it could be made to appear like a direct sale of seats from the Irish to the Liberal party.[26] Squabbles such as these were a blow to the reputation of the Irish leadership and, coming so quickly after Rosebery's harmful declaration on Home Rule, further discredited the Liberal alliance.

But these two instances were only part of a larger difficulty; that presented by Healy. His disagreement with the majority party, in which he obtained the support of a small number of M.P.s (some of them relatives and mostly representing the Cork region) was to persist for the rest of the lifetime of the parliamentary party and was to be a serious danger up to the early years of the new century. Arguments within the leadership caused a great deal of dissatisfaction among the British League organizers. At the 1894 conference one delegate called for 'some very plain speaking' because 'the cause of Ireland [is] suffering very much [from these] dissentions'. Bluntness is not what he got. O'Connor merely asserted that 'Irish M.P.s could be relied upon as one man' and he also praised the bracing air of Liverpool.[27] This was not sufficient and, as a result of conference complaints, enquiries were begun about the attitude of League branches towards Healy. Delegates and organizers must have believed that if they were sufficiently mature to work with Liberals in local politics then the leadership ought to be able to resolve its internal differences. To secure a strong party, free from personal ambition, had been one of the motives behind the opposition to Parnell. Now criticism centred on Healy. J.F.X. O'Brien and O'Connor received numerous complaints both from local organizers and their branches and from influential Irishmen in Ireland blaming Healy and demanding his removal from the offices he held in the I.N.L.G.B. and in the party generally. From this information it is reasonable to conclude that Healy's charge that O'Connor conducted a personal 'vendetta' against him was incorrect. O'Connor had been fair to Healy over the Parnell divorce issue. It was

[26] For the Tweedmouth affair see Banks, *Blake,* pp. 88-117 and Lyons, *Dillon,* pp. 162-3; for mid-Ulster see Lyons, pp. 165-6.

[27] *D.P.,* 14 May 1894.

Davitt, just as in the earlier dispute with Parnell, who was the most insistent, perhaps sharing with other correspondents from the rank and file of the movement the belief that Healy threatened democratic processes. O'Connor did show concern about 'this drifting policy' and did forward his correspondence on the matter to Dillon but it was not until October 1895, after the 1895 conference and after the election, that O'Connor had Healy expelled from the I.N.L.G.B. and then in November helped to have him removed from the Irish Federation and from the committee of the parliamentary party.[28] Carefulness, consideration before acting, showed that O'Connor was looking for some way to end the dispute with the least damage and goes some way to substantiate the genuineness of his frequently expressed distaste for faction.

Unfortunately, although he may have removed Healy from offices close at hand (and could do nothing about Healy at the hustings or in parliament), O'Connor's own political difficulties were not removed. His election at Liverpool in July 1895 had not been a very impressive affair. He faced, first of all, increasing criticism from the Unionist press, which included some of the local Liberal press which had changed sides since 1892. A paradox in O'Connor's representing the Liverpool seat now became more apparent, or was no longer regarded as agreeable. This was not the obvious paradox of an Irish Nationalist sitting for an English constituency, though undoubtedly that was the essential cause of dissatisfaction. Rather, the grievance appeared to be that O'Connor was a wealthy and cosmopolitan politician, supposedly a more populist choice than the Conservatives who dominated the politics of the city. But whereas the Conservatives, of comparatively modest means and certainly more parochial in their outlook, made a point of fostering democratic toryism (the line laid down by A.B. Forwood and even more by his successor Archibald Salvidge, the leader of the Liverpool conservative Workingmen's Association), O'Connor appeared to have little to do with his constituency. Something of the flavour of these criticisms can be seen in O'Connor's entry in *Liverpool's Legion of Honour*, a sort of local *Who's Who* first published in 1893. This identified him as 'prominent among those Home Rule Irishmen who interrupt their opponents with yells and howls, and retard the work of that great assembly by choosing the most offensive epithets in their extensive vocabulary'. This was at a time when O'Connor, who had never approved of obstruction, was blaming Chamberlain and the Unionists for their

---

[28] See Dillon Papers, MS 6740-4, f. 20, letters to O'Connor dated 19 Sept. 1894 and J.F.X. O'Brien Papers, MS 13432 (8), letters on Healy to J.F.X. O'Brien dated from Apr. 1894 to Nov. 1895. Cf. Healy, *Letters*, ii, 423-4.

delaying tactics (though employing the epithet 'Judas' once again) and he was himself one of the most ardent supporters of the government. Nevertheless such criticism was elaborated in the years which followed. By 1895, for instance, the Liverpool *Porcupine* noticed that O'Connor had

> the hardihood to present himself to his native constituents . . . ask[ing] them to return him to parliament again. For a public man to ingratiate himself into the graces of half washed and wholly uneducated men and women . . . then to wink the other eye in the back office of the *Sun* is a scandal.

O'Connor at this time might well have wished to be rid of the *Sun* but the further question, 'what have you ever done for your Scotland Road paddies?' was something to which he might have given more thought even though, in the face of provincial dullness, it is little wonder that he spent so much of his time in London. Before the election of 1895 O'Connor was in Liverpool only long enough to make certain that the details of the organization were satisfactory before going on to Ireland and he returned only briefly for the poll. His majority in Scotland division was halved, to a mere 637 votes, and the Liberals lost Exchange division to a Unionist (and were not to regain it until 1906).[29] Part of the trouble may have been dissatisfaction among Catholics, who opposed Liberal education policies and were looking with more favour on Unionist proposals – a feature which was to become more evident. But there was, too, a general disillusionment with the Liberal-Irish alliance and amongst this could probably be found a protest at O'Connor's neglect of his constituency.

Neglect of another sort was a charge O'Connor had to deal with when it came to I.N.L.G.B. affairs. After the election, in February 1896, McCarthy had obtained his long-held ambition to resign from the chairmanship of the majority party and he was replaced by John Dillon. Under Dillon discipline increased, but to such an extent that the accusation that personal rule was reappearing in the Irish party could legitimately be made. Healy, for one, lost no time in suggesting that the committee of the party did not meet again after he had been removed from it, and also claimed that Dillon and O'Connor were effectively in charge of Irish policy. Accusations that O'Connor

[29]B. Guiness Orchard, *Liverpool's Legion of Honour* (1893), p. 529. This also remarked on the rareness of O'Connor's visits to Liverpool; *Porcupine*, 6 July 1895; *D.P.*, 27 June, 24 July. O'Connor's constituency also received some bad publicity in the *Daily Graphic* (21 Dec. 1896) because of the drink problem in the area, supposedly highlighted in evidence given before the Royal Commission sitting at that time. When the Commission reported no undue prominence was given to Liverpool (*Royal Commission on the Laws Relating to the Sale of Intoxicating Liquors* (1899), pp. 81, 82, 95).

domineered over the I.N.L.G.B. also probably originated from Healy and the Healyite press. At the 'race' convention which met in Dublin in September 1896, a meeting calling together the American, British and Irish Leagues in place of their usual annual conferences, O'Connor saw the opportunity to defend himself. The charge was that

> The Irish National League of Great Britain was constantly referred to as T.P. O'Connor's organization . . . there was a picture drawn of him as a ceaseless and incessant wire-puller, who spent his nights and days in sending instructions to all parts of the country and in carrying out a correspondence multi-tudinous in size and machiavellian in dishonesty . . . [On the contrary, he continued] I have not written a letter in the last five years to any member [of the I.N.L.G.B.] regarding organization.

J.F.X. O'Brien, the General Secretary, would have agreed with this and had complained to Dillon about the difficulty of getting hold of O'Connor. Even when O'Connor was contacted, as he was for instance over an enquiry concerning an election petition in 1892, he could be found referring the matter to 'Mr Denvir or some other member of the staff'. O'Connor's preoccupation with journalism or his absence at European health resorts played a part – and as late as September 1902 he asked to be excused from any engagements for the following month, writing from Vichy.[30] O'Connor's correspondence with O'Brien was sparse (and he found O'Brien 'narrow'). But the impression of a wire-puller was still there and was repeated, perhaps predictably, in the Liverpool press. It semed to go with the office and with the personality. Perhaps in actuality O'Connor restricted his main efforts to the presidential rostrum (and perhaps it could be said that, as in journalism, he jibbed at detailed or routine work). Real manipulation takes place by word of mouth not from what is put down on paper so there is no likelihood of proving the case one way or the other. At any rate, O'Connor did not increase his supervision of the I.N.L.G.B. but, probably with some justification, left day to day work to O'Brien. The convention at Dublin appeared to be satisfied with his back-handed defence (aimed, after all, at Healy). There was less satisfaction with the more important issue of the state of the parliamentary movement. The gathering at Dublin was presumably intended to put new heart into the cause and a considerable renewed effort was required because, as O'Connor said, 'depression and lethargy had taken the place of the old hopefulness and energy'. O'Connor refused to regard the verdict of the 1895 election as final but electoral prospects looked so black that during the convention and

[30]Healy, *Letters,* ii, 423; *D.P.,* 5 Sept.; J.F.X. O'Brien Papers, MS 1343-2 (8), O'Connor to O'Brien, 19 Nov. 1892; *ibid.* O'Connor to O'Brien, 7 Sept. 1892.

at the League conference at Manchester the following June he could do little more in public than urge the League to stand firm. Much opinion in the League might have agreed with the Glasgow delegate who in 1896 had said that 'in 1890 the Irishmen of Great Britain had remained almost solid while forty per cent of the Irish party went away'. In private, O'Connor looked as though he agreed. Writing to Dillon at the end of 1897 after an unsuccessful intervention in a by-election contest in Liverpool Exchange, he calculated that 'we very nearly did the trick' (which was true, the Unionist majority was 54); the voters 'would probably have come up better if there were the stimulus of a strong and united movement at home. All the same it would be well if there were even an approach in the spirit in Ireland to the spirit we have here.'[31]

Yet in the prevailing mood of the country there was little that O'Connor or any other of the parliamentary leaders could do. A convention could draw the converted closer together but it did not inspire them to go on the offensive. This is the picture also presented by an article O'Connor wrote for the *Contemporary Review* in August 1896, before the convention, where he began by remarking on the 'deadlock' in parliament. He admitted Irish division and apathy in the Commons, and called the election result 'disastrous' (but blamed it on the 'weakness' of the Liberal government). Yet the main theme of the article was that Home Rule, the settling of Irish grievances, was necessary for the well-being of the Empire.[32] Such an argument was not lacking in perception, especially in not offending fashionable susceptibilities, but it was obviously defensive and long term. If O'Connor himself by now had more regard for the Empire (and it is possible, though if so it did not go very deep, as events in the next couple of years were to show) he was also for a time bowing to the inevitable.

Imperialist sentiment, apart from such special pleading, clearly made the political task more difficult and in the last part of the decade much of the activity of the parliamentary party (or what was left of it after internal dissensions) went into criticizing the details of Unionist legislation, and not to any great effect. Examples of this in O'Connor's case sometimes showed a more detailed interest in constituency matters. The Belfast Corporation Bill of 1896 was criticized because, according to O'Connor, the provisions for Belfast council discriminated against Catholics and he compared Belfast unfavourably to Liverpool

[31] *D.P.*, 5 Sept. 1896, 7 June 1897; Dillon Papers, MS 6740-4, f. 45, O'Connor to Dillon, 21 Nov. 1897.

[32] 'Home Rule and the Irish Party', *Contemporary Review*, 70 (Aug. 1896), 179-90.

in this respect. Gerald Balfour, who had become Irish Secretary in 1895, said O'Connor's remarks were 'exaggerated'. O'Connor also intervened in such matters as a Liverpool Cattle and Markets Bill (again in March 1896) which he opposed unless the market was put under public ownership, and spoke on a Bill extending the powers of the Mersey Docks and Harbour Board which 'gave the labour of the city a very large amount of work to do'. In August 1898 he also championed the cause of the Liverpool branch of the Seaman's Union which was protesting against inadequate crew accommodation. Two years later he supported their objections to the use of Lascar seamen. Any M.P. might have done as much for his constituency (though possibly not so vehemently) and O'Connor had done something similar for Galway City, but it was a departure for O'Connor and Liverpool.[33] At the same time he continued to show his interest in national and imperial matters, in the military estimates (which as a good radical he often greeted with dismay), foreign affairs (especially the issue of Crete), and expenditure within the House (especially any signs of waste).

Of even more interest to his constituents and to Irishmen in Britain generally was the issue of education. Catholic schools were 'voluntary' schools in the same way as those provided by the Anglican church and their funding was a source of considerable and continuing controversy. From the 1890s the Catholic community began to be more demonstrative. Their schools were not in any way so well endowed as those provided by the Anglican establishment and Catholic spokesmen welcomed any government assistance. This presented a political problem which may have lost O'Connor votes in the 1895 election, which he referred to in his article for the *Contemporary Review*, and which was to cause him difficulties from here on. The Irish party had supported the second reading of the Unionist's Education Bill of 1896 which proposed to give state support for voluntary schools. Unionists were always more sympathetic in this regard than the non-conformist wing of the Liberal party who opposed any state subsidy for denominational education. O'Connor made a reasonable distinction between politics and religion and it was a stance he was to continue to adopt but this never convinced those who made no distinction between the two, and even to the Liberal party in general it may have seemed politically unrealistic. O'Connor's part in the 1896 debate was further complicated because it was an English Education Bill but he had to plead for his Irish constituents. His support was grudging, in

[33] *Hansard, 4,* 38 cols 334-6, 6 Mar. 1896; *ibid.* col. 723, 12 Mar. 1896; *ibid.* 156, col. 1180, 22 Apr. 1898; *ibid.* 64, col. 912, 11 Aug. 1898; *ibid.* 82, cols. 856-9 and cols. 1403, 1436-7, 4, 11 May 1900.

order to obtain 'whatever small concessions it gave to Roman Catholic schools' whose deficiencies he then detailed. Government spokesmen had no sympathy for him, were perhaps gratified to overlook that he spoke for an English constituency, and were not oblivious of the political advantages of education issues. The Bill, it was said in reply, 'does not primarily affect Ireland'. Most of the Bill was, as it turned out, lost because of Chamberlain's non-conformist objections, but O'Connor returned to the issue some three years later when he took the opportunity of a routine debate on the education estimates to draw attention to the needs of the Irish in Britain. These were, he said, 'a large class of the community [which had] the unique distinction of being oppressed with almost equal injustice by both sides of the House'. Disillusion with the Liberals was again evident, as was a sense of grievance, that he was 'the sole representative' of the migrant community. More specifically, 'his own constituency was inhabited by undoubtedly one of the poorest populations in the United Kingdom. . . . He could scarcely trust himself to express the feelings [their] schools produced on his mind. . . . The poorest of the poor [were] kept up largely by the expense of the poor.' Impatience with political stalemate was evident and the Irish party did not escape from blame either; O'Connor could complain that only one other Irish M.P. had spoken on the Education Bill.[34] In June 1898 at the League conference held in Birmingham, he asserted Irish 'independence of British parties' but then pledged support for 'Gladstonian' candidates. By the time of the conference in Bradford the following May, although claiming that the 'worst days' of the organization in Britain were over, he was now more ready to argue publicly that 'dissension in Ireland was disastrous and almost fatal to the success of the movement in Britain' and he demanded more 'consideration of their views' by those in Ireland.[35] This was to some degree a response to criticisms made in earlier years from the floor of the conference, and some of the concern for Liverpool and interest in education might have been due to pressure, but it also showed a genuine disquiet on O'Connor's part. Not that involvement in the education issue was to prove anything but a thankless task.

Other concerns of the Irish party which had less to do with the Irish in Britain also arose because of Unionist initiatives, and equally showed the Irish party at a disadvantage. These were, further land purchase proposals, a debate on Irish taxation, and the extension of

[34] 'Home Rule and the Irish Party', *Contemporary Review,* 70, 185-6; *Hansard, 4,* 38, cols. 1205-14 for the speech; col. 1205, 12 Mar. 1896; *ibid.* 40, col. 1205, 12 May; *ibid.* 70, col. 853, 28 Apr. 1899.

[35] *D.P.,* 30 June 1894; *ibid.* 22 May 1899.

local government in Ireland. Land purchase, which arose again in the Act of 1896, put the leaders of the majority party in the difficult position of accepting beneficial legislation while constantly affirming that nothing would be satisfactory but a full measure of Home Rule. The Liberal party was no help and the Redmondite party cooperated with the Unionists in committee and gained considerable advantages. William O'Brien, active once more in the west of Ireland, was even more inclined to concentrate on the practical benefits of reform. Over taxation, the Royal Commission on taxation in Ireland set up by Gladstone in 1894 reported in 1896 and revealed considerable over-taxation. There was some desultory debate in the House at the beginning of 1897 and much public interest in Ireland but, when it proved impossible to cooperate with the Unionists, the Irish party let the matter drop. This was a far cry from the confidence of the 1880s and all that the issue did was to provide additional ammunition for Nationalist speakers. The Irish Local Government Act, passed by the Unionists in 1898, appeared in the same light. Full responsible powers in local matters were extended to Ireland by the Act, thereby also allowing the Nationalists to break the ascendancy's paternalistic hold on the Irish provinces. Nationalists did make full use of these powers in the years that followed but Dillon, as was customary with him and other parliamentarians, regarded the Act as an attempt to subvert Home Rule. While there was some justice in this, O'Connor's objections were more eccentric. He argued that the Act merely allowed 'poor Kerry to assist poor Kerry' and tried to turn the debate into a discussion on emigration. This prompted the Unionist member for East Down, J.A. Rentoul, to remind him that they were both 'emigrants to our great advantage'.[36] There was little attempt at a detached, constructive criticism; all the running was made by the Unionists.

Where the Irish did take the initiative their comparative isolation could often make them appear futile, an irrelevance beside the great issues of Empire. This was not completely true of objections in cases that arose out of the continued application of coercive legislation in Ireland, and O'Connor here could still make detailed objections as well as attempting to raise the whole issue of distress and coercion in a frequently indifferent House. But effectiveness in debate here came from long practice; the subject was almost customary and Irish objections were just as often ignored. Nevertheless, even in this unpromising but, for Irishmen, serious area, O'Connor was more

---

[36]*Hansard,* 4, 57, col. 326, 4 May 1898.

active than were most Irish politicians.[37] Some Irish concerns could appear quixotic or antiquarian, the archetypal case here being, at first glance, Irish opposition to the Cromwell memorial at Westminster, a dispute which arose in February 1900. Here though, O'Connor derived some mischievous amusement out of reminding the Commons that Irish susceptibilities had to be considered because the Irish were 'still members of this House'. Irish objections to the Jubilee celebrations of 1897 which arose, according to O'Connor, because 'Irishmen would not lie to the world with regard to their own feelings and their own country' could be dismissed with impatience, but it took some persistence to oppose the festivities. O'Connor's opposition to Unionist policy in southern Africa was of a different order; it came early and it did not waver. During the debate on Uitlander grievances in August 1899 O'Connor tried to convice the Commons that 'there was a disposition among fair minded men to look at the position from the Boer as well as the British point of view', that 'a needless war was a criminal war', and that it was better to wait 'a quarter of a century to secure by [a] natural growth of opinion a peaceful and tranquil settlement than embark once more on a needless war'.[38] These were good liberal sentiments and required some moral courage, though perhaps even more was shown by Liberal 'pro-Boers' like Lloyd George. Opinions such as these were expected of Irishmen (though not all were immune from imperial sentiment: a Liverpool Irish militia battalion served in the Boer war, on the Imperial side), but the war fever and Irish criticism, led by O'Connor, did help to revive Nationalist ideals and self-confidence.[39]

Probably more directly beneficial was the reunification of the party after a wearying decade. Negotiations to bring the party together were complicated and lasted from 1898 to 1900, though even then it can hardly be said that the party was as united as it had been in Parnell's heyday. The vehicle for reunification was William O'Brien's United Irish League, first established as an agrarian movement in

[37] On coercion and related matters see *Hansard, 4,* 60, col. 440, Treason-felony prisoners, 28 June 1898, *ibid.* 61, cols. 419, 429, Kelly case, 8 July 1898, *ibid.* 69, col. 1585, Criminal Law and Procedure (Ireland) Repeal Bill, 19 April 1899, *ibid.* 66, col. 1496, Distress in the West of Ireland (supporting an amendment of Davitt's), 20 Feb. 1899.

[38] *Ibid.* 79, col. 970, 23 Feb. 1900; *D. P.,* 7 June 1897; *Hansard, 4,* 76, cols. 270-1, 9 Aug. 1899.

[39] For the Liverpool battalion see Frank Forde, 'The Liverpool Irish Volunteers', *Irish Sword* 10, 39 (Winter, 1971), 106-31. A Volunteer battalion was first raised in 1860. The battalion served in the Boer war along with a London Irish battalion because there was no Volunteer movement in Ireland to provide reserves for Irish regiments. See chapter 6, p. 221 for the battalion in the first world war.

January 1898. Dillon, though continually suspicious of the Parnellites, and of Healy's influence over O'Brien, forced the pace by resigning from the chairmanship in February 1899. A conference in April and then further conferences in November and in January and February 1900 decided the issue and at the final conference John Redmond from the Parnellite camp was elected chairman of the parliamentary party in time for the start of the new parliamentary session. Dillon absented himself from all the meetings except the final ratification meeting. O'Connor was busy with his new paper *M.A.P.* (Mainly About People), founded in June 1898, but as his many heartfelt comments since 1895 would suggest, he was more anxious than Dillon to obtain unity, and probably more aware of the popular annoyance with faction. His chief concern was that reunification would prove a reality and he successfully urged on Dillon to support Redmond as president of the U.I.L.[40] This was accomplished in June, thus bringing together all parts of the movement and leaving Healy isolated but undismayed. O'Connor had resolved his political difficulties to a large extent, though his activities latterly had been something of a mixed bag. It remained to be seen how effective the party could be at the polls and here O'Connor had a shock in store.

'Mainly About People', 1900-5

The election campaign in the autumn of 1900 was the most uncomfortable O'Connor ever had to fight and it was fortunate, though perhaps unforseen, that the affairs of the party and O'Connor's fortunes did recognizably improve after this. He probably did not envisage defeat but, even so, he may have been only marginally more confident than when he fought his first contest in Galway. Trouble came from a much more vociferous Unionist campaign in Liverpool and a more formidable electoral challenge from their camp. More dangerous still was the prospect that a rival nationalist candidate, Austin Harford, a Liverpool Irishman, would be nominated. More generally, there was the problem of what attitude to take to Redmond's leadership, a continued difficulty with the Catholic Church, and the need, as O'Connor saw it, to clarify relations with the Liberals.

Unionist opposition in Scotland division was usually, and with some justification, regarded with contempt by O'Connor. He tended to see their candidates as young hopefuls serving their apprenticeship

[40] Dillon Papers, MS 6740-4, f. 75, O'Connor to Dillon, 12-13 June 1900.

before moving on to fight safe seats. In 1900 however, the candidate was a local man, W. Watson Rutherford, and he put forward a long manifesto on local issues to do with pensions, compensation for accidents, business and trade, housing and, most dangerous of all, schooling. O'Connor, despite his work in the last parliament, could not, or at any rate did not, pay any attention to local matters in the election. Added to this was the passion aroused by the Boer War. This probably did not lose O'Connor support but, at this early stage in the war especially, it encouraged more positive enthusiasm among the Unionists. Some of the contradictions in O'Connor's social and political life could also be exploited, more so than in the election of 1895. The *Porcupine* in particular could always find space for something on O'Connor: he was good copy and its criticism increased throughout 1900. 'As a journalist', O'Connor was told, 'you are as loyal as John Bull himself in the pages of *M.A.P.* and the *Sunday Sun*' but there was none of 'this unctuous fealty to the Saxon when you fulminate on a Home Rule platform'. In society, or 'the London halls of dazzling light', he indulged none of the 'rhetoric of the sort which would raise cheers for Kruger'. He was said to earn, variously, £5,000 or £6,000 a year (March) or more than £10,000 (September). He was reputed to be mean, and was difficult to find 'when he's wanted'. The fuller flavour of these attacks can only be given by a final example;

> He lives in a fine style, keeps a carriage and footman, and moves in the most swaggering society of modern Babylon. His non affluent constituents of Scotland division only see him once in a blue moon, and he's not in the habit of compensating for his absenteeism by sending an occasional cheque to help the poor and needy among his constituents. All things considered, I do not think this disinterested Home Ruler will be ruined for love of the old country.[41]

Much of this was clearly partisan and, so far as O'Connor's wealth was concerned, a relative and speculative judgment. Some of the criticism was fair comment and would normally have been safely ignored. But while it is doubtful whether his constituents were quite so puritanical or begrudging as Unionist journalists, such attacks may have expressed in an extreme form the dissatisfaction with O'Connor personally which had gained ground and which could be summed up in the charge of neglect. This probably accounts for Austin Harford's

[41] Watson Rutherford's election notice is in *Porcupine,* 29 Sept. 1900; The articles in the *Porcupine* from March to October 1900 are listed in the bibliography; the long quotation is from 'T.P. and his £s'. The writer may have been incorrect in referring to the *Sunday Sun,* which was supposed to have been merged in the *Weekly Sun* in 1893 and O'Connor, equally, was said to have had no connection with this newspaper after 1898; see above, p. 129.

candidature. Harford and his brother Frank had come into local prominence in 1898 and 1899 when Frank, after a petition, had defeated G.J. Lynskey in south Scotland ward and Austin had won the other Scotland ward seat. Hartford supposedly represented a more popular type of nationalist, more 'extreme' (compared to Lynskey at any rate), and above all local. His step from local to national politics was a speedy one and had shown some belief in local support and some self-confidence, 'vanity' as O'Connor styled it. O'Connor was clearly astounded by this development, coming so shortly after the I.N.L.G.B. had met in Dublin, been re-founded as the United Irish League of Great Britain, (or U.I.L.G.B.) and re-elected him as president. Writing to Dillon he first expressed the fear that he would be beaten but then on the same day wrote to say that 'I think I shall beat both Harford and the Tory but only on condition of remaining in the constituency and fighting it out. It is an infernal nuisance.'[42] Letters which he wrote to Dillon throughout the campaign provide the only account O'Connor ever gave of a specific election contest, but the occasion was different in another way in that O'Connor usually did not fight his entire campaign in Scotland division itself. Aside from any accusations of neglect, it had, since 1885, been as a politician of national standing that O'Connor had attracted support and his enforced residence in Liverpool presented a real problem because it meant that on this occasion he could not so easily see to the operation of the Irish vote throughout Britain, nor could he help in Ireland. He had to write to Dillon a few days later regretting that he would not be able to help in 'the great fight' in the Irish constituencies.[43]

Very soon O'Connor's surprise turned to fury. Despite an initial lack of help he was assured that 'the priests' would be 'neutral' (though one source says that he had their help), and he then believed that 'even those who were behind Harford in the fight with Lynskey are with me now'. Harford was then persuaded by Redmond to withdraw though this did not happen until near nomination day and O'Connor was therefore kept in Liverpool. O'Connor's embarrassment and outrage were dwelt on with great relish by the Unionist press which held its breath (and held back any disparagement of Harford) while there was a chance of a split anti-Unionist vote. Then there was regret that 'the retirement of Harford had practically spoilt the chances of a real good owld [sic] Donneybrook Fair style of argument' with the result that 'the only explosions were the rhetorical cries of Tay Pay and the other speakers'. O'Connor therefore won

[42] For Frank Harford see *Porcupine*, 22 Apr. 1899; *D.P.*, 23 June 1900; Dillon, Papers, MS 6740-4, f. 90, f. 91, two letters O'Connor to Dillon, 25 Sept. 1900.

[43] *Ibid.* f. 94, O'Connor to Dillon, 28 Sept.

the seat and was carried shoulder high, despite his protests, by 'a dozen stalwart Hibernians'.[44] But the divisions during the election, the long years of disagreement and the continued ascendancy of the Unionists, all meant that O'Connor obtained his lowest majority ever. At 556 it was lower than his majority in 1895, half that of 1885, and a third of the majority he was to receive in 1906.[45] Electoral statistics can be misleading however; the fact that O'Connor's support went into a trough in 1895 and 1900 only, and then improved dramatically, may show the importance of the fortunes of Home Rule as distinct from O'Connor's presence among the electorate. And, as O'Connor suggested to Dillon, the battle within Liverpool was not over and would have to be continued in the municipal elections coming up the following November. Local matters were still a novel distraction for O'Connor and it was a sign that he had at least to take more care.

How the Irish vote should be used nationally, and in O'Connor's absence while he was unable to travel, give detailed reports or supervise, was of equal concern. Redmond's attitude was crucial and he was still an unknown quantity. It took some time for personal relations here to become more cordial. As late as March 1900 when the Irish leaders had travelled up by train to attend the St. Patrick's day festivities in Liverpool, O'Connor had refused to share a carriage with Healy and Redmond (as Healy gleefully recorded, although it may not have been Redmond O'Connor was set on avoiding). Redmond's intervention with Harford was not received by O'Connor with much enthusiasm; it was, so O'Connor wrote to Dillon, 'very curious' and 'instead of doing me good, was calculated to get my enemies decently out of their hole.'[46] All this is a sign of uneasiness at least, and in the conduct of the election generally O'Connor found Redmond's policy unsatisfactory. Redmond, as a Parnellite and as a new leader, wanted to stress the independence of the party. O'Connor,

---

[44]*Ibid.* f. 91, O'Connor to Dillon 25 Sept; *ibid.* f. 94, O'Connor to Dillon, 28 Sept.

[45]O'Connor's majorities and percentage of the votes cast were;

1885	1,250	64.9
1886	1,480	67.0
1892	1,190	65.3
1895	637	59.0
1900	560	57.9
1906	1,691	71.5
Jan. 1910	2,167	79.1
Dec. 1910	1,769	78.1

Electorate: 1885 7,076; 1906 5,761; 1910 5,326
(McCalmont, pp. 157-8, F.W.S. Craig, *British Parliamentary Election Results* (1974), p. 143).

[46]Healy, *Letters,* ii, 448; Dillon Papers, MS 6740-4, f. 94, O'Connor to Dillon, 28 Sept.

closest to the Liberals, wanted the vote to go to Liberal candidates and he wrote in a circular which he sent to Redmond and the other members of the executive of the U.I.L.G.B. that he (O'Connor) 'wanted to make it as easy as possible for our people to vote for the Liberal' and believed that the League ought to discourage voters 'pressing the Liberal candidate too closely on the question of Home Rule'. In reply only P.A. M'Hugh of the executive fully agreed with O'Connor, relying on O'Connor's expertise. Swift MacNeill wanted a pledge for Home Rule if the Irish voters held the balance in a contest, J.F.X. O'Brien wanted abstention where there was no Home Ruler, and Redmond's telegram declared against 'general instructions to support Liberals; should only support when Home Rule declaration unequivocal'. O'Connor's comment when forwarding these responses to Dillon was that Redmond's attitude was 'by no means a surprise to me' but that he regretted O'Brien's 'narrow views' and he disparaged the policy of 'demanding the Home Rule pledge in season and out of season'. O'Connor's view was, he said, a practical one. In the circular he had made a comparison with the election of 1885 where, so he claimed, Irish instructions had been intended to bring the Conservatives closer in strength to the Liberals. In his comments to Dillon he now thought it possible 'from what I see here in England' that the Conservatives would receive a large majority. The Irish ought to work against this to bring about an approximation of the two parties and 'give us our chance of making terms when the time comes'.[47] In the abstract there was much to be said for O'Connor's interpretation but influence on the Liberals had not been effective since Gladstone's resignation and the Liberals, although now under the determined leadership of Campbell-Bannerman with Herbert Gladstone as chief whip, were noticeably undecided about Home Rule. O'Connor's views may have been a rationalization of his concern for Liberalism (Dillon does not appear to have replied to endorse O'Connor's opinion) and although he was by now the expert on the use of the vote, it may have been a case of familiarity breeding over-confidence. Redmond's instinctive preference for independence might have been the right policy because it would be a salutary warning to the Liberals. In any case it was Redmond's policy which was followed and the Irish do not appear to have supported the Liberals *en bloc* during this election. These alternatives, a sharp reminder of Irish demands, or a more discreet pressure, set out early on the dilemma presented by the

[47]N.L.I., Redmond Papers, copy, O'Connor to Redmond and the executive of the U.I.L.G.B., 26 Sept.; Dillon Papers, MS 6740-4, f. 95, O'Connor to Dillon, 28 Sept.; for Liberal attitudes see H.W. McCready, 'Home Rule and the Liberal Party, 1899-1906', *I.H.S.*, 13, 316-48.

Liberals which was to remain with the Irish party for the rest of its existence. At least in 1900 it looked as though a new start could be made.

Much of what followed in O'Connor's career and in the fortunes of the Irish party up to the Liberal landslide of 1906 was an extended commentary on the problems and choices revealed in the earlier election of 1900. But apart from this, the context was one of growing confidence. The fact that choices could be made was an improvement and implied some anticipation of success. O'Connor, after the shock and then annoyance of the election (and perhaps his disgruntlement at having his advice ignored by Redmond and the U.I.L.G.B. executive) was full of what can only be described as Edwardian zest. A weight off his mind must have been the sale of the *Sun* to Bottomley in 1900. He had ended his connection with the *Weekly Sun* two years earlier and, also in 1898, had founded *M.A.P.* (Mainly About People being originally the title of a column in the *Star* showing, like his journal *P.T.O.,* a fondness for acronyms) and this was a project which, so O'Connor claimed in the first issue of the paper, he had 'had in mind for at least eight years'. This was something of a departure for O'Connor, a journal, modelled, according to Fyfe on *Truth*, but mixing political comment and social gossip with O'Connor's literary reviews; the emphasis throughout was on O'Connor's personal view and on personalities. The product was clearly more lightweight than his earlier newspapers, less of an editorial burden (and O'Connor began to pare down what was left, as was his habit). O'Connor remained fertile in ideas but was still put off by routine work or the necessity to attend the office. The finances of the paper remained just as complicated as those of the *Star* and the *Sun* had been but publication and the majority shareholding was vested in the firm of C. Arthur Pearson. O'Connor also had to deal with a determined manager of the Pearson enterprises in Peter Keary and the correspondence between Keary and O'Connor, lasting from 1902 to 1909, has survived almost intact.

Up to 1906 O'Connor kept and even increased a large personal following both in *M.A.P.* and, in possibly the most celebrated paper he founded, *T.P.'s Weekly.* The latter, first issued in November 1902, was not controlled by the Pearson group, at least not up to 1908, and was even more O'Connor's personal creation with an almost complete dependence on literary matters. Both journals are good examples of what one literary historian has described as 'the rich, diversified book publishing and journalism' which Edwardians were beginning to enjoy. O'Connor's products were foremost among those journals giving the impression that 'it was a pleasure to be alive with a strong pair of eyes in those peaceful, entertaining, and fiercely competitive years'.[48] Meredith, O'Connor's old friend, had announced in the first issue of *T.P.'s Weekly* that this marked the onset of 'the age of democracy in literature' and this was, equally, one of O'Connor's themes, although he was not always explicit about how it would be achieved. The magazine also obtained testimonials from Thomas Hardy, W.W. Jacobs and H.G. Wells. Although *T.P.'s Weekly* did not often reach the highest standards of scholarship, particularly not in O'Connor's long exhaustive reviews, what it did offer was far superior to the popular trivialities of the Harmsworth press and it did provide guidance and clarity for that large Edwardian public interested in self-improvement and, in an area of endeavour which was, and has remained, somewhat Jamesian, it was not noticeably patronizing. New as well as celebrated talent was encouraged and contributions from Wells, Arnold Bennett, Conrad and Chesterton were included; they were not paid generously because *T.P.'s Weekly*, contrary to appearances, made a more modest profit than *M.A.P. T.P.'s Weekly* had a long life; it lasted up to the first world war and was revived after the war, the title being altered to *T.P's and Cassell's Weekly* in 1927. O'Connor remained nominal editor until his death when the journal was renamed *John O'London's*.[49]

Some of the material in these journals, particularly the society gossip in *M.A.P.*, could leave O'Connor open to attack (as remarks made in the Liverpool press showed) and this was to continue. Perhaps in perspective it is difficult to equate the radical and nationalist with such information as 'the doyen of lady mountaineers is Miss Lucy Walker' or such articles as 'The Queen of Spain by Lady Violet Grenville'[50] but O'Connor was either unaware of, or unperturbed by the comparison. He gained additional prestige by his journalism, as even the Liverpool press grudgingly admitted, and this operated even in parliament where one of the longest (certainly the most entertaining) speeches he made at this time was in response to a campaign by the non-conformist wing of the Liberal party to impose additional

[48]'About Ourselves and Our Readers', *M.A.P.*, 18 June 1898. Fyfe (pp. 186-92) gives descriptions of features in the paper; Derek Hudson, 'Reading' in Simon Nowell-Smith, *Edwardian England*, p. 326.

[49]*T.P.'s Weekly*, vol. 1. no. 1, 21 Nov. 1902; Fyfe, *Sixty Years*, pp. 51-2. O'Connor may also have refused James Joyce a job; Joyce and his father visited London in May 1900 and paid a call on O'Connor (Richard Ellmann, *James Joyce* (1966), pp. 80, 766).

[50]*M.A.P.*, 18 June 1898.

PLATE 1. Waking the Liberal lion, December 1885

"T.P.'S" RETURN FROM THE STATES.

PLATE 2. *Sitting*, left to right: J. O'Shea, T.P. O'Connor, Austin Harford

Standing, left to right: a journalist, Frank Harford, M.E. Kearney, J.C. Taggart, W.J. Loughrey

IRISH LEADERS VISIT THE PREMIER

MR. JOHN REDMOND and MR. T. P. O'CONNOR paid a visit to the Premier at Downing-street, probably in connection with the Home Rule statement Mr. Asquith is to make on Monday. Judging from the smiles on the faces of the Irishmen, photographed as they left, the result of the interview was not unsatisfactory to them.

PLATE 3.

PLATE 4. O'Connor in old age

censorship on the London theatre and its 'grossly immoral' plays. In parliament, O'Connor was imagined to be 'a great authority on this matter' but his attitude was a good deal more practical and was a liberal or permissive one. Objectors 'need not go to the plays' and he recognized the futility of the House of Commons setting itself up as a guardian of either literature or morality.[51] Surprisingly perhaps, there is no sign that O'Connor had lost any of his taste for literature, or that his energy in his journalistic pursuits had diminished. On the contrary, he could still introduce novelties and his enthusiasm was reawakened in the new century in just the same way as his radicalism persisted and then found new expression.

Perhaps this was also helped by his domestic circumstances. Realization on both sides that the marriage had been a mistake occurred about 1898 and this might have been a relief and could have led to a more equable home life. For all his involvement in Society, it seems clear that O'Connor did not share his wife's concern for its more pretentious aspects, at least this is what Fyfe reports. There is a suggestion, for instance, that he was ready to attack the overall pretentiousness of someone such as Oscar Wilde, rather than any specific transgression. For a time Wilde even appeared to believe that he was being persecuted by O'Connor but there seems little sign of vindictiveness on O'Connor's part (and, perhaps realising this, by 1898 Wilde entertained the idea that O'Connor might publish *The Ballad of Reading Goal*, and write an introduction for it). Not all politicians who had matrimonial difficulties had to face publicity (Lloyd George kept his adventures quiet) and for the most part O'Connor did manage to keep his personal troubles out of the newspapers. But the Liverpool press on occasions could treat him like public property. The Liverpool *Porcupine*, as well as noticing that O'Connor could afford to hire Madame Patti 'to sing at his wife's "at homes"', also reported on O'Connor's bad temper at having to leave his club (he was a well established clubman by this time) to 'give his opinion on a passage in his wife's play'. By 1905 the same newspaper was wondering whether Mrs. O'Connor was going to return to the U.S.A.[52] O'Connor also had a friendship with a Mrs. Crawford (a Greek lady, widow of a Scotsman, so not, presumably, the Mrs. Crawford who had figured in Dilke's divorce) and this may have been

[51] *Hansard, 4,* 83, cols. 276, 287, 299, 289, 15 May 1900.

[52] Fyfe, p. 197; Rupert Hart-Davis (ed.), *Letters of Oscar Wilde,* pp. 328, 370-2, 662-3, 733; *Porcupine,* 6 Oct. 1900, *ibid.* 4 Aug. 1900, *ibid.,* 'Mrs. Tay Pay in a Quandary', 25 Nov. 1905. O'Connor was a member of the National Liberal, City Liberal, and Bath clubs (note in O'Connor's, *The Phantom Millions.* This was another pot boiler and examined the career of Madame Humbert).

entirely platonic. He figures in the gossip of Max Beerbohm as something of a *bon viveur* in company with the actress Evy Green in Dieppe; and asking Beerbohm not to tell his wife. Elizabeth O'Connor did stay with her husband for longer than Fyfe implies. Sometime in 1904 she can be found writing from Brighton to Edmund Downey that 'Tom is one of the best fellows in the world, but he is *human*, and I trust him accordingly'. She also wrote to Keary in August 1904 enquiring about a journal called *Chic*, which she proposed to edit, and announcing that she had been elected unanimously as President of the Society of Women Journalists, both posts probably deriving from O'Connor's influence.

A more complete separation came between 1905 and 1908 and O'Connor left the house in Chelsea (the house in Brighton was probably sold) and gave his wife an income, though not perhaps with complete regularity. After a few temporary arrangements, he moved into a flat in Morpeth Mansions in Victoria Street, Westminster, where he lived for the rest of his life. This clearing of the air and agreeing to differ, probably suited O'Connor and as a result there is perhaps a discernible change in O'Connor's attitude towards his affairs. Perhaps he had become more melancholic, indulged sometimes in self-pity, and entertained a passing mood of cynicism. But he managed to control his emotions, as he usually did, with a great deal of activity. One acquaintance of O'Connor's, J.J. Horgan, described the O'Connor household as one where feast or famine ruled (with, on one occasion a reception being held by Elizabeth O'Connor at the front while the bailiffs removed furniture at the back).[53] This has the ring of truth. O'Connor may sometimes have given the impression of ostentatious prosperity but he was not the comfortable wealthy man his political enemies liked to portray. Perhaps his daily routine calmed down slightly with the separation from his wife (when he may have obtained more of the domestic calm he had hoped for in marriage), but he was also diverted by the new journals. These entailed a lot of writing but less supervision than the Pearson establishment would have liked, so that difficulties and arguments began and can be seen in his correspondence with Keary from about

[53] Lancaster, *Brian Howard,* p. 316. There is also a reference here to O'Connor's being 'enamoured of a certain lady' (p.8) who may have been Mrs. Crawford; N.L.I., O'Connor-Downey correspondence, MS 10040, n.d. Mrs. O'Connor to Downey; N.L.I., O'Connor-Keary correspondence, MS 16839-40, Mrs. O'Connor to Keary, 29 Aug. 1904; Lancaster, *Brian Howard,* p.8, says that the separation came 'after twenty years' which would place it about 1905. O'Connor's last note from Oakley Lodge (to Dillon) is dated 6 Jan. 1907. Addresses of flats in central London follow in O'Connor's correspondence and he appears to have first written from Morpeth Mansions in May 1910 (Catalogue description of O'Connor correspondence in Dillon Papers, T.C.D.); J.J. Horgan, *Parnell to Pearse* (1948), pp. 152-3.

1904 onwards. In addition, at the end of 1904, he began discussions with Edmund Downey, who appears to have been a Pearson employee but who acted in this case in a private capacity, to start yet another journal, the *London Reader*. After some correspondence over an advertising campaign, it does not look as though this venture made much progress. More than this, O'Connor devoted an appreciable part of his time to lecture tours (where his subject was, predictably, usually something to do with parliament). This may have been a regular feature of his career but specific evidence only comes to light for the end of 1903 in letters to his tour agent, Gerald Christy, regarding bookings. Writing from Leeds at the end of 1903, he told Christy that he 'could not stand another trip to Liverpool', that he was tired of 'standing up'. The pace, and his other commitments, especially in politics, began to tell and O'Connor was seriously ill at the end of 1903, 'very near a dangerous collapse' as he wrote to Keary. He would have been well advised to cut down on his engagements for most of 1904.[54] If anything, O'Connor had become busier than ever since the turn of the century, so much so that it is doubtful whether his political colleagues were aware of any change in his circumstances, except for the better. Politics was where he became most active, where he found greater purpose and more reason for confidence.

Priority was given to Liverpool. As he had promised Dillon (though Dillon showed no great interest), O'Connor intended to deal with Harford, 'settle the fellow and his gang' at the following municipal elections and he characterized them as 'the Healys of Liverpool'. He went onto the offensive immediately in October 1900 as his letters to Dillon indicate. He blamed not only the Harford brothers and their principal supporter, J. O'Shea, but also Michael Conway, an ex-Parnellite M.P. whom he regarded as a particular centre for intrigue and discontent and who, nevertheless, had earlier asked O'Connor to help him become an organizer for the U.I.L. O'Connor also blamed the Diamond press (which published local variants of the *Catholic Herald*, including a Liverpool edition) and the *Leader*, both of which had, he claimed, been running a campaign against him, sometimes based on reports of bogus meetings. His objection is instructive. He told Dillon 'I detest these things – not

---

[54] O'Connor-Keary correspondence, MS 16839-40, O'Connor to Keary, 24 Feb. 1904; O'Connor-Downey correspondence, MS 10040, letters from O'Connor to Downey, 1903. Last mention of the *London Reader* appears to be in a letter of 22 Sept. 1903; N.L.I., O'Connor-Christy correspondence, MS 5381, O'Connor to Christy, 15 Nov. 1903. O'Connor was up and about by Monday 6 February but wrote that 'every time I attend a long sitting in the Commons I find myself bad again' (O'Connor to Keary, 10 Feb. 1904).

because I really mind attacks, as you know I am accustomed to it by this time – but because the *Herald* is one of the permanent sources of discord in Liverpool'.[55] For O'Connor to bring the matter up might be an indication that he was not immune from annoyance, but the real objection did appear to be the political consequences of the attacks – the *Herald* had influence with his constituents, the *Porcupine* did not. By the time O'Connor left Liverpool after the election, alternatives to the Harford group had been suggested for the local elections, though not with any great hopes. Plans to set up a new central body which would bring in Irishmen elected to public bodies other than the city Council, thereby putting Harford and his followers in a minority, were also agreed by O'Connor and a 'great public meeting'. However, it was not until a full year had passed that O'Connor could feel easier in his mind, and perhaps by then passions had begun to cool. In October 1901 O'Connor again visited Liverpool and the large meeting held on 5 October was obviously regarded as of some importance – this was the meeting dealt with at length by 'Brother Sam' in the Liverpool *Review* and it was noticed in *The Times* where it was described as convening the 'reunited branches of the U.I.L.'. This meeting approved the newly formed central organization and Harford was brought into line by agreeing (there was little else he could do) to work with the new structure. A shift of emphasis by O'Connor from Ireland to Liverpool was noticeable; so was O'Connor's continued, perhaps even augmented, support among ordinary voters (although he had the reputation of being arrogant or impatient with local politicians). As 'Brother Sam' remarked, bringing up a suspicion already touched on, which might though be groundless, 'Mr. O'Connor may be an astute man and an expert wire-puller, but on the platform the illusion (if there be any) is complete; there he is a patriot [sic] .... At the same time you feel that he understands you and your case, and sympathises with you and esteems you – such is the undefinable, instinctive regard which circulates unseen between persons whose natures are blest with that greatest of qualities, sympathy.'[56]

Much the same could be said of O'Connor's relations with the U.I.L.G.B. generally. O'Connor's correspondence with J.F.X. O'Brien did not increase. About the only routine work in which he did appear to take an interest was the appointment of officers. Conway wrote to him in the summer of 1902 withdrawing a further application,

[55] Dillon Papers, MS 6740-4, f. 94, O'Connor to Dillon, 28 Sept. 1900; *ibid.* f. 91, O'Connor to Dillon, 25 Sept.; *ibid.* f. 99, O'Connor to Dillon, 15 Oct.

[56] *The Times*, 7 Oct. 1901; 'Brother Sam', 'At the Feet of T.P.', Liverpool *Review*, 12 Oct. 1901.

this time for the secretaryship of the League, although this might not have been the end of his ambitions. O'Connor also appeared to push the prospects of a Mr. Byrne of Oldham – perhaps he kept on the lookout for talent – although it is not clear in this case what the outcome was. The General Secretary's post became vacant in 1903, probably through O'Brien's retirement and, once Conway was out of the way, perhaps it was largely O'Connor who was instrumental in having Joseph Devlin appointed as secretary in July 1903.[57] Devlin was to prove his ability and go on to become M.P. for Belfast West in 1906 – one of the few young recruits to the parliamentary party. In 1905 F.L. Crilly, from Merseyside, became General Secretary and kept the post for the remainder of the League's existence.

Conferences of the U.I.L.G.B. continued to go well from 1900 onwards, whatever interruptions there had been from Liverpool. O'Connor in his presidential addresses showed satisfaction about the improvement of party finances and what might be expected from the Liberals, so long as Irish unity was maintained. At the 1901 conference at Bristol attention was concentrated on the Boer war and in the public meeting afterwards O'Connor protested at increased taxation which meant that 'a mighty world-wide empire might rob a few thousand people in two small states of the liberties they had acquired by emigration'. O'Connor was recognized as a dangerous opponent of the government in this area and the morale of the Irish movement generally could only improve as the war dragged on into its final repressive stages. In 1902 the conference, held in Manchester, was celebratory and unremarkable. O'Connor praised efforts in registration and fund raising (the former largely in Britain, the latter in America), and again emphasized the need for unity. He also took the opportunity to warn the Liberals about the effect of Irish intervention in by-elections which, so he claimed, had caused the recent defeat of a Liberal Imperialist in North East Lanark and returned a Home Ruler for Bury.[58] What followed in 1903, when the conference met in

[57] J.F.X. O'Brien Papers, MS 13458, Conway to O'Connor, 8 May 1902. Conway had been an organizer for the I.N.L.G.B. in Lancashire before the Parnellite split and M.P. for North Leitrim until 1892. Opposition was not necessarily a bar to advancement, Harford became head of the central organization in Liverpool in 1903, a position he held until 1923; on Byrne see J.F.X. O'Brien Papers, MS 13432 (6), D. Boyle to O'Brien, 20 Sept. 1896, *ibid.* MS 13432 (6), O'Connor to O'Brien 21, 26 Dec. 1900. Boyle reported that Byrne drank too much. O'Connor appears to have left it to O'Brien to settle; for Devlin see O'Connor's remarks to Dillon that 'the more I see of Devlin the more confidence I have in his intelligence' (Dillon Papers, MS 6740-4, f. 129, 19 Dec. 1903); letter of acceptance by Crilly, J.F.X. O'Brien Papers, MS 13432, 13 Apr. 1905.

[58] *D.P.*, 27 May 1901; *ibid.* 19 May 1902. A motion was also passed against Irishmen joining the army or navy.

Liverpool, was a curiosity. Motions were put forward to exclude from the U.I.L.G.B. all those who were not Irish by birth, to keep out of the clubs 'low class Englishmen' who attended 'for the sake of drink'. This was a sort of parallel to O'Connor's new found interest in Liverpool, the League suddenly realizing how acclimatized it was to Britain and, in this case, reacting against it. It was a fact that the 'Irish' community contained a majority who were not Irish-born (and this change may have taken place as early as 1891). Irish-born among the League officers might also have felt threatened by 1903, although they were still in fact very much in control. But O'Connor could not give way to these fears and objections. The League, he said, should accept 'gentlemen who . . . if they were not Irishmen themselves, had Irish connections'. An additional factor, one which was not touched on, was that some of them might be voters. Feeling in some quarters must have been strong, particularly about the no doubt symbolic issue of drink in the clubs, because the matter was raised again by a number of branches in the conference of 1904 when O'Connor himself perhaps felt obliged to talk of 'low Englishmen who indulged in betting and drinking'. It may have been because he was a teetotaller himself that he 'regretted that he could not take up an extreme temperance attitude' but a fine compromise was reached when O'Connor proposed that no new branches should allow drink, and this was accepted.[59]

But in 1904 and 1905, with the approach of a general election, the attention of the conferences was far more on national politics and they looked forward to the use of the Irish vote. Here, in 1904, O'Connor had to deal with rebellious branches, such as those in Lewisham and in Gateshead, which voted against Liberal candidates whom they suspected of being unfavourably inclined towards Catholic education. O'Connor doubted whether this was a good way to defend their faith, but was otherwise surprisingly mild in his comments, as he was in the conference held at Finsbury in June 1905, the final conference before the election. At this conference he appeared to favour negotiation being left to local leaders and he spent more time on giving an account of the Irish vote, stressing (as was the case) that in some areas it could have a 'dominating influence', and once again he talked of the benefit of a 'weak' Conservative government.[60] Perhaps he thought that circumstances required the application of a velvet glove, or he may have drawn a lesson from the 1885 election, or Liverpool in 1900, and

[59]*Ibid.* 1 June 1903; *ibid.* 23 May 1904. Some such change was clear to commentators. See the article, 'The London Irish', *Blackwood's Magazine,* 170 (July 1901), 124-34, *passim.*

[60]*D.P.,* 23 May 1904; *ibid.* 12 June 1905.

it may have been the wrong one, unsuited to the circumstances of 1906. The religious-education issue was the only serious difficulty O'Connor faced in these years. But though he might look forward to the election with confidence he still had to weigh up the impact of the Church and, to a lesser extent, Labour, and then decide what could be expected overall from the Liberals. The decision made in 1905 had its roots in matters that went back to 1900 at least. The more the decision is examined the more difficult it is seen to be and the more it can be said that, partly through O'Connor's influence, the decision arrived at was lacking in imagination, possibly fatally incorrect.

Religion and education had proved a difficulty since 1895. Even in the 1900 election, although receiving some assistance from priests in Liverpool, O'Connor may have lost some support because of the education issue. Elsewhere he tried to deal with demands coming principally from the bishops of Nottingham and of Salford that Catholics should vote Conservative when instead he put the emphasis on Home Rule. Contradicting bishops was a dangerous business but O'Connor 'had no hesitation in saying that the Bishop [of Nottingham] was wrong' while in the case of Salford he went to the length of issuing a special manifesto to the Irish voters of Manchester and Salford calling for 'Home Rule and Home Rule alone'. A similar manifesto was issued in the Gateshead by-election in 1904 when O'Connor asked the voters 'are you for Ireland or against Ireland?'[61]

The difficulty increased as a result of Balfour's Education Act of 1902 which, like the abortive proposals of 1896 but this time on a larger scale, proposed to fund voluntary schools within a national education system. Catholic spokesmen, especially Cardinal Vaughan, demanded the assistance of Irish M.P.s and O'Connor, as before, tried to draw attention to the complexity of the issues and the disadvantages experienced by Catholics in Britain and he did this immediately the Bill was introduced in March. It was left to Dillon to speak at greater length during the second reading. Despite this concern it proved difficult to satisfy Catholic opinion. The *Tablet* described the Irish M.P.s support for an amendment which would allow public support for any school where a religious test was not applied as 'perfect madness' and 'raving lunacy' (even though the alternative appeared to be no funds). O'Connor was perhaps more aware than Dillon of the urgency of the problem since it directly affected his own constituents and the fortunes of the Irish in Britain. Perhaps Dillon was given precedence because O'Connor was identified

---

[61]*Ibid.* 4 Oct. 1900; *ibid.* 2 Oct.; N.L.I. Redmond Papers, copy of manifesto of Devlin and O'Connor to the Gateshead electors, 15 Jan. 1904.

as too much of a radical. Where this issue was concerned O'Connor had always concentrated on social justice and he had always been interested in education. Faith received less priority. In face of continued dissatisfaction and ingratitude O'Connor became exasperated and wrote to Dillon in September suggesting that they attend no further debates on the Bill. He took the same abstentionist line at the League conference which followed in 1903 where, although he expressed 'strong remarks' against priests hostile to Home Rule, he also opposed the proposal for an enquiry into 'the hostile attitude of the clergy in certain districts', winning over his audience by suggesting that 'there were certain things which wise politicians did their best to ignore (laughter and hear hear)'.[62] While the U.I.L.G.B. conference, composed of full time nationalists, might be hostile to Church attitudes, O'Connor must have known that this was not representative of all Irish opinion throughout Britain, and the defeats of Liberals in by-elections (at Gateshead and at Lewisham) to some extent justified his caution. In such a case the best policy was to ignore as much as possible and say as little as necessary and this was the policy pursued until Home Rule prospects improved in 1905.

A waiting game was sensible because it soon became clearer that the Unionist government's days were numbered (even though it survived for longer than was anticipated). Balfour's reforms, such as the Education Act, might have been of benefit to the nation but they did not pull his party together. A similar comment could be made about Irish land reform. George Wyndham, who had become Irish Secretary in 1900, introduced his land purchase proposals in March 1903, after a land conference which had met in the autumn of 1902. To Dillon especially, this more comprehensive reform, which went a long way towards settling the problem of the land by introducing peasant proprietorship on a large scale, was still something to treat with suspicion. At the time the Irish party, including O'Connor, gave the land proposals a rough ride even though in O'Connor's case, and paradoxically, they substantiated his argument that much could be gained from a reforming Conservative ministry – a claim he made on numerous occasions up to 1905. So grudging was the reception that this led to a break with William O'Brien who left the party in November 1903 and then became as isolated as Healy. O'Brien particularly accused O'Connor of hypocrisy, of shedding 'tears of ink' when Wyndham was finally broken by Ulster Unionist opposition to his devolution proposals in 1904 and 1905. Although O'Connor originated the phrase 'devolution is the Latin for Home Rule', co-

[62]*Hansard, 4,* 105, col. 951, 24 Mar. 1902; *Tablet,* 12 July 1902; Dillon Papers, MS 6740-4, f. 123, O'Connor to Dillon 15 Sept. 1902; *D.P.,* 1 June 1903.

operating with the Conservatives had proved difficult in practice and the devolution dispute had shown that some parts of the Irish problem were intractable.[63] Taken with the tariff reform crisis precipitated in the Unionist ranks by Chamberlain from 1903 onwards, it was a sign that the Unionist hegemony was beginning to crack. This was what was important to the Irish; to O'Connor it may have seemed that they could not lose and that even if the Unionists' opposition continued after the election, further reforms would come. It might also be that support for a weak Conservative administration was half intended as a ploy to disguise Irish intentions and to threaten the Liberals; in practice though, all the overtures were made towards the Liberals.

Liberal attitudes towards the Irish and to Home Rule remained unresolved until late in the day. Campbell-Bannerman was popular with the Irish both because of his easy-going exterior and his underlying toughness (shown in his unrelenting opposition to the Boer War) and Herbert Gladstone, the chief whip, could be relied upon to continue the policy of his father. Along with Morley, they had to be singled out by O'Connor as worthy of support against the equally influential Liberal Imperialist circle around Rosebery which included Asquith, Haldane and Grey. Continuing Liberal divisions were one reason why the Unionists were able to hang on to power. Added to which the Irish sometimes had to put more bite into their co-operation with the Liberal opposition. While the Irish abstained on the second reading of the Education Act for their own reasons, O'Connor was not above making this appear a *quid pro quo* for Liberal support against further Irish coercion, and he wrote to both Campbell-Bannerman and Morley to this effect in October 1902. By-election results also played their customary part. By 1905 the Liberals, in something like a re-run of the 'flowing tide' up to 1892, were to gain 24 seats in by-elections. But throughout these years, while the Liberals were so uncertain and had not, since 1900, had the formal support of the Irish vote, it was possible to suggest that their success could be advanced even further not only over the education issue where, as in Lewisham and Gateshead in 1903 and 1904 Liberal non-conformists could prove unpopular, but also where the Liberal was lukewarm over Home Rule. In a by-election victory in North Leeds in July 1902 for instance, O'Connor could say that the gradualist or 'step by step' policy towards Home Rule advocated by the Liberal victor, R.H.

[63] William O'Brien, *The Irish Revolution* (1923), p. 27. Anthony MacDonnell, the Permanent Under Secretary, had attended Queens College, Galway at the same time as O'Connor (Fyfe, p. 215); M. Macdonagh, *William O'Brien* (1928), p. 170.

Barran, would 'play the deuce, not only at Leeds but elsewhere'.[64] On other occasions, where the Liberal candidate was a staunch Home Ruler, O'Connor could pledge full support, as he did for 'Loulou' Harcourt in January 1904. Herbert Gladstone, for one, had always taken the Irish vote seriously, estimating that it had an influence in over 130 British seats and could help the Liberals to win 40 seats in addition to those already held with Irish assistance.[65] In drawing together Liberal electoral forces after their long years of discordance, and while coming to an agreement with the infant Labour Representation Committee in 1903, Gladstone and Campbell-Bannerman must also have been aware of the importance of the Irish factor, especially as it was generally believed (with the exception of O'Connor on one, perhaps unusual, occasion) that the general election verdict would be a close one.

But while O'Connor must also have been aware of the many imponderables in deciding electoral strategy and in determining relations with the Liberals, more was involved than calculation. By now co-operation with the Liberals had about it a sense of inevitability, derived in O'Connor's case from his long friendships with some Liberal leaders, and his own share of liberal views; it had become a habit of mind. At the same time, he did keep options open to a surprisingly large extent in his dealings with the League, the Church, and the Conservatives. Possibly his subtlety here has been overlooked precisely because he was by now such an accomplished politician and did not advertise the fact. Healy believed at this time (1902) that 'T.P. seems chiefly to inspire the tactics of the party' and, allowing for some exaggeration, Healy may have been correct.[66] O'Connor could defer to Dillon and could even write to him, as he did in December 1903, admitting a naivety in parliamentary matters. But this was probably the result of self-depreciation and the care, later tact, with which he approached Dillon's considerable intellectual integrity and lack of compromise. He also wrote this when he was on the verge of grave

[64] For the development of Liberal policy see McCready, loc. cit; B.L., Campbell-Bannerman Papers, Add., MS 41237, f. 47, O'Connor to Campbell-Bannerman, marked 'private and confidential', 18 July 1902; ibid. MS 41223, f. 101, O'Connor to Morley, 25 Oct. 1902; ibid. MS 41216, f. 23, Campbell-Bannerman reporting a conversation with O'Connor to Herbert Gladstone, 18 July 1902.

[65] Bodleian Library, Harcourt Papers, dep. 437, fol. 64, O'Connor to Harcourt, 26 Jan. 1904; Viscount Gladstone Papers, Add. MS 46107, ff. 28-35 lists seats influenced by the Irish vote. This is undated but appears to have been first compiled before the election of 1895. McCready, loc. cit. 338 does not appear to have made enough allowance for two member seats in his total tally. Bryce's estimate was lower and put the total in addition to those already held at ten to twenty seats.

[66] Healy to his brother, 26 July 1902, Letters, ii, 459; Dillon Papers, MS 6740-4, f. 129, O'Connor to Dillon, 19 Dec. 1903.

illness and near collapse. The innocence he confessed to was, more accurately, to do with the electoral strategy of the party, about which he observed to Dillon; 'All that we can definitely know is that there is a big majority and a big minority and that in the uncertainty of the future we can only go on that fact. This means of course that we ought to support the Liberals. This policy will not be accepted without difficulties.'[67]

O'Connor may have learnt his lesson about being too definite in the election of 1885 and the 'difficulties' and the 'uncertainty' were apparent but, equally, his somewhat opaque phraseology (opaque at least after the passage of time) may have had a more definite purpose. There is a suggestion of O'Connor introducing the theme that he personally wanted to follow in the election, namely, to support the Liberals. And it was not as though Dillon, who was not so concerned about the Liberals as O'Connor, had any alternative. It is true that by October 1905 Dillon suggested that the vote ought to go to Labour except where the Liberal candidate was, in the words of Dillon's biographer, 'an old and tried friend of the Irish cause' but this was merely a gesture, interpreted liberally and resulted in only seven Labour candidates in the election being supported against Liberals.[68]

Support for Labour might have been a way of making more of the fluid circumstances leading up to the 1906 election, using Irish pressure to more effect, and it might have been supposed that O'Connor more than anyone else in the Irish party would have been sympathetic. It was not as though the idea was a new one. Davitt had suggested such support in the 1880s and O'Connor had then, before the 1885 election, followed such a policy himself. But some of the difficulties and second thoughts have been noted. Apart from the special circumstances existing in the elections of 1885 and 1886, O'Connor had then, in his *Star* days, largely followed the Liberal line. The British League had rejected proposals from J.G. Taggart in 1891 that Labour should be supported. O'Connor had himself intervened to put down Sexton's 'Bootle Rebellion' in 1890, and then, consistently through the 1890s, the British League had proved unsympathetic to Labour candidates in by-elections. O'Connor himself had for a long time been strangely aloof from labour disputes, even those affecting seamen and dockers in his own constituency (for instance a Liverpool seamen's strike in 1889 and a dock strike in 1889-90). Latterly, perhaps as part of strengthening his ties with Liverpool, he had been

[67] Dillon Papers, MS 6740-4, f. 129, O'Connor to Dillon, 19 Dec. 1903, cited also in Lyons, *Dillon*, p. 244.

[68] Lyons, *Dillon*, p. 279.

more active. In parliament he supported Sexton's campaign to have dock workers brought under the protection of the Factory and Workshop Acts. Although Archibald Salvidge, the Liverpool Conservative leader had also helped, it was O'Connor who apparently did more to make the campaign a success and the dock workers' union showed its appreciation by presenting O'Connor with a gift and an address of thanks when he visited Liverpool in October 1901. Sexton later was on close terms with O'Connor but still saw him as something of an old political hand, able to 'convince the rank and file of any movement that they were the real authors of any plan he put forward'. Even in 1906 when Sexton fought a Liverpool seat for Labour he found it difficult to obtain U.I.L.G.B. support and many Catholic voters were League supporters first, and only then swayed by the politics of economics.[69]

Lack of support for Labour continued to be the rule and, though it might be supposed that Labour's electoral agreement with Herbert Gladstone had solved the matter, this was clearly not so as far as Labour's relations with the Irish were concerned, especially not in by-elections. Here too O'Connor went to some lengths to keep the Irish vote uncommitted. At the end of 1904 in the sensitive Lancashire seat of Accrington where Labour (in addition to independent socialists) was making a great effort, O'Connor visited the constituency and one of his speeches was printed separately as a pamphlet of advice to voters for the forthcoming general election. In essence, the printed speech was the clearest indication to date of a refusal to help Labour although in presentation it was disingenuous, being prefaced with fulsome and probably sincere sympathy for Labour. A distinction made between the 'English working classes' and the Irish in Britain was merely one argument in the speech which Labour supporters might have been unable to stomach. Slightly earlier in the year O'Connor had been even more antagonistic in his opposition to Labour candidates in the old testing round of North East Lanark, saying that the Irish would not let 'the grass grow under their feet' while the Labour party was 'growing towards strength and power'. Despite Hardie's newspaper whistling to keep its spirits up and declaring that 'almost for the first time the Irish organization looks foolish', Labour was to find that the League, and nationalist sympathy among Irish voters, were more formidable obstacles than they might have appeared at first sight and this was only the beginning of

[69] For the background see E. L. Taplin, *Liverpool Dockers and Seamen, 1870-1890; Hansard,* 4, 95, col. 142, 11 June 1902; S. Salvidge, *Salvidge of Liverpool,* p. 43; *The Times,* 7 Oct. 1901; Sexton, *Sir James Sexton,* pp. 80, 192, 196.

disagreements between the two movements which were to last up to 1914.[70]

In every respect the place of Labour was not so dangerous a difficulty as the religious-education issue and the attitude in this taken up by the Liberals. There was time to let these matters mature in 1904. This was fortunate for the Irish because their leadership was weakened by the resignation of William O'Brien, the illness of Edward Blake, the absence on convalescence of Dillon for most of the session, and O'Connor's illness at the beginning of the year. The dog-days of the Unionist government did still allow O'Connor to write a series of biographical sketches on political figures for *Everybody's Magazine,* including studies of Balfour and Salisbury, but otherwise there was time to look to the future. O'Connor was left with Redmond. The latter had opposed the Liberals in 1900 and it would have been in the Parnellite tradition to, at the least, drive a hard bargain. But by now Redmond was far more amenable and Herbert Gladstone reported to Campbell-Bannerman as early as February and May 1905 that Redmond saw that the Liberal leadership could not put forward a specific policy which could be given to Irish voters as justification for support. Redmond may have been influenced by O'Connor. Certainly it was due to O'Connor's initiative that he and Redmond (described as a 'friend') met Campbell-Bannerman over a working breakfast on 24 November, shortly before the Liberal leader took up the challenge set by Balfour by agreeing to form a caretaker government. At this notorious meeting the terms for Irish support were agreed upon. Campbell-Bannerman admitted that a commitment to a full Home Rule Bill in the next parliament was not possible but did hold out the strong possibility of a measure which would be 'consistent with and leading up to' Home Rule. He also promised to restrain the more revisionist supporters of Asquith. It is fair to emphasize that what had occurred was that the Liberal party had shifted from the Gladstonian pledge of a Bill to a 'step by step' policy and this had been publicized in Campbell-Bannerman's speech at Stirling on 23 November.[71] However, even this was opposed by Rosebery in his speech at Bodmin on 25 November. There would be no help for the

[70] N. L. I. Pamphlet collection, I 94109, U.I.L.G.B. Leaflets, no. 8 *Speech delivered by Mr. T.P. O'Connor at Accrington on October 27th 1904; Glasgow Star,* 6 Aug. 1904, *Labour Leader,* 13 Aug. 1904. The speech at Accrington was the one recorded occasion when O'Connor predicted a great Liberal victory, which seems paradoxical in view of his simultaneous reserve towards Labour.

[71] For the *Everybody's* articles see the bibliography; Campbell-Bannerman Papers, Add. MS 41217, f. 221, Gladstone to Campbell-Bannerman, 26 May 1905; for a description of the working breakfast see O'Connor, *Campbell-Bannerman* (1908), pp. 72-5; McCready, *loc. cit.* 341.

Irish there, while Campbell-Bannerman did have the support of Asquith and Grey for his proposal. All that the Irish seemed able to do was to rely on Campbell-Bannerman. Their trust was not entirely misplaced but it is possible to see that an opportunity to exert greater pressure was lost and this inability to assert themselves was to be the first example of an enduring weakness of the Irish party in its relations with the Liberals in the years to follow. For all O'Connor's awareness of the uncertainties of electoral calculations, the decision appears to have rested, too, on the widespread belief that the result would be a close one. The Liberal landslide left the reasoning behind the decision to a large extent redundant and the Irish could not begin to exert effective pressure again until 1910. Redmond might have been more demanding. But to O'Connor, who had perhaps sometimes been excessive in his understanding of the Liberals, it was a minor triumph. He had come through the searing and ennervating experiences which had lasted since the fall of Parnell, overcome that disorientation and with some determination seen a natural order restored. Failure to pursue the Liberals in 1894 might have been a mistake but O'Connor's courage remained undimmed. Whether his persistence would prove justified was now to be put to the test but he and the Irish movement in 1905 had every reason for feeling optimistic again.

5

HOME RULE, ULSTER, LAST APPEARANCES, 1906-14

For all the doubts about O'Connor as a politician, such as Parnell's early hints about his limitations and the doubts expressed in his own correspondence with Dillon, the period after the great Liberal victory of 1906 put him in the forefront of the Irish leadership and his influence had never been greater. The faults he was perhaps too ready to admit did not, in practice, inhibit him in his relations with the Liberal government and he was for all of this period, whatever the reservations of his critics, the chief link between the Liberals and the Irish party. It may well be true that he quite properly left the ultimate responsibility with Redmond and Dillon, the Irish leaders from Ireland – and the distinction he could make between Ireland and the Irish in Britain became more noticeable from here on. But lack of power in his own party and lack of ability were not the real problems or the major difficulty. All politicians lack ability somewhere, it is why they resort to what is possible. Perhaps the Irish leadership was too old and set in its ways – but this applied less to O'Connor than to other Irish leaders. The problems themselves were what tested O'Connor's ingenuity and taxed his patience. These were two-fold; to preside (as he virtually did) over the progressive 'alliance' of Liberals, Labour and Irish and keep them more or less united and, more important, to keep Home Rule in the forefront of the Liberals' mind and finally pass it through parliament. In both O'Connor succeeded. His encouragement and occasional orchestration of the anti-Unionist alliance was, along with the undoubted self-interest that kept the parties together, more than adequate although it came in for increasing condemnation first from Labour and then from the new forces of nationalism in Ireland. So far as the latter was concerned, O'Connor was all confidence, unperturbed by visionaries in politics, somewhat contemptuous of them. Home Rule, too, was passed through both the Commons and the Lords and that, given the obstacles, was a monument to political skill among all supporters of the government. For a man entering into his sixties the achievement was considerable and showed his great reserves of courage and, in some ways, imagination. This was especially so because his work in journalism did not diminish; if anything in these years his experience, his fertile memory, and his wide reading (often brought together at excessive length in his reviewing), along with a few grey hairs, turned him into something of an oracle in public affairs and, at any rate so he hoped, in the world of letters. His energy did not diminish; there were three trips to raise funds in the United States and Canada, the work of the U.I.L.G.B. (though mostly still confined to his presidential address), by-elections, attendance at crucial and sometimes peculiar debates in parliament and, as always, new schemes for magazines. Yet all this did take its toll. There is more than a suggestion of his increasing pessimism, the same old struggle to finance his outwardly well-appointed style of life. Past disappointments were only part of the reason, there were more than enough new developments in politics to cause concern and impatience. For all his appreciation of the difficulties of keeping popular forces together, serious unrest in the ranks of labour took him largely by surprise when this occurred both in his own constituency and in Ireland. Of newer nationalism he remained more ignorant, and continued to be more dismissive than Redmond and Dillon, the leaders who had kept roots in Ireland. Such scepticism was perhaps justified up to 1914, or perhaps even later, and it was a mark of his being more and more the British politician. But finally there was the parliamentary victory for Home Rule which turned out to be pyrrhic and where O'Connor totally underestimated the force of Unionism and, the other side of the coin, was betrayed by his natural belief in the efficacy and supremacy of parliament. O'Connor's career now partook of the puzzle of the Edwardian age; optimism, positiveness on the one hand, the forces of uncomprehending idealism and chaos on the other. To begin with, in 1906, O'Connor was faced with the problem of the Liberals' enormous majority and even when the Irish became more obviously effective, after the elections of 1910, the difficulties with his Liberal ally did not diminish. Throughout it all, O'Connor persisted, fired often with his old sense of righteousness, to be left in 1914, more disconcerted but still not without hope.

Testing the Liberals, 1905-9

O'Connor conducted the 1906 election campaign from Liverpool, a lesson he may have learned from the previous election. There was no suggestion now of his being more useful in Ireland or being needed to suppress faction. With his League officers, especially F.L. Crilly and now including Austin Harford, he controlled the use of the vote throughout Britain. Partly through greater attentiveness, but mostly because of the context given by the Liberal landslide, his own contest was a greater success than he might have anticipated, more completely successful than any previous campaign in Scotland division, including that of 1885, though O'Connor was by now less than enthusiastic about electioneering. In the case of the Liberals the success was greater than he would have wished. Unionist opposition to O'Connor had not changed in character since 1900 though it was less self-assured and more strident in this election. O'Connor's opponent, A.A. Tobin, was a barrister and a local man who had taken over the contest with O'Connor from F.E. Smith, who had himself been nursing the constituency with little success since 1904.[1] Routine electioneering stuff asserted that Tobin would 'wrest Scotland division from the enfeebled grasp of T.P. O'Connor'. Then, once the close co-operation, the 'secret bargain', between the Liberals and the Irish became clear, it was described as a plan 'to hand over the destinies of the north of Ireland to a disloyal and recalcitrent rabble. . . an implacable and anti-English band of disguised rebels'.[2] Then, too, there followed the usual complaints, that O'Connor neglected his constituency and neglected Catholic schools. O'Connor brushed most of this aside. On at least three occasions he observed that Scotland division was fought by Unionists anxious to be rewarded for their effort by promotion in the legal profession, a charge that was treated with some impatience by the Unionists, probably because it was correct. Tobin was also of Irish extraction but this did him no good because, according to O'Connor 'if in some prehistoric period in the history of Ireland [Tobin] had some ancestors located there (laughter and applause). . . why was he not on the Irish side?' As for Tobin's plans for Catholic schools, O'Connor took it for granted that the Unionist was therefore 'a weekly communicant and president of the St. Vincent de Paul Society'. Tory fears for Catholic schools cut no ice in Liverpool, had less effect than in 1895 or 1900, when it was evident that the most vociferous support for Tobin came from Orangemen. O'Connor's confidence in Liverpool was justified. He more than trebled his majority and there were the customary festivities when he was returned, viewed with distaste by the Liverpool *Porcupine.*[3]

More generally, outside Liverpool, the campaign proved un-complicated and beneficial. On the schools issue O'Connor appeared

[1] William Camp, *The Glittering Prizes* (1960), pp. 37-8; Earl of Birkenhead, *F.E., the Life of F.E. Smith, First Earl of Birkenhead* (1933, rev.ed., 1959), pp. 166-8; Salvidge, *Salvidge of Liverpool,* p. 62, citing Smith to Salvidge, 12 Jan. 1905 where Smith suggested Tobin as a candidate. Smith went on to fight Liverpool Walton division and sat for that constituency for most of the rest of his career.

[2] 'Tobin for Scotland', *Porcupine,* 23 Nov. 1905; *ibid.* 'Tay Pay Under the Liberals', 6 Jan. 1906.

[3] *D.P.,* 3 Jan.; 'T.P.s Chestnuts', *Porcupine,* 9 Dec.; *D.P.,* 8, 13 Jan. In the latter case he listed his opponents over the years; *D.P.,* 8 Jan.; 'T.P. as King Mob', *Porcupine,* 20 Jan.

to have had more qualms than he had admitted in the Liverpool election. Writing to Redmond in October he had gone so far as to describe the 'English priests' as 'hopeless', had anticipated great opposition from them and had 'given up all hope of reasoning with them'. Even after the election, at the end of January 1906 when the Liberal Education Bill was in prospect, he wrote again to Redmond that Archbishop Bourne of Westminster, the successor to Cardinal Vaughan as chief Catholic spokesman, would certainly be an opponent and that he (O'Connor) was 'not trusted by him', a judgement that turned out to be over-cautious.[4] During the election, despite the reservations of some leading English Catholics and despite real fears of what the Liberals might do to the 1902 Act, no Catholic vote against the Liberals materialized. In the League manifesto issued by Redmond and O'Connor in London and covered by the press on 1 January, the Irish party was presented as the champion of Catholic education but the matter was not given prominence. In the Liverpool contest, apart from his dismissal of Tobin, O'Connor felt able to reassure the voters about Liberal intentions when he campaigned in support of R.R. Cherry (a barrister shortly to be promoted) in Liverpool Exchange. According to O'Connor 'the Liberal government [were their] best friends who would suport the Roman Catholic schools and would assist the Irish party to secure educational advantages for Ireland which had been denied them by the Conservatives'.[5] This was a large claim and the Liberals', and Cherry's, lack of enthusiasm on this score was to make O'Connor's electoral task more difficult in future. But, in general, promises about the Liberals appeared to be less important to most Catholic voters than hopes for Home Rule and there was no disruption of the Irish vote during the election.

Labour did not prove a difficulty. While the election was remarkable for the emergence of a Labour vote, the Irish vote re-emerged equally strongly, so much so that it is perhaps possible to discern some Catholic suspicion of 'socialists' and some reluctance to vote for Labour candidates even where there was a straight fight with a Unionist. Such was the case in Ince and in Manchester North East (where the Labour candidate, J.R. Clynes, was himself of Irish extraction). In contrast, and more typically, O'Connor and the

[4]Redmond Papers, O'Connor to Redmond, 25 Oct. 1905; *ibid.* O'Connor to Redmond, 26 Jan. 1906.

[5]*D.P.*, 8 Jan. 1906. For the Catholic issue in 1906 see also A.K. Russell, *Liberal Landslide, the General Election of 1906* (1973), pp. 187-9.

League made something of a display of sympathy for Labour.[6] This followed on from Dillon's suggestion to Redmond. O'Connor's manifesto appeared to go further in claiming the Irish had always been 'steady and consistent supporters of the claims of labour' and it promised support 'in all areas where the Labour candidate is sound on the question of Home Rule'. This seemed a considerable advance on Dillon's proposal except that the manifesto immediately added that any Liberal who was an 'old and trusted friend of the Irish' would be supported and that the Labour candidate could not be supported where 'it would assure the return of the Unionist candidate'. Labour was right to be sceptical; it was, as the *Labour Leader* said, a case of 'thank you for nothing when we get down to details'. O'Connor here, as in his advice following the disagreements in the Accrington constituency in 1904, showed a preoccupation with Labour which may have mirrored the mingled apprehension and generalized good wishes felt for the new political force among both Irish leaders and Irish voters. The manifesto of 1906 had come after a further meeting between Campbell-Bannerman and O'Connor, which increased Irish commitment to the Liberals. At about the same time Keir Hardie had made his second bid for an alliance between the Labour party and the U.I.L.G.B., a union which he thought would 'dominate the political situation' in industrial areas during elections. This was dismissed because Redmond did not share Hardie's belief that the Liberals were on the point of disintegration.[7] The upshot was that only twenty Labour candidates were supported by the League and thirteen of these were in straight fights, probably also covered by the 1903 agreement between the Liberals and the L.R.C. Irish voters in Britain supported 168 Liberals and must have contributed particularly to the 46 Liberal gains in the north of England and Scotland. Overall, the final result showed the Liberals with an unprecedented 400 seats, the Unionists with 157, the Nationalists with 83 and Labour with 30.[8]

Put crudely, the overwhelming Liberal victory was a disadvantage to the Irish since they could no longer put pressure on the Liberals so easily. Neither O'Connor nor the other Irish leaders expressed it quite so bluntly. Immediately in 1906 co-operation between the Irish, the Liberals and Labour was genuine; any doubts about the Liberals

[6] Catholic and Irish attitudes to Labour are referred to in P.F. Clarke, *Lancashire and the New Liberalism*, pp. 253-4. Clarke suggests that such reservations were rare and that more typical was James Sexton's straight fight in Liverpool Toxteth against the Unionist. Sexton was unsuccessful.

[7] Manifesto of U.I.L.G.B., *D.P.*, 1 Jan.; *Labour Leader*, 5 Jan.; Redmond Papers, Hardie to Redmond, 11 Nov., 26 Dec.

[8] Russell, *Liberal Landslide*, p. 193.

would take some time to work out. Even then O'Connor had fewer doubts than Redmond or Dillon, or isolated rebellious spirits such as William O'Brien, who later was to claim that the Irish had given away their bargaining power and yet had received no guarantees on Home Rule. O'Connor's manifesto, apart from its concern for Labour, had blamed the Unionists for always using the 'Irish bogey' which had 'succeeded in inflicting enormous injuries on the people of Great Britain [by] a monstrous programme of subordinating all British political issues to the anti-Irish campaign'.[9] A cynic might see something odd in this coming from an organization whose sole purpose was to exert pressure to win Home Rule. Such an emphasis was an attempt to disarm criticism and it reflects an impatience to be found within the progressive 'alliance' with the old politics. It was as though O'Connor at least wanted to be seen subordinating the old demands of the Irish electorate, but it also shows perhaps a wider interest in British issues and a genuine sympathy with the new forces of radicalism which the election had revealed. O'Connor in particular, once more observing the House of Commons, celebrated the advent of the new Labour party in his journal *M.A.P.* When it came to the League conference of that year, which was held in Manchester in June, the Irish vote, having done its work more effectively than at any other time, including the election of 1885, was soft-pedalled. O'Connor admitted that in some parts of the country and in some circumstances the vote could be effective but attributed the election victory to 'a strong tide of British feeling which swept all before it'.[10] Once again, part of this might have been calculation, but it also represented O'Connor's satisfaction with the clean sweep made of the Unionists. Another source of satisfaction was seen in his founding of a new journal, *P.T.O.*, also in June 1906 and less than a fortnight after the League conference. Although he was now fifty-eight, and gave the impression of greater age by suggesting that he had seen it all before, the new radical parliament represented his own sentiments to an extent that perhaps no previous parliament had done. Trouble would come over details of who was to be given priority. In this invigorating atmosphere O'Connor could see disagreement merely as a matter of detail (although this then became an argument he was to use continually up to 1914). But difficulties soon arose, over education in 1906, and over devolution policy in 1907 which was to result in the ill-fated Irish Council Bill.

Education and its political overtones caused O'Connor more difficulty than devolutionist proposals which is perhaps another,

[9]O'Brien, *Irish Revolution*, p. 35; *D.P.,* 1 Jan.
[10]*M.A.P.,* 10, 17 Mar.; *D.P.,* 4 Jan. 1906.

slight, sign that his attention was turning to British domestic issues. As quickly as possible in the 1906 session the Liberals introduced an Education Bill which, as anticipated, was a counterblast to the Act of 1902. This had been one of the main promises of the election campaign and, as Augustine Birrell the engaging education minister remembered it, 'the non-conformists were as happy as they were on the day of Queen Anne's death'. In such circumstances it was clear that the Irish could not support the Liberals, while at the same time they could not afford to antagonize their allies and give support to the Unionists at the very beginning of the new parliament. Both Dillon and O'Connor therefore intervened and spoke at length on the second reading of the Bill in May, though once again to explain their difficulties to the Liberal backbenchers and to try and moderate the Bill's effect on Catholic schools. O'Connor spoke before Dillon, as it was proper he should with a constituency interest at stake. Dillon dealt more with abstractions, the principle involved, and at one stage was forthright enough to declare his preference for an efficient education system over a 'Bible' education. While O'Connor undoubtedly shared these views, he could not afford to be so forthright; as it was he was regarded by the Church authorities as far less of a respectable figure than Dillon. Instead O'Connor stressed, again, the social interest of the Irish in Britain who, he said, in the Famine years 'brought no money with them, no education in their heads, no training even of their hands'. He also emphasized that Catholic feeling in Britain had never been 'so deeply stirred as at this moment'. Possibly few members made so many references to their constituency as O'Connor was to do in the new century although, as events were to show, perhaps he did not make enough. He was also fully aware of the political implications and revealed them in his speech, asserting, for instance, that there was 'no spirit of partisanship as between the two parties' over religious education, a laudable sentiment which both sides of the Commons would agree with in public and one which, if it had been true, would have made O'Connor's task a lot easier. He gave full credit to the Liverpool education authorities and always continued to do so, even though the Liverpool Conservatives used his difficulties here as a political weapon during elections. Other local authorities were condemned for their 'pig headed obstinacy' and 'denominational bigotry'.[11] The Liberals were unimpressed, the Unionists saw the issue as too good an opportunity to miss. The Bill was one of the first to be blocked by the Lords and became a dead letter. But the problem did not go away. The

[11] Augustine Birrell, *Things Past Redress* (1937), p. 184; Lyons, *Dillon*, p. 285; *Hansard, 4,* 156, cols. 1047, 1041, 1046, 7 May.

Catholic authorities under Bourne had been sympathetic and O'Connor's worst fears had not been realised, but this patience could be strained and the political difficulties increased in the years that followed.

Devolution proposals created more of an immediate crisis but the record appears to indicate that this was less of an immediate concern to O'Connor. As early as the King's speech in 1906 the Irish, especially Dillon, had been attempting to clarify Liberal intentions and the Unionists too had attempted to provoke the government into revealing its plans. O'Connor was involved early on in a number of squabbles with the Unionist benches such as the Irish Unionist leader Colonel Saunderson's protest about a visit of O'Connor's to Belfast in which he and Devlin, speaking at the Sun Hall had, according to Saunderson, painted a false picture of Ireland's economic ills. This led to counter-charges from O'Connor on the 'orgies and debaucheries of jobbery' which had occurred at the end of the previous Unionist administration in Ireland. O'Connor also remarked on how the Ulster Unionist benches were 'crowded and enthusiastic' in a way they had not been for the previous twenty years but then added, with less confidence perhaps than when he had first made the claim in the 1880s, that the heyday of religous conflict in politics in Ireland was passed. This was the clear implication in his attack on 'a gang still left in Ireland. . . some of them sincere with the fanaticism of bigotry' when he spoke in one of the squalid debates forced from time to time by Protestants on the inspection of religious establishments.[12] His public attitude to the Ulstermen often lacked the minimum of sympathy for fellow countrymen which other Irish nationalists may have felt and this may bear witness to his long absence from Ireland. But he was in no way showing prescience about opposition to come. He was merely commenting on a disappearing phenomenon for the benefit of his Liberal allies and Englishmen generally.

Over the real issue which had, according to O'Connor, encouraged the Ulstermen to attend, namely, devolution, O'Connor was curiously detached. All that the King's speech promised were plans for 'associating the people' with government in Ireland. After that O'Connor appeared fully content to wait and see. In the meantime he turned his attention elsewhere and stressed the urgent necessity for the Liberals to introduce legislation to help trade unions, another

---

[12]*Hansard, 4*, 152, col. 376; 21 Feb.; *ibid.* col. 155, col. 1451, 24 Apr.; *ibid.* col. 1450; *ibid.* 153, col. 171, 5 Mar.; *ibid.* 159, col. 802, 26 June. Cf. Birrell, *Things Past Redress*, p. 185, 'Never have I drawn breath in so irreligious an atmosphere as that of the House of Commons when discussing religion'.

prominent election promise. Here too he protested against Ulster Unionist opposition. At the U.I.L.G.B. conference in 1906, while giving priority to British popular feeling, he had also begged for patience from Irish audiences over devolution proposals. His reason was, 'I am not free, nor are any of my colleagues free at this time, to state the reasons which influence the policy we recommend to our countrymen'.[13] Such an explanation had also been used by O'Connor when Home Rule negotiations were in the air in 1886 but, although confidential negotiations were increasingly required of the Irish and often engineered by O'Connor in the new century, they were not entirely a source of satisfaction to the Irish public and possibly went against O'Connor's instincts as a publicist. In October O'Connor visited the United States, his third visit, and apart from some coolness among splinter groups in New York, probably the most friendly and successful. He thereby followed up Redmond's visit of 1905 and once again raised money for the party, whose funds had been exhausted by the election. Back in England in December he supported Cherry, who had been given a ministerial post, at the by-election in Liverpool Exchange, then turned his attention to devolution.

Lloyd George had suggested to Redmond in November that Irish legislation in 1907 would be minimal but at the same time, in the event of any obstruction by the Lords, parliament would be dissolved. The latter prospect was no consolation to the Irish since it would further delay legislation. Morley also attempted to gain Irish support in 1907 in return for Irish legislation in 1908. So alarmed did the Irish leaders become that they put forward their own proposals for a Bill which was discussed by the cabinet on 15 December. O'Connor played some part in these discussions, chiefly reporting his conversations with Lloyd George to Dillon. The difficult task of interpreting Lloyd George was to loom larger in O'Connor's life in the years that followed. Apart from reporting that John Burns, or even Churchill might replace James Bryce as Irish Secretary (while indicating his own preference for Birrell), O'Connor revealed his own concerns in relation to the coming legislation:

> with the English people [he wrote to Dillon] our antecedents are not the very best fighting ground. The line of least resistance I have always thought with the English masses, is that what is given to Ireland is mere local administrative work, which is not only not legislative but scarcely political in the Imperial sense... I simply throw in these opinions, not as the opinions I would

[13] *Hansard*, 4, 164, col. 867, 9 Nov.; *D.P.*, 4 June.

express except among ourselves and as something we should keep in our minds.[14]

Dillon was probably less concerned with the niceties of tactics here and might not have seen why any priority ought to be given to English susceptibilities in a piece of specifically Irish legislation, which was itself merely an instalment on a larger promise. Moreover, while O'Connor might have been dwelling on what approach to take up, some of his real attitude to devolution, and perhaps even to Home Rule, might have been revealed here.

At Westminster it was revealed that Birrell would replace Bryce. The latter had proved unsatisfactory to the Irish while Birrell had won their good opinion over the Education Bill. It then became clear that a Bill proposing the setting up of an Irish Council would be forthcoming in 1907 and such a Bill was introduced in May. While the Irish had won substantial concessions, there was still doubt about the proposal and as a result a 'race' convention, similar to that of 1896, was convened to meet in Dublin in the same month and was to include American branches of the League as well as the U.I.L.G.B. Feeling there, and in Ireland generally, was against the Bill. O'Connor in his speech to the convention now enlarged on the government's 'profound and invincible ignorance of national sentiment in Ireland' and on the 'badness' of the Bill, a view that was shared by the U.I.L.G.B. delegates and even more by the American delegates whose violence of language may have disturbed the convention as much as it dismayed the Liberals in Britain. Opposition probably arose because the Bill might have appeared in the guise of a final settlement, an alternative to Home Rule. Whatever the cause, neither O'Connor nor the Irish movement in general emerges with a great deal of credit. Redmond and O'Connor had accepted the 'step by step' policy. Moreover, in O'Connor's study of Campbell-Bannerman which was published the following year, O'Connor made no apology for Irish attitudes. He described how the breakfast discussion with the Liberal leader had been 'brief, for there was complete agreement as to both policy and tactics', and Campbell-Bannerman's Stirling speech on the instalment policy was, O'Connor further suggested, 'all that the Irish party could have expected at that moment'. Later in the work he simply described the Council Bill as a 'ghastly and almost immediate failure'. This may have been a 'popular' biography but in that case there was all the more reason for some defence of the Irish position. If the Irish were ready to accept instalments on Home Rule then they ought not to have

[14]Lyons, *Dillon,* pp. 291-2; Dillon Papers, MS 6740-4, f. 136, O'Connor to Dillon, 28 Dec. 1906.

complained when a large measure was not served up in the first Bill. O'Connor possibly realized all this: he had been the chief architect of the policy. Liberals, for their part, blamed O'Connor for appearing to have promised Irish acceptance of the Bill and they may even have gone so far as to demand a different intermediary with the Irish party.[15] This may have been the first occasion when the full meaning of the policy was brought home and the strength of the rejection in Ireland may have been a surprise to the Irish leaders. In that case O'Connor was, and was to continue to be, at a greater disadvantage than other Irish spokesmen because of his distance from opinion in Ireland.

The Council Bill crisis shows O'Connor's difficulty: how to keep on good terms with the Liberals while still exerting pressure. After this, and up to the first election of 1910, it is not hard to see that Irish policy moved towards exerting pressure, but O'Connor for the most part trailed behind, reluctant to be on bad terms with the Liberals. He became more critical of the Liberals in parliament when Irish issues were at stake and used the vote in Britain more demonstratively during by-elections. But over non-Irish issues his chief complaint became that the government were not living up to their radical promises and in this he may have spoken for many on the Liberal backbenches. Opposition in Westminster centred chiefly around education issues. First of all there was the vexed question of university education in Ireland which came up again when Bryce's commission of 1906 reported in July 1907. Its main proposals, to authorize two colleges in Dublin – Trinity College and one other to be the basis of a new national university – proved unsatisfactory both to Nationalist and to Unionist sentiment. O'Connor accused the government of trying to impose English ideals on Ireland and this 'was not his idea of true Liberalism'. His criticism was not very much to the point. He was concerned about education in Ireland but he was making a political gesture and his chief political interest was still the provision for education in England and Wales. There was no Education Bill in 1907 but Reginald McKenna, Birrell's successor as President of the Board of Education, tried to get round the difficulty by the expedient of a short statute disallowing payment for religious education. O'Connor called this 'a declaration of war against a certain type of school' and was driven to say, as before where this issue was concerned, 'a plague on both your houses'. McKenna's strategem did not succeed and it was dropped by the end of the year, but not

[15] D.P., 23 May 1907; Campbell-Bannerman, pp. 73, 75, 131; Fyfe, T.P. O'Connor, pp. 217-18. Here O'Connor was also criticized as being 'all things to all men'.

forgotten. At the end of 1907 McKenna promised further legislation and a Bill was introduced in February 1908. This Bill was seen as more disadvantageous to the Catholics than had been previous Liberal efforts in that it attempted to carve up England and Wales into areas of non-conformist and Anglican special interest. All O'Connor could do was reiterate, with some desperation and to a near empty House, the arguments he had used before. He made a special plea for his own constituency. As he put it, 'nothing was more tragic or pathetic than the spectacle of the Irish poor in the slums and lanes of England' and, as a matter of social justice, education 'ought to be cheaper for them and more efficient'.[16] He was ignored but the Bill was dropped due to wrangling among the Anglicans and the immediate threat to Catholic schools was removed. However, Birrell had a scheme for university education in Ireland accepted after much debate and this was applied at the beginning of 1909.

Such continued threat, year after year, made O'Connor's task more difficult but this was disguised at first in the attempt to put pressure on the Liberals. As before, this was done through the medium of by-elections and the most spectacular examples here were the contests in Jarrow in June 1907 and the more drawn-out affair involving the candidature of Churchill in Manchester North West in January 1907 and April 1908. Jarrow was a remarkable case because here the Irish put forward their own Nationalist candidate, J. O'Hanlon, something not seen in Britain since 1885 (and then only in O'Connor's and Redmond's case), although Crilly made the demand during the by-election for two additional M.P.s for the Irish community in Britain (a demand, equally, not heard since 1885). Athough O'Hanlon came bottom of the poll he received over 2,000 votes and the Labour candidate, Peter Curran, himself of Irish descent, won the seat from the Liberals as a result. It was a not inconsiderable demonstration of the continuing effectiveness of the Irish vote (and a contrast to the modest attitude taken at the U.I.L.G.B. conference the previous year) and designed, so O'Connor said, 'to bring back Liberalism from temporary aberration', a warning of Irish dissatisfaction over the Council Bill.[17]

The more notorious Manchester contest was also a more complicated affair and proved less satisfactory, to O'Connor

[16]*Hansard*, 4, 177, col;. 971, 4 July 1907. For the clearest account of education issue 1906-8 see E. Halevy, *A History of the English People in the Nineteenth Century* (1934, rev.ed. 1961), vol. vi, p. 69, pp. 71-3, *Hansard*, 4, 178, col. 146, 11 July, *ibid.*; 189, cols. 322- 3, 20 May 1908.

[17]*Jarrow Express*, 27 June. The by-election, which was a celebrated one, can be followed in *The Times*, 5 June to 6 July. See below p. 208 for the effects on Labour.

personally, and as a means of demonstrating effective Irish pressure.
A contest would arise in Manchester North West if Churchill were
given the cabinet post he had long desired and deserved. This
possibility was of long-standing and had first arisen in the cabinet
reshuffle of January 1907. At that stage O'Connor was not very
sanguine about Churchill's chances. Both O'Connor and Crilly had
canvassed the constituency and the effect of Liberal proposals, the
abortive Education Bill, and local Catholic antagonism was uppermost
in O'Connor's mind when he reported to Dillon. In O'Connor's view
'what they [the priests] will do with their "Te Deums" over the defeat
of the Education Bill it is impossible to say'. To Redmond O'Connor
confided that the clergy was 'a very formidable force' and that if the
by-election were conducted on the issue of education, and not on the
'national issue', then the wishes of the parliamentary party might be
ignored.[18] Because of these difficulties, in a marginal seat which had
been Conservative up to 1906, Campbell-Bannerman was urged to
delay the promotion of Churchill and this was agreed by 16 January.
But the question of Churchill's promotion, not unnaturally, arose
again in the spring of 1908.

O'Connor had been immediately interested in 1907, he was even
more fully involved in 1908, as the voluminous correspondence in
both letters and telegrams to Redmond, Dillon and Devlin testifies. In
essence, O'Connor's case was now that if Churchill would pledge his
(and as he was about to be made a cabinet minister, possibly the
government's) support for a full measure of Home Rule ('an Irish
parliament for the management of purely Irish affairs with an
executive responsible thereto'), and if Churchill would agree that this
ought to be put before the electors at the next general election, then he
ought to be supported. What is evident in all of O'Connor's exchanges
is his closeness to the Liberals, perhaps particularly to Churchill, a
protective attitude in not wanting the Irish organization to be
superseded by Catholic pressure (Manchester always having been
more of a problem here than Liverpool), and an important tactical
opportunity. The chance of applying pressure here had increased
because Campbell-Bannerman, after a month of illness, resigned on 6
April 1908 and died a fortnight later. It was his successor Asquith
who particularly wanted to promote Churchill from a non-cabinet
post (under-Secretary for the Colonies) to a cabinet post (as it turned
out, President of the Board of Trade). Despite the disappointments of
the Council Bill, the Irish had shown great faith in Campbell-
Bannerman and had liked him personally. The same could not be said

[18]Dillon Papers, MS 6740-4, f. 141, O'Connor to Dillon, 2 Jan. 1907; O'Brien
Papers, MS 13458, O'Connor to Redmond, 18 Jan. 1907.

for Asquith, the originator of the 'step by step' policy. O'Connor impressed on Redmond that support for Churchill on Irish terms was 'a magnificent opportunity' to force Asquith's hand on Home Rule and thereby retrieve 'an impossible situation'. Redmond at first affected, perhaps, not to be so convinced and in the course of a speech on 15 April had said that 'I do not see how we could consistently or wisely ask the Irishmen of Manchester to vote in favour of the representative of the government'.[19] This may have increased the pressure. Churchill lobbied the Cabinet and a pledge was forthcoming from Asquith that Home Rule would be dealt with in the next session of parliament, and a promise was also given on Catholic schools. Redmond's reservations were withdrawn. League support was put fully behind Churchill, yet on election day, 23 April, he was defeated, though by only 429 votes, and had to go on and gain a place in one of the Dundee seats in May (where he also had to face the opposition of Catholic voters). Whatever the reasons for Churchill's defeat – the marginality of the seat, the many pressure groups involved besides the Irish – Asquith's pledge was undoubtedly minimized by the defeat and, indeed, Dillon reported to Redmond shortly afterwards that Asquith appeared wholly unenthusiastic about a resolution on Home Rule put before the House.[20]

Whether or not the Irish vote (as in 1885 and 1886) was used as a scapegoat (and the local Liberal chairman did blame the Irish in Manchester for Churchill's defeat), it was clear that matters had begun to go badly for the Irish, and the Irish in Britain, in 1908 and this uncertainty lasted into 1909. In Manchester it was the case that the local Catholic bishops of Manchester and Salford had by 20 April declared, according to the report of one Irish organizer, that 'Catholic electors would be justified in voting Tory'. Catholic-Irish relations had deteriorated since 1906, largely because of the education issue. So much so that shortly after the by-election, on 9 May, O'Connor and the League executive met to discuss the result and then issued a manifesto deploring the intervention of 'English Catholic Associations' whose activities were described as being directly opposed to 'the best interests of the Catholics'. Such bad feeling may also explain why no

[19] The two questions put to Churchill are in O'Brien Papers, MS 13458, O'Connor to Devlin, 13 Apr. 1908. This collection contains the fullest account of the contest; Redmond Papers, O'Connor to Redmond, 15 Apr.; O'Brien Papers, MS 13458, Telegrams to Dillon, 15 Apr.; *The Times,* 16 Apr.

[20] Peter de Mendelssohn, *The Age of Churchill* (1961), vol. i, pp. 338-9; Denis Gwynn, *The Life of John Redmond* (1932), pp. 160-1. For additional descriptions of the by-election see Mendelssohn, pp. 338-42 and R. S. Churchill, *Winston Churchill,* (1967-1973 continuing), vol. ii, pp. 253-61; Dillon to Redmond, 23 Apr. 1908, cited in Lyons, *Dillon* p. 304.

League conference appears to have been held in 1908. At the conference the following year held, appropriately by that time, in Manchester at the end of May, O'Connor, though facing more immediate discontent from Labour, concentrated on the Catholic difficulty and it was here that he made the most explicit attack he was ever to launch on Catholic influence.

> In a recent election [he said] efforts were made to make disastrous and absolutely unnecessary conflict between the claims of faith and fatherland. . . . [I am] a little impatient and a little angry to find ministers of the Catholic Church, some of them English and some of them Irish, throwing doubt on the loyalty and fidelity of the Irish people after their centuries of sacrifice for the Catholic cause (cries of 'Shame').[21]

Nothing here about being diplomatically deaf and dumb, and Labour by comparison received a certain amount of, admittedly distant, praise. O'Connor's radicalism became more evident here, as it was in parliament where, in the sessions of 1908 and 1909 with Home Rule in the doldrums, he appeared to find almost an equal interest in the social reforms, abortive or otherwise, of the Liberal government. Put another way, he was increasingly exasperated by the inaction of the government, especially in face of Unionist obstruction. Apart from his increasing interventions in education debates (which he approached almost from the point of view of a social reformer), O'Connor continually protested at the conduct of the Unionists. On the Old Age Pensions Bill in June 1908 he blamed the Unionists for the government's proving unable 'to deal with long overdue measures of reform' and his temper was scarcely improved by Balfour's reminder of his own obstructionist record.[22]

His own position was made more uncomfortable in the summer of 1909 by another reminder from the politics of the past. Late June 1909 saw one of the worst examples of sectarian rioting which Liverpool had ever experienced, and it was largely confined to O'Connor's Liverpool Scotland constituency and the neighbouring division of Exchange. There had been outbreaks of, largely Orange, unruliness at the beginning of the century, in 1902 and 1903, but Salvidge, the Conservative leader, had thought that he had nipped this trouble in the bud. Yet the 1909 rioting arose principally because of

[21] The Irish vote in Manchester North West was said to be about 1,000. They could all have voted for Churchill and he could still have been defeated. P.F. Clarke sees good reason for believing that the Liberal view was correct (*Lancashire and the New Liberalism*, p. 254; O'Brien Papers, MS 13458, P. Hickey to Devlin, telegram, 21 Apr.; text of manifesto in *The Times* 11 May 1908; *D.P.*, 31 May 1909.

[22] *Hansard*, 4, 190, col. 905, 11 June 1908.

the agitation of George Wise and his Protestant Reformist Church and began with an attack by Protestants on a large Catholic procession which was thought to be displaying religious artefacts declared illegal under the Emancipation Act of 1829. O'Connor detested this scarcely hidden aspect of Liverpool politics, and had often appeared to be trying to ignore it in Liverpool while attacking sectarianism in Belfast. But his intervention, perhaps out of necessity, was somewhat partisan, questioning the Home Secretary, Herbert Gladstone, on 28 June in order to obtain the guarded opinion that local Catholics had behaved with 'restraint'. O'Connor also attacked the marked attachment of many local Conservative politicians to the Orange order – Colonel Sandys the M.P. for Bootle, for instance, who was also a Grand Master of the Orange Order, and Watson Rutherford, who had contested Scotland division and who was now M.P. for Liverpool West Derby. In his new and popular column for *Reynolds's Newspaper* O'Connor compared them unfavourably with the 'many influential Catholics' who were attempting to prevent counter-demonstrations.[23] On the insistence of the Orangemen Herbert Gladstone set up a Commission to enquire into the disturbances and particularly into the conduct of the police and this reported in 1910. The report was marginally in favour of the Catholics, if they wanted to interpret it this way, but nobody came out well in such a squalid business. O'Connor had, so the Orangemen thought, played his provocative part by being guest of honour at a mass meeting to welcome Captain O'Meagher Condon, a Fenian leader of 1867, in St Martin's Hall in Scotland Road in September 1909. O'Connor had also obtained permission for O'Meagher Condon to visit the grave of the Manchester Martyrs inside Manchester prison, although the Orangemen knew nothing about this, O'Connor insisting, through Crilly, that 'the matter must be kept absolutely secret'.[24] What O'Connor felt about all these petty demonstrations it is difficult to say; perhaps it was a tedious obligation, but to the Orangemen O'Connor was still the Catholic champion and a species of rebel. O'Connor tried to keep his distance but the disturbances and his exasperation with Ulster Unionists in parliament were only a foretaste of greater difficulties. So too was the introduction of Lloyd George's budget, approved by the cabinet early in the spring of 1909

[23] Salvidge, *Salvidge of Liverpool,* p. 47; for a full account see L.R.O. 'Police (Liverpool Inquiry) Act, 1909, transcript of proceedings and report'. A narrative largely based on this report is in Eric Midwinter, *Old Liverpool* (1971), pp. 172-87; *Hansard,* 5, 7, col. 35, 28 June 1909; *R.N.,* 24 Oct. 1909.

[24] Police Act, transcript, p. 85; O'Brien Papers, MS 13458, O'Connor to Denis Johnstone, 6 Oct. 1909; *ibid.* Crilly to Johnstone, 5 Oct. indicates the need for secrecy. Presumably, O'Connor obtained permission from Gladstone, the Home Secretary.

and debated in the Commons until November 1909. Here, O'Connor gave more full-hearted support but his Irish colleagues did not share his enthusiasm. About the best that could be said for the budget controversy so far as most Irish M.P.s were concerned was that it rapidly assumed the proportions of a general election issue and this might break the deadlock in parliament and clear the ground for Home Rule.

'P.T.O.' and 'T.P.'s Weekly', 1905-14

To explain O'Connor's resilience by 1909 by reference to his journalistic work creates an antithesis that was in fact less apparent then than it had been in an earlier period, during the late 1890s and the early years of the new century. An enthusiasm for journalism, education through literature, was augmented by the great Liberal landslide of 1906. From 1906 much of O'Connor's writing once again took as its theme the revived interest of politics and this preoccupation paralleled (as once before, in the 1880s) whatever fortunes or misfortunes he encountered in the more public world of politics or the platform and meant that he had the resources or objectivity, at least to begin with, to regard them as little more than passing irritants. As a man of ideas, though no intellectual, he saw the battle in parliament in a wider context than did most Irish politicians and his commitment was now much more with Britain. He saw affairs much more, though not entirely, as a British politician would. This meant that he was on the moderate side where nationalism was concerned but more tenacious than Redmond, Dillon or Devlin in wanting Westminster to prove its worth. O'Connor became even more the lynchpin in continued negotiations with the Liberals. To see O'Connor as a man of letters helps to show him in the round and further explains a subtle change that had been germinating since the 1890s.

One of the easiest developments to identify in his journalism was the founding of his new journal *P.T.O.* which was first issued in June 1906. But this, paradoxically, shows the least truly creative side of O'Connor and was a continuation of the sort of lack of ability in detailed financial management, and impatience with editorial work that had dogged O'Connor in the case of the *Star* and the *Sun*. If he had been wiser, and not thought he needed the money, he could well have left this sort of venture behind him. His correspondence with Peter Keary, the manager of the Pearson group, which had been occasionally acrimonious in 1904, did not revive on a more or less equable basis until the end of 1905 when O'Connor suggested yet another scheme. Writing from Biarritz, and outlining his further engagements, he

188

suggested that he and Keary should buy out the *Daily Express*, which he believed was about to be amalgamated with the *Evening Standard* (both being owned by Sir Arthur Pearson). O'Connor was convinced that 'London is ripe, indeed crying for a new half penny daily on broad democratic lines'. This came to nothing but the same friendly tone could be seen a few months later when O'Connor confirmed that he would write for *M.A.P.* until the end of his contract in June 1906, and when he also admitted his 'sense of relief at escape from a position that I find unbearable', presumably the editorship of *M.A.P.*[25] This was almost a re-run of his last days with the *Sun*, and his founding of a new journal (about which he does not appear to have informed Keary), occurred in the same month as his contract with Pearson ended and is also reminiscent of the way he left the *Star* and founded a rival newspaper. Once again he began the paper with a declaration of intent in the first issue and he also involved his readership in a mood of realism for,

> Three times I succeeded in making a paper into a property of value on the day it was started and to those who remember what a slow, tiresome, heart-breaking process it used to be in the old days to establish a journal, and to those who know how nine out of ten new journals fail within a short time of their appearance, this experience [the founding of *P.T.O.*] will mark a new epoch in journalism.

This was personal journalism with a vengeance and clearly assumed a wide and faithful following, one concerned to know what he went on to say, that although it would be a 'one man journal' it would also allow him to be 'free from all inept interference; from all stupid wrangling; from the fret and fume of divided responsibility' – all references to his days on *M.A.P.* The new journal promised much. There was, for instance, a long review of Upton Sinclair's *The Jungle* by Winston Churchill, one of the new rising stars of politics, in the first issue with a second instalment in the second number.[26] But the note of peevishness and disillusion might test the most faithful of followers and the journal soon turned out to be the mixture as before. The market for such a paper was probably glutted (which had been the major problem when the *Sun* was founded) and it is more than probable that O'Connor's negligent style of editorship proved an additional hazard. For all his awareness of the problems of finance his capacity here did not

[25] N.L.I., MS 1639-40, O'Connor to Keary, 5 Sept. 1905; *ibid.* 21 Mar. 1906, 5 Apr. 1906.

[26] 'The Story of my Newspaper; its Inception and Purpose', *P.T.O.*, vol. i. no. 1, 16 June 1906; 'The Chicago Scandals' *P.T.O.*, 16, 23 June 1906.

increase. Although *P.T.O.* was not as onerous a responsibility as the *Sun* or *M.A.P.* had been, it was not a financial success. By January 1908 O'Connor was once more in correspondence with Keary, the general theme of an extremely complicated exchange being on what terms O'Connor could re-establish himself with the Pearson group.

From January to May terms were hammered out and for all O'Connor's impracticality in financial management and despite the fact that he was bargaining from a weak position he drove not so much a hard bargain as an exasperating one. This might illustrate why, at least by this stage in his life, managements could not easily co-operate with him and why, in another sphere, Liberals and the Labour party could sometimes find him annoying as a negotiator. At one stage, in February, he could be found saying that 'the new agreement is much worse'. Later he tried to insist on 'no provision with regard to where or how I do my work', provision for compensation if he left the paper, insurance on his life and compensation for the backers of *P.T.O.*, Bass and Newbould. For all the detail of these negotiations, it is not entirely clear what the final settlement was but by April it seems that Pearson was also to take over *T.P.'s Weekly*, that there would be separate accounts for O'Connor and the Pearson management, and that O'Connor would be able to draw £1,000 a year monthly on account of profits (O'Connor inserting in the contract that this figure would be 'a minimum'). Even by 21 May O'Connor, apologizing for the delay owing to pressure of business in the House of Commons, then suggested that one or two points, his minimum pay and the amount of compensation were 'different from which they were to be', that further consultation was needed, but that he foresaw no difficulty and that it would be well 'to finish the job and have it off our minds'.[27] Possibly all financial transactions have an element of what appears in retrospect to be niggardliness or neurosis. Pearson remained equable, and it must be said that to secure the amalgamation of *M.A.P.* and *P.T.O.* would be a valuable outcome, as would the acquisition of the moderately prosperous *T.P.'s Weekly*. (It is not clear which of the financial terms refer to the latter, although a letter from Pearson to Keary of 29 January suggests that O'Connor could have a share in the profits of this paper for seven years, not for life as O'Connor wished). O'Connor might emerge as suspicious and difficult (more so than in politics) and extremely careful with his own money but this might, equally, be a distortion of what was a fight for his livelihood. For all the detailed preparation, however, O'Connor's coming back into the Pearson fold did not prove successful. He edited *M.A.P.* ('incorporated'

[27] O'Connor to Keary, 9 Feb. 1908; Keary to Pearson with typed list of proposals added, 13 Apr.; O'Connor to Keary, 21 May.

with *P. T. O.*) from June 1908 and announced at once that 'conditions of management ensure the permanency of my editorship'. Although the correspondence with Keary was usually agreeable, disagreement on the policy of the paper continued and Keary appeared to want a more sensational tone. By the end of 1909 O'Connor can be found saying that he did not understand a letter of Keary's and meeting criticism about *M.A.P.* 'doing badly'. At this juncture, so Fyfe suggests, O'Connor broke with the paper because he objected to a series of articles on the White Slave Trade and was bought out, on what terms it is not known, but probably the break was a relief all round.[28]

O'Connor's enthusiasm for founding newspapers did not entirely dissappear. Even during the negotiations with Keary he had wanted Pearson to put in a bid for the *World* and the *Onlooker*. In September 1910 he founded *T.P.'s Monthly,* which made little impact, and during the war years (from 1915 to 1916) he ran *T.P.'s Journal* which, again, quickly ran into financial difficulties. These ventures, far less promising even than *P. T. O.,* show even more the irrepressible, perhaps even irresponsible, side of O'Connor. But, equally, it has to be acknowledged that activities of this kind require a great expenditure of nervous energy as well as continual assertions of confidence which do not always read well afterwards. Above all, they require creativity, both in original idea or impulse, and in supplying the continuing ideas by which the popular press especially is sustained. It was remarkable for a man entering his sixties to be so active and full of new ideas and, as before, O'Connor's blind spot and some of his discontent might be located in his inability to transfer the vision into practice. O'Connor recouped some of his fortunes by concentrating more on articles for other newspapers, the *Chicago Tribune,* for which he began writing in about 1908 and the *Daily Telegraph* to which he also began to contribute in 1908. One of his articles for the latter was augmented to form his study of Campbell-Bannerman which, as in the case of his biography of Parnell, was published very soon after its subject's death.[29] Most celebrated of all was his political column for *Reynolds's Newspaper* which began in September 1909 (coinciding with the budget crisis which saw the turn in the fortunes of the Irish party) and

[28] *M.A.P.,* 20 June 1908. Fyfe is therefore incorrect in saying that the merger with *P. T. O.* took place 'within a year' (*Sixty Years of Fleet Street,* p. 51). It had lasted almost exactly two years; O'Connor to Keary, 9 Dec. 1909; Fyfe, p. 192. *M.A.P.* did not prosper and lasted only until 28 October 1911 when it became the *Watchdog* and still proved unsuccessful.

[29] Keary to Pearson, 29 Jan. 1908; 'My New Magazine' (*T.P.'s Monthly*), *T.P.'s Weekly,* 3 Sept. 1910; Fyfe, pp. 237-8. For *T.P.'s Journal* see Chapter 6. p. 223; O'Connor to Keary, 4 Jan. 1908.

lasting up to 1917. This is a constant source for O'Connor's political views from here on, not markedly different from what he said in private, arguably the most able popular political column of its day, while showing at the same time a great sense of personal conviction.

The conduct of O'Connor's papers shows that once again his interests had come together, though he sometimes appeared to want to deny it, and deny the importance of politics. This was apparent in his last work for *M.A.P.* in 1906 and his first work for *P.T.O.* later in the same year when he welcomed the advent of a new radical House of Commons which, equally, gave his journalism new life. In February he welcomed 'the vast transformation' in the House (on a par with his celebration of the popular result while speaking at the League conference the same year). In March he wrote of its 'bold, not to say daring experiments in social life far beyond what has even been attempted before at Westminster' and he attributed much of this to the Labour party, who also owed their election to 'character' and not to 'influence'. He also remarked on how the Labour men were not modest, twenty-six of them had 'already made their maiden speech'. Such a social transformation had one consequence for O'Connor, that it was no longer necessary to keep both a town and a country house, with two sets of servants, 'always one of the things which add to the miseries and difficulties of life'. This may indicate when it was that O'Connor sold his house in Brighton, for far more complex reasons than the demands of a radical parliament. Soon he was giving the new members advice on how to 'conduct themselves' and was quick to notice that the House 'as is often the case [is] far more radical than the ministry' that ministers became 'sober with responsibility' and (in his column 'At the Bar of the House' in *P.T.O.*) 'a radical only knows what he wants, while the minister of a government knows the difficulties'.[30]

This was experience talking and it quickly proved correct. Experience made O'Connor well worth reading but it also meant that he could be bored by politics and would turn to other things. Elections, those contests described in such mock-heroic terms by some of the Liverpool press, he could now openly condemn. In 1906 he wrote of the strain of having to face 'large crowds pretty constantly', and, a note of self-pity again, confessed that 'even those who were supposed to be fortunes' favourites and the spoiled children of success have their dark sombre moments. . . few politicians are free from these moments of despondency'. This was an attitude he returned to after the second election of 1910, when he would have good reason for being tired, and when, in a long piece for *T.P.'s Weekly*, he enlarged on the occasions of a politician's innocence and experience. A politician's first election was 'one of the most delightful and even intoxicating of experiences'. Then, 'to the hardened and experienced electioneer' it was 'one of the hardest and most exasperating' of circumstances.[31] O'Connor's worst disillusionment with parliament had passed by 1900 but it would be too much of a simplification, and would underestimate his endurance, to overlook the fact that his attachment to parliament was by now something of a love-hate relationship. There were disappointments enough in the parliaments up to 1909. For a start, he must have quickly become disenchanted with the Labour party, not only because their greatest weakness was lack of proficiency in parliamentary debate, but because O'Connor had begun by making the direct comparison with the Parnellite incursion (and that of the elite of 1880, not the men of 1885 or 1886), and the Labour party turned out to be far less able and far less constructively or obstructively irreverent, a view he still held as late as 1918. In practice, he was to continue to prove unhelpful to Labour, especially in by-elections where the League's fortunes were involved. Moreover, his ambiguous attitude towards parliament could be gauged in comments he made during debates. After an exchange with Balfour in August 1907 he said, ' I am a parliamentarian and would regard the failure of the House of Commons to excite the nation as a grave national disaster'. The following month he remarked on 'the obstinacy and unwillingness to accept any new proposals which had been in the line of rulers since the days of the Old Testament' and admitted that he 'never found the House of Commons half so interesting as when he was about fifty or a hundred miles from it'.[32] Although these are taken out of context, the context was one of increasing Liberal inactivity, apparently successful obstruction by the Unionists and the Lords. O'Connor's exasperation (the one word which continually arises to describe the years from 1906 to 1909 and which would be even more applicable to his attitude in 1913 and 1914) was because he saw more clearly than most, had seen something similar before, and both feared and ignored what had then ensued. O'Connor's attachment to parliament was, in other words, realistic (though his grasp of politics was not so perceptive as he thought). Knowing what he did, remembering the failure of the 1890s it was necessary to be active and to prevent the case going by default.

---

[31] 'Studies in Temper and Temperament', *M.A.P.*, 13 Jan. 1906; 'The Psychology of an Election', *T.P.'s Weekly*, 4 Dec. 1910.

[32] Fyfe, pp. 288-9. For an initial comparison with the Parnellites see *M.A.P.*, 17 Mar. 1906; *Hansard, 4*, 180, col. 1642, 15 Aug. 1907; *ibid*. 186, cols. 1311, 1314, 24 Mar. 1908.

A half cynical, half angry attitude to parliament, part of which might have been a pose, could also explain the undoubted emphasis he now put on his life as a 'man of letters'. This seems paradoxical at first sight because from 1909 onwards the political situation began to clear, but his increasing absorption in 'letters', given that his political concerns did not diminish, was a sign that he saw literature as something of a refuge, some consolation, which is, in practice, how many men of affairs regard the arts. Not that O'Connor was exactly retiring, or even consistent. In June 1909 he could be found as one of the guest speakers at the Imperial Press Conference, along with Lord Milner, Morley, Augustine Birrell, and Churchill. There he attempted to deny that there was any distinction to be made between literature and journalism, and perhaps even that 'work done under the inspiration and fire of the moment' was better than the 'deliberate' work of the man of letters, a large and coat-trailing claim suitable for a public occasion. In reality, the 'deadline', the never-ending struggle for money was, as O'Connor knew, what prevented his being a more accomplished writer either of political studies or of imaginative fiction, what at about this time had made his study of Campbell-Bannerman so slight. There is an art in journalism and O'Connor was one of its greatest practitioners but it was, and is, transitory, and it was becoming (in contrast to the 1880s) more obviously divorced from letters, and more separate too perhaps from the world of political influence. Morley, who spoke at the same conference affected to be less sanguine than O'Connor and, as J.A. Spender recollected, Morley believed that 'journalists and writers were out of place in political affairs [but] did not apply the maxim to himself'.[33] The following year in an enlightening and sympathetic interview for *The Bookman*, written by Ashley Gibson, O'Connor was more genuine, more ready to recognise the claims of literature. As Gibson recorded, 'Mr. O'Connor himself has told me that he is weary of being discussed as a politician or of being discussed as a journalist, and that in both capacities he has been "written to death". He would have preferred instead to have gained some credit for *T.P.'s Weekly*, a "penny journal that has done much to make good literature popular".' The latter claim was certainly true, back numbers of the *Weekly* can still be entertaining and, along with various spin-offs from the magazine, such as *T.P.'s Monthly* and 'T.P.'s Weekly Circles' (discussion and rambling groups meeting in the provinces of Britain, and in such exotic places as Paris and Toronto), bear witness to O'Connor the teacher. Those who were more harsh in their judgement might have regarded

---

[33] *D.P.,* 11 June 1909; Fyfe, pp. 138, 228; J.A. Spender, *Life, Journalism and Politics* (1927), i, 225.

him as a cultural entrepreneur. O'Connor never achieved his ambition to be regarded as a man of letters. A more common view might have been that represented by T.M. Healy (a political opponent into the bargain), who was described as 'a lover of literature to whom Mr. T.P. O'Connor, the "popular educator" of our times is anathema'.[34]

The fate of the popularizer is often oblivion, especially where so much prestige is involved and fanatically fought over. O'Connor appeared to recognize as much and more in a retrospective article, 'Our tenth birthday', which was published in *T.P.'s Weekly* in 1912. Here he seemed more disenchanted. Of the *Weekly* he noted that 'like most new ideas it got little encouragement. Very few men who have introduced anything novel into this world have ever found anything but discouragement from their neighbours' – accurate enough but more worthy of the *Star*. He went on to pay tribute to the 'broader spirit of humanitarianism which is one of the signs of our times' and this was equally true and the *Weekly* is one of the best examples of cheerfulness and zest which in retrospect, in the knowledge of what was to come, make such statements all the more arresting. But there was also some awareness that the imagination of the age was troubled by new ideas and great expectations. Here O'Connor made two perceptive comments. One was that 'politicians will not make these ideas prevail', and especially not the idea of a free development of nations, because politicians were 'too deeply committed to the difficulties of the hour'. Here it was politics that was made to seem ephemeral, and it was a shrewd politician speaking. Yet his second comment was that 'there is no peril I fear more constantly than looseness of feeling or sloppiness of expression. Sentimentalists have done as much harm in the world as good. This could well have been aimed at socialists, who were causing him some trouble, or, to a lesser extent, the 'new' nationalists associated with *Sinn Féin*. It is an unanswerable puzzle to speculate just how far literature fuelled the more intransigent nationalism which was growing in Ireland but which still lacked political effectiveness. Perhaps it remains astonishing that, until it was too late, O'Connor did not make any detailed assessment of the great Anglo-Irish literary revival associated with Yeats and his circle, and that when he did finally pass judgement his argument was incorrect. Such a lack of insight was not merely because he was growing older and more hardened in his taste, but perhaps derived more from a refusal to recognize that literature might not be concerned with rationality, as

---

[34] Ashley Gibson, 'T.P. O'Connor as Author and Journalist', *The Bookman*, Feb. 1910; Healy described in the *Sunday Times*, 12 Jan. 1913. Healy must have agreed with this because he quoted it in his memoirs (*Letters*, ii, 511).

his piece in the *Weekly* had hoped, but, both in Britain and in Ireland in the new century, might be obsessed with the wilder shores of human feeling. An exception which proves this rule is that O'Connor, like the young Joyce, was a devotee of Ibsen. That O'Connor was not actually associated with the Anglo-Irish movement is not surprising given that school's contempt for parliamentarians (even though Yeats admitted at the time that the parliamentarians appeared to be the only men in Ireland who could be effective in politics, and even though Yeat's aloofness did not stop his being deceived by an adventurer such as, of all people, F.H. O'Donnell).[35] As in politics proper, the enigma of the relationship between art and action needed some years yet for its fulfilment. Yet the 'fact' remains, that here was one of the few (if not the only) instance in the English speaking world where politics owed a debt to literature and O'Connor, who had once grasped this unity, failed to see it. Instead his preoccupation, as he himself had said was true of politicians, was small-scale and specific. For instance, he called a debate in parliament on 21 April 1910 on the publication of Sir Robert Anderson's memoirs. O'Connor condemned the memoirs because Anderson, while still a civil servant, had been allowed to propagate the Irish Unionist case. In particular, Anderson had assisted in *The Times's* campaign against Parnell and had even been the author of articles on 'Parnellism and Crime, 1887' in *Blackwood's Magazine*, where the memoirs were also serialized. O'Connor had as his target the whole Dublin Castle administration, which had much to hide – Anderson was a minor example. Dilke's testimony was that O'Connor's speech, in a long debate, was 'most terribly crushing in its grim, ruthless exposition'.[36] And it was in instances such as this that O'Connor, looking backwards, made the connection between letters and politics. In the debates to come, on the budget, the powers of the Lords, and Home Rule, the press had a customary but augmented role as a chorus and interpreter The importance of J.L. Garvin of the *Observer* on the Unionist side, and J.A. Spender of the *Westminster Gazette* and C.P. Scott of the *Manchester Guardian* on the side of the Liberals, bears witness to this.[37] O'Connor understood and relished

[35] Yeats, so a fragment of autobiography reveals, thought that the parliamentary party 'alone had any political training'. For this and for Yeats and O'Donnell see W.B. Yeats, *Memoirs* (1972) (ed. Denis Donoghue), p. 110 and pp. 115-6.

[36] *Hansard,* 5, 16, cols. 2335-55 for the debate; Gwynn and Tuckwell, *Dilke,* ii, 550. Anderson's memoirs were first published in *Blackwood's* Apr. 1910 and then reprinted as *The Lighter Side of My Official Life* (1910). The background to O'Connor's attack is given in Leon Ó Broin, *The Prime Informer* (1971), pp. 120-9.

[37] For Garvin see A.M. Gollin, *The Observer and J.L. Garvin* (1960), Spender remarked of the period from 1910, especially with reference to Irish matters, that it resembled more 'a Balkan blood quarrel than the political contention to which Englishmen were accustomed' (*Life, Journalism and Politics,* pp. 2-3).

this necessary task of journalism and by the end of 1909 he was playing his part in his articles for *Reynolds's Newspaper* and in the publicity he handled for the Irish cause generally. He was not to know that extremism and mischance would make much of this seem redundant by 1914; it was meanwhile his task, and the task of all responsible politicians, to see that constitutional politics worked.

Approaches to Violence, 1909-14

O'Connor's part in the budget crisis was a crucial one because he was the Nationalists' link with the Liberals (Redmond's 'chief scout') as the Master of Elibank, the Liberal chief whip from 1910, put it). It was a long crisis lasting, at least, from the autumn of 1909, through the first election of 1910 and until the following spring and was the first of many such alarums, both constitutional and domestic, in which O'Connor was closely involved up to 1914. The story of the budget crisis and those which followed has often been told and the Irish part has been detailed by Redmond's biographer and more recently by the biographer of John Dillon.[38] So far as O'Connor was concerned (and an analogy might be drawn here with 1900 and 1905-6), his task was to keep together the alliance between the Liberals, the Labour party and the Irish. This was not an assertive policy and it would have been modified had Redmond or Dillon so wished. Wherever the Liberals were not pushed hard enough it could be said, but only in retrospect perhaps, that the alliance had considerable disadvantages. but the fact that the alliance did survive must owe something to O'Connor's patience and, with a few understandable lapses, his good humour; he bore his task too lightly to be regarded as dogged.

There was little at first to indicate that difficulties over the budget would be important or that they might, after some extreme discomfort, cause the log-jam in Anglo-Irish relations to be broken and clarify the position over Home Rule. Certainly, so far as O'Connor was concerned, there was little realization at first of these implications. Initially, it was the radical aspects of the budget which O'Connor, along with British radicals but unlike many of the Irish party, insisted on approving. As late as September in his column for *Reynolds's*, he emphasized the bonus for democracy in supporting the budget against the Lords.

[38] A. C. Murray, *Master and Brother, Murrays of Elibank* (1945), p. 23; for the Irish background in 1910 see Gwynn, *Redmond*, pp. 174-87, which quotes extensively from O'Connor's letters to Redmond, and Lyons, *Dillon*, pp. 310-20, which gives excerpts from O'Connor's letters to Dillon and to Lloyd George. Lyons gives a detailed chronological exposition of the crisis.

If the Lords want to produce chaos, let them do so and bear the consequences. Revolutions can't be fought or resisted with rosewater.... I would welcome such action on their part. It would give the democracy an unequalled chance of making the government of England really democratic. This odious, selfish, and stupid anachronism which lies like some hideous vampire over the aspirations of England and its toiling masses; over Ireland demanding Home Rule; over Wales asking for religious equality; over Scotland praying for land reform. . . [would be] delivered into the hands of the people.[39]

Accepting that this was written in a radical journal, it still shows a real enthusiasm for change and the old antagonist against the House of Lords did not miss his opportunity. By comparison, Irish objections against the excise duties on the Liquor trade which were contained in the budget were matters which Healy and O'Brien had had the freedom of action to oppose throughout 1909. Possibly late in the day the majority party realized the general opposition in Ireland to the new duties, which it was thought would harm a not inconsiderable part of the Irish economy. O'Connor realized the danger later still. Healy reported in November that O'Connor's attitude was a willingness to sacrifice 'a few thousand publicans'.[40] This was probably malicious but it is true that O'Connor was chiefly, and justifiably, concerned at the effect of the budget on the future of the alliance. Lloyd George, whom O'Connor had helped briefly in the election of 1892, had by the time he was made Chancellor, become a close friend of O'Connor's. Writing to him on 25 September O'Connor instanced the difficulties the Irish party already faced, namely, Healy himself and what must be regarded as a resurgent opposition from the Catholic church. He feared that great damage would be done to the alliance if the Irish had to vote against the third reading of the budget and, in a marked departure from the policy Redmond and Dillon would be obliged to advocate, O'Connor hinted at abstention ('hinting to some of the men that they need not vote when things were so critical'). This was a dangerous line for O'Connor to follow, as he admitted to Lloyd George, and it shows the lengths he was prepared to go, and that uppermost in his mind was the consideration of 'how disastrous I consider it to be ever to divide the democratic forces in the two countries'. O'Connor impressed on Lloyd George in this letter and in one which followed at the end of October, the strength of feeling

[39] *R.N.,* 19 Sept.

[40] Healy to Maurice Healy, 1 Nov., in *Letters,* ii, 489. Healy described 'T.P.'s Letters to a Chicago paper' (probably the *Chicago Tribune*) which at one stage O'Connor is supposed to have asked 'what is the ruin of a few thousand publicans to the ruin of half a million tenants'.

against the budget which had begun to affect the other Irish leaders and he genuinely could not understand why the Liberals were prepared to put so much at risk for the sake of 'these wretched license duties' which would bring 'nothing either in finances or reputation'.[41] He reserved his criticism for the Liberal attitude but in many ways he saw the problem as a radical might see it, explaining the Irish position partly to himself, a psychological process which was never wholly absent from the remainder of his time at Westminster. But, more immediately, his fears were avoided. Irish opposition was pre-empted by the Lord's rejection of the budget on 10 November. In the run-up to the election which followed Asquith in his Albert Hall speech of 10 December pledged the Liberals to Home Rule in a more decisive and apparently more enthusiastic way than he had done in 1908.

O'Connor's worst forebodings in the January 1910 election were therefore not realized. He had, when writing to Lloyd George, particularly pointed to the disruptive tactics of Healy, the opposition of *Sinn Féin* (a rare mention this, and the *Sinn Féiners* were not to loom so large again for O'Connor until the Roscommon by-election of 1917) and, most of all, the Catholics under Archbishop Bourne and the effect they might have, especially in Lancashire. A campaign was launched by the Catholic Federation during the election which involved asking test questions of Liberal candidates. But, if anything, such intervention, acceptable in a by-election, proved counter-productive. Instead, Irish voters were given instructions by the League which in effect urged them to vote for the Liberal, whatever the Labour party's attitude to Home Rule, and they needed little urging after Asquith had made his more forthright statement on Home Rule.

In Liverpool the Conservatives once again attempted to make an issue of education but this was unsuccessful. O'Connor himself came late to the contest in Liverpool. In the middle of October 1909 he had set off once more to America to raise funds, returning to Liverpool at the end of December when, according to the representative of the *Catholic Herald,* he 'looked very worn' and he took a week's rest under medical care before returning to Liverpool on 10 January, confident that 'Scotland division is quite safe in the hands of my

---

[41] H.L., Lloyd George Papers, c/6/10/1, O'Connor to Lloyd George, 25 Sept.; *ibid.* c/6/10/2, O'Connor to Lloyd George, 'Saturday' (dated by Lyons 30 Oct.). O'Connor's friendship with Lloyd George is indicated at the end of the latter where he said 'You know I would not think of bluffing with a friend so close as you'. See also Fyfe, pp. 220-1. O'Connor made out a convincing case in the September letter that there was precedent for differential treatment for Ireland but the Liberal rank and file appeared to be obdurate on this matter and saw any change in the budget duties as the equivalent of destroying the budget. A conversation between Spender and Redmond particularly suggested as much (Spender, *Life, Journalism and Politics,* p. 233).

friends'. When he did return he spent most of his time campaigning for the Liberal, Max Muspratt, in Exchange. Here he claimed that the Liberals had had a change of heart over education and that 'their schoomaster was T.P. O'Connor' and Muspratt seemed more enthusiastic than O'Connor about the issue. Although the Conservatives did win back Abercromby division, and although Sexton's campaign proved unsuccessful again in West Toxteth, O'Connor's confidence proved justified. He obtained a majority of over 2,000, the largest majority he ever received, Muspratt was returned for Exchange, and there were signs of increasing Liberal support in other Liverpool divisions.

Over Britain as a whole the Liberals had not kept their massive majority (though their losses were not so great as by-election losses up to 1909 appeared to threaten). O'Connor in *Reynolds's* put Liberal setbacks down to defections in the south of England and its 'sleepy hollows', 'bribery, intimidation and motor cars, outvoters and stupidity' and in the north 'insane divisions among the progressive forces'. But there was little need to explain overmuch the reversal of the 1906 landslide.[42] In Ireland the result had not been so decisive as had been hoped with seventy Redmondites elected and eleven independent nationalists (including the followers of Healy and O'Brien), but it was a creditable performance in view of the difficulties over the budget (which had still to be resolved). Finally, and most important for the Irish, the Liberals with 275 seats to the Unionists 273, even if they might sometimes have the support of the forty Labour M.P.s, had lost their overall majority. More than that, Redmond was now in a stronger tactical position than Parnell had enjoyed. The outcome of the election was the sort of result O'Connor had hoped for ever since 1885 (and had particularly expected in 1906) although, tactics and numbers of seats aside, much else had changed since 1885. Such a result had not been planned for or expected in 1910, although the Irish might have believed that the Liberals' strength would be diminished.

O'Connor played an important part in the complicated negotiations which followed, especially in February and May, and which tried to establish what should be the proper consequences of the election. The budget and the powers of the House of Lords still had to be dealt with. For all Asquith's statement on Home Rule had eased the situation for the Irish during the election, the particular benefit would have to be established, Liberal resolve had to be gauged, as would the sort of hold, if any, that the Irish had over the Liberals. The Irish position, held

[42]*D.P.*, 2 Jan, 10 Jan.; Liverpool *Catholic Herald* 1 Jan.; *D.P.*, 11 Jan.; the Catholics and the Irish in the first election of 1910 are discussed in N. Blewett, *The Peers, the Parties and the People* (1972), pp. 349-53 and in Clarke, *Lancashire and the New Liberalism*, pp. 256-8; *R.N.*, 6 Feb.

with some resolution by Redmond and Dillon, was that the Irish would have to oppose the budget unless there were public assurances from Asquith before this vote that the power of the Lords, their so-called 'veto', would be curtailed. This promise was the more urgent because it was revealed by Asquith in the Commons by 21 February that he had received no 'guarantees' from the king prior to the election that peers would be created; it is now known that the king had specifically refused to give such a guarantee until after the result of a second election.[43] The Irish had to be sure of Liberal intentions so they then went on to insist that veto resolutions regarding the Lords had to be introduced at the same time as the budget was reintroduced.

O'Connor's role in all this was two-fold; to keep the Liberals, chiefly through Lloyd George, fully aware of Irish fears, and to influence both the Liberal party in the Commons and Liberal electors through *Reynolds's*. In the first case O'Connor wrote urgently to Lloyd George from Ireland on 9 February, informing him that the budget would be opposed if satisfactory assurances were not given to the Irish. He appeared once again almost like a commmentator, at least marginally in sympathy with the Liberals' dilemma, thinking 'it only right that I should give you this information at once'. O'Connor is said to have written in a similar cautionary vein to Morley the following day and this was passed on to Asquith who informed the king. The letter to Lloyd George was the first formal notification of the difficulties. O'Connor, apart from attending on Redmond when they both met Lloyd George on 12 February, then continued to act not so much as a negotiator putting pressure on the government but as a constructive intermediary, passing on Lloyd George's information that Healy and O'Brien had suggested a compromise on the budget, and keeping his lines of communication open to Ireland. Yet O'Connor was perhaps more effective elsewhere. He kept up the attack in *Reynolds's* against 'dallying or wavering' and condemned any suggestion that ordinary government business should continue (which would require the passing of the budget) as 'irrelevant, conventional and empty nonsense in the midst of a great fight like this. . . the phrases by which the "bon bourgeois" has always tried to stop the advance of a revolution'. He regarded Asquith's admission over the guarantees as the 'darkest night for the anti-Lords majority'.[44] O'Connor was equally active in private. Austen Chamberlain wrote

[43] The constitutional issue is described in Ensor, *England 1870-1914*, pp. 417-30, and Halevy, *History*, vol. vi., pp. 305-68.

[44] Lloyd George Papers, c/6/10/3, O'Connor to Lloyd George, 9 Feb.; negotiations down to April are fully described in Lyons, *Dillon*, pp. 314-17; O'Connor to Morley, 10 Feb. cited in J.A. Spender and Cyril Asquith, *The Life of Herbert Henry Asquith*

to his father that it was only the good offices of Dillon and O'Connor that was preventing the Irish vote in St. Georges in the East going against the minister, W.W. Benn, in the contest caused by his taking office. Chamberlain also reported that O'Connor had said the Irish had 'replenished their war chest' and might choose, again according to O'Connor, to defeat the government on an issue other than the budget. By April O'Connor could be found suggesting that if Asquith resigned over the veto proposals it could lead up to Balfour demonstrating an inability to form a government. This was the small change of parliamentary rumour but activity such as this, persistent lobbying, most of which has gone unrecorded, was one of the O'Connor's strong suits. The Master of Elibank, the Liberal whip, paid tribute to O'Connor's effectiveness on this score just at this juncture especially among the ranks of radical and northern Liberal M.P.s. O'Connor had the ear of Sir John Simon, Percy Alden, Charles and Noel Buxton, and about fifty other Liberals and such moves were dangerous to the government. Elibank's broad-minded view in later life was that O'Connor's 'friends were everywhere and [his] enemies no one ever found'. Such advantages played a part in convincing the Liberals that something must be done to placate their allies, to deal with the question of the Lords in the order required by the Irish, although the decisive element was probably the determination of Redmond and Dillon not to give way on this matter. Accordingly, resolutions modelled on earlier proposals of Campbell-Bannerman's indicating what policy would be implemented if the Lords proved recalcitrant were passed in the Commons by 14 April. On the same day Asquith announced that he had received the necessary guarantees from the King that peers would be created if the Liberals were successful after a subsequent election. The Parliament Bill to deal with the Lords was introduced into the Commons on 27 April and by 28 April the budget had passed both Commons and Lords. Irish ability to exert pressure on the Liberals had been demonstrated but it had also possibly reached its limits. What would happen when the issues were not of such crucial importance to the Liberals had yet to be demonstrated.

O'Connor had good reason to feel satisfied by the time of the Easter recess. His oldest enemy, the Lords and their adherents, appeared to be on the run and he had scored some telling points against them in the debate on the resolutions at the beginning of April ('all the great men of history [were] children of commonplace parents', 'some illustrious descendants of illustrious names contradict

(1932), i, 272; *R.N.*, 6, 20, 27 Feb., 20, 27 Mar.; Letters of Austen Chamberlain to his father, 25 Feb., 21 Mar., 10 Apr., quoted in A. Chamberlain, *Politics from the Inside* (1936), pp. 206, 235, 247; Murray, *Master and Brother*, pp. 35, 23.

me from above the gangway'). His comment on Asquith's declaration of April was that never in all his long parliamentary career had he seen such 'a great spring tide of joy' among the radicals and the Irish.[45] The cause of his impatience had been removed and prospects were fair for a direct attack on the Unionists, and particularly the Lords. These thoughts would have refreshed O'Connor during the holiday he took in early May at a villa on Lake Como in company with the Master of Elibank and Lloyd George, all looking forward to a more constructive parliamentary session. But then the death of King Edward VII on 7 May caused new uncertainties and was to result in a good deal more difficulty for O'Connor than he had experienced earlier in the year. After his yearly presidential task of speaking to the U.I.L.G.B. conference, held confidently rather than provocatively in Belfast on 15 May, he had to return to Westminster and once again took up the slack between the Liberals and the Irish.[46]

A delay in the battle with the Lords was thought proper, allowing time for the royal funeral, for King George V to take up his duties and, unfortunately for the Irish, giving space for consideration of alternative solutions. Geoge V agreed to uphold his father's guarantee but wanted the Lords to discuss the Parliament Bill. A constitutional conference was also set up which met from June to November. In these circumstances the Irish might justifiably fear that all their gains would be eroded. Dillon's suspicion of Lloyd George, shown in letters to and from O'Connor, was particularly justified since by the time of the conference the Chancellor's fertile imagination had thought of the now notorious proposal of a coalition between the government and the Unionists. The prospect of a Liberal fall from power, or such a coalition, was what might be said to have put limits on Redmond's use of Irish pressure. To avoid the worst, the two principal Irish leaders, Redmond and Dillon, decided to sit out the crisis in Ireland. Perhaps, as Dillon's biographer had remarked, this was a wise policy and prevented an embarrassing compromise or disruption from Dillon. But it was a poor reflection on Irish parliamentarians that their chief value could lie in their absence. Needless to say, it also made O'Connor's life more difficult. His letters both to Redmond and to Dillon, which came as a result of meeting variously with Lloyd George and the Master of Elibank, were both detailed and tackled developments with more calm than Dillon could manage (partly on account of temperament, partly because O'Connor sympathised

---

[45] *Hansard*, 5, 16, cols. 55, 54; *R.N.*, 17 Apr.

[46] *D.P.*, 16 May. O'Connor particularly attacked O'Brien (holding a conference at the same time in Skibbereen).

more with the Liberals). O'Connor's worry was shown in his constant and usually unavailing requests that the Irish leaders attend negotiations in London: Lloyd George, wrote O'Connor, 'presses for it vehemently', their absence 'at such a critical moment' was 'a misfortune', and O'Connor later thought it 'desirable – more, necessary that you should be here'. Such a situation, which was going to be repeated during other tactical absences of the Irish leaders in years to come, showed that O'Connor might have disliked taking ultimate responsibility, but in any case was not empowered to do so, and was given detailed instructions by both Dillon and Redmond which he was not in a position to follow. At the same time, while trying to keep some sort of talks going he was, according to Redmond's biographer, suspected by Dillon of being too sympathetic to the Liberals and of not pressing Dillon's and Redmond's views with sufficient determination.[47] O'Connor's patience was extraordinary, though he was still in awe of Dillon, if not of Redmond. His calmness was, perhaps fortuitously, to prove justified. The Parliament Bill was delayed on second reading in the Lords and the constitutional conference had proved abortive by 10 November. Asquith, partly on the confident advice of the Master of Elibank, (who was more optimistic about the outcome of yet another election than the Irish had been earlier in the year) announced the dissolution of parliament for 28 November.

Before the constitutional conference had finally broken down, O'Connor had prefaced his part in the election by touring north America to collect funds – this time concentrating on Canada while Redmond toured the United States. This was the most rewarding tour financially with $100,000 being collected for party funds and for the election campaign.[48] The tour attracted a considerable amount of criticism in the Unionist press, perhaps because it was so successful, and this was a foretaste of the attack made in the election where O'Connor was concerned. He returned to Liverpool at the end of November and found that he had to face the opposition not only of the local Conservative dignitaries and a strident Unionist press (both probably at their most exuberant during this election), but also the scrutiny of F.E. Smith, who had discovered a loyalty to Ulster's

[47] This exchange in June includes letters to Redmond on 4, 6, 17 June (copies to Dillon) which are quoted in full in Gwynn, *Redmond,* pp. 175-81, and Dillon to O'Connor, 5 June, Redmond to O'Connor 5 June, giving instructions to O'Connor about the Irish position which O'Connor passed on to the Master of Elibank (copies in Elibank Papers, MS 8802, ff. 69-75, N.L.S.). See also Lyons, *Dillon,* pp. 317-20; Dillon's warning about O'Connor is in Gwynn, *Redmond,* p. 178.

[48] Gwynn, *Redmond,* p. 184, A.J. Ward, *Ireland and Anglo-American Relations* (1969), p. 18.

cause, and Edward Carson who had become leader of the Irish Unionists in February 1910 and who campaigned in Liverpool before going on to Ulster. Smith gave O'Connor some witty, and not undeserved, knocks, such as saying that O'Connor was someone 'who in the character of politician desired to destroy the dukes but who in his capacity as a journalist was entirely dependent upon the duchesses (laughter). He would sell every single Catholic school in the city for a housemaid's tittle-tattle about a lady of title (renewed laughter and applause).'[49]

This was good platform stuff and perhaps a case of what often had been felt but never so well expressed. Yet the language of the Conservative campaign generally was deplored by the Liberal *Daily Post* and O'Connor too found that the sectarian aspect of the contest was worse than usual both in Warrington and in Liverpool, where he said that it was all the more regrettable because that city had 'just emerged from a disgraceful and disastrous series of riots produced by Orange bigotry' – the disturbances of 1909 soon to be investigated by A.J. Ashton's tribunal on police conduct. The Conservative candidate for Scotland division, T.O. Ockleston, made some good points about the economic irrelevance of Home Rule to Irish working men living in Britain (many of those Ockleston addressed might not, by this date, have even been born in Ireland). Similar arguments were being put forward by socialists, perhaps' with greater sincerity.[50] But the concentration on Home Rule appears to have been received with enthusiasm by Irish voters in Britain, the British voters possibly being somewhat bored by constitutional issues. Both in *Reynolds's* and in the manifesto of the U.I.L.G.B. published on 23 November, O'Connor had concentrated on 'the intolerable claim of the aristocrats' to rule the country and had prophesied, with some accurancy, that the Irish vote would be united as never before.[51] The Catholic interest, warned off in January 1910, played no part in the election. In Scotland division, the result was to give O'Connor a majority of 1,700, lower than the first election of 1910 but higher than in 1906. Nationally, the Liberals lost two seats to remain level with the Unionists at 272. The Labour party gained two seats, increasing their number to forty-two and the majority Irish party gained seats with ten nationalists remaining independent.

[49] *D.P.*, 1 Dec.

[50] *Ibid.* 1 Dec. 1910; *R.N.*, 4 Dec., The *Manchester Guardian* in its leader on the election results also compared Liverpool to Belfast (*M.G.*, 6 Dec.); see speech of Ockleston in *D.P.*, 2 Dec. and compare the attitude of the socialist Glasgow *Forward* where it described Irish voters as 'wage earners on British soil, sharing the hopes and suffering of their fellow workers' (*Forward*, 17 Dec.).

[51] *R.N.*, 13, 27 Nov.; *D.P.*, 23 Nov.

While both the Liberals and the Irish might feel well satisfied with the result, the Irish had had some warning of the difficulty of influencing the Liberals in the first part of 1910. For all of 1911 this problem was disguised because the Liberals were fully occupied with passing the Parliament Bill into law, and, after a fierce contest, it was passed through the Commons by May and through the Lords by August. Here the Irish took a back seat, and this included O'Connor even though the issue of the Lords was his pet subject. Irish involvement would have complicated the issue since Unionist objections were precisely centred on a fear of the implementation of Home Rule once the Lords' powers were restricted to ones of delay. Yet while matters appeared to be going well for the Irish, the 'alliance' faced another test, this time from Labour. For O'Connor, always concerned with co-operation within the alliance, the problem took two forms. Firstly there was the impatience of the Labour party, occasioned partly by dissatisfaction with its own electoral and parliamentary performance (in which the obduracy of the Irish League in Britain played a part), and also due to dissatisfaction with the Liberal leglislative record, especially after 1911. This was the more prolonged and heavier of O'Connor's burdens. Secondly, and the more immediate threat, there was the unprecedented industrial unrest which had been growing since 1907 and which broke out in a series of bitter and prolonged strikes in the summer of 1911. One of the most crucially affected areas was Liverpool and strikes and disturbances there among seamen, dockers and other port workers, and among railwaymen and other transport workers, caused widespread disturbance in the city from the middle of June to the end of August, with the strike reaching a peak and becoming general between 13 and 19 August.[52]

There is no doubt that O'Connor was taken by surprise by the strike and by the unrest in general, as he admitted in *Reynolds's,* a surprise which he said was shared even by 'men in the labour world', by whom he probably meant politicians and established trade unionists. Yet O'Connor, rather than the Irish movement, was particularly involved because most of the disturbances took place in his dockland constituency and his constituents' interests were at stake. O'Connor had some reputation as a conciliator in labour disputes by this time, though the record remains obscure. His work here probably began during the 1890s when he intervened on behalf of

---

[52]Descriptions of the strike can be found in Tom Mann's newspaper the *Transport Worker,* Sept. 1911 and these are repeated in his *Memoirs,* pp. 24-9. For a fuller description see H. R. Hikins, 'The Liverpool Transport Strike, 1911', *T.H.S.L.C.*, 113 (1961), 161-95.

the seamens' union and this had been augmented by his work for the dockers' union in 1900, a gesture which was favourably remarked on as late as the by-election in Exchange division at the end of 1906.[53] By the end of 1907 his interest or ability here was sufficient for Lloyd George, as President of the Board of Trade, to offer him the post of Government Arbitrator in labour disputes, a post which O'Connor had to refuse because his membership of the Nationalist party prevented him from accepting office, although the possibility of a government office was to come up again. Labour disputes in Ireland in 1907, particularly that associated with James Larkin's first foray into Belfast to organize dockers and transport workers, then gave rise to a curious incident recorded in the recollections of G. R. Askwith, who was appointed Arbitrator instead of O'Connor, which may indicate that O'Connor had a realistic view of Irish labour which bordered on cynicism.[54]

Further involvement with industrial disputes is hidden; by its nature industrial conciliation is as complex as international diplomacy although less complete records are kept. When the worst of the crisis broke in 1911 some indication of O'Connor's efforts behind the scenes is indicated by what he said in the debate in parliament on 16 August, where he attributed the strike to 'tyranny and various circumstances which I attempted to mitigate and control – a thing which I failed to do'.[55] The debate in parliament came immediately after the 'Bloody Sunday' incidents of 13 August when police had baton-charged a crowd in front of Liverpool's St. George's Hall. The unsettled state of the city was then the occasion for some sectarian rioting (all located in or near Scotland division) and this was seized on

[53]*D. P.*, 6 Dec. 1906. O'Connor often held his constituency meetings and 'surgeries' in the 'Morning Star' public house. A platform was set up on the bar on which O'Connor sat (Liverpool oral tradition).

[54]Halévy, *History,* vol. vi, p. 107. The possible reference to O'Connor in Askwith's work (Lord Askwith, *Industrial Problems and Disputes* (1920), p. 110) reads: 'We arrived at Belfast on the morning of August 13 [1907] not encouraged by meeting a distinguished Irishman on the boat who I thought might be a possible arbitrator if one became necessary. This hope of impartiality was stopped by his remark at breakfast that he knew his countrymen; I had no chance settling the dispute, even if I was not shot, as I probably should be and Larkin ought to be hanged.' Halévy, in connection with O'Connor and the government post of arbitrator said (*History,* p. 107). 'Lord Askwith has kindly explained. . . a passing allusion in the text (of *Industrial Problems)*'. This appears to be the allusion and this would identify the Irishman as O'Connor. It is possible that Askwith's leg was being pulled.

[55]*Hansard,* 5, 29, col. 1970, 16 Aug, 1911. O'Connor also admitted that most of the disturbances had taken place in his constituency, but did not protest at Winston Churchill's attributing the unrest to 'the hooligan class . . . roughs from the adjoining Irish district, always ready for an opportunity to attack the police'. *Ibid.* cols. 1969, 1989.

by the local press who were perhaps unduly alarmist or perhaps trying to prove a case. O'Connor's own attitude veered between a detached sympathy for the strikers and a concern for law and order. In the debate in August he offered his services as a conciliator and a Commission of Enquiry was set up on 18 August which comprised O'Connor, Kyffin-Taylor, the Conservative M.P. for Liverpool Kirkdale division, and D.J. Shackleton, the Senior Labour Advisor to the Home Office, and which began work almost immediately, enquiring especially into the food supply. The strike was over by 24 August but the Commission remained in being, probably as a result of O'Connor's initiative, and partly through the influence of the Lord Mayor of Liverpool, Lord Derby, who no doubt saw this as a means of implementing the suggestion of the police enquiry of 1909, that a permanent committee should be set up to work to prevent civil disturbance in the city. O'Connor may have felt vindicated in his attacks on Unionist sectarianism (though he made no mention of this in 1911 since it might have been thought provocative, and he was not entirely guiltless in this regard even though his attitude towards nationalist display in Liverpool was more defensive). O'Connor did believe that the authorities in some instances had over-reacted and he had settled some disputes personally so that Askwith came in as arbitrator at the end of the dispute and praised his ability in 'managing the Irishmen'. But O'Connor's conclusion in *Reynolds's* was that *'it was a near thing'.*[56]

There is marginally more direct evidence for O'Connor's acting as a mediator in labour disputes in the years which followed, mostly through the Liverpool conciliation committee and dealing with local industries such as the Liverpool United Gaslight Company and the Mersey Docks and Harbour Board.[57] But he had no major part to play in the labour dispute which followed some years later and which, unlike the labour unrest in Britain, threatened the Nationalist movement directly. This was the strike and lockout of Dublin

[56] Hikins, *loc. cit,* 187-9, 191 where the violence and the sectarianism is described as minimal; Askwith, *Industrial Problems,* p. 171; Randolph Churchill, *Lord Derby, King of Lancashire* (1959), p. 137; David A. Roberts, 'Religion and Politics in Liverpool since 1900', (unpublished M.Sc. thesis, University of London, 1965), pp. 60-1; *R.N.,* 20, 27 Aug., italics, or rather capitals in original. The setting up of the commission is mentioned in Churchill's reports to the King, quoted in R.S. Churchill, *Winston Churchill,* vol. ii, companion part iii, p. 1287.

[57] O'Connor acted in a dispute with the Mersey Docks and Harbour Board over working conditions *(Hansard, 5, 65,* cols. 783, 796-8, 23 July 1914) and in a dispute with the Liverpool United Gaslight Company over union recognition *(ibid.* col. 782). In March 1915 he also intervened to bring a strike of Liverpool coal-heavers to an end 'after some rowdy opposition' *(The Times,* 4 Mar. 1915). The latter strike was thought to be unpatriotic.

transport workers which reached a crisis in September 1913 and which lasted until January 1914. Other nationalists were involved, notably William Martin Murphy who was the owner of the Dublin transport company around which the strike began, and his friends T.M. Healy (who was also related to him) and Richard McGhee. The majority party, while having no financial interest to defend, was either hostile or, apparently, indifferent to the strike. Dillon, when writing to O'Connor, regarded Larkin as a 'malignant enemy'. O'Connor did not commit himself but probably considered Larkin a wild man in labour affairs and a danger to the Nationalist movement. In replying to Dillon's letter, which had urged O'Connor not to attend a meeting of the Gaelic League in London called to express sympathy with the strikers, O'Connor agreed that it was better to pass no opinion 'on the merits of the struggle' but he also added 'though honestly all my sympathies are with the strikers'. Later, when he came to write his memoirs, O'Connor seemed, if anything, to be hostile to the memory of Larkin and praised Murphy's 'fearlessness' but this is no clear guide to his feelings at the time because he grew to associate 'Larkinism' with any kind of violent unrest, including that of the Dublin Rising of 1916.[58] O'Connor's emphasis was clearly on the Nationalist movement and how Larkin would affect it, not only in Ireland but also in Britain. Whatever the views of British trade union leaders, the Irish in Britain, overwhelmingly part of the industrial working class (like Larkin himself who came from the Liverpool Irish community), must have sympathized strongly with the Dublin strikers.

Violence and bitterness such as that shown in the Dublin strike was a bad advertisement for the supposed omnipotence of Home Rule and it intruded just where the forces of Nationalism, Liberalism and Labour met. Perhaps this explains the antagonism shown by Dillon. It also helps further to identify the balancing act performed by O'Connor in his relations with the Labour party. In 1914, during the third reading of the Home Rule Bill in parliament, O'Connor used the Dublin strike as an example of how self-government would not mean monolithic government, that there would be a labour and a capitalist interest in Dublin and, probably a more important implication, the Unionists need not fear that they would be unable to declare their interest.[59] Needless to say the Unionists were not convinced and

[58] Dillon to O'Connor, 16 Oct. 1913 cited in Lyons, *Dillon*, p. 335; Dillon Papers, MS 6740-4, f. 208, O'Connor to Dillon, 17 Oct.; *Memoirs*, ii, 56-7 where Larkin was described as attempting to be 'dictator of Dublin'. For O'Connor, 'Larkinism' and the Easter Rising see Chapter 6, p. 228.

[59] *Hansard*, 5, 60, col. 1440, 2 Apr. 1914. O'Connor had made a more specific plea to the Unionists on this point before the Dublin labour dispute, on the second reading of the Bill in January 1913 (*ibid.* 46, col. 1042, 7 Jan. 1913).

neither, with almost as good reason, were the Labour party and the various champions of socialism in Ireland and in Britain. In the latter case it was not so much that they feared that there would be no room for argument in a Dublin parliament but that the Nationalist hegemony would prevent the development of Labour. There was good reason for this fear. Labour had not been helped much by the Irish in 1906, the Irish vote went uniformly to the Liberals in the two elections of 1910. For a long time after this, when things looked increasingly bleak for Labour, the Irish vote, Irish support from working class Irish voters, was still not forthcoming because of the Irish League.[60] Socialists were not slow to protest, realizing that neither the government's survival nor Home Rule was in jeopardy during by-elections. But O'Connor was not slow to assert the need to prevent 'divisions' in the progressive ranks and, less publicly, he urged the need not to antagonize the Liberals.[61] The matter did not stop there. Increasingly, even as Home Rule approached, O'Connor accompanied his fairly general praise of Labour at League meetings (as in the conference of 1909) with somewhat dubious claims about the improved economic circumstances of Irishmen in Britain (as he did in Cork in 1911) and coupled this with an insistence on the separateness of the problems of the Irish in Britain. At the Belfast conference in 1910, and then again with increasing emphasis in the Dublin conference in 1913 and the London conference of 1914, he combined promises that Home Rule was all but achieved with the not entirely consistent demand that the future of the Irish organization in Britain had to be discussed. His claim at the 1914 conference was that 'the Irish in Great Britain still had to assert themselves and fight for their proper recognition and proper place'. James Connolly may have been expressing a general view when he said, in response to argument such as this, that in the future the problem of Ulster would be used to sustain the U.I.L.G.B. as well as the Nationalist organization in Ireland, even though the League according to Connolly, had already 'paralysed' the labour movement 'for a generation'. There was, indeed, everything to suggest that O'Connor saw himself continuing to lead the Irish movement in Britain after Home Rule was obtained.[62]

[60] Examples of by-elections before 1910 are Jarrow and Manchester North West; after 1910 there were the contests in North East Lanark (Mar. 1911), Kilmarnock (Sept. 1911) and Leith (Mar. 1914). See Glasgow *Forward*, 4 Mar. 1911 and 21 Oct. 1911 and O'Connor in *R.N.*, 1 Mar. 1914.

[61] There are numerous criticisms of O'Connor from Labour and socialist spokesmen in these years. See *Forward*, 17 Dec. 1910, James Connolly in *Forward*, 18 Mar. 1911, Herbert Morrison in *Forward*, 6 Mar. 1914.

[62] *D.P.*, 5 June 1911; *ibid.* 16 May 1910, 13 May 1913, 1 June 1914. O'Connor returned to this theme after the war. See Chapter 6 p. 251; James Connolly, 'The Exclusion of Ulster', *Forward*, 24 Apr. 1914.

Industrial unrest and the demands of Labour politics caused a running squabble both immediately before and then during discussions on Home Rule. But O'Connor was well able to contain the trouble and turn his main attention to the Bill itself where he soon found enough other difficulties. The third Home Rule Bill was introduced in parliament on 11 April 1912. After all the preparations, emphasis, and anticipation caused since the Liberals had once more seemed a likely means to pass Home Rule, the stop placed on the Bill by 1914 now seems the cruellest anti-climax in the whole of O'Connor's career, especially given all the advantages which, on paper, Redmond's party had after the elections of 1910, and given (perhaps the cause of the trouble) that his party were scrupulous to obey due constitutional process. The course of events has frequently been described and it is only necessary to add how disillusionment set in and how O'Connor met it.

Disillusionment is perhaps too strong a term because O'Connor, like all the other Irish M.P.s, entered into the struggle over the Bill with high hopes and it is still not clear how far these had been dissipated by the autumn of 1914. O'Connor's optimism was bound to be stronger because he had put more faith in the Liberals. In December 1910 he had performed his usual function of passing on details of a conversation with Elibank to Redmond where, although stressing the need for 'reticence', and admitting that 'of course we shall have difficulties with the details of the Bill', he believed that the Liberals would be 'reasonable'. With the onset of the Bill, O'Connor did admit to the readers of *Reynolds's* that he was ready to expect the worst, he had 'been disappointed so many times'.[63] This may express a real conviction or a passing mood; it reads more like the political equivalent of touching a rabbit's foot. He also had to face some barbed attacks in parliament where the Ulster Unionists concentrated on how his position as an Irish nationalist for an English constituency was becoming more and more anomalous. One Unionist suggesting, for instance, that the problem of Ulster, and incidentally the problem of O'Connor, could be solved by an exchange of populations between the north of Ireland and Liverpool Scotland division, the sort of black humour often appreciated by Irishmen. O'Connor had little difficulty in debate, at least before it came to the question of Ulster and even then his embarrassment arose largely because of events outside parliament. Otherwise he was well able to deal with wrecking amendments, on the use of Irish in a Dublin parliament, on

[63] O'Connor to Redmond, 22 Dec. 1910, quoted in Gwynn, *Redmond*, p. 184; *R.N.*, 7 Apr. 1912.

proportional representation, and on the control of judges with a great deal of good humour, saying in reply to the first, as might be expected, that 'the language of Shakespeare was good enough for him'.[64]

Unfortunately for O'Connor, debates in the Commons were not now a decisive element in the fortunes of Home Rule. Debates on the first and second readings in 1913 and 1914 were generally acknowledged to be formalities and were in effect a means of implementing the Parliament Act. These debates were incidentally, all appearances to the contrary, the first time many of the Irish party, including O'Connor, had had a chance to speak at any length on such a Bill, the first Home Rule Bill having been more a matter of establishing a principle, and the second not having been criticized in any detail by the Irish majority party. In such circumstances it was not a matter of controversy if the Bill was decided in the main by detailed negotiations between the cabinet and the Irish leaders, since that had been the policy followed in 1886 and 1893. O'Connor, for one, was very much accomplished at such negotiations and in normal circumstances would have relished them. But the problem was made worse for O'Connor personally because, once again, he had to deal with the judicious absence of the other Irish leaders from the scene of the negotiations when the future of the Bill was not only passing out of the Commons but out of the control of parliament altogether as a result of direct appeals both by Unionists and then militant nationalists to irreconcilable opinion in Ireland. To do justice to the complexity of attitudes on both sides would require a separate study but at least it can be said that the refusal of the Irish parliamentary party to accept that the Ulster Unionist opposition was any more than a 'bluff' was a testament to a belief in parliamentary principles. O'Connor had taken such a view as early as 1906 when dismissing the activities of the Ulster Unionists under Saunderson. Since then he had attacked the manifestations of Orangeism in Liverpool, both in the 1909 disturbances and in the two elections of 1910. The steps towards extremism in 1912 included the setting up of the Ulster Volunteer Force in January, Bonar Law's blank cheque to Ulster opposition in his notorious Blenheim speech of 27 July, and the signing of the Ulster Covenant in September 1912. The Nationalist leaders were impressed by none of this. O'Connor, in common with much radical opinion, dismissed the Covenant in particular and many have been equally

[64]*Hansard, 5*, 37, col. 228, 16 Apr. 1912; *Hansard, 5*, 42, col. 2022, 22 Oct. 1912; *ibid.* 43, col. 918, 4 Nov. for proportional representation; *ibid.* 44 cols. 2141-4, 3 Dec. where he made a comparison with Irish bishops and quoted Swift to the effect that 'on their way through Hounslow Heath the bishops were taken out of their coaches. . . highwaymen were put in their place' (col. 2141).

scathing about F.E. Smith's and Carson's celebration of Orange support in Liverpool immediately after Carson's return from Belfast. This was one of the most histrionic demonstrations to take place in England in modern times where Smith promised armed men from Liverpool to support the Ulster Unionists (something of a departure from the intentions of the conciliation committee formed scarcely a year previously).[65] Such scepticism, mixed with an increasing anger, persisted throughout 1913 and became apparent in the debates in the Commons, especially in that of 9 June 1913 where, according to William O'Brien, O'Connor showed 'one of those rare lapses to which the most genial of Irishmen was subject' and launched an attack ('a poisonous stream of provocative bitterness') against the Irish Unionists which, to Unionists both then and on a less obvious occasion in a debate the following month, was used to prove the point that Protestants had much to fear from the 'ferocity of the dominant party' under Home Rule.[66] The vocabulary of the speech in June certainly gives the impression that O'Connor had lost his temper but it ought to be equally obvious what an incredibly tortuous dilemma both he and the Irish party were in. Orange intransigence, whether justified or not, was paying dividends. When O'Connor referred to Protestant intolerance (which was his way of replying to Orange charges) he was accused of aggravating the situation. Similarly, when Healy condemned O'Connor, whom he described as the Irish party's 'press agent', for 'mishandling' the campaign against Carson and showing 'great unwisdom' this, while essentially true (in O'Connor's underestimation both of Carson and the force of his threats), overlooks O'Connor's faith in the Liberal government, and it is possible that any other policy would have been equally criticized by Healy.[67]

---

[65] Liverpool *Forward*, 4 Oct. 1912 and for a fuller description see A.T.Q. Stewart, *The Ulster Crisis* (1967), pp. 66-7. O'Connor's dismissal of the Covenant can be found in a letter to Winston Churchill where he made the somewhat over-precise claim that 'the Covenant was not signed by 25 to 40 per cent of the Protestants of Ulster over 25 years of age' (O'Connor to Churchill, 22 Oct. 1913 in Churchill, *Winston Churchill*, vol. ii companion part iii, p. 1405).

[66] William O'Brien, *Irish Revolution*, p. 193; Lord Case in parliament, *Hansard, 5*, 53, col. 1319, 9 June 1913. See also the retort the following month that O'Connor's 'bitterness' was obvious 'however well he disguises in words which were carefully chosen, his real meaning' (*ibid.* 55, col. 110, 7 July).

[67] Healy, *Letters*, ii, 557. It is clear from O'Connor's letters that he did underestimate Carson. See, for instance, O'Connor to Churchill, 7 and 22 Oct. 1913, where he spoke of 'Carsonism' 'breaking up' (quoted in Churchill, pp. 1401-2 and p. 1405. Similar remarks occurred in his letters to Dillon and Devlin, 1 Oct. 1913 where he said that 'the English tories have at last begun to realize the hole into which Carson has got them' (quoted in Gwynn, *Redmond*, p. 229). See also Lloyd George Papers, c/6/10/7, O'Connor to Lloyd George, 3 Apr. 1914.

Ulster undoubtedly became the stumbling block and the absence of Dillon and Redmond from discussions on the matter provided, as in 1909 and 1910, additional burdens for O'Connor. The first minor crisis came in the autumn of 1913 when it became clear that Churchill would take the opportunity of a constituency speech at Dundee (given on 8 October) to come out against any coercion of Ulster and would propose the exclusion of part of Ulster from the Home Rule Bill. Many Liberals were concerned about the Ulster case but O'Connor, writing to Dillon, enclosing a copy to Devlin and asking them both to get in touch with Redmond, was reassuring about the firmness of Liberal intentions. Dillon in reply, as his biographer suggests, was vague, Churchill was answered to some extent by a speech of Redmond's at Limerick, and many in the Irish party, though not O'Connor, thought that that was the end of proposals making special provision for Ulster. O'Connor, still not best pleased at his intermediary role, was driven to lose his temper with Dillon on this occasion, and read him a lesson in the basics of negotiation, that in this case their Liberal friends had merely wanted to be informed and might have opposed Churchill more vigorously if they had known Redmond's attitude.[68] There was little sign here that O'Connor, compared to Dillon, was lacking in negotiating or parliamentary skills.

Whether O'Connor was excessively naive here is also open to doubt. He was aware that Lloyd George, in cabinet, had been in favour of some form of 'temporary' exclusion for Ulster as early as 1911: what may have been more ominous was that Lloyd George had said very little about Ireland since. O'Connor at this stage shared the general view that exclusion of any part of Ulster was unacceptable and he had written to Churchill that 'postponement' would be better than 'mutilation' and that 'no proposal was more resented' than exclusion.[69] But he did his best up to the end of 1913 to keep lines of communication open to Lloyd George because he feared that Lloyd George might believe that the issue of Ulster threatened the break-up of the Liberal party. O'Connor's friendship with Lloyd George was still a close one. Amidst the political discussions O'Connor could be found passing on the good wishes of an Irish American organization to Lloyd George, trying to secure 'Anatole France for tea', and using Lloyd George as an intermediary with Sir Edward Grey in an attempt to obtain government sponsorship for English paintings to be sent to the San Francisco Exhibition. In January 1914 O'Connor went on a

---

[68] O'Connor to Dillon and Devlin, 1 Oct. 1913 in Gwynn, *Redmond*, p. 229; O'Connor to Dillon, 13 Oct. quoted in Lyons, *Dillon*, p. 334.

[69] O'Connor to Churchill, 7 and 13 Oct. quoted in *Churchill*, pp. 1402, 1405.

holiday with Lloyd George to Algiers (though O'Connor would have preferred Palestine).[70] O'Connor's good offices with Lloyd George were not needed immediately because in December Asquith came up against Bonar Law's refusal to negotiate on the basis of temporary exclusion. Then, by March, O'Connor, now in welcome company with Redmond, Dillon, and Devlin, met with Asquith, Birrell, and Lloyd George where the Irishmen were obliged to agree to temporary exclusion of four Ulster counties on the understanding that no more concessions would be required of them. These proposals were announced by Asquith when the Home Rule Bill began its third reading on 9 March.

Despite their concession, the move towards extremism on the Unionist side continued, with the Curragh mutiny occurring in March 1914 and the Larne gun-running in April. Nationalists, while enraged at the Curragh mutiny, an anger shared by Liberals and radicals, advised against government intervention against the Ulster Volunteers after Larne on the grounds that it might prove provocative both to Unionists and to nationalists for Westminster to seek to re-establish close control of Irish affairs on the eve of Home Rule. One insight into O'Connor's attitude however is given by a conversation he had with C.P. Scott, where O'Connor said that the advice of the Irish had led to too much leniency and that this was always a danger 'with a weak government like this'.[71]

In the Commons in May the Home Rule Bill passed its third reading and in June an Amending Bill was introduced to allow temporary exclusion for parts of Ulster. Discussions on the latter had only just begun when the Howth gun-running to the National Volunteers (since June under the nominal control of Redmond) led to the Bachelor's Walk massacre in the centre of Dublin. O'Connor's reaction to this in *Reynolds's* showed the distance between him and the new nationalism in Ireland but also his distance from the Liberals because his 'first impression was that it might be the end of all things [and that] our people might well have lost their heads'. He then demanded 'that at all costs we should drive out of office a ministry under which such things were possible'.[72] With the Home Rule Bill shortly to be put on the statute book, but suspended during the European war, and with the Amending Bill abandoned, Home Rule came to a ragged, uncertain halt. The supremacy of the Nationalist

[70]Lloyd George Papers, c/6/10/4, 5, and 6, O'Connor to Lloyd George, 10 and 13 June, 16, 10 and 13 Dec.

[71]B.L. C.P. Scott Papers, Add. MS 50901, f. 119.

[72]*R.N.*, 2 Aug. 1914.

party was still evident but, as is now apparent, it had been seriously questioned for the first time since the 1880s by the alternative of force. There is little reason to believe that O'Connor's disappointment was because he had lost, for a time, the opportunity of being elected to an Irish parliament, though he had implied something of the sort in one debate.[73] Instead there was the bitterness of hope yet again deferred; but still a resolve. This faith and determination did much to answer the critics he had met with in his long parliamentary career and the enemies he was likely to find even more in evidence by this time in Ireland itself. O'Connor was certain in his belief

> which ought to be preached now and then [that there is] no commoner, no more vulgar mistake, than to imagine that men engaged in political life are, as a rule, self seekers without principle and without any other [aim] than to line their purse, fill their stomachs and feed their voracious appetites. [There is] more unselfishness among politicians than among any other class in society. . . none have to suffer more humiliations, more insults and more misconstructions than those on the side of popular rights. . . but if you be a real man you go right on.[74]

This was a conviction about constitutionalism which had been severely tested if not disproved by 1914, and it was to come under greater strain in the years which followed when all the old landmarks were obliterated and all the old parliamentarians scarcely comprehended the magnitude of the change.

[73]*Hansard,5*, 60, col. 1443, 2 Apr. 1914.
[74]*R.N.*, 18 Jan 1914.

6

A LONG FAREWELL, 1914-29

Sir, you are a member of the Saxon parliament. I would have you
remember that you are talking to a member of the provisional
government of the Irish Republic.[1]

In the years of continual setback and disaster after 1914, the
declaration of war, the Easter Rising, the destruction of the parliamentary party in the election of 1918, and the Anglo-Irish war from
1919 to 1921, it would be easiest to take the view that O'Connor's
apparent awareness of the need for stoicism in the right course was
fully justified. Certainly, the impression given by his involvement in,
for instance, the drawn out negotiations with Lloyd George's government after the Rising, is chiefly one of incredible powers of endurance.
This ability to endure may have been an integral part of O'Connor's
character but, even so, when viewed not in the long term but in the
day-to-day activity of a politician and, still, a man of letters, it
becomes overlaid by a more obvious fertility of imagination where
negotiation or new proposals were concerned, what a critic might
regard as too much activity, too much fuss. An inner pessimism, for
which there is occasional testimony, and which was fully justified by
events, was nevertheless at odds with a no doubt perverse zest for life.
Although he was an old man, and in his mid-sixties when the war
began, his energy remained so remarkable that his occasional
complaint or the brief interruption of his work through illness is,
paradoxically, what causes the surprise. This is another way of
suggesting how much O'Connor was taken for granted. The Rising,
the 1918 defeat, and the guerrilla war in Ireland did not break
O'Connor, though Redmond was destroyed, Dillon withdrew into
bitter exile, and Devlin, the isolated Nationalist leader in Ulster,
became more desperate. O'Connor was less deeply involved, or
perhaps compelled by his nature to see the surface of things, having a
horror of extremity in his own feelings to match his distaste for
extremism in politics. He was, too, a survivor, and with the onset of
the European war emerged more clearly as a British as well as an Irish
politician by conviction and interest. Whether this makes his defeat
any less remarkable is a matter of taste and opinion. His own plans
then came to nothing, whether they were his increasingly quixotic

---

[1] W. O'Brien, *Recollections*, p. 507, Dominick O'Mahoney, a Fenian, speaking to
O'Connor.

ventures in journalism or his hopes for a continuing Irish political presence in Britain. Yet he was not to know the end to his political hopes until the final decade of his life, and even if he never saw an end to complexity perhaps he would have been at a loss if matters had been made simple. It was a politician's defeat and power and appearances were never given up easily.

The War Effort, 1914-16

O'Connor's attitude towards the outbreak of war was, to begin with, intimately bound up with his hopes for Home Rule. This was obviously the case with the other Irish leaders, yet it is fair to say that O'Connor's awareness of the implications of the war was stronger and that afterwards his involvement in the war effort as a British M.P. was far more marked than that of the other Irishmen; he here made a choice without perhaps fully realizing that he had done so. Asquith's formula for Home Rule, arrived at by September, was to put Home Rule on the statute book and suspend its operation during the war. This largely followed the wishes of Redmond, expressed in a memorandum to Asquith, and O'Connor had suggested a similar line of action both in letters to Lloyd George and in his column for *Reynolds's*. One difference however was that O'Connor had advised Lloyd George that an Act of Parliament suspending the Home Rule Bill (such as transpired) would be 'false' and he had proposed instead as 'the only safe course' an 'arrangement by parliamentary pledge' which would, presumably, be more binding and take less away from the Nationalists. What was best for the Nationalists was clearly given priority by O'Connor but he genuinely saw no distinction between this and what was best for Britain in her hour of need. News that the Home Rule Bill was on the statute book would, he told the readers of *Reynolds's*, 'bring a thrill of joy to the U.S.A. and to the colonies', the clear implication being that support for Britain would be increased.[2]

Yet he was more cautious than Redmond and was apprehensive about Redmond's total commitment of Ireland to Britain's cause. Although O'Connor was, as Redmond's biographer suggests, 'more sympathetic to the cabinet than any other member of the [Irish] party', it is also clear that O'Connor's immediate instinct was to advise Redmond not to intervene in the foreign affairs debate on 3 August. As

[2]Lloyd George Papers, c/6/10/10,, O'Connor to Lloyd George 21 Aug.; *ibid.* c/6/10/11, memorandum of Redmond to Lloyd George 22 Aug., outlining alternatives and favouring suspension. Copy sent to Lloyd George by O'Connor; *R.N.,* 9 Aug.

the purpose of the debate was to allow Grey to explain the danger of diplomatic developments, and as he had already remarked in his speech on the improved Irish situation, there was no necessity for Redmond to speak. Perhaps Redmond was carried away by a very emotional debate. O'Connor's appraisal was cooler. A day earlier in his newspaper column he had recognized 'the necessity of closing up our [British and Irish] ranks' in face of the German threat, but he had also emphasized that the Irish 'had made every sacrifice that could have been asked from us. . . . What further sacrifices . . . could we in fairness be asked to make?' In the emotionalism of that debate and those few weeks O'Connor was wary, his distrust of excess of feeling showing to good effect. Perhaps, too, he was surprised, as he was when he reported to Dillon Redmond's speech had been greeted with enthusiasm, and that Unionist M.P.s had thanked Redmond afterwards 'literally with tears in their eyes'.[3] Whether O'Connor reported this dryly it is now too late to say, but it is evident that Dillon was disturbed by Redmond's pledge while Devlin, with his greater fears for the future of Ulster, was enraged. The speech once made, O'Connor enlarged on its 'epoch making utterances', as indeed they were and were to remain, as O'Connor was to remind an indifferent Commons in the years after 1916 when Redmond and the Irish party were increasingly pushed to one side. There was, from the outset, a hint in O'Connor's testimony that something of the Irish position was irrevocably given away.

O'Connor was probably equally surprised at the general enthusiasm for the war. He had taken more of an interest in foreign affairs than any other Nationalist M.P., more so even than Dillon, whose strictures on Grey and the policy of entente he may have regarded as naive. O'Connor's interest in foreign policy had in fact preceded his concern for Ireland; his biography of Disraeli had shown that. Yet he retained a radical's debunking pacifism, had shared many of the views of Labouchere who in his day had been regarded as the most extreme critic of official policy. O'Connor, too, had a greater first-hand knowledge of Europe than had Dillon, his education and his journalistic work had fitted him for wider horizons, and his literary interest had made him sympathetic to France even though he had latterly become aware of its growing 'exasperated patriotism'. By comparison, he soon reversed his favourable impression of Kaiser

---

[3]Gwynn, *Redmond*, pp. 354-5; *R.N.*, 2 Aug. This was in the column that discussed the Bachelor's Walk incident; Dillon Papers, MS 6740-4, f. 223, O'Connor to Dillon, 4 Aug. It is not exactly the case that Redmond 'had to make the most vital decision of his life on his own' (Lyons, *Dillon*, p. 354).

Wilhelm. With the outbreak of hostilities he put the best, and a reasonable, gloss on events, stressing the provocative growth of the German navy, declaring his support for 'the sacred principle of nationality', which had dated somewhat, and for 'the rights of small nations'. Finally, and for all his admiration for Russian literature, he made no bones about his detestation of one of the allies, 'the autocracy of Russia'.[4] Despite all this, it is difficult not to sense a lack of enthusiasm, a realization which was by no means common that the war would be a bloody and long ordeal. Before Redmond's speech and the declaration of war O'Connor had deprecated 'the conditions which might drag this country into what might be the greatest and the worst continental war of modern times'. Apart from sharing in the radical inability to do anything effective to stop Britain's involvement (and to be fair to O'Connor he was fully engaged elsewhere) what is also apparent is the extent to which he identified himself with Britain, writing of 'our' country and the peril which 'we' faced. Admittedly he was writing for a British newspaper, but some of his sympathies were engaged. Something comparable is shown in his correspondence with Lloyd George where he remarked, again partly perhaps in surprise, at the enthusiasm shown in Ireland, the 'depth of feeling of friendship to England now existing among our people' and citing bishops' pastoral letters, a sermon Redmond had heard in Balbriggan, and the 'cheers and bands' accompanying soldiers leaving for France, the latter all the more remarkable because they included the Scottish Borderers who had been involved in the Bachelor's Walk incident.[5] He also suggested that these sentiments were shared by Irish American opinion. Part of this was, no doubt, intended to convince Lloyd George and the cabinet of the worth of the Nationalist case but, equally, the fact that he should transmit such enthusiasm was a sign that he too was ready to be convinced. Much of O'Connor's attitude to the war in the years down to 1916 could then be described as committed and little short of enthusiastic. Such an example, which might signify a hasty change of mind, is now easy to criticize but it would be a condemnation that would have to be almost universal and would have to include many other radicals and socialists as well as many recruits to the colours. Although other Irish leaders were not as closely involved in the war effort, the precedent had been set by Redmond and, with Home Rule on the statute book, there was a sort of moratorium on discussion of Ireland in the Commons. The best way to further ensure Home Rule appeared to be by redoubling Ireland's efforts in fighting the European war.

[4]Fyfe, *O'Connor*, pp.170, 233-4; *R.N.*, 9, 2, Aug.

[5]Lloyd George Papers, c/6/10/10, O'Connor to Lloyd George, 21 Aug.

Almost a celebratory announcement of O'Connor's adhesion to the war was his attendance and spirited speech at a large patriotic and recruiting rally at the Tournament Hall, Edge Lane in Liverpool on 21 September 1914. Here he shared the platform with Winston Churchill, who called for a million men for the new army, and F.E. Smith, O'Connor's old Liverpool adversary. By this date and in the city where his real power and support lay, he was ready to follow the lead given by Redmond. Part of his speech marks a distinct change, where he touched on 'Our Empire, founded on freedom, on free institutions, on the respect for nationality. We ask no man to abandon his language. We ask no man to swerve in his faith. We ask no man to swerve in his individuality. Our flag flies over a wide world and a free Empire.'[6]

This speech was taken by many, including the Liberal *Daily Post* when it looked back on his life, to be the occasion on which O'Connor truly became a Liverpool rather than an Irish politician who made mysterious visits to his own peculiar constituency. Whether this was entirely the case, bearing in mind his long co-operation in Liberal ventures in Liverpool Exchange division, and the heated battles against Unionists in elections since 1906, it does mark a change of emphasis and a new duality of loyalty which may have been shared by his Liverpool Irish constituents. The recollections of one inhabitant of the Scotland Road area reveal that the war began with patriotic celebrations (as it did in Ireland, especially in the Dublin described by Sean O'Casey).[7] In retrospect it seems that the war did more for peace within Liverpool than all the efforts of the conciliation committee and it was as though the belligerency drummed up by Unionists since 1912 had found a less divisive outlet. Relations between O'Connor and other Liverpool politicians, especially Smith, improved considerably; even prior to this they had not always been as strained in private as debates on the floor of the House had suggested they must be.

Nevertheless O'Connor did not achieve so much credit or influence for his efforts here as he might have expected. This was not because of any sluggishness in recruiting. On the contrary, he was

[6]Barbara Wittingham-Jones, *Liverpool Politics* (1936), p. 128. The meeting is dated in Churchill, *Winston Churchill*, vol. iii, companion part i, p. 218.

[7]*D.P.*, 18 Nov. 1929; P. O'Mara, *The Autobiography of a Liverpool Irish Slummy* (1934, 1967 ed.), p. 140. A few Liverpool Irishmen and other Irishmen resident in Britain (whether of Irish birth or of descent) did choose to go to Ireland and join the Irish volunteers. These are noted in Thomas P. Coffey, *Agony of Easter* (1970), p. 35 and Margery Forester, *Michael Collins, the Lost Leader* (1971), pp. 37-8 which gives a description of the 'Liverpool Lambs'. The numbers involved were inconsiderable compared to those who volunteered for the British Army.

active and Irish recruits from Britain were abundant. He began to hold recruiting meetings throughout Britain, especially in the northern cities, immediately after the Tournament Hall meeting, calling for a special Irish effort for brigades being raised on Tyneside and in Liverpool. O'Connor, as one of the most able platform speakers of his day, was proving his worth in this work as much as any other radical or labour leader. By December 4,000 recruits had been gained from Irishmen in Tyneside, or almost a full brigade, and the figure may have been comparable in Liverpool (although the Liverpool Irish battalions were an older territorial creation and not inspired by O'Connor, or much mentioned by him), and this was apart from Irishmen who joined other British regiments. These were the Irish equivalents of the 'Pals' battalions and flourished in the same spirit of optimism. Recruitment appears to have continued at a high level into 1915, and O'Connor could be found at recruitment meetings in this year too, though by then mainly in the London area.[8] Where the problem lay was with the War Office which appeared, to O'Connor and Redmond at least, to be unwilling to give Irishmen their due recognition. Partly no doubt this was due to administrative incompetence, an inability to cope with the influx of recruits except by the old territorial pattern, but partly too there is evidence to suggest that Unionists in the higher reaches of the army at one and the same time both did not want O'Connor's recruits and yet complained that it was proving difficult to fill the 'Irish' division recruiting in Ireland. Sir Lawrence Parsons, the Anglo-Irishman in command of the Irish division complained frequently to O'Connor and F.L. Crilly but also refused to accept Irish recruits from Britain. He told neither O'Connor nor Crilly of one of his motives, which was that such transfers 'would mean filling us with Liverpool and Glasgow and Cardiff Irish who are slum birds that we don't want'. Meanwhile the recruits that Parsons did want, the 'clean, fine, strong, temperate, hurley-playing country fellows', proved more and more reluctant to enlist and, of these, O'Connor had admitted to C.P. Scott that *Sinn Féin* was having some success in limiting recruiting in the south and west of Ireland by suggesting in its propaganda that Nationalist Irishmen were being asked to join the colours 'in order that they may be conveniently killed off'.[9] Meanwhile, too, the Ulster division was allowed to recruit as it

---

[8] Gwynn, *Redmond*, p. 407; figures given in O'Connor to Bonham Carter, Asquith's secretary (probably 29 rather than 20 Dec. given in Gwynn, *Redmond*, p. 407) copy in Lloyd George's Papers, c/6/10/2; O'Connor spoke at recruiting meetings at Wimbledon, Hyde Park, and Croydon in 1914 and 1915 (*The Times*, 19 Oct. 1914, 12 July 1915, 20 Nov. 1915) and these may have been merely the major occasions in a fuller programme.

[9] Gwynn, *Redmond*, p. 400; Scott Papers, Add. MS 50901, f. 180, Diary, 27 Nov.

wished and was a virtual conversion of the Ulster Volunteer Force, officers and all.

O'Connor complained almost at once about what, from the point of view of efficiency alone, was a preposterous situation. He did this both in a letter to Asquith and in a covering letter to Lloyd George in December 1914 but, although the two Liberal leaders then intervened with Kitchener, little additional recognition was given to the Nationalist contribution. O'Connor, with some insight into the problems of propaganda and a certain amount of style, suggested that to transfer Irish troops raised in Britain to Dublin would boost the morale of the troops, would entrance Dublin, and would counteract any efforts against the allied cause originating from Irish American publicists; but this scheme was ignored.[10] Some of O'Connor's urgency here does smack of a new found zeal for the martial arts (which had been noticeably lacking during the Boer war crisis), especially, for instance, where he talked of how he could 'command' so many recruits to serve as troops for the Irish division. So far as the cabinet was concerned, it might be claimed that it had more important things on its mind, except that the conduct of the war generally was still lethargic and amateurish. The entire dispute, which has been given only in outline, now appears something of a lilliputian squabble in view of the tragic end of precisely these battalions, including those comprising the Ulster division, in the summer of 1916. Accepting the patriotic atmosphere of the first years of the war, the Irish did have a grievance, one particularly resented by O'Connor. He and others claimed that by October 1914 50,000 Irishmen were in the army (whether as regulars or as new recruits is not clear), that by February 1915 115,000 Irishmen from Britain had volunteered, while the figure given for the end of 1915 and up to the spring of 1916 was 150,000.[11] Yet it was only by constant pressure that something like an Irish division was created and given slightly more freedom in recruiting. This may have been achieved by the threat of a debate and the idea for this may have originated either with O'Connor or with Lloyd George. Nevertheless,

[10]Lloyd George Papers, c/6/10/12, O'Connor to Lloyd George, 30 Dec. and copy of the letter of 29 Dec. to Bonham Carter for Asquith's attention (c/6/10/2). See below p. 235 for the Liverpool and the Tyneside Irish battalions in 1916.

[11]Figures are obviously difficult to decide with any precision because some recruits were Irish-born and some not, some enlisted in Ireland and some in Britain and they may have joined territorial battalions which were not 'Irish'. Some figures are given in Fyfe, pp. 241-2. The figure of 150,000 was claimed by the Irish Nationalist party in Liverpool (*D.P.*, 9 Nov. 1915) and by O'Connor (*R.N.*, 6 Feb. 1916). See also the totals of 150,183, and 265,000 given in *Royal Commission on the Rebellion in Ireland* (1916), p. 124 and see below p. 226.

it looks as though no specifically Irish recruiting rallies were encouraged either in Newcastle or in Liverpool.[12]

Insult was added to injury so far as Liverpool Irishmen were concerned when great publicity was given to the so-called 'emigration riots' which took place in Liverpool in November 1915 when a body of 600 Irishmen from the west of Ireland attempted to embark for the U.S.A. on the *Saxonia*, and at the same time there was another party hoping to leave from Glasgow on the *California*, all finally prevented by the Foreign Office.[13] This was the occasion for Nationalists in Liverpool to protest about the attentions of the press and to claim that, out of the high total of Irishmen who had enlisted, 20,000 had been Liverpool Irishmen. Had the Nationalists made a more public protest against military administration and publicity earlier, much of their difficulty might have been removed. O'Connor himself was restrained by Redmond's total pledge to the war effort and it also seems the case that not all the other Irish leaders were concerned to take a stand on the issue. Yet, even so, O'Connor's activities were in pursuit of greater efficiency and above all showed a commitment to the war. He had a greater 'British' interest and closer contacts with the cabinet than other Irish leaders and his attention was not only concentrated on recruiting. In his journalistic work the war caused the closing down of *T.P.'s Weekly* and prevented a revival of *M.A.P.* which he had planned despite all his earlier experiences with that paper. But he did bring out *T.P.'s Journal*, designed as a war paper, in 1915; it lost money heavily and soon had to be discontinued. An aggressive line in anti-German press articles came from him almost at once, 'responsive', so his biographer believed, 'to the national mood' and this was to continue and perhaps become more blatant up to 1916. In spite of all that had happened in the interim he could write in August 1916 of 'the only way with Germany' or, in October, of 'the whining of the hun'.[14] To be entirely fair, it may be that by this latter date the work was uncongenial and that it bears witness to O'Connor's continuing awareness of the importance of propaganda, especially when directed to the

[12] The suggestion about a debate occurs in O'Connor to Redmond, 27 Feb. 1915, quoted in Gwynn, *Redmond*, p. 414. Fyfe (p. 242) said it was O'Connor's idea whereas O'Connor said that Lloyd George had first proposed the idea to Dillon and then to O'Connor. Fyfe also said that no rallies were allowed in Liverpool or Newcastle (p. 242).

[13] *D.P.*, 8, 9 Nov. The Foreign Office announced that passports issued by their office would be required for all men over the age of nineteen. The crew of the *Saxonia* (mostly Liverpool Irishmen), went on strike against the emigrants, the disturbances were caused by attacks on the emigrants by the local, largely Liverpool Irish, population. No recruits were gained.

[14] Fyfe, p. 234; *R.N.*, 6 Aug. 1916, 8 Oct. 1916.

U.S.A. Here, he had helped to modify the inflexible censorship scheme first put forward by F.E. Smith. He visited France on a number of occasions, especially in the latter part of 1915 and early in 1916, aiding French morale at the time of the opening of the battle of Verdun. He was put in charge of an Anglo-French Joint Parliamentary Commission to effect closer co-operation between the allies, and when he wrote to Bryce at the end of 1915 he was sanguine both about the prospects for the commission and the results of an interview he had had with the French premier, Briand. Feeling in France as a whole he found 'excellent'. Of his visits to the front and to the wounded little can be said with any certainty; soldiers may have found him indistinguishable from the other visiting politicians whom legend has it they so much disliked. He himself was agreeably surprised at their lack of hatred for the Germans. It might also be said here that he made a great many attempts to help in individual cases, as when he tried to have the young, and far from robust, T.M. Kettle brought back from the trenches (although Kettle was killed before the transfer could be made) and he helped too with pensions, in assisting with the resettlement of Belgian nuns and priests in Ireland and in Britain (which is detailed in O'Connor's correspondence with Herbert Gladstone), and he intervened with Lloyd George in an attempt to lessen antagonism against naturalized British citizens of German or Austrian origin.[15] The war was his close concern and by 1915 and 1916 this can be illustrated by a comparison. In January 1916 Dillon, who like most of the Irish leaders now spent most of his time in Ireland, told C.P. Scott that he was glad that the Irish had continued to oppose conscription because it showed that they 'were not selling their principles'; in March 1915 O'Connor could be found at lunch with Lloyd George discussing ways to overcome the munitions crisis.[16] O'Connor wanted the Irish effort to have its reward and it is clear that he was personally fascinated by the conduct of a great war. But then, too, the Irish effort, the numbers of Irish recruits was to obtain a particular resonance in comparison to the Rising in Dublin and also because of the anonymous fate of the new battalions in France in 1916. O'Connor was let down badly but it might be added that, in common

[15]*Hansard*, 5, 65, cols. 2207, 2230, 2263-4, 8 Aug. 1914; *ibid.* 66, cols. 738-42,10 Sept.; Fyfe, p. 240; Bodleian Library, Bryce Papers, UB 23, O'Connor writing from Paris to Bryce, 31 Dec. 1915; Fyfe, pp. 246-7; 'Great and Important Lessons Learnt by visits to the Wounded', *R.N.*, 27 Feb. 1916; Viscount Gladstone Papers, Add. MS 46080, f. 105, f. 138, O'Connor to Herbert Gladstone, 11 and 14 Jan.

[16]Lloyd George Papers, c/6/10/14, O'Connor to Lloyd George, 12 May 1915; Scott Papers, Add. MS 50902, f. 86, Scott in conversation with Dillon, 10, 11 Jan. 1916; *ibid.* Add. MS 50901, f. 193. 15 Mar. 1915.

with other politicians at the time, his political and wider imagination proved sadly lacking.

The Dublin Rising, in Place of Literature

The Easter Rising of 1916 surprised the Irish leaders (in O'Connor's case in a way in which he had been surprised before), fatally weakened the claim that the Irish could make in return for their part in the war effort, and was the major cause of the break (though by no means apparent at the time, nor inevitable) between the parliamentary party and Irish public opinion. O'Connor's part in all this was somewhat paradoxical and is in some ways difficult to explain. Along with the Irish party generally he had been aware of the forces of extremism. To some extent the party had been outbid by Ulster extremism prior to 1914 but were still justified even during the first years of the war in dismissing *Sinn Féin* as faddist and disruptive and, on the evidence of its performance at the polls, no political threat. Even the irreconcilable minority of the National Volunteers which broke away under Eoin MacNeill to form the Irish Volunteers persisted in following a policy of waiting on events. Moreover the distance of parliamentarians from public opinion can be exaggerated. Dillon was sensitive to the least sign of nationalist impatience, there was a unity of purpose between Devlin and all shades of nationalist opinion in the north of Ireland, and Redmond still gathered the loyalty and respect of the overwhelming majority of Irishmen. O'Connor, more than most, was accused of distance from the new forces of nationalism, principally because of his long absence from Ireland. But the difficulty went deeper than absence and lessening awareness; it had not worked this way in the case of many Irish Americans and, even if it were true, O'Connor could claim that he was primarily responsible for the Irish in Britain. And O'Connor was aware of popular moods, including the mood of Ireland, and knew that it had not appeared to be moving in support of *Sinn Féin*. At the same time, it is curious that his conversation and correspondence at the beginning of the war did warn of the danger of extremism to an extent that is not noticeable in the case of other Irish politicians. In his correspondence with Lloyd George in August 1914 he touched on the visit of Patrick Egan from the U.S.A. and how his support for the allies would counteract 'the campaign of John Devoy'. He returned to this theme in December, talking of 'the pro-German campaign in America' and the activities of Kuno Meyer in support of the German cause in America. In November 1914, while in conversation with Scott, he attacked the extremists in Ireland, including Roger Casement who (a rare sidelight on what might have been known of Casement in some close circles) he described as 'both bad and mad', and he showed a singular vehemence against the 'treasonable Irish weekly press' which he suggested ought to be dealt with by martial law. More than anyone, he was used to rating press influence highly and might deplore this extremist campaign in particular because it was, so he claimed, 'directed principally against the Nationalist party and only secondly against Great Britain', and because much of its abuse was directed against him personally. As late as March 1916 in conversation with Scott he could say that 'the *Sinn Féiners* [were] very active and malevolent', and could give details. Yet the conclusion encouraged by the twists and turns of the desperate gamble of the Rising is that in these circumstances O'Connor's warnings often appeared melodramatic or worrisome, the grumblings of one professional to another. Above all, what mattered, what O'Connor was concerned with, was the war effort, not any threat to the parliamentary party (at least this is how the matter was presented in conversations with British ministers and other men of affairs). To Scott, supporting, with good reason and on Nationalist advice, a disengaging policy in Ireland, a lack of any great concern on the part of the British was equally justified.[17]

What caused the general surprise when the Rising took place was, to begin with, that the gamble was so great, indeed irrational, and on the part of Patrick Pearse and his secret military council within the Irish Volunteers, calculatedly so. The numbers involved clearly indicate the extent of the gamble; scarcely 1,600 followers of Pearse and Connolly took part in the Rising in Dublin while, according to the most recent investigation, the number of Irishmen serving in one capacity or another with the British forces was 265,000 (not including those of Irish descent).[18] Numbers are important in indicating why the parliamentary leaders could have ignored a possible threat and why, speaking for the Irishmen of Liverpool, and representative of most Irish opinion in Britain, Austin Harford could quickly denounce the Rising for, among other things, being 'insignificant, unrepresentative and irresponsible'. If anything, majority opinion in Ireland began by

[17]Lloyd George Papers, c/6/10/10, c/6/10/12, O'Connor to Lloyd George, 2 Aug., 30 Dec.; Scott Papers, Add. MS 50901, f. 180, 27 Nov. 1914; *ibid.* Add. MS 50902, f. 188.- For a fuller explanation of government lack of interference see Leon Ó Broin, *The Chief Secretary, Augustine Birrell in Ireland* (1969), pp. 161-204.

[18]F.S.L. Lyons, *Ireland Since the Famine* (1971), p. 366; *Royal Commission*, p. 124 and see also F.X. Martin 'Eoin MacNeill on the 1916 Rising; Select Documents xx', *I.H.S*, 245. The larger figure here includes not only those serving with the army or with the police but also the National Volunteers and the Ulster Volunteers. MacNeill's total force amounted to 16,000 men of whom about 1,300 took part in the Rising along with about 200 of the Irish Citizen Army under Connolly.

being even more hostile, and this was particularly so in Dublin. Much British opinion, too, began by appreciating this, and the justice of Redmond's statement of 27 April disassociating the Irish people from the Rising in the strongest possible terms. Perhaps British reaction here was unusually perceptive, given the strains of war, perhaps, though, it owed even more to what bordered on an accusation put forward almost at once by O'Connor. He had, wisely, refused to comment until the news of the Rising was made clearer except that he could safely say that 'these painful events are the most eloquent vindication of Home Rulers that History has yet recorded'. This was an argument he continued to pursue while the post mortems on the Rising went ahead and he became more insistent in his charge that the Irish party had been neglected. By the end of the first week in May he was ready to claim that 'the only forces . . . that can stand between southern Ireland and anarchy are Mr. Redmond and the Irish party'. At the meeting of the Irish party called for 9 May, the successful resolution, which shows signs of having been drafted by O'Connor and which was a more moderate one than that demanded by Dillon (who had been in Dublin during the Rising) stressed how the Irish party during the 'past ten or fifteen years' had been 'subjected to the fiercest and most unjust attacks' had faced 'every weapon of faction, of personal hate, [and of] journalistic insincerity', and, in summary, had not had 'the vigorous support they were entitled to demand'.[19] Opinion in Britain, especially official and parliamentary opinion, may have felt guilty. O'Connor too was correct to concentrate on opinion if anything were to be retrieved. Beside this practical politics, Redmond was too full of despair, Dillon of anger. But then events began to justify their attitudes further and already, in private, O'Connor had been more alarmed than he could publicly admit. When news of the executions of the leaders of the rebellion first reached Britain on 5 May O'Connor's reaction, without any first hand knowledge, was vehement. Scott described him

> just in from seeing [Lloyd] George and greatly excited about the position in Ireland which he declared was being ruined by Maxwell [commander of the British forces in Dublin] and martial law. 'Before the executions', as he rhetorically put it, 99 per cent of nationalist Ireland was Redmondite; since the executions 99 per cent is *Sinn Féin*. He could find no words strong enough to denounce the whole proceeding and Maxwell he denounced as a wooden headed soldier.[20]

[19] Austin Harford in *D.P.*, 3 May; *R.N.*, 30 Apr. *ibid.* 7 May; *D.P.*, 11 May.
[20] Scott Papers, Add. MS 50903, f. 20, 5-8 May.

An instinctive reaction like this shows that O'Connor, along with almost any other nationalist, would realize the implications of the executions. But almost immediately the difficulties of his particular position became clearer. Scott could think O'Connor rhetorical and British politicians were much too sensible to believe that changes could ever take place suddenly. Besides which they, and it must be emphasized, O'Connor, were preoccupied with the European war and regarded the Rising as incidental. After speaking to Scott from the heart, O'Connor felt he had to collect himself and dwell on the difficulties now facing the implementation of Home Rule with the exclusion of six Ulster counties, even though he admitted that it would be 'folly' to reject such a proposal. Yet there was as yet no strong evidence that the coalition government did intend to implement a compromise at such a dangerous juncture.

In other words, O'Connor's understanding of the Rising was far more perceptive than commonly supposed. It is true that at one stage he virtually attributed the Rising to 'Larkinism' in Dublin, a comparison which is unusual rather than entirely improbable.[21] But this was incidental to his larger perception that 'men of letters' had worked for the Rising and that 'no men could shrink more from the sanguinary consequences of their preaching' than these. The first is true, the second it would be agreeable to believe was obvious but more recent experience suggests that it is far from the case. O'Connor, by virtue of his long experience of politics and literature, had the imagination to grasp at what had happened when few of his political contemporaries, Irish or British, might have been aware that literature could move men to such actions. Had O'Connor known it, the dispute between Eoin MacNeill and the minority around Pearse had been precisely on a point where O'Connor would have taken a comparable view to MacNeill's, that the idea of a 'blood sacrifice' for Ireland to reaffirm the separateness of Irish national identity was romantic nonsense. Yet in conclusion, O'Connor, having understood so much, was then incorrect. He understood the 'contempt' many Irish intellectuals had for the parliamentarians, and he was right to say that 'the work of politicians' had made cultural nationalism possible, and that 'people in despair and in material want don't listen to singers, to playwrights, and to archaelogists'. But he failed to see, or more probably refused to admit, how the imagination could, and did, catch fire.[22] As in his conversation with Scott, as in the long years since the death of Parnell, in his fear of intransigence and in his distaste for much that passed for

[21] *R.N.*, 7, 14 May.
[22] *Ibid.* 18 May. On literature and the Rising, see the bibliography.

literature in the new century, what he perceived he could not, as a creative politician, then accept and so he transformed it instead into his worst fears – something to avoid, not something to work against. Yeats could catch the horror surrounding the executions, the new argument of 'MacDonagh's bony thumb', just as Yeats had had the freedom to see what the death of Parnell could very probably mean. To O'Connor, this could still be poetic licence or criminal indulgence and might yet prove innaccurate because it depended upon events. He was, finally, imperceptive and this was part superficiality but also came from civilized standards, an unfamiliarity with psychological horrors which have since become more commonplace. Some courage was also involved, and his customary stubbornness in wanting a return to reason, the rule of law and of parliament, especially as his concern was not reciprocated by the British government. His charges against both Unionists and the new nationalists were complaints, recrimi-nations and, after the first shock of the Rising had died away and had been replaced by a renewed concern for the war effort, these did not prove effective in provoking a new spirit of government or Unionist generosity. Such a demand for redress had little practical influence among the new politics of deceit and brutality.

O'Connor, therefore, in the years immediately after the Rising, is seen more than at any other time as both more limited in what he could achieve, disheartened and stoical in equal measure but, equally, persistent and concerned. The reminder he had given to the readers of *Reynolds's* before the war about the necessity to 'go right on' was now proving true with a vengeance. Admittedly, O'Connor had less to lose and his British connection could stand him in good stead as a reason for never refusing to negotiate. Redmond, by comparison, had had to bear the full brunt of the challenge to his authority, and his leadership never fully recovered. Dillon had begun to think this of him as early as May, and Dillon for his part had returned to a greater antagonism towards the government. Dillon had been in Dublin and was a witness to the Rising and, while emphasizing his lack of sympathy with the rebels, had spoken in the debate in the Commons in May when he recognized that those who took part in the Rising had fought a clean fight, an attitude which deeply shocked the Commons and dismayed O'Connor.[23] In retrospect Dillon's attitude is perhaps easier to understand than O'Connor's. The other leading Irish politician, Joseph Devlin, was in the most difficult position of all. He had his strongest support among Ulster Nationalists but even an immediate

[23]*Hansard*, 5, 81, col. 2512 for the debate and Dillon's speech. For reactions, including that of O'Connor see Lyons, *Dillon*, p. 382.

implementation of Home Rule would affect him most closely since Ulster still provided the difficulty just as it had done prior to the war.

A settlement along Home Rule lines was what was suggested by Asquith's announcement in the Commons that Lloyd George would take charge of negotiations to implement self government, and Lloyd George himself quickly produced another scheme to serve as the main basis for discussion. This scheme allowed for a parliament in Dublin to administer twenty-six counties, retention of Irish M.P.s at Westminster, and exclusion for six north-eastern counties to be governed by a Secretary of State. The detailed discussions which followed until the final break with first Lansdowne for the Unionists and then Redmond by 21 July have recently been detailed elsewhere.[24] Not only was the essential problem as intractable as when negotiations were broken off and Home Rule put on the statute book in September 1914, but all that occurred since, and especially the circumstances of 1916, made matters more difficult, particularly for the Nationalists. Unionists and Ulster Unionists were now in Asquith's coalition cabinet and southern Ireland was in such a ferment that without great good fortune the Nationalists would find it impossible to obtain acceptance for a modified Home Rule bill, especially as it transpired that more concessions were required of the Nationalists. Added to this, British opinion and the cabinet was preoccupied with the war, on the one hand would welcome a settlement only if it were achieved quickly and removed what they might regard as a nuisance, on the other would not recognize any settlement that appeared in any way to threaten British security. A final and crucial difficulty, which has been highlighted by Dillon's biographer, was that Lloyd George presented his scheme, with its proposals for the exclusion of Ulster, in different ways to the interested parties; to the Nationalists it was made to appear a temporary expedient where the question of Ulster could be resolved later, to the Unionists it appeared as a permanent solution which would give Ulster the guarantee which the Unionists required.

To O'Connor, none of these difficulties appeared to cause much hesitation: negotiations themselves were a blessing. The fact that his old friend Lloyd George was in charge of them was an additional source of something approaching confidence. O'Connor's apparent equanimity was so pronounced that it led to an outburst of impatience from Dillon before the negotiations began – a rare display of temper towards O'Connor but wholly understandable given the great weight of despair, bitterness and, above all, awareness, that Dillon carried. O'Connor, by comparison, does appear here as more detached, thick-

[24] See Lyons, *Dillon,* pp. 386-402.

skinned and less concerned about Ireland (and probably less familiar with the difficulties there) than Dillon. O'Connor still had an eye on the war. He told the readers of his newspaper column that 'the future of the war depends to a very large extent on whether the Irish question is settled or not', though he also tried to convey the changed mood in Ireland, the 'resentment [which] no good democrat can fail to understand', and he had a scathing aside reserved for 'men who have tried to embarrass and weaken the Irish party' who had then 'come forward as super patriots and have demanded a settlement'. His concern for the war was also a concern for Britain and this was also presented as the chief concern of 'those two and a half million of my countrymen in Great Britain'. Because of this he could not himself act as a negotiator. As before, in 1913 and 1914, he was one of those who did most to encourage negotiations and once again he was the chief intermediary between the Irish and the cabinet. It remained a burden he had to carry by himself at Westminster when, through most of June, Redmond, Dillon and Devlin stayed in Ireland for the usual tactical reasons and when once more O'Connor had to urge on Dillon, 'you ought to come over here at once, indeed I regret to think that already your coming over here has been too much delayed'.[25]

O'Connor's influence was therefore apparent in keeping negotiations going, performing the indispensable task, arduous enough in itself, of explaining Irish circumstances to Lloyd George and putting Lloyd George, for whom he still retained a considerable personal regard, in the best possible light with the Irish leaders, attempting to overcome Dillon's not unjustified suspicions of the Welshman. It does seem, too, as though O'Connor had an influence with Lloyd George and through him the cabinet, not so great an influence as O'Connor might have anticipated, but one which made perhaps as great an impact as the events in Ireland. This is how it is possible to interpret O'Connor's increasingly detailed reports to the cabinet and to Lloyd George which began with his letter to Lloyd George of 9 June. It was here that O'Connor protested so effectively against the military government of General Maxwell (putting into effect his earlier condemnation in the conversation with Scott) that it caused Lloyd George to pass on and augment these protests to Asquith and then caused the prime minister to urge once again on Maxwell the 'necessity of going slow and of creating no "incidents" '.[26]

[25]Dillon's attack on O'Connor, on 27 May, is mentioned in Lyons, *Dillon*, p. 386; *R.N.*, 4, 18 and 26 June; O'Connor to Dillon, 28 June, copy in Lloyd George Papers, D/14/3/44.

[26]Lloyd George Papers, D/14/2/23, O'Connor to Lloyd George, 9 June; *ibid.* D/14/2/22, Lloyd George to Asquith, 10 June; D/14/2/23, Asquith to Lloyd George, 10 June.

O'Connor also passed on two lengthy accounts of what must, in the circumstances, be regarded as a brief stay in Dublin. This arose out of his attendance in Dublin at a party meeting called to discuss Lloyd George's proposals. He sent Lloyd George a long and, as he later indicated, 'hurried memorandum' of Sunday 11 June and further typed particulars dictated on 13 December after his return to Britain which were intended to be circulated to the cabinet. These, briefly, emphasized the change of mood in Dublin (a change which O'Connor had anticipated would accompany the executions; it was a different thing to experience the change in actuality). He described the dignified and exemplary conduct of the rebels, how the leaders of the rebellion had all but been turned into saints (this was O'Connor's terminology), how the entire Rising had been given a religious colouring which in turn had spilt over into religious services being held in Dublin, how secret societies had revived (compared by O'Connor to the 'Invincibles' of Fenian days), and how, despite the end of the executions, matters were continually aggravated by the harrassing conduct of the military under martial law. O'Connor's main recommendations were that certain officers should be withdrawn and martial law as a whole removed, and that Ireland could adequately be governed under the safeguards provided by the Defence of the Realm Act.[27] What effect this had on the cabinet is not clear but it is possible that this was the only non-military or non-Unionist information about the situation in Ireland that the cabinet was receiving. Perhaps this explains the touching detail that O'Connor gave, such as his re-telling of the tale of a child praying to 'St. Pearce' (sic). To try to make sense of such a monumental change of mood after such a brief visit to Dublin taxed the imagination and instinctively, as a journalist, O'Connor knew that this could best be done by giving particular circumstantial detail and it was the imagination on which O'Connor concentrated in order to get the message home to the cabinet. Perhaps, too, he was defending himself against too much realization of the total change of circumstances, or he may, by now, have simply been seeing things as a stranger or visitor to Dublin would see them. At any rate, although it does not say much for the cabinet's grasp on events that they were prepared to accept this information as important, the fact that they did

[27]*Ibid.* D/14/2/27, O'Connor to Lloyd George, 'Sunday' (11 June) from Dublin; *ibid.* D/14/2/35, O'Connor to Lloyd George, 13 June. O'Connor also made a personal appeal on behalf of the Kent family; *ibid.* D/14/3/5, O'Connor to Lloyd George, 16 June. O'Connor's discussion of these incidents also occurs in O'Connor's recorded conversations with Scott (Scott Papers, Add. MS 50903, f. 51, 12-17 June) but as O'Connor was dictating the memorandum for the cabinet while also speaking to Scott, it is possible that Scott merely ran the two together when he came to write up his diary. Whatever the merits of O'Connor's choice of incidents, it is curious how they have stuck in the imagination.

so also indicates that they did not themselves put O'Connor in quite the same category as the other Irish leaders: he was more of a British politician, almost an impartial witness.

O'Connor, among all the Irish leaders, while not exactly taking the British line, appeared to be more aware of the context – a time of general crisis in the conduct of the war. This made him all the more persistent about the continuation of negotiations and more sanguine about the results. He played no major part in formulating the terms to be negotiated, but then neither did Redmond or Dillon; Lloyd George kept such things to himself. It might be said that O'Connor shared Lloyd George's belief that negotiations must be kept going at all costs, irrespective of their contents. Lloyd George was then able to persuade Dillon to enter into the negotiations by the dire picture he painted of the struggle facing Britain on the western front and how this might make opinion in Britain less patient with Irish problems (a reminder which bears some comparison with Lloyd George's tactic during the final negotiation of the Anglo-Irish treaty in 1921). The basic problem remained that to the Nationalists the terms had to be temporary, to the Unionists they would only have any merit if they were permanent. For a time this approach worked. Despite anguish on O'Connor's part over Dillon's pessimism, and the considerable difficulty of opposition from the Catholic church in Ireland, and the Nationalists of Ulster to even a temporary settlement, it seemed as though, on the threat of resignation of all the Irish leaders, including Redmond and Devlin (who had done most to persuade northern Nationalists), an agreement to the proposals had been reached on the Irish side by 23 June. O'Connor was less dismayed about possible Unionist reactions and appeared to believe, with what might be regarded as even less justice than when he had adopted a similar attitude before the war, that Unionists, even the Unionists within the cabinet, would not prove a threat. But although this had been a constant theme of O'Connor's, perhaps there was some justification for it just at this time. Redmond was firmly convinced that Lloyd George had pledged his political future on the settlement and O'Connor in his numerous accounts of the position in the cabinet which he sent to Redmond and Dillon expressed the clear conviction that Unionist recalcitrants in the cabinet were in a minority and that Lloyd George would push the matter through despite their opposition. On 13 June he reported to Dillon that Walter Long was opposed and that Lord Lansdowne would probably resign, on 21 June he wrote that Lloyd George was prepared to go so far as to bring up his own resignation in order to keep his hands free in the negotiations, and to stiffen Asquith's resolution, and on the following day in a letter accompanying one sent by Lloyd George to Redmond he suggested that Lloyd George was prepared to accept the resignation of Lansdowne, Long, and Lord Selborne. The Irish were then called upon to make further concessions to safeguard imperial defence in Ireland during the war, allowances which O'Connor thought probably justified but which were also a further irritant to nationalist sentiment. But the settlement which seemed attainable because of sacrifices such as these was destroyed by Lansdowne's insistence in the Lords on 11 July that the terms must be permanent, Redmond's rebuttal published on 21 July, and then the government's acceptance of the permanence of the settlement on 22 July which led to Redmond's angry denunciation of the negotiations in the Commons on 24 July. Such open intransigence was what O'Connor had chiefly worked against, though his efforts were directed towards Nationalists, advising Lloyd George on 11 July, for instance, that Dillon and Devlin would have to be treated 'very tenderly', but he was impatient with Asquith and aware of the implications of Lansdowne's speech. The failure of the negotiations did not enrage or embitter him as it did Redmond and Dillon. He was, as he told Scott, 'much more sorry for the failure of the negotiations as he had expected more from them'. Neither had he been much perturbed at the conduct of Lloyd George. If he recognized Lloyd George's emphasis on talks before substance (and it is difficult to believe that he did not, it was merely that he did not enlarge on such things), then he also saw the advantages. Redmond remained justified in his anger. Dillon could claim, as his biographer indicates, that he had been right to regard co-operation with the coalition government since 1915 as a mistaken policy, and he reverted to his earlier intransigence. O'Connor, privately, might have been unimpressed, and he described Dillon's attitude to Scott as one of 'morbid suspicion'.[28] Politics from this view was still about reaching agreement. Given the difficulties in Ireland it was either a superficial or a courageous view but in any event it was a logical view for a politician. For similar reasons O'Connor still approved of Lloyd George; disillusionment there was still to come.

However great the opportunity missed in 1916, it remained inexorably the case that the function of the Irish party was to secure a settlement in Ireland. Sympathy for the Irish party might have meant that this was the best time to achieve consitutional settlement on the

[28]Lloyd George to Dillon, 10 June 1916, quoted in Lyons, *Dillon,* p. 391; Redmond's view is given in Gwynn, *Redmond,* p. 506; O'Connor to Redmond, 20 June quoted in Gwynn, *Redmond,* pp. 509-10; Dillon Papers, MS 7640-4, f. 335, O'Connor to Redmond, 21 July, copy to Dillon; Lloyd George Papers, E/2/22/1, O'Connor to Lloyd George, 11 July; Scott Papers, Add. MS 50903, f. 65, 27 July.

old lines, but negotiations dragged on fitfully until the end of the war. O'Connor played the major part in these moves because he was least dismayed of all the Irish leaders, because he remained more or less permanently at Westminster, and because he was more attached to the British cause in the war. The latter soon meant that Ireland was relegated in importance. It was in the middle of the summer negotiations of 1916 that the Somme offensive opened up and it was from here on, at least for the rest of 1916, that O'Connor's attacks on the 'hun' were at their most lurid in his *Reynolds's* column.[29] It was also on the first day of the battle of the Somme, 1 July, that the battalions raised among the Irishmen of Britain and the Ulster division suffered their most grievous, appalling, casualties, the Tyneside Irish battalions in particular meeting, according to a recent historian of the battle, 'a bizarre and pointless massacre'.[30] Against such a background Lloyd George's warnings to Dillon become clearer. To O'Connor, who may or may not have appreciated the full extent of the tragedy or may, like much of the population, have become inured to casualty lists, this could only have increased his distance from the new nationalism of Ireland. While he made no extensive public references to the losses of the Tyneside Irish, Liverpool Irish, or similar battalions, he did co-operate with Redmond in publishing a work entitled, somewhat unfortunately, *Irish Heroes in the War*. O'Connor's essay on 'The Irish in Britain' in this collection was written in 1916 and the book was published in 1917. While the chief purpose of this was to draw attention to the part played by the Irish (and especially the Irish in Britain) in the war effort, it may also have been intended to offset the effect of the Rising and it is, incidentally, further evidence of O'Connor's attachment to the Irish in Britain, 'more patient, more tolerant. . . broader in [their] outlook', rather than the Irish in Ireland.[31]

This emphasis, together with a new hope for negotiations, was seen more clearly by the end of 1916 when Lloyd George finally replaced Asquith as prime minister and at the head of a new coalition government. O'Connor may have been indifferent to the manoeuvres which had preceded Lloyd George's elevation. More accurately this appears to have been the attitude of most of the Nationalist party, or those of them who were still active which meant, like it or not, that O'Connor and the Nationalists were kept out of the making of the new government and received no pledges on policy, an opportunity which

[29] Articles in *R.N.*, 9 July, 6 Aug., 8 Oct.

[30] John Keegan, *The Face of Battle* (1976), p. 249.

[31] Felix Lavery (ed.), *Irish Heroes in the War* (1917), p. 32.

any strong Irish party, without drawing too heavily on the lesson of Parnell would never have let slip. At the time of the formation of the coalition government in May 1915 O'Connor, so a diary of the Asquith cabinet records, expressed some sympathy for Asquith and some doubts about Lloyd George's trustworthiness. This may have represented the Irish party's regard for the old Liberal leader, but the harsher reality might be that O'Connor and others were little concerned to defend the outgoing coalition government. O'Connor, above all, was more aware of Lloyd George's ability and, when the victor was clear, sent an immediate letter of congratulation which was coupled with an appeal for the release of the Irish Volunteer prisoners from Frongoch and a suggestion that this could mark a new start in Irish policy. At the same time, O'Connor accepted a very minor government post as President of the Trade Board of Film Censors, which helped to augment his ever precarious finances. He may have regretted the fact that the Irish party had not involved itself more closely in the promotion of Lloyd George. His sympathies at this instant were clear, indeed earlier in the year, before the Rising, he had been prepared to go further and speaking to Scott had thought it 'very desirable. . . to have had a representative [of the Nationalist party] in the coalition government' and had himself in mind 'as representing an English constituency'. Dillon, 'the determining factor in all these matters' had vetoed that idea and Dillon and Redmond were now even more antagonistic towards the government headed by Lloyd George. At the outset Redmond clashed with Lloyd George over the latter's delay in releasing the prisoners and it was left to O'Connor to smooth over the prime minister's frayed nerves.[32]

Obviously Ireland was only one among the many problems facing the new prime minister, and at this juncture Lloyd George did not see it as a very pressing problem. Yet he was not above trying to hold out hopes of improvements in Ireland and O'Connor's initiative in this respect did not come out of a vacuum. Lloyd George had invited both O'Connor and Dillon to his home at Walton Heath on Sunday 3 December, and 'opened his mind very fully to them' as Scott recollected after a conversation with Dillon.[33] Dillon, never one for play-acting in politics, declined to advise him. O'Connor's reaction was not given but he showed every sign elsewhere of being enthralled by Lloyd George's performances. Equally, O'Connor kept at his

[32]C.E.H. Hobhouse, *Inside Asquith's Cabinet,* ed. Edward David (1977), p. 249; Lloyd George Papers, F/42/2/1, O'Connor to Lloyd George, 11 Dec. 1916; *The Times,* 11 Dec; Scott Papers. Add. MS 50902, f. 188, 6-8 Mar; Lloyd George Papers, F/42/2/2, O'Connor to Lloyd George, 20 Dec.

[33]Scott Papers, Add. MS 50903, f. 114, 4 Dec.

thankless post as chief intermediary between the government and the Irish party, writing to Dillon on conversations with Lloyd George on the possibility of conscription being applied to Ireland as recruitment dried up, a policy which O'Connor opposed vehemently, and, on the other side, after the Nationalist party's defeat at a by-election in North Roscommon, persuading Redmond in February 1917 not to publish the text of a manifesto attacking *Sinn Féin's* policy of abstention, a manifesto which could have been interpreted as a formal announcement of the end of the parliamentary party.[34] Such a familiar role as go-between was one which O'Connor was obliged to fill for the rest of the war years and up to the election of 1918 and he did this with great ability and long sufferance, complaining only when he felt he could not, practically, act as a negotiator in the absence of the other Irish leaders. As before, these complaints were brushed aside.

The one exception to this somewhat passive function (forced on him by his close connections with the cabinet) was when he himself tried to bring about a debate in the Commons on Home Rule on 7 March 1917. Despite his friendship with Lloyd George, O'Connor could not fail to know that the prime minister was not preoccupied with Ireland. A conversation of O'Connor's with Sir Henry Duke, the Chief Secretary for Ireland since July 1916, revealed, so O'Connor wrote to Devlin, that Lloyd George 'had not given any serious attention to Ireland' since coming into power.[35] Nevertheless O'Connor went ahead with his motion calling on the government 'without further delay to confer upon Ireland the free institutions promised her'. He had been nervous about taking such a step, as a conversation with Scott reveals, and Scott for his part urged postponement; both may have been aware that the debate would be unpopular in the midst of the war crisis. O'Connor then went on to try to clear the ground with Lloyd George, reporting this at length to Redmond, where the chief difficulty appeared to be that by now Lloyd George, although sympathetic to Ireland, was more impressed by Carson's power within the cabinet. On the eve of the debate O'Connor sent Lloyd George a six-page letter, both personal and political, apologizing for this interruption into the prime minister's many responsibilities, asking in the end only for benevolent neutrality, indeed advising that the prime minister 'ought not to be there [in the Commons]' and anticipating, perhaps apprehensively, 'a flood tide' of

[34] O'Connor to Dillon, 23 Jan. 1917, cited in Lyons, *Dillon*, p. 408; Gwynn, *Redmond*, p. 539.

[35] O'Connor to Devlin, 15 Feb. copy in Redmond Papers, quoted in R.B. McDowell, *The Irish Convention, 1917-18* (1970), p. 68; O'Connor to Redmond, 5 Mar., quoted in Gwynn, *Redmond,* p. 540.

support from the press. The letter was remarkably percipient in emphasizing that the present Irish policy meant only the old policy of coercion, that O'Connor could hardly bear the prospect of Lloyd George being 'hated, distrusted, reviled by Irishmen', and that Lloyd George would have to choose once the war was done between 'the reactionaries and the democratic forces'. But look forward was what Lloyd George at this crisis could not do, and the avoidance of real choice was something he had achieved since 1910 and was to sustain until 1922 when nemesis struck with all the more force for being so long delayed. So the debate was to no avail. O'Connor's opponents, headed by Sir John Lonsdale, the whip of the Irish Unionist party, attacked O'Connor for bringing up the matter because it would 'embarrass the government in the prosecution of the war'. Lloyd George blamed divisions between Nationalists and Unionists for lack of progress, the 'old position' which Lloyd George had brought up with O'Connor before the debate and which O'Connor had impressed both on him and on Redmond would be 'a disaster'. Redmond was even more bitter and dismissive than in July 1916, warned the government 'not [to] ask us in to your back parlours for any more negotiations', and he led his party out of the Commons at the end of his speech, an action which marked the end of any large organized Irish presence in the Commons working for Home Rule.[36] O'Connor's venture, which had been markedly moderate, and in which he had done little more than rehearse the commitments entered into by both sides since 1914, ended in a blank stalemate. There were special circumstances perhaps, but nothing so clearly shows the limits of rationality when faced with the language of power. More specifically it showed the decline in political morality which had come with the war. It may also have been the decisive blow in ending O'Connor's friendship with Lloyd George; his personal correspondence with Lloyd George ended with the letter of 5 March and he does not appear to have written to him again until 1922 and then only in formal terms on a matter to do with the crisis in Greece.

Negotiations which followed, leading up to the Irish Convention in the summer of 1917, proved equally futile. Not that Lloyd George was perturbed at the possible consequences of his treatment of the now politically less powerful Irish leaders. At the end of April he invited all of them to his home at Walton Heath but, following Redmond's warning about back-parlour negotiations, they all, with the exception of O'Connor, turned down the invitation. O'Connor

[36]*Hansard*, 5, 91, col. 425, 7 Mar.; Scott Papers, Add. MS 50903, f. 180, 29 Feb.; Lloyd George Papers, F/42/2/3, O'Connor to Lloyd George, 6 Mar.; *Hansard*, 5, 91, cols. 472-81 for Redmond's speech.

then merely reported Lloyd George's fears which were still dominated by the thought that Carson might resign; Redmond and Dillon must have tired of hearing this. O'Connor was still represented by Scott as being 'very sanguine' about further negotiations, but if this were so O'Connor was virtually on his own. Lloyd George continued to give enough grounds for scepticism. In the spring and summer of 1917 he either could not or would not be definite, putting forward plans favourable to the Nationalists (and to O'Connor in particular) of allowing county option only for Ulster and making even this subject to a time limit, and then reverting to the 'clean cut' (of all Ulster counties) which would benefit the Ulster Unionists, at least territorially. Some of this probably bewildered O'Connor. He reported to Redmond on 10 May that a 'clean cut', to be inevitably replaced when its unpopularity was demonstrated by county option, was the best that the Nationalists could hope for, while shortly afterwards, on hearing that Lloyd George appeared determined to apply the 'clean cut' and nothing else, he confided to Scott 'Well I think the little devil (meaning Lloyd George) has done it now'. Much of O'Connor's conversation with Scott may have been designed to put Scott at his ease or, occasionally, gently to rib him. After his closeness to Lloyd George he probably felt unable to denounce him and, again in conversation with Scott, the most he would say was that Lloyd George was 'a hard bargainer; you had to allow for a certain amount of bluff'. O'Connor perhaps did remain more optimistic than other Irish leaders. There was no disguising the seriousness of the position for the Irish party but O'Connor still took negotiations seriously, more so than the 'extreme men' of the party, by which he meant, in conversation with Scott at least, Dillon and Devlin, neither of whom would have been so regarded in Ireland.[37] There the Nationalists suffered another by-election defeat in South Longford in May, when the first *Sinn Féin* candidate was 'returned' and when Redmond threatened the resignation of the Irish party *en masse*.

O'Connor was still left with the most disagreeable part to play of all the Irish party, remaining in London for negotiations and here his patience was tested as never before. The events of the Irish Convention which first met in the summer of 1917 and which lasted into 1918 have been well covered elsewhere.[38] O'Connor's part was an exasperating one. He was required to stay in London during May and June to report on developments at the Westminster end while the

[37] Scott Papers, Add. MS 50904, f. 6, 7 May; O'Connor to Redmond, 10 May, quoted in McDowell, *Irish Convention*, p. 69; Scott Papers, Add. MS 50904, f. 55, 17 May; *ibid.* Add. MS 50904, f. 6, 7 May; *ibid.* 17 May.

[38] See McDowell, *Irish Convention*.

Convention, which was grandiloquently intended to settle Ireland's future, or, as many Irishmen believed, designed by Lloyd George to catch world attention, prepared to meet in Dublin. Redmond, Dillon, and the other Irish leaders meanwhile stayed in seclusion in other parts of Ireland. Lloyd George's high-handed pronouncements continued to nullify any attempt at persuasion on O'Connor's part. At one and the same time he had to face the complaints of the British at the absence of his colleagues, and to restrain his own impatience at their absence in circumstances which became more and more uncompromising. He was then given an even more arduous task. Redmond in July asked him to visit the U.S.A., once more to raise funds for the Irish party, specifically for the party organ, the *Freeman's Journal*.

Concern for the *Freeman's Journal* had long been uppermost in Dillon's and Redmond's minds. The newspaper's offices and machinery had been destroyed in the Rising, it was encumbered by debt, and although revived it was making considerable losses. A newspaper defending the Nationalists against William Martin Murphy's *Irish Independent* and the *Sinn Féin* press was indispensable in the coming propaganda war in Ireland, without it the Nationalist party might as well admit defeat. Dillon had turned to O'Connor for help on 6 June 1916; O'Connor was, as Dillon's biographer remarks, the natural choice. But O'Connor had been involved in the *Freeman's* affairs prior to this. O'Connor's friend Alderman (later Sir) Alexander Maguire of Liverpool had been persuaded to try and reorganize the ailing newspaper in 1915 and 1916. O'Connor had also responded to pleas from Redmond to help its finances by trying unsuccessfully to raise money from an unknown 'friend', probably Sir Basil Zaharoff. When O'Connor received Dillon's further pleas on the paper's behalf O'Connor, in a manner reminiscent of his involvement in the Tweedmouth affair in the 1890s, approached Lloyd George, much to Dillon's horror since the independence of the paper would be compromised. O'Connor, perhaps having learnt not to be choosy about newspaper finances and yet not having, on closer examination, an impressive record in making them pay, took little notice of Dillon and continued to write to Lloyd George (on 19 and 28 June) about a project for raising money, adding only that it would be necessary 'to leave the Irish leaders in absolute control of its policy'.[39]

[39] For Maguire and the *Freeman's Journal* see Fyfe, p. 265; O'Connor to Redmond, 3 June, quoted in Gwynn, *Redmond*, p. 514; for Zaharoff see Fyfe, p. 237; Lloyd George papers, D/14/2/17, O'Connor to Lloyd George asking for an interview, 7 June 1916; Dillon Papers, 6740-4, f. 314, O'Connor to Dillon, 7 June; Lloyd George Papers, D/14/3/15, D/14/3/44, O'Connor to Lloyd George, 19 and 28 June.

Such strategems or makeshifts must have been wearing thin by the middle of 1917. Even if Lloyd George and his friends had helped the paper, they would hardly be required to do so after his accession to the premiership and the cooling of relations with O'Connor by the spring of 1917. A fund raising tour in America seemed a far preferable way out. Yet for all his equally well-developed knowledge of the United States and apparent awareness of Irish extremism there, which he had had to overcome in his previous visit in 1910, (which was all apart from his reluctance to embark on such a tour at his age and at the height of the war), O'Connor was totally unprepared for the first shock of a widespread Irish American hostility towards the Nationalist party. Writing to Redmond from the United States, he said that 'feeling here about the executions and England was far more violent than ever in Ireland' and he was inundated with abusive letters and attacks on the Irish party, one of which styled him 'the Benedict Arnold of the Irish movement'. In face of such hostility O'Connor decided not to attempt a speaking tour but instead to put the Nationalist case through the press and to raise money by personal contact with wealthy Irish Americans, where he showed considerable ability and persistence. The entry of the United States into the war did not diminish the activities of Irish American republican groups, headed by *Clan na Gael*, but O'Connor did think, with a perceptive and possibly cynical piece of calculation, that his task would become easier as war fever increased and when the U.S.A. received her first casualty lists. In the meantime he had to sit tight, which meant enduring lonely hotel rooms in New York in sweltering summer weather, an unfortunate task for a man nearing the age of seventy and one who had latterly not enjoyed the best of health or attention, and for once this pricked the consciences of the other Irish leaders.[40]

O'Connor had to persist in this trying commission for more than a year, facing to begin with a constant campaign of abuse which stressed, among other things, that he was an English M.P. for an English city, and (because of his film censor's post) a paid official of the English government, some commentary on the notion of an Irish 'race' when second or third generation Americans could accuse other emigrés and their children of not qualifying.[41] For O'Connor it was also a disillusioning experience after his earlier enlivening experiences of America. At first he had hoped that his stay would be a relatively short one, up to the end of 1917. But by December only £8,000 of the

[40] O'Connor to Redmond, 9 July 1917, quoted in Gwynn, *Redmond*, p. 563. See also J.F.X. O'Brien Papers, MS 13458, O'Connor to Devlin, 1 Aug., written from the Knickerbocker Hotel, New York.

[41] Fyfe, pp. 272-4, which quotes extensively from a pamphlet attacking O'Connor.

£20,000 target he had set himself had been collected and he prolonged his stay for a further six inhospitable months. News from Ireland, the deadlock in the Convention and, even more of a shattering blow, the death of John Redmond in March 1918, did little to alleviate his more gloomy moments. But then, in April 1918, it became known that Lloyd George intended to extend conscription to Ireland. Irish parliamentary opposition revived to something like its old form and O'Connor wrote from the U.S.A. joining in the protests, an attitude which, paradoxically, helped to re-establish him to some small degree in the U.S.A. At the same time he interpreted American attitudes to the cabinet and, on his return, to his own party and to the Commons generally (and yet on none of these occasions was he particularly optimistic about relations with the U.S.A.).[42]

When O'Connor returned to England in July 1918 he came back to a House of Commons which few members of the Nationalist party now bothered to attend and to a situation where, according to O'Connor, Lloyd George 'appeared to be aiming at the destruction of the Irish party, which he said was played out'. O'Connor was also appalled at the policy of the government in Ireland which caused him to describe it as 'more of a militaristic and coercionist government than at any time since the days of Balfour'. Lloyd George he described as 'more dupe than Machiavelli' and he laid the blame on Orangemen who had come into power at Dublin Castle, an estimate that perhaps overlooks the fact that Lloyd George was not particularly interested in Ireland in 1918. It was against this background that O'Connor, apparently unabashed by his experiences in the debate of March 1917, introduced a resolution in the Commons on 5 November calling for Irish self-determination, no longer referring to the Home Rule Bill of 1914 but instead attaching his demand to President Wilson's ideal plan for European nationalities.[43] In the turmoil of approaching allied victory in Europe and coming at the end of years of growing distaste for Irish affairs in the Commons, it had little impact, making less impression than the general principle of self-determination made on statesmen at Versailles. Accordingly, if Lloyd George wanted a showdown with the extremist forces in Ireland, O'Connor along with Dillon was often convinced that an election at the end of 1918 would grant him his wish. But they were also hoping against hope (as

[42]O'Connor reported in *M.G.,* 11 Apr. 1918; Lloyd George Papers, F/6/2/60, Washington embassy to the cabinet reporting conversations with O'Connor, 7 May 1918; Fyfe, p. 279; *Hansard, 5,* 109, col. 1439, 7 Aug. 1918. The speech to the Commons was then published separately before the year was out, see bibliography.

[43]Scott Papers, Add. MS. 50905, f. 70, 26 July; O'Connor to Samuel Insull, n.d., quoted in Fyfe, p. 277-8; *Hansard, 5,* 110, col. 1962, 5 Nov.

O'Connor had done in many ways since 1914) that because of their long experience of Irish affairs this need not be so, and need not mean the destruction of the Irish party.

A Refuge in Britain

By the time of the 1918 election O'Connor was entering his seventieth year in circumstances which, to all appearances, might have appeared too novel and too disappointing for an old and much tried politician. Remarkably, particularly after yet more disasters in Anglo-Irish relations, this was not the case. There was always an element of self-deception along with his habit of resilience. O'Connor was certainly aware of how things had changed for the worst. With regard to the United States, for instance, he enlarged on what he saw as an irreversible antipathy between the Americans and the British (among whom he appeared to include himself) when he gave Scott his version of the American tour – all a far cry from his earlier experiences of the United States. However, very soon after the ordeal of his tour (which was not his last trip to America) there was considerable recompense in Britain. The first inkling of this was when he visited his Liverpool constituency, where he celebrated his seventieth birthday on 5 October. His reception could almost be described as a royal tour where the *Manchester Guardian* described him as 'sitting out a sort of perpetual levée', meeting the Lord Mayor and other dignitaries, touring his constituency, and making a series of enthusiastically received speeches.[44] Perhaps instinctively, O'Connor was returning to his political power base but his support, equally, may have proved more enthusiastic than he had anticipated. Writing to Dillon he had indicated how Harford, still head of the Liverpool U.I.L.G.B., had wanted to run things quietly, had hoped that Liverpool would 'back me up', and had indicated the necessity of introducing himself to his new voters (the electorate under the 1918 Reform Act having, he supposed, increased five-fold, from 6,000 to 30,000).[45] This also shows that O'Connor was assured of a political future of some sort whereas the same could not be said of any other Irish Nationalist M.P.

Dillon was greatly pleased at O'Connor's reception in Liverpool, recognizing that it was 'a recompense for what you have endured and

[44] Scott Papers, Add. MS 50905, f. 93, 8 Aug. 1918, where he said, 'The Americans did not really like us – not even the best of us. He had the feeling that in our hearts, however modest outwardly, we gave ourselves airs'; *M.G.*, 8 Oct.

[45] Dillon Papers, MS 6740-4, f. 535, O'Connor to Dillon, 19 Sept.; *ibid.* f. 540, 30 Sept.; *ibid.* f. 545, 7 Oct.

so bravely faced in recent years – and during your American tour' but clearly had little cause elsewhere for satisfaction. It is true that he and O'Connor attempted to collect every crumb of comfort they could from the volatile conditions of the election. Dillon had written to O'Connor in August suggesting that the party might survive given half a chance. O'Connor, still active politically in Britain, had gone further in still believing that Lloyd George might, as O'Connor had suggested in his letter to the prime minister in December 1916, choose the radical side and the cause of Ireland in the polarized politics of post-war Britain. Lloyd George continued to postpone the choice and Dillon remained sceptical. O'Connor, too, was over-optimistic about the chances of pushing *Sinn Féin* to one side, writing to Scott in October that '*Sinn Féin* is on the downgrade' (a view which he also put forward in a *Daily Chronicle* article and which he appears to have sincerely believed). In November he also proposed to send a telegram to American supporters attacking the idea of an Irish Republic and 'the insane policy of abstention' and offering the certainty of passing Home Rule 'within one or two years' if a strong Irish party were returned to parliament. Dillon, with his greater exposure to Irish realities, turned down the idea; O'Connor had to be restrained to some extent.[46]

Nevertheless, both came together in an attempt to retrieve the organization of the party. And the one part of the movement which they appeared to imagine could still provide a nucleus for a fresh effort was the organization of the Irish in Britain. This initiative appears to have been completely overlooked in accounts of the last years of the party. On 26 October there was a meeting of Irishmen from Great Britain held in Manchester at the Free Trade Hall. Devlin and Dillon, the latter now in effect leader of the party, were at the conference and O'Connor acted as chairman. The meeting was not advertised as a reconvened conference of the U.I.L.G.B., such a move would perhaps have been thought too insensitive in view of the considerable changes which had taken place since 1914, but it was probably an attempt to revive the old organization and to test whether there was a groundswell of opinion in Britain in favour of the parliamentarians. As it happened, nothing very decisive came out of the meeting but the intention remains clear nevertheless. Dillon was given pride of place and he produced a long, closely argued speech which denied any alliance with the Liberals, and attempted at the same time to prevent any total commitment to Labour. Neither of these pleas was entirely

[46] *Ibid.* f. 540, O'Connor to Scott, copy in O'Connor to Dillon, 30 Sept. The letter to Dillon refers to the *Daily Chronicle* article; *ibid.* f. 550, O'Connor to Dillon, 21 Nov.; *ibid.* f. 553, Dillon to O'Connor, 22 Nov.

satisfying; the audience could not be expected to know all that had happened in parliament between the Liberals and the Irish party, and no alliance (such as the one strenuously advocated by Glasgow delegates with the Labour party) would involve, or ever had involved, a complete unanimity of view. Nothing positive was decided by the meeting but it undoubtedly emerged as an attempt to determine electoral strategy on the old scale. At the same time O'Connor, as astute and accommodating as ever and more able than Dillon to understand meetings in Britain, won support for a resolution declaring 'friendship to all the friends of Ireland and independence of all English parties'. This phraseology was reminiscent of the election of 1885 but now designed to achieve, and achieving, a breathing space and also giving the Irish organization in Britain, or what was left of it, the right to pick and choose among British candidates, a fact Dillon recognized when writing to O'Connor the following month.[47]

After the Manchester meeting however, Dillon's and O'Connor's fortunes, in the election and in the longer term, diverged and they were never again able to come together in political activity. Indeed they saw each other rarely after this with Dillon remaining in isolation in Dublin though corresponding perhaps more frequently with O'Connor. In the election, O'Connor, as he confessed to Dillon with perhaps a twinge of conscience, became absorbed in Liverpool and other British affairs. By 7 December he admitted of the Irish in Liverpool that 'we here in England are so absorbed in our own struggle that few of us pay the least attention to Ireland'. The contest in Liverpool was given additional zest because although O'Connor was given a walkover (and never again had to fight an electoral contest in Scotland division), the Irish in the city became 'incensed' by lack of consultation when the Liberals nominated their candidate for Exchange division, and they proceeded to put forward their own candidate, Austin Harford. By 5 December the Liberals, recognizing the strength of the Irish vote, had withdrawn their candidate and left Harford, who styled himself an Independent candidate, with a straight fight with the Unionist, Sir Leslie Scott. O'Connor shared this annoyance with the Liberals over, as he wrote to Dillon, 'a seat that really belong to us' and threw himself into supporting Harford with all his old energy. He also visited, or reported on, the Irish in London (where Whitechapel, St. George's and Limehouse caused some difficulty), Manchester, and Glasgow,

---

[47] Reports of the conference in *M. G., D. P., The Times,* 28 Oct. The latter called it a 'demonstration' and suggested that the meeting was a rowdy one. Cf. Fyfe, p. 280 where he remarks that O'Connor turned down a proposal of Austin Harford's to hold a conference of the U.I.L.G.B. in Liverpool; resolution given in *M. G.* report; Dillon Papers, MS 6740-4, f. 547, Dillon to O'Connor, 15 Nov.

where he attended a convention on 16 November which apparently brought the Scottish delegates back from their total commitment to Labour. This was rounded off by a manifesto, published on 10 December and signed by O'Connor and F.L.Crilly, which listed the candidates whom Irish voters should support. Of these candidates, thirty-eight were Labour, twelve Liberal, and three including Harford, were Independents. This slight diversification, though recognizing the strength of support for Labour among Irish voters (which would probably be especially marked among the voters newly enfranchised in 1918) also showed the freedom of manoeuvre O'Connor had gained by the Manchester conference. It was also clear, however, that the British League had declined considerably, many branches having ceased to function during the war. What was also noticeable was that the manifesto was restricted to constituencies in the north-west of England so that, whether O'Connor realized it or not, the Irish had lost their greatest leverage in no longer being able to rely on a spread of voters throughout Britain which could affect constituencies held with small majorities. What the effect of this initiative in the old style was it is difficult to say. In Liverpool, Leslie Scott was exasperated with, and abusive towards, Harford and O'Connor, attempting to associate them with *Sinn Féin*, a clear sign that he was apprehensive. In the event he was able to defeat the Liverpool Irishman by a small margin.[48] Otherwise, although this was by no means the end of O'Connor's ambitions for the Irish in Britain, an appeal to the Irish vote was never again to be made so explicit.

O'Connor had no part to play in the electoral campaign in Ireland. The most he could do was to write to inform Dillon of the campaign in Britain, try to keep up Dillon's spirits, and hope that 'you will get the necessary 20 or 25 seats to continue the movement'.[49] Dillon had sufficient cause for pessimism but hung on, sometimes allowing himself a share of O'Connor's enthusiasm but warning him of the direness of the position in Ireland. The result was worse than Dillon had feared. *Sinn Féin* won seventy-three seats, the Unionists twenty-six, and the Nationalist party returned only six M.P.s, five of these in Ulster as a result of agreements with *Sinn Féin*. Only one seat was won in the south of Ireland, at Waterford, where Redmond's

[48] *Ibid.* f. 569, O'Connor to Dillon, 7 Dec.; *D.P.*, 29 Nov. Harford had failed, against Conservative opposition, to become Lord Mayor earlier in November (*ibid.* 11 Nov.); references to O'Connor's visits to various parts of Britain can be found in Dillon Papers, MS 6740-4, f. 549, f. 550, f. 554, O'Connor to Dillon, 20, 21 and 26 Nov.; Manifesto in *D.P.*, 10 Dec. and seats listed in Appendix D. O'Connor appears to have advised Irish voters in other parts of Britain to vote Labour, as at Southampton (*The Times*, 10 Dec.); *D.P.*, 6 Dec.

[49] Dillon Papers, MS 6740-4, f. 564, O'Connor to Dillon, 5 Dec.

brother, Captain William Redmond, won the contest. Dillon was defeated by Eamonn de Valera in Mayo. In the new House of Commons to represent Irish nationalism once *Sinn Féin* had abstained and set up their own *Dáil*, there was now only Devlin returned for Belfast West, four other Nationalists from Ulster, William Redmond, and O'Connor. Such an outcome was no firm basic for an active part in politics and yet, as before, O'Connor remained active and ready with ideas both in politics and in his own affairs. He was far from being dismayed by the new political and social landscape of the post-war world however much he may have misunderstood it. There was still up to 1922 or 1923 the problem of Ireland, deteriorating into nightmare where every political habit of O'Connor's told him that he ought to intervene, there was his political future in Britain, all tied up with the future of the Irish in Britain, and there was the ever present problem of his own chaotic finances and his journalistic ventures.

Ireland was a dangerous ground for the few Nationalists in parliament since their policy had been so clearly defeated in the election. Dillon, who had presided over the disaster, advised silence and caution to both O'Connor and Devlin. To a large extent this was advice they did not need. It remains possible that O'Connor might have now regarded himself as chief Irish spokesman. More probably, he was only too well aware that he had been cut off from Ireland since 1914 to such an extent that it would be difficult for him to act on the subject in any public way, even though he was identified as the leading Irish representative as far as British opinion was concerned. He also had to recognize the position of Devlin, to whom he had had to defer over the substance of negotiations and who still had a stake in Ireland. There may, however, have been some difference of view on tactics between the two veteran parliamentarians, relations were sometimes strained. O'Connor had begun the 1918 campaign in a euphoric mood but had then agreed with Dillon about the need for caution or, 'had come to the same conclusions myself already'.[50] O'Connor's appraisal of the political outlook by 1918-19 was, in other words, more subtle, realistic, and detached than Dillon's detailed advice (written under the strain of living in Dublin through the Anglo-Irish war) might suggest.

Similarly, it must have been apparent to O'Connor that his old friendship with the prime minister was by now a dubious advantage.

[50]Cf. Lyons, *Dillon*, pp. 459-60 which gives Dillon's view of O'Connor's constituency, Dillon's advice, and O'Connor's coolness towards Devlin. O'Connor's attitude is seen in the letter quoted to Dillon of 7 Oct. (Dillon Papers, f. 545); Fyfe makes the point that by the time of the first world war O'Connor 'represented Ireland in English and in Scottish eyes more adequately than Redmond or Dillon' (Fyfe, p. 246).

The first sign of disenchantment had come at the end of 1917. Since then O'Connor's dealings with Lloyd George had not ceased, but there was nothing to compare with the earlier blow by blow accounts of negotiations and sometimes effusive personal regard for the prime minister to be found in the few final letters. Instead, as has been indicated, the only correspondence from O'Connor kept in the Lloyd George papers after 1917 was a memorandum of O'Connor's based on a conversation with the Greek Prime Minister Venizelos which was forwarded to the prime minister in June 1922. This was aimed at securing support for the Greek cause in the final settlement of the Near East where, ironically, Lloyd George needed very little persuading and over which, in the Chanak crisis, Lloyd George was to fall irrevocably from power scarcely more than three months later.[51] A break with Lloyd George had become open by 1919, when O'Connor was avoiding him socially and ready to mention 'my resentment against him personally' and he agreed with Dillon that any association with Lloyd George would be harmful for Ireland. This cut deep; Lloyd George was the one politician with whom O'Connor, usually tolerant to a fault, refused to be reconciled.[52]

Some of this antagonism would have been occasioned by post-war developments. It was evident that Lloyd George, although making vague promises about Home Rule for Ireland, gave the matter no priority until forced in that direction. He was, more immediately, preoccupied with treaty-making at Versailles. Where once O'Connor would have been sympathetic, now his questions in the Commons were pointed ones about the validity of plebiscites, the rights of minorities, and the principle of self-determination. There was no reply when O'Connor, hearing that Lloyd George was off to visit the Bretons, asked whether there would be any mention of 'the glories of the Celtic race. . .[and] the self-determination of races'. No statement was forthcoming on Ireland until 22 December 1919 and then only in a few items of possible intent mentioned in an adjournment debate at the end of the session. Dillon, in exile, and Devlin and O'Connor had got wind of these proposals, they all equally regarded them as unsatisfactory, and both Devlin and O'Connor refused to attend the debate. O'Connor's view, expressed in conversation with Scott, was that the proposals 'substitut[ed] something much less good' for even the Home Rule Act of 1914, and he was aware, if Scott was not, that the demand in Ireland was now for independence. This contempt

[51] Lloyd George papers, F/42/2/5, O'Connor to Lloyd George, 27 June 1922, enclosing a memorandum of a conversation with Venizelos of 27 June.

[52] O'Connor quoted in Fyfe, p. 287; *ibid* p. 332.

came after a year in which Devlin and O'Connor had attended the Commons on only one occasion to add anything specific or substantial on Ireland. This had been in April when they had spoken in a routine debate on the Irish estimates, an occasion and a subject which would allow them to criticize the government while not compelling to act as spokesmen. O'Connor's opinion on the latter point, whether influenced by Dillon or not, was apparently quite clear when he emphasized that 'I do not claim, I cannot claim to speak in the name of Ireland'. O'Connor's part in the debate was to remind the House of, or to introduce new members to, the historical record of broken promises. Although recently installed as Father of the House, a place in the life of parliament which gave him genuine pleasure and which also may have appealed to his sense of humour, there was no room for sentiment in the hard-faced reply he received from the Coalition benches, that they had heard it all before and that it did not help matters at that moment. O'Connor in reply seemed to sum up more than an opinion of the speech when he said 'nobody is more tired of it than I am'.[53]

In 1920, when the Anglo-Irish war began in earnest, the tiny Nationalist contingent at Westminster refused to involve themselves in Lloyd George's Government of Ireland Bill. Apart from thereby avoiding condemnation from Irish public opinion, they also evaded a curious, anachronistic, though possibly by now traditional fate which Lloyd George had prepared for them. Because, even if they had proved 'conciliatory', Lloyd George had planned that they should not have 'a great deal conceded to them'. Lloyd George's strategem had taken leave of reality; the Irish did not attend the debate. Their only comment was, finally, when the Bill had reached its third reading, to protest in advance against the debate on the Bill being held on Armistice Day, viewing it as an insult to the Irishmen who had died in the war. Nevertheless, it was apparent that the prime minister was more sensitive to Unionist opinion, to the Ulster Unionists still in the coalition. It was here that the real anguish for O'Connor might have been located. He had never favoured abstention on anything and must have known that even an Irish party reduced in size (to, say, the twenty to twenty-five members hoped for in 1918) could have played havoc with the government, going much further in attack than the Labour party was entitled to do over the subject of Ireland. O'Connor's instinct was to attack. For all the difficulties about intervening in debate, and the warnings against even attending the Commons which the I.R.A. issued in the autumn of 1920, O'Connor's gorge rose when

[53]*Hansard*, 5, 119, col. 207, 18 Aug. 1919; Scott Papers, Add. MS 50905, f. 220, 21 Dec. 1919; *Hansard*, 5, 114, col. 1438, 3 Apr. 1919; *ibid.* col. 1550.

the war in Ireland became more obviously a barbarous one. Far from dwelling on the past, and at a time when his own political hopes were at a discount, he, along with Devlin, grilled the Irish Secretary Hamar Greenwood. In November 1920 he asked the Irish Secretary for information on sixteen separate cases involving military or police misconduct as well as following up other civilian complaints, and insisted that he would not rest 'until I have dragged out the truth'.[54]

When it came to the final negotiations in 1921, which led up to the 'Treaty' between the British government and the *Dáil* at the end of the year, neither O'Connor nor any other Nationalist had a major part to play. Even so, on at least one occasion O'Connor did use his influence with Lord Derby – dating from the days of their co-operation over industrial disputes, sectarianism, and recruitment – to moderate British demands with regard to the Irish contribution to the Imperial exchequer.[55] Perhaps as a result of this exclusion much was, inevitably, lost. For most of Ireland a greater amount of formal, constitutional independence was obtained than the Nationalists had ever aimed at and possibly parliamentary action by itself would never have achieved such a result. But the major problem of Ulster was left in deep freeze and, while the Nationalists (and O'Connor in particular) had come round to seeing the necessity for some sort of separate accommodation for the north-east of Ireland, their knowledge and skill as negotiators would never have allowed such an anomalous arrangement as was provided for the six north-east counties to appear permanent. Nevertheless, to O'Connor watching half ruefully and half cynically from the sidelines, it was the enforced ending of a lifetime's work. The cruelties of the Civil War which followed in Ireland between pro-Treaty and anti-Treaty forces only increased his disenchantment. Replying to a letter of Herbert Gladstone's in February 1923, he summed up his feelings in a way that can be even more readily understood after the more recent horrors of the 1960s and 1970s in Ireland.

> Like you I look back on the old days in which you and I were workers in the same cause with a sort of melancholy retrospect. Our cause won, though it won by other methods and by other men; and the very way in which it ultimately succeeded is the very best defence of the very different methods which your father recommended to his countrymen; and the very neglect of his

---

[54]Scott Papers, Add. MS 50906, f. 16, 7 Apr. 1920; *Hansard, 5,* 134, col. 1193, 10 Nov. 1920, protest of Jeremiah MacVeagh, Devlin and O'Connor. O'Connor's cross-questioning of Greenwood came shortly before this (*ibid.* col. 134).

[55]L.R.O., Derby Papers, O'Connor to Derby, 8 July 1921.

counsels has brought the bloody harvest both to Ireland and to England.[56]

This was not a final testament even though he confided to Gladstone that he would have to confine himself in future to 'a few words now and then on causes that still appeal to me'. He was at the same time 'engaged on the terrible task of starting a new paper', in fact a revival of *T.P.'s Weekly*. Paradoxically, the settlement in Ireland, or rather the removal of Ireland from British politics, appeared to clear the ground for his plans for the Irish in Britain. This, for a time, represented a political future for O'Connor and it was something he had seized on at the very beginning of his exchanges with Dillon in anticipation of the 1918 election. In September of that year he had written that 'it is about time we should let the people at home know that Irishmen in Great Britain have their own opinions and own point of view and God knows it is about time we in England should think about such things when our people are in such a condition'. Later in the same month he reminded Dillon of the many war casualties among his Liverpool constituents.[57] What appears a sudden emphasis on his constituents (which could be taken to mean all of the Irish in Britain) could, to a critic, appear an instinct for survival. A more sympathetic view would be that the Irish in Britain had indeed sacrificed much of their interest in social policies for the sake of Home Rule and it may well be that it was the further sacrifices of the war which brought about more clearly the distinction between the exiles (and their children) and the Irish in Ireland and meant that attention to their own needs could be no longer delayed.

Whichever was the more important element in what was a mixture of motives it was apparent, as has been seen, that O'Connor and his constituents concentrated on their own affairs in 1918. O'Connor went further in referring to claims for larger representation for the Irish in Britain, what he called the 'curious fact' (which it certainly was) that he had been informed that it had been Irish abstention during the period of the conscription crisis in 1918 which had led to the defeat of proportional representation, a system which would have given the Irish 'perhaps 20 to 23 seats in Great Britain'. Dillon, as his biographer has shown, viewed all this with some alarm. Yet it is difficult not to come to the conclusion that in many respects Dillon

---

[56] Viscount Gladstone Papers, Add. MS 46085, f. 116, O'Connor to Herbert Gladstone, 6 Nov. 1923.

[57] Dillon Papers, MS 6740-4, f. 535, O'Connor to Dillon, 19 Sept. 1919; *ibid.* f. 540, O'Connor to Dillon, 30 Sept.

could not grasp O'Connor's intentions, that he was inconsistent in his own attitude, and it is possible that Dillon's objections have been given an incorrect emphasis. Dillon had been given pride of place in the Manchester conference of October 1918. At one stage, towards the end of November, he offered up the opinion to O'Connor that 'the Irish in Great Britain are proving more than at any previous occasion that they are the best politicians. . . and the most level headed of the race', a view which O'Connor had expressed as early as 1916'. Clearly, the views of Irish parliamentarians towards those who had stayed loyal to the movement were not unbiased, but it also indicates at least an awareness of the potential, and the political potential at that, of the community in Britain. Dillon went on to warn O'Connor, and by extension the voters in Britain, against too close a tie with Labour. O'Connor was aware of the popularity of Labour, especially with new voters, but it was O'Connor who had shown the greater acumen in retrieving something from the Manchester conference, and then in his visits to Irish communities during the election. By comparison, Dillon's attitude appeared merely provocative.[58] Then, in the years that followed down to 1922, it was probably not the case, as has been suggested, that O'Connor wanted to use the Irish vote within the Labour movement and was otherwise uninterested in a separate movement. It was the case that O'Connor, compared to Dillon, was less suspicious of the Labour party and had earlier been more sympathetic to trade unionism, and his options here were restricted by Irish voters' support for Labour which O'Connor compared on one occasion to the 'Niagara tide'. But O'Connor had also, in December 1918, declared to Dillon that there were some aspects of Labour policy, such as nationalization, which he could not support, that 'our people' would not support 'the extreme socialistic section' of the Labour party but that what remained were 'enough materials for working alliance'. Then, when the Treaty of 1921 had finally cleared the ground (and it may well be that O'Connor had looked forward to this with some impatience), it was O'Connor who wanted to persist with a separate organization and Dillon who then proved lukewarm, warning that such an organization would have no other political context but to act for or against *Sinn Féin* and republicanism, and that politically the Irish in Britain could not exist separately from the Irish in Ireland. There was some good sense in this latter opinion, one which would have been applauded by many British politicians, but it was O'Connor who, ever optimistic, ignored

---

[58] *Ibid.* f. 569, O'Connor to Dillon 7 Dec. 1918; *ibid* f. 557, Dillon to O'Connor, 28 Nov.

Dillon's advice as he had done before, and had to be proved wrong in practice.[59]

O'Connor was unable to do this openly until the end of 1921. In the meantime his belief in the Irish in Britain as a political force was evident, as was his concern for their social welfare, which may have been mixed with some sense of guilt over their long neglect.[60] But there were also more immediate problems posed by republicanism. O'Connor had noticed some sympathy for *Sinn Féin* even in his own constituency in the municipal contests of 1918 and he warned Scott that, under the guise of Art O'Brien's Self Determination League, it was 'gaining ground everywhere'. By the summer of 1920 he began to doubt whether his own parliamentary seat was safe. Although this was probably unduly pessimistic, there was some I.R.A. activity in Liverpool which cannot have been received with much enthusiasm by the Liverpool Irish population. At the end of 1920 and the beginning of 1921 this resulted in I.R.A. attacks on Irish emigrants bound for the U.S.A. (almost a re-run of the emigration troubles of 1915 though the local population might this time have found them difficult to understand). Twenty warehouses near the Liverpool waterfront were burned down, and plans were discovered and passed on to a grateful Irish Secretary which disclosed that the I.R.A. planned to destroy the Liverpool dock system and that Liverpool was the 'military centre' for I.R.A. activity in Britain. Devlin in the Commons dismissed the plans as a forgery, but the Liverpool press took the threat more seriously and the plans appear to be genuine.[61] O'Connor, probably acutely embarrassed (as he had been during earlier upsets in his constituency)

[59] *D.P.*, 9 Dec.; Dillon Papers, MS 6740-4, f. 579, O'Connor to Dillon, 18 Dec.; *ibid.* f. 840a, Dillon to O'Connor, 1 Aug. 1921. For an alternative interpretation which puts great emphasis on O'Connor's close links with Labour see Lyons, *Dillon*, p. 460, pp. 473-4. There is possibly some inconsistency in Lyons's argument in saying first that O'Connor wanted virtually to merge the Irish organization with Labour and then that O'Connor wanted to persist with a separate organization. Perhaps it ought to be equally emphasized that the political situations in 1918 and 1921-3 were markedly different, the former preceding the defeat of the Nationalist party, the latter when *Sinn Féin* principles were firmly established in the government of Ireland.

[60] See Fyfe, pp. 287, 299, 333-4, 341. The final chapters of Fyfe's biography make frequent references to O'Connor's desire to improve the social conditions of the Irish community, especially in providing better educational facilities, and the quoted comments referred to here may derive either from conversations with O'Connor or from speeches O'Connor made when, as was frequently the case in his last years, he was guest of honour at banquets.

[61] Scott Papers, Add. MS 50905, f. 220, 21 Dec. 1918; *ibid.* Add. MS 50906, f. 23, 4 June 1920; E.M. Brady, *Ireland's Secret Service in England* (1928), pp. 11, 45, 60; Devlin in the Commons, *Hansard, 5,* 135, col. 507, 24 Nov. 1920. Cf. another account which says that the I.R.A. was at least considering a campaign in Britain, D. Neligan, *The Spy in the Castle* (1968), p. 119.

did not attend the debate on the captured documents and made no public comment elsewhere on I.R.A. activity.

Such dangers from republicanism were largely removed by the Treaty and, almost immediately, O'Connor sounded out Dillon on the prospects for a new organization. Undeterred by Dillon's warnings, he sent out circulars from the old U.I.L.G.B. offices to the old League branches in September 1922, just prior to the election, and he called for suggestions about a conference. Shortly afterwards he spoke of how the Treaty had 'liberated' Irish voters 'for more concentrated attention on advancing the interests of our own race in Great Britain' and again he called for a conference.[62] No record of such a conference has survived, but O'Connor revealed his hopes for the Irish presence just as strongly in the support he gave to Devlin as the Independent candidate for Liverpool Exchange during the election of November 1922. Sir Leslie Scott, the sitting Unionist M.P., was predictably incensed and described Devlin as 'unexpected, unsought, and I trust, unwelcome' and O'Connor he referred to as 'that flotsam and jetsam of the Irish Question left here in Liverpool by the passage of the tide, high and dry'. Devlin's candidacy was possibly too opportunistic and he was defeated by 3,000 votes. But O'Connor did not yet give up his ambitions completely. Another circular suggesting a conference was sent out in March 1923 proposing that a conference be held at Leeds, equidistant from the main centres of Irish population, but if this conference met it had no noticeable effect.[63] By 1923 O'Connor appears to have been finally convinced. It was true that in some areas the Irish vote was still a force to be reckoned with. In Liverpool, for instance, disagreements with Labour in municipal contests led to a setback for Labour in 1922 and the formation of a separate Catholic Centre party in 1924 which was under the leadership of Harford. In 1923 a rogue candidate, Alderman William Grogan, put up for Liverpool Exchange in the general election and even though he was denied the support of the local Irish machine (which suggests that there was some sort of extremism or republicanism in his candidacy), he was only narrowly defeated, by 219 votes. But O'Connor, without the hope of some impact in national affairs, now showed how little was his interest in municipal politics and how little sympathy he had for the

[62] Circular of the U.I.L.G.B., 29 Sept. 1922, signed by O'Connor, copy in Dillon Papers, MS 6740-4, f. 897; O'Connor reported in *M.G.*, 4 Oct. 1922; *ibid.* 22 Oct.

[63] *D.P.*, 7 Nov. 1922; circular of U.I.L.G.B., 29 Mar. 1923, signed by O'Connor, copy in Dillon Papers, MS 6740-4, f. 923. This is followed by a printed memorandum to branch secretaries, dated 10 Apr. 1923, announcing the suspension of funds pending the announcement of a conference, which it was hoped would meet in May. This appears to be the last document issued by the U.I.L.G.B.

sort of 'Catholic' politics favoured by Harford. In the elections of
1923 and 1924 he threw his weight behind Labour and campaigned
for Labour candidates in St. Helens and in Widnes as well as in
Liverpool and was given a walkover in Scotland division. When
Devlin once again appeared in Liverpool, in 1924, when he hoped to
gain the Labour nomination for Exchange, O'Connor reported to
Dillon that Devlin had been duped into making the attempt, said that
'Joe's appearance gave me a great deal of anxiety', and he had to
dissuade him from standing.[64] By 1923 the attempt to resurrect or
recreate an Irish organization in Britain was over.

From 1924 onwards O'Connor was regarded as above party in
Westminster and began to look more like the Father of the House. Up
till then his activity, his business in politics, had not decreased. In
1921 Lloyd George, perhaps annoyed because O'Connor refused to
act his part in the last performance over Home Rule, had described
O'Connor as a 'futile person' but even Healy, who reported the
comment to his brother, did not agree, perhaps remembering how
effective his old adversary had been underneath the sunny aspect.
O'Connor himself summed up the position more accurately after the
election of 1922 when he met Asquith in the lobby and confided that
his 'new slogan' was 'I'm damned if I'll be buried before I'm dead'.[65]
His energy in politics, in electioneering increasingly for Labour, in
attempting to revive the Irish organization, proved that this was not
mere bravado. But, apart from politics, his activity in journalism
remained scarcely undiminished up to his final years. During the war,
as if he did not have enough to do, he had brought out a syndicated
column to replace the work he lost when the *Chicago Tribune*
cancelled his regular contribution and he had begun *T.P.'s Journal* in
1915, even though it did not prove much of a success. His work for
Reynolds's Newspaper, some of the best journalism he had ever
produced, stopped at the end of 1916 at his own request and was
replaced for a time by contributions to the *Daily Chronicle*. After
the war he became chief obituary writer for the *Daily Telegraph* (a not
uncommon sideline for established politicians) which he described in
private as 'T.P.'s meditations among the tombs', and his column for
the *Sunday Times*, 'Men, Women, and Memories' was the forerunner
of the 'Atticus' column. At the end of 1923 he revived *T.P.'s Weekly*
which became *T.P.'s and Cassell's Weekly* in 1927 and he remained
attached to the paper until 1929. He kept his lively touch.

[64] Dillon Papers, Add. MS 6740-4, f. 969, O'Connor to Dillon, 1 Dec. 1924. Devlin
was elected for a west Belfast constituency in the Stormont parliament in April 1925.

[65] Healy to his brother Maurice, 6 Dec. 1921, quoted in *Letters* ii, 645; Lord Asquith,
Letters of Asquith to a Friend (1934), p. 43, letter dated 15 Feb. 1923.

His work as film censor was uneventful, apart from a squabble with Marie Stopes in 1923 over a film about birth control. He was liked on all sides, especially when Ireland was out of the way, as his numerous appearances at celebratory banquets testified. His finances, despite the parliamentary income, the income from the post as film censor, and from his journalism, did not become secure until the very end when, in 1929, a fund was opened for him which reached £10,000. His hopes for achieving something more substantial, both financially and as a literary testament, were not to be realized in his memoirs. Although he worked hard on them, encouraged by Dillon, they provided neither an adequate record of his life nor a convincing history of the Irish parliamentary party: they have been described as little more than a repetition of earlier sketches for the *Weekly Sun*. Recognition, perhaps belated, came from other quarters. He was made a Privy Councillor by the Labour government in 1924 (which alarmed Dillon needlessly), refusing the peerage which would have been too much at odds with his long opposition to the House of Lords. His last years were full. In the Commons he was listened to with respect though obviously not with any urgency. In 1926, during the general strike, he pleaded for compromise, though this had also been his instinctive reaction when he had been more fully involved in labour troubles. His attempts to speak on the questions of Catholic schooling and the social disadvantages of the Irish in Britain were similar to attempts he had made since the 1890s and they continued to be largely ignored.[66] Outside the Commons, his contacts with a wide variety of London society remained almost unimpaired, though his contacts with Liverpool were more tenuous after 1924, and he was active in many charitable works. When he was entering his eightieth year he felt sufficiently in command of himself to venture on a last, brief, visit to the U.S.A., in February 1928, where his reception was at any rate a more pleasing one than that given him in the war years. In May 1929 he went to Liverpool for the last time and was greeted with greater adulation than ever before and once again was given a walkover. But illness took its toll even of his incredibly resilient constitution. His last years were interrupted by crippling bouts of rheumatism and more serious attacks of diabetes. He died peacefully at his Westminster flat on 18 November 1929.

It is impossible to summarize anyone's life; there is often a sense of let-down about the lives of politicians who have sacrificed to action

[66]*The Times*, 19 Nov. 1929; Keith Briant, *Marie Stopes* (1962), pp. 163-4; Fyfe, p. 301; *Hansard*, 5, 195, col. 328, 5 May 1926; *ibid.* 198, cols. 2751-6, 2 Aug. 1926, on voluntary schools.

the more creative, unspectacular accretions of a life's work which can only be seen clearly in retrospect. O'Connor, beneath all the furious activity of even his later years, believed that he had been a failure, particularly where it hurt most, in the world of letters. A disappointment that emerged in his by no means infrequent bouts of melancholy may have become doubly strong when he had more time for reflection in old age. Yet, although he is often seen as primarily a journalist, and although his enthusiasm and innovations in journalism, especially with the *Star*, were what had most impact and were crucial in creating the popular face of British journalism, politics was his life. Conferences, elections, negotiations, were all managed with skill, though perhaps by their very nature avoided passion. His tolerance and good humour deceived even his colleagues, his grasp of the personalities of politics was often detailed to the point of femininity. Perhaps, too, the English confused his good humour with a lack of earnestness and a harsher generation of nationalists in Ireland regarded it as a political weakness. His death was virtually ignored in Ireland, a matter which was commented on sourly by Devlin who wrote that 'there was a time when the death of T.P. O'Connor would have filled the Irish people with a feeling of deep sorrow. . . almost of national disaster'.[67] He had latterly worked hard for the reconciliation of the British and the Irish but the Irish in Britain, during his lifetime and after, remained, more of 'a people apart' and, in effect if not in intention, this was to some extent due to the various Irish political Leagues which O'Connor presided over from 1883 to 1914. Yet he was remembered in Scotland division with affection, a rare emotion in politics. What he had wanted for his constituents and for the Irish in Britain generally was never remotely realized in his lifetime; perhaps his own efforts here came too late. Clearly, he was no martyr for his people, but they would not have welcomed him in such a guise. At the same time, he sacrificed his own best chances for the sake of his fellow countrymen and he gained few honours and, as once he had feared, much insult and the fate of obscurity. In a way that his constituents recognized and others have not, he truly represented their self-reliance, their hard-won scepticism, and their wit.

[67] *D.P.*, 18 Nov. 1929.

APPENDICES

Appendix A

From Police and Crime Records, Police Reports, 1850-1920, Irish State Paper Office, Dublin Castle.

Thomas Power O'Connor M.P.
  Scotland Road [sic] Liverpool [Erased]

Son of a billiard marker residing in Athlone. [Erased. Replaced by] native of Athlone Educated at Queens College Galway.

Took an active part in the Land League agitation and addressed a number of meetings throughout the country. He received £300 from the Land League Funds on 7th August to 7th Septr. 1882.

Information received that O'Connor was sworn into the I.R.B. Organisation at the time he was elected MP for Galway in 1880.

The Priests of Galway opposed O'Connor at this election and were it not for the assistance and influence of the I.R.B. section, he would have been defeated.

Mentioned in Special Commission charges. See official Report.

Is an Anti Parnellite, since split. Was a member of the O'Brien-Dillon Mission, 1890, to America to collect funds for Campaign tenants, which was frustrated by the split in November 1890.

Appendix B

Manifesto of 21 November 1885 (excerpt)

The Liberal party are making an appeal to the . . . electors on false pretences. . . . To Ireland more than any other country it bound itself by . . . solemn pledges and these it most flagrantly violated. . . [enacting] a system of coercion more brutal than that of any previous administration, Liberal or Tory, . . . as if Ireland were Poland and the administration of England a Russian autocracy. . . . The last declaration of Mr. Gladstone was that he intended to renew the very worst clauses of the Coercion Act of 1882. . . . The Liberals began by menacing the Established Church, and, under the name of free schools made an insidious attempt to crush the religious education of the country, to establish a system of state tyranny and intolerance, and to fetter the right of conscience which is as sacred in the selection of the school as in the free selection of one's church.... The two last cries of the Liberal party are the so-called reform of procedure and a demand to be independent of the Irish party... a new gag and the application to all enemies of Radicalism in the House of Commons of the despotic methods and the mean machinery of the Birmingham caucus. The specious demand for a majority against the Irish party is an appeal for power to crush all anti-Radical members in Parliament, then to propose to Ireland some scheme doomed to failure because of its unsuitability to the wants of the Irish people and finally to force down a halting measure of self-government upon the Irish people by the same methods of wholesale imprisonment by which acceptance was sought for the impracticable Land Act of 1881. Under such circumstances we feel bound to advise our countrymen to place no confidence in the Liberal or Radical party, so far as in them lies to prevent the Government of the Empire falling into the hands of a party so perilous, treacherous and incompetent.... except in some few cases in which courageous fealty to the Irish cause in the last parliament has given a guarantee that the candidates will not belong to the servile and cowardly and unprincipled herd that would break every pledge... in obedience to the call of the whip and the mandate of the caucus. The executive of the National League will communicate the names of the candidates whom they think should be exempt from the terms of this manifesto...

T.P. O'Connor, President
Justin McCarthy
Thomas Sexton
T.M. Healy
J.E. Redmond   Executive
James O'Kelly
J.G. Biggar
Irish National League of Great Britain

Appendix C

The beginning of O'Connor's speech on the first Home Rule Bill, 3 June 1886 (*Hansard, 3,* 306, cols. 847-50)

Sir, I am sure an Irish Member has no great need to appeal to the indulgence of the House when he rises to speak on the Bill now under discussion. It is a measure which most deeply concerns the future of his country, and is the embodiment of his hopes and opinions during many years of severe struggle; and on its acceptance or rejection depends issues for his country of momentous and solemn importance. I have further, Sir, to ask for indulgence because this Bill appeals to the deepest and strongest political convictions and passions of an Irishman; and while frankly I desire to put some restraint on myself lest I should be betrayed into any expression which might wound the just susceptibilities of even the opponents of this measure, I desire to criticize freely the attacks on the Bill, but, at the same time, to criticize them in a courteous spirit. Now, Sir, I may be allowed to reiterate the surprise of many others at the forms which the criticism of this measure has taken. It is the first time in my experience that a Bill has been objected to on the second reading stage, not so much because of its central principle, as because of its details. I listened with the attention it deserved the other night to the speech of the right hon. Gentleman the Member for the Border Burghs (Mr. Trevelyan); and it is not an unfair description of his speech to say that the greater part of it was taken up with a denunciation of the largeness of the tribute, which, under this Bill, Ireland is expected to pay to England. Well, Sir, we on these Benches gave to that part of his speech an attentive and a sympathetic hearing. Does he suppose that we, in voting for the second reading of this Bill, preclude ourselves from making the most earnest struggle for a reduction of the tribute? My hon. Friend the Member for Cork (Mr. Parnell) is in no way more distinguished from other politicians than in his resolve and his power to drive for his own people and his own side the hardest bargain it is in human power to drive. No Irish farmer, Connaught farmer, at a County Mayo fair, drives a harder bargain for his cow than does my hon. Friend for the rights of his country; and when we come to deal with the question of tribute, my hon. Friend will be true to his invariable traditions, and fight for a reduction with a tenacity of which in his Parliamentary career he has given the House such abundant examples. I trust that when we reach that stage of the Bill we may have the able assistance of the right hon. Gentleman. Then some Members *Hiberniores Hibernis ipsis,* object to the constitution of the proposed Legislative Assembly. Sir, I would think that in logic, as well in Parliamentary Order, it would be right that we should first decide whether we are to have a Legislature at all before we discuss what that Legislature is to be like. We, on these Benches, do not profess to regard the constitution of the new Irish legislature as a foregone conclusion when we vote for the second reading of this measure. We shall subject the details of the scheme to searching criticism, and we shall welcome, as the Prime Minister doubtless will welcome, any light that the keen intelligence of the right hon. Gentleman or any Member of the House can throw upon it. But this much I must say upon the constitution of the new Legislature. The right hon. Member for West Birmingham (Mr. Chamberlain) has denounced that legislature as a thing that the sturdy Liberalism of Birmingham would not pick out of the gutter and that because of the restrictions it places upon the rights of the democracy. We do not take this view. We are ready to accept any restrictions on the rights of democracy at the start of this grave enterprize; our first work is to weld the different classes of our people into a perfectly harmonious whole, to undo the evil work of centuries of a policy, the fundamental principle of which was to divide and to conquer, above all to soften and finally to extirpate that estrangement of different creeds which has been not the natural growth of. . . Irish hearts of all creeds, but of such appeals to religious rancour by foreign and unscrupulous tongues as we have heard within the last few months. To foster this idea of common nationhood above our strong Party differences, our class hatreds, and our distinctions of creeds will be the first work of Irish statesmanship; and by way of starting that work favourably and accelerating its progress, we are quite willing not merely to submit to, but even to welcome, restraints on the rights of majorities, which in ordinary circumstances we would reject. We might as "a down-trodden majority" appeal for sympathy to the right hon. Gentleman the Member for West Birmingham; and for a while, perhaps, we might obtain it by references to his speech of Bristol already quoted, and his recent speech to the Birmingham Two Thousand; but we could not count upon that sympathy for long, as the right hon. Gentleman is liable to remember that in some of the epistolary gems with which he has so abundantly favoured the public, he has condemned the Bill for its treatment of the minority; so that this measure contains not merely in this but in many other respects, of which more by-and-bye, faults of an entirely contradictory character. It is a creature of such awful mien and such abnormal and unusual atrocity that it oppresses a down-trodden majority and enslaves a crushed minority. But, Sir, on this question of the Orders, the proper property qualifications, and other details of the proposed Irish Legislature, I have a right to bar all criticism at this stage. It appears to me the demand of logic and of reason, no less than of Parliamentary procedure, that we should first decide whether we are to have an Irish Legislature at all before we go on to discuss what kind of Legislature it should be. Let us catch our legislative hare before we worry our heads over the form in which it shall be cooked. Nor, Sir, do I think that we need waste much time over the legal and Constitutional arguments of which we have had so much during these debates from the Gentlemen of the Long Robe. In spite of all the subleties to which we have listened, all the debate on this point seems to me to be very simple, and that it can be put into a nutshell. The supremacy of Parliament is said to be destroyed, but a power is not destroyed which is suspended; a power does not cease to exist because it is not exercised. The right hon. and learned Gentleman the Member for Bury (Sir Henry James) says that he cannot recognize any distinction between a right and an abstract right, or as I would put it, between a power in reserve and a power in use. This may be good law, but is appears to me to be uncommonly bad sense. Surely the entire working of our Constitution depends on the difference between power in reserve and power in exercise. I believe there are lawyers still who would claim that the Sovereign had a right to veto any legislation, though passed by both Houses of Parliament, to which she objected; the veto of the Crown certainly is not yet an exploded superstition, but the veto is not exercised. Several times during the agitation on the Irish Church Her Majesty was appealed to from the same quarters as are now threatening her with treason, to refuse her assent to an Act of the Legislature which violated her Coronation Oath, trampled on the Christianity of the country, and was even a revolt against Divine Providence. But everybody knows that if the Queen had exercised her veto on that occasion in the direction suggested by her so-called friends, the result would have been very serious. The right hon. and learned Gentleman the Member for Bury may now know the difference between a power in reserve and a power in exercise; but Her Majesty, who is not a man of law, but a woman of good sense, does, and, accordingly, though she had the power of veto, she left that power in reserve, and did not exercise it.

Appendix D

Manifesto of 9 December 1918: list of constituencies

O'Connor and F. L. Crilly advised Irish voters to support candidates for the following constituencies

Labour

Accrington
Barrow in Furness
Birkenhead East
Blackburn
Liverpool Edge Hill
Liverpool Fairfield
Liverpool Kirkdale
Liverpool Walton
Liverpool West Derby
Liverpool West Toxteth
Manchester Ardwick
Manchester Blackley
Manchester Clayton
Manchester Gorton
Manchester Rusholme
Nelson and Colne
Oldham (one seat)
Preston (one seat)

St. Helens
Salford North
Salford West
Southport
Wigan
Altrincham
Chester
Crewe
Stalybridge and Hyde
Farnworth
Fylde
Heywood and Radcliffe
Mostey
Newton
Royton
Waterloo
Westhoughton
Rochdale

Liberal

Eccles
Leigh
Manchester Exchange
Manchester Withrington
Oldham (one seat)
Preston (one seat)

Rossendale
Salford South
Warrington
Darwen
Lancaster
High Peak

Independent

Ashton under Lyne
Blackburn
Liverpool Exchange

All these seats are in the north west of England.

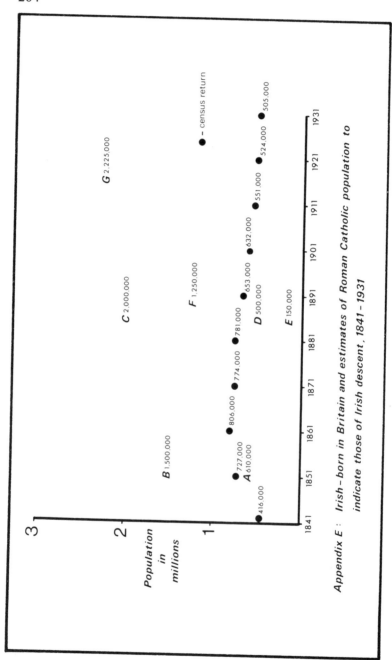

Appendix E : *Irish-born in Britain and estimates of Roman Catholic population to indicate those of Irish descent, 1841-1931*

Notes to Appendix E

Irish-born

These are from census returns but are not likely to be wholly accurate because of the migratory nature of the population and re-emigration. The total also includes Irish Protestants.

Roman Catholic population

This includes Irish-born but is not synonomous with those of Irish descent even though the latter formed the bulk of this population; the total also includes non-voters.

A, B and F are cited in E.R. Norman, *Anti-Catholicism in Victorian England* (London, 1968), p. 17.

A   Estimate of Horace Mann for 1851 on the basis of A. Hume, *Results of the Irish Census of 1861* (London, 1864), p. 12.

B   T.C. Anstey in parliament, *Hansard, 3,* 114, col. 93, 4 Feb. 1851.

C   T.P. O'Connor in parliament, *ibid, 3,* 296, col. 1073, 29 Apr. 1885. The suggestion was that these were all adult voters.

D   Shaw Lefevre in parliament, *ibid.* col. 1079.

E   *Ibid.* and in his *Gladstone and Ireland*, p. 284, that this was the number of Catholic Nationalist voters.

F   K.S. Inglis, *The Churches and the Working Classes in Victorian England* (London, 1963), p. 123. Estimate for the end of the 1880s.

G   O'Connor in 1916, *R.N.*, 26 June.

Appendix F

Total population and Irish-born in the borough of Liverpool

	Total population	Irish-born	percentage
1841	286,487	49,562	17.3
1851	375,955	83,813	22.3
1861	443,938	83,949	18.9
1871	493,405	76,761	15.6
1881	552,508	70,977	12.9
1891	517,980	47,243	9.1
1901	684,958	45,673	6.7
1911	746,421	34,632	4.6

(Source : census)

BIBLIOGRAPHY

A.   Genealogical and Biographical Sources
B.   Works by T.P. O'Connor
    1. *Books*
    2. *Newspapers*
    3. *Miscellaneous*
C.   Manuscript Sources
D.   Printed Sources
    1. *Parliamentary Papers and official publications*
    2. *Newspapers and pamphlets*
E.   Political History of Britain and Ireland
    1. *Contemporary works*
    2. *Later works*
F.   Journalism, Letters, and Sociological Works
    1. *Contemporary Works and narrative histories*
    2. *Later works*
G.   Migrant and Liverpool History

(place of publication London unless otherwise indicated)

A. Genealogical and Biographical Sources

Information on T.P. O'Connor's family background suffers from the handicap common to all Irish genealogy that central records for Roman Catholics began later than in England (1864) and that many family records prior to that date (including census returns) were destroyed in the burning of the Dublin Public Record Office in 1922. O'Connor had a radical's scepticism over genealogy ('O'Connors are as plentiful in the west of Ireland as raindrops in a storm; my father was just one of them', quoted in Fyfe, p. 15). There is little reason to suppose that O'Connor had any ulterior motive for being so down to earth, though there remains some lack of clarity about his early life. One source for the O'Connor family in Athlone is the Roman Catholic baptism register of St. Peter's parish (copy on microfilm in the National Library of Ireland) which has been consulted for the period 1848-64 for O'Connor's baptism and for those of his brother and sisters. The name O'Connor appears to have been fairly numerous among shop-keepers and tradesmen in the town of Athlone. Apart from O'Connor's father, there was a lodging-house keeper, an eating-house keeper and a clerk to the Board of Guardians in Athlone in the 1840s. These are all indicated in *Slater's National Commercial Directory for Ireland* (Manchester and London, 1846) and the 1879 and 1891 editions gave further information about O'Connor's father and the family's financial position, as did *Griffith's Valuation of County Westmeath* (1854).

Details on the Power family are also difficult to come by. Michael MacDonagh in his essay on O'Connor for the *D.N.B.* noted that O'Connor's mother was 'the daughter of a non-commissioned officer in the Connaught Rangers' (*D.N.B., 1922-30*), while Fyfe promoted Power from the lieutenant for whom there is some evidence to a captain, made him at least known to the Duke of Wellington, and portrayed him pointed out to one of the Duke's lady admirers as a suitable case for religious conversion, though whether from Roman Catholicism to Protestantism, or from Anglicanism to militancy is not indicated (Fyfe, p. 15). Records in the National Army Museum (*Army Lists 1810-1814*) indicate a Geoffrey Kane Power appointed as an ensign in the 88th, the Connaught Rangers, in January 1808. He served with the Connaught Rangers throughout the Peninsular War (and thus provides a tenuous link with the anecdote cited above), was promoted to lieutenant in September 1809, and appears to have left the army in 1814. No additional detail was obtained by a search among army records in the Public Record Office for Power's service papers. There is no record of Power's application for his commission in the Commander in Chief's memoranda (W.O. 31), and no return exists for officers' services for the Connaught Rangers in the period in question. No other officer by the name of Power was commissioned in the Connaught Rangers in the entire period 1793-1922. Mention of a Colour Sergeant Thomas Power does occur in the Public Record Office regimental returns for the Connaught Rangers. He was a weaver from Waterford who enlisted in 1807 and who was discharged in 1830 (Soldiers' Documents of Chelsea Hospital Out Pensioners in the Connaught Rangers, W.O. 97/975). O'Connor in his entry for *Dod* named him as Thomas O'Connor, though he styled him 'esq', if that means anything. It is possible that other N.C.O.s named Power might have served in the Connaught Rangers who did not receive a Chelsea pension, and who therefore are not listed in the most accessible records. It was not possible in the absence of any indication of Theresa Power's place of birth, or her mother's maiden name, to pursue the connection with Waterford any further since Power is one of the most common Waterford names. O'Connor's relatives in Galway city may have been Powers, but a search in the Roman Catholic marriage register of St. Nicholas 1840-8 revealed no entry for Power. *Griffith's Valuation of Co. Galway* (Manchester and London, 1855) reveals one Power entry, Michael Power, with a house and a yard having a rateable value of £13, rented from Michael Perrin, located in Church Yard, St. Nicholas Ward. There is also an entry for a Power in the Tithe Applottment Book for Rahoon, Galway city. A search in the Church of Ireland registers for St. Peter's Athlone, and St. Mary's Athlone, reveals no entry for a Power, although entries for this period are scanty. No information was available from the church of Ireland, St. Nicholas records, Galway. I am grateful for the help of those indicated in the acknowledgements for this genealogical scrutiny. Perhaps new information on O'Connor's family might be revealed as a result of this study.

There does not appear to be any surviving collection of O'Connor's papers. This is probably owing to his untidy domestic circumstances during his last years rather than the result of any conscious design. Little sign of any reference to private papers emerges from his memoirs and he did not keep a diary. He must, however, have left an appreciable amount of material to be dealt with by his executors, his friend Sir Alexander Maguire and his solicitor F. S. Parker. Enquiries among the successors to Parker failed to reveal any papers relating to O'Connor and it does not appear as though Maguire left, or had control of, any such collection. It is probable that Hamilton Fyfe had access to a collection of O'Connor material (especially O'Connor's copies of letters to Lloyd George) when he was writing his biography but it has not been possible to trace any such papers in this way. O'Connor was survived by his two sisters and two nieces, the daughters of William O'Malley. His nieces lived most of their lives in England, did not marry, and appear to have left no family papers. It also proved impossible to trace any papers of the Howard family which might have a bearing on O'Connor. Reliance has been placed on letters of O'Connor's kept in other collections (see Manuscript Sources below). These have turned out to be sufficient and the lack of a central collection has not been a great disadvantage so far as this study is concerned. Apart from Hamilton Fyfe's biography, *T.P. O'Connor* (1934), the most consistent personal descriptions of O'Connor, among a great many such descriptions are in the autobiography of his wife, Elizabeth O'Connor, *I, Myself* (1910), and the autobiography of his brother in law, William O'Malley, *Glancing Back* (1933).

Biographical sketches and anonymous articles on O'Connor:
'Who's T.P. O'Connor?', Liverpool *Porcupine*, 21 Nov. 1885.
Orchard, B.G. (ed.), *Liverpool's Legion of Honour, 1893* (Birkenhead, 1893), biographical notice of O'Connor, pp. 529-30
Lynch, Arthur, *Human Documents, Character Sketches of Representative Men and Women of the Time* (1896), chapter on O'Connor.

'Men of the Week; T.P. O'Connor', Liverpool *Review*, 25 Mar. 1899
'An Open Letter to T.P. Leave Ireland Alone', Liverpool *Porcupine*,
31 Mar. 1900
'Tay Pay, High and Mighty', Liverpool *Porcupine*, 14 Apr. 1900
'T.P. O'Connor, a Little Arbitration', Liverpool *Porcupine*, 21
July 1900
'The Rambler', 'Imaginary Interviews; Tay Pay', Liverpool
Porcupine, 4 Aug. 1900
'T.P. and his £s', Liverpool *Porcupine*, 1 Sept. 1900
'Is T.P. a Mean Man; How he Bluffs the Paddies', Liverpool
Porcupine, 6 Oct. 1900
'Brother Sam', 'At the Feet of T.P.', Liverpool *Review*, 12 Oct.
1901
'Men You Know; T.P. O'Connor', Liverpool *Review*, 4 Jan. 1902
'Tay Pay's Chestnuts', Liverpool *Porcupine*, 9 Dec. 1905
'Tay Pay Under the Liberals', Liverpool *Porcupine*, 6 Jan. 1906
'T.P. as King Mob', Liverpool *Porcupine*, 20 Jan. 1906
Gibson, Ashley, 'T.P. O'Connor as Author and Journalist', *The
Bookman*, Feb. 1910, 217-24
O'Learly, Con., ' "T.P." The Story of a Great Journalist', *Everyman*,
28 Nov. 1929
Fallon, W.G., 'The Great "Tay Pay"', *Irish Independent*, 28
Dec. 1961

B. Works by T.P. O'Connor

1. Books

Benjamin Disraeli, Earl of Beaconsfield (1878), published
anonymously 'By T.P. O'C'; published first in serial form.
Lord Beaconsfield, a Biography (London and Belfast, 1879)
Gladstone's House of Commons (1885), reprinted from the *Pall
Mall Gazette* and the *Freeman's Journal*
The Parnell Movement (1886), reprinted from the *Freeman's
Journal*; various American and Australian editions in
collaboration with local editors.
Charles Stewart Parnell, a Memory (1891)
Sketches in the House, the Story of a Memorable Session (1893),
reprinted from the *Weekly Sun*
Some Old Love Stories (1895)
Napoleon (1896)
*The Phantom Millions, The Story of the Great French Fraud,
Being Incidents in the Career of Madame Humbert and
Others* (Bristol, 1902)

Sir Henry Campbell-Bannerman (1908)
Memoirs of an Old Parliamentarian (2 vols., 1929)

2. Newspapers

Star. O'Connor was editor from its inception in January 1888 until March-April 1890
Sunday Sun, May 1891-1893 when it became the
Weekly Sun, 1893-1898, when it passed out of O'Connor's control.
Sun, June 1893-1906 or 1910. O'Connor sold his interest to Horatio Bottomley in 1900.
M.A.P., June 1898-October 1911 when it became the *Watchdog.* O'Connor had ceased to be editor at the end of 1909.
T.P.'s Weekly, 1902-1914, revived 1923-7 when it became *T.P.'s and Cassell's Weekly;* after O'Connor's death it became *John O'London's.*
P.T.O., June 1906-June 1908 when it was incorporated with *M.A.P.*
T.P.'s Monthly, Sept. 1910-1914
T.P.'s Journal 1915-1916

3. **Miscellaneous** (works of editing, pamphlets, speeches, and articles; not including the numerous introductions and forewords which O'Connor wrote for other authors; for those see B.M. Catalogue).

'The Present Condition of Austria', *Dark Blue,* vol. 3. 15, 1872
The Cabinet of Irish Literature, vol. 4. ed. 'T.P. O'C' (1879)
'The Rule of the Purse', *Contemporary Review,* 37 (June 1880), 990-1003
'The Land League and its Work', *Contemporary Review,* 38 (Dec. 1880), 981-99
Mr. T.P. O'Connor in Chicago, Unanswerable Statement of the Case for Ireland, Fellowship Club reception, n.d. (1881-2)
'Ireland in 1883', *American Catholic Quarterly,* vol. 8. 68, 1883
'Ireland, Present and Prospective', *American Catholic Quarterly,* vol. 9. 523, 1884
'Crisis in England', *American Catholic Quarterly,* vol. 10. 488, 1885
The Home Rule Debate, Speech of Mr. T.P. O'Connor M.P., June 3rd, 1886 (1886)
'Ireland. . .', *American Catholic Quarterly,* vol. II. 682, 1886
Reid, Andrew, (ed.), *Ireland, a Book of Light on the Irish Problem* (1886), chapter by O'Connor

'The Needs of Ireland and English Parties', *American Catholic Quarterly,* vol. 12. 121, 1887

'The Immediate Prospect for Ireland', *American Catholic Quarterly,* vol. 12. 518, 1887

with F.H. Hill, 'Ireland in 1888', *Universal Review,* 1. 161. 309, 1888

'The Candour of Mr. Gladstone', *Contemporary Review,* 56. (Sept. 1889), 361-9

'The New Journalism', *New Review,* Oct. 1889

'Representation of Ireland in the Imperial Parliament', *Subjects of the Day,* vol. 3. 38, 1891

'Structure, Rules and Habits of the House of Commons', *Harper's Magazine,* 88. 34, 1893

'Home Rule and the Irish Party', *Contemporary Review,* 70 (Aug. 1896), 179-90

'Home Rule, Some Objections', *Time,* 14. 641, 1896

'Celebrities of the House of Commons', *Harper's Magazine,* 95. 111, 1897

'Some Absurdities of the House of Commons', *North American Review,* 171. 265, 1900

'Robert Cecil, 3rd Earl of Salisbury', *Everybody's Magazine,* 6. 3, 1901

'Some Metropolitan Stars', *Overland Monthly,* n.s. 39. 568, 1901

'Arthur J. Balfour', *Everybody's Magazine,* 7. 265, 1902

'Henry Labouchere', *Everybody's Magazine,* 9. 476, 1903

'D'Arcy Thompson', *Educational Review,* 28. 536, 1904

'The Immediate Future of Ireland', *Fortnightly Review,* 8, 608, 1904

Speech Delivered by Mr T.P. O'Connor at Accrington on October 27th 1904, Advice to Irish Electors in Great Britain, U.I.L.G.B. leaflet no. 8 (1904)

Address to the President of the French Republic. . . 30th April 1915 (1915)

'The Irish in Great Britain' in F. Lavery, *Irish Heroes in the War* (1917), 113-36

The Irish Mission to America, Speech of Mr T.P. O'Connor at the House of Commons 6 August 1918 (Dublin, 1918)

C. Manuscript Sources

Bodleian Library, Oxford
Letters from O'Connor in Bryce Papers, UB 23, and in Harcourt Papers, dep. 437

British Library
Letters to and from O'Connor are in the following collections:
Campbell-Bannerman Papers
Dilke Papers
Viscount Gladstone Papers
W. E. Gladstone Papers
C.P. Scott Papers (reference to O'Connor in Scott's Journal)
G.B. Shaw Papers (catalogued provisionally at the time of consultation)
British Library of Political and Economic Science
Diary of G.B. Shaw, transcribed by Blanche Patch, entries for 1888-90

House of Lords Record Office
Lloyd George Papers, mostly letters of O'Connor to Lloyd George, 1909-17, with an additional memorandum on Greece sent in 1922
Liverpool Record Office
17 Earl of Derby Papers, a few letters from O'Connor to Derby on the war and the Irish matters, 1919 and 1921
National Library of Ireland
n. 695, p. 4693, correspondence between O'Connor and Edward Blake, photostats of Canadian material
MS 5381, letters of O'Connor to Gerald Christy
MS 10040, letters of O'Connor to Edmund Downey
MS 4360, letters of O'Connor to James Hooper and four letters of S. Bennett to O'Connor
MS 708, Minute Book of National Directory of U.I.L.G.B., 1904-18
MS 9756, Minute Book of Fr Purcell branch of I.N.L.G.B., 1892-5
MS 16839-40, letters of O'Connor to Peter Keary
MS 13432 (8) and MS 13458, letters from O'Connor in J.F.X. O'Brien papers
MS 15735, letter of Parnell to O'Connor, 1885
John Redmond Papers
National Library of Scotland
Blackwood's Correspondence, MS 4280, letters of O'Connor to John Blackwood, 1871, 1875
Public Record Office
Army lists, 1810-14
Sheffield University Library
Mundella Papers, Mundella-Leader correspondence, 1878, 1881
State Paper Office, Dublin Castle
Police and Crime Records, 1850-1920
University of Dublin, Trinity College Library
Dillon Papers MS 6740/4, letters of O'Connor to John Dillon

D. Printed Sources

1. Parliamentary Papers and official publications

Borough Electors (Working Classes), Return P.P. 1866, lviii.

Liverpool *Council Proceedings,* 1870-1920

Final Report of Her Majesty's Commissioners Appointed to Enquire into the Operation and Administration of the Laws Relating to the Sale of Intoxicating Liquors (1899)

Medical Officer of Health, Report to the Health Committee of the Borough of Liverpool on the Health of the Town, 1847-1880

'Police (Liverpool Enquiry) Act 1909, Before Mr Arthur J. Ashton K.C. Transcript and Shorthand Notes of the Proceedings and Report of the Commissioners', typescript in Liverpool Record Office

Report of the Proceedings of the Irish Convention (1918)

Report of the Select Committee on the Liverpool Election Petition H.C. 1852-3, xv.

Report of the Select Committee on Parliamentary and Municipal Elections H.C. 1868-9, viii.

Report of the Select Committee for the Registration of Voters in Boroughs H.C. 1868-9, vii.

Royal Commission on the Rebellion in Ireland, Minutes of Evidence and Appendix of Documents (1916)

Special Commission Act, 1888, Reprint of the Shorthand Notes and Speeches, Proceedings and Evidence Before the Commissioners Under the Above Named Act vol. i-xii (1890)

Unemployed in the City of Liverpool, Report of the Commissioners (1894)

2. Newspapers and Pamphlets

So far as local newspapers are concerned, indexes (such as those existing for *The Times* and the *Manchester Guardian*) are badly needed. Some indexes, used as a working reference for journalists, may survive in local newspaper offices. Where they don't their compilation would be an invaluable work of research. National British newspapers are on file at the British Library, Newspaper Library, Colindale, Irish newspapers in the National Library of Ireland, Liverpool newspapers mostly on microfilm in the Liverpool Record Office.

Catholic Herald (London, Manchester, Newcastle, Welsh, and Liverpool editions)

Catholic Times

Liverpool Critic

Liverpool Daily Courier
Liverpool Daily Post
Dublin Evening Telegraph
Dublin Express
Liverpool Forward
Freeman's Journal
Liverpool Irish Herald (one copy in L.R.O. for 1885)
Irish Loyal and Patriotic Union, Leaflets (1886) collected in
    Pamphlets, Irish Question, Sydney Jones Library, University of
    Liverpool
Liverpool Irish Programme and *Nationalist*
Irish Times
Journal of the Home Rule Union
Journal of the Home Rule Union, leaflets 1888-90 in British Library,
    Bloomsbury
Labour Leader
Liberal Home Ruler
Liverpool Echo
Manchester Guardian (on microfilm, along with manuscript index, in
    Manchester Central Library)
The Observer
Pall Mall Gazette
Liverpool Porcupine
Liverpool Protestant Standard
Liverpool Review
Reynolds's Newspaper
Scotland Road Packet (Sept. 1933-Nov. 1934 on file at Colindale)
The Tablet
The Times
The Transport Worker
Truth
United Irish League of Great Britain, leaflets, 2-8, National Library
    of Ireland
Liverpool United Irishman (on file at Colindale)

E. Political History of Britain and Ireland

1. Contemporary works

Addison, C., *Politics from Within* (1929)
Anderson, Sir Robert, *The Lighter Side of My Official Life* (1910)
Asquith, Herbert Henry, 1st Earl of Oxford and Asquith, *Letters of
    the Earl of Oxford and Asquith to a Friend* (1934)
Askwith, George Ranken, 1st Baron, *Industrial Problems and
    Disputes* (1920)

Bennett, S., *William Ewart Gladstone and What he has Done* (1890)

Birrell, Augustine, *Things Past Redress* (1937)

Bryce, James, *Studies in Contemporary Biography* (1903)

Chamberlain, Austen, *Politics from the Inside* (1936)

Davitt, Michael, *The Fall of Feudalism in Ireland* (1904)

Devoy, John, *Devoy's Postbag*, ed. W. O'Brien and D. Ryan (2 vols. Dublin, 1948)

Eversley, 1st Baron, George J. Shaw-Lefevre, *Gladstone and Ireland, the Irish policy of Parliament from 1850-1894* (1912)

Gardiner, A.G., *The Life of Sir William Harcourt* (2 vols., 1923)

Garvin, J.L., *Joseph Chamberlain* (3 vols., 1932)

Gladstone, Viscount, *After Thirty Years* (1928)

Gwynn, D., *The Life of John Redmond* (1932)

Gwynn, S. and Tuckwell, G., *Sir Charles Dilke* (2 vols., 1917)

Healy, T.M., *Letters and Leaders of my Day* (2 vols., 1928)

_____ 'The Irish Parliamentary Party', *Fortnightly Review*, (Nov. 1882), 625-33

Hobhouse, C.E.H., *Inside Asquith's Cabinet*, ed. Edward David (1977)

Horgan, J.J., *Parnell to Pearse* (Dublin, 1948)

Leslie, J.R.S., *Henry Edward Manning, his Life and Labours* (1921)

Lucy, Sir Henry, *A Diary of Two Parliaments* (1886)

_____ *Diary of the Home Rule Parliament* (1896)

_____ *Diary of the Unionist Parliament* (1901)

_____ *Later Peeps at Parliament* (1904)

McCarthy, Justin, *Reminiscences* (2 vols., 1899)

_____ *Story of an Irishman* (1904)

MacDonagh, Michael, *The Home Rule Movement* (Dublin, 1920)

_____ *William O'Brien* (1928)

MacKnight, Thomas, *Ulster as it Is* (2 vols., 1896)

Mann, Tom, *Tom Mann's Memoirs* (1923, reprinted 1967)

Morley, John, *The Life of William Ewart Gladstone* (3 vols., 1903)

_____ *Recollections* (2 vols., 1903)

Murray, A.C., *Master and Brother, Murrays of Elibank* (1945)

O'Brien, William, *The Irish Revolution* (1923)

_____ *Recollections* (1905)

O'Donnell, F.H., *A History of the Irish Parliamentary Party* (2 vols., 1910)

Russell, Sir Charles, *Speech before the Parnell Commission* (1899)

Sheehy-Skeffington, F., *Michael Davitt* (1908)

Smith, George Barnett, *The Life and Speeches of the Rt. Hon. John Bright* (2 vols., 1881)

————— *The Life of the Rt. Hon. William Ewart Gladstone* (2 vols., 1879, 6 vols., 1880-2)

Spender, J. A. and Asquith, Cyril, *The Life of Herbert Henry Asquith* (1932)

Temple, Sir Richard, *Letters and Character Sketches from the House of Commons,* ed. Sir Richard Carnac Temple (1912)

Thorold, A. L., *The Life of Henry Labouchere* (1913)

2. **Later Works**

Altholz, J. L., 'The Political Behaviour of the Engish Catholics, 1850-1867', *Journal of British Studies,* 3 (1964), 89-103

Arnstein, W. L., *The Bradlaugh Case* (Oxford, 1965)

Banks, Margaret, *Edward Blake, Irish Nationalist* (Toronto, 1957)

Birkenhead, Earl of, *'F. E.', The Life of F. E. Smith, First Earl of Birkenhead* (1933, rev. ed., 1959)

Blake, Robert, *Disraeli* (1966)

Blewett, N., *The Peers, the Parties, and the People, The General Elections of 1910* (1972)

Boyce, D. G., *Englishmen and Irish Troubles, British Public Opinion and the Making of Irish Policy* (1972)

Camp, William, *The Glittering Prizes, A Study of the First Earl of Birkenhead* (1960)

Churchill, R. S., *Lord Derby, King of Lancashire* (1959)

Churchill, R. S. and Martin Gilbert, *Winston S. Churchill* (3 vols., 1966-71 continuing) and *Companion Volumes* (1967-73)

Clarke, P. F., 'Electoral Sociology of Modern Britain', *History,* 57 (1972), 31-55

————— *Lancashire and the New Liberalism* (Cambridge, 1971)

Clarkson, J. D., *Labour and Nationalism in Ireland* (1925)

Coffey, Thomas, P., *Agony at Easter, the 1916 Irish Uprising* (1970)

Cooke, A. B. and Vincent, J. R., *The Governing Passion, Cabinet Government and Party Politics in Britain, 1885-86* (Brighton, 1974)

Cunningham, Hugh, 'Jingoism in 1877-78', *Victorian Studies,* 14, no. 4 (1971), 429-53

Curtis, L. P., *Coercion and Conciliation in Ireland, 1880-1892* (Princeton and Oxford, 1963)

Foster, R. F., *Charles Stewart Parnell, the Man and his Family* (Brighton, 1976)

Glasier, J. F., 'Parnell's Fall and the Non conformist Conscience', *Irish Historical Studies,* 12 (1960-1), 119-38

Greaves, Desmond C., *The Life and Times of James Connolly* (1962)

Hamer, D.A., *John Morley, Liberal Intellectual in Politics* (Oxford, 1968)
_____ *Liberal Politics in the Age of Gladstone and Rosebery, a Study in Leadership and Policy* (Oxford, 1972)
Hammond, J.L., *Gladstone and the Irish Nation* (1938)
Hanham, H.J., *Elections and Party Management, Politics in the Time of Disraeli and Gladstone* (1959)
Hind, R.J., *Henry Labouchere and the Empire, 1880-1905* (1972)
Howard, C.H.D., 'The Parnell Manifesto of 21 November and the Schools Question', *English Historical Review*, 62 (Jan. 1947), 42-51
Hughes, Emrys, *Keir Hardie* (1964)
Hurst, Michael, *Joseph Chamberlain and Liberal Reunion* (1967)
Hyde, H. Montgomery, *Carson* (1953)
James, R.R., *Lord Randolph Churchill* (1959)
Jenkins, R., *Asquith* (1964)
Jones, Andrew, *The Politics of Reform, 1884* (Cambridge, 1972)
Joyce, Patrick, *Work, Society and Politics; The Culture of the Factory in Later Victorian England* (Brighton, 1980)
Koss, S.E., *Sir John Brunner, Radical Plutocrat, 1842-1919* (Cambridge, 1970)
Lloyd, Trevor, *The General Election of 1880* (Oxford, 1968)
Lyons, F.S.L., *Charles Stewart Parnell* (1977)
_____ *The Fall of Parnell, 1890-91* (1960)
_____ *The Irish Parliamentary Party, 1891-1910* (1951)
_____ *John Dillon, a Biography* (1968)
_____ *Ireland Since the Famine* (1971)
McCready, H.W., 'Home Rule and the Liberal Party, 1899-1906', *Irish Historical Studies*, 13 (1962-3), 316-48
McCaffrey, Lawrence J., *Irish Federalism in the 1870s, a Study in Conservative Nationalism*, Amer.Phil.Soc.Trans., new ser. lii (Philadelphia, 1962)
Maccoby, S., *English Radicalism, vol. iv, 1884-1914* (1953)
_____ *English Radicalism, vol. v, The End?* (1961)
Macintyre, Angus, *'The Liberator', Daniel O'Connell and the Irish Party* (1965)
McDowell, R.B., *The Irish Administration 1890-1910* (1964)
_____ *The Irish Convention 1917-18* (1970)
Mansergh, N., *The Irish Question 1840-1921* (1965)
Martin, F.X., 'Eoin MacNeill on the 1916 Rising; Select Documents xx', *Irish Historical Studies*, 12 (Mar. 1961), 226-71
Mendelssohn, Peter de, *The Age of Churchill, Heritage and Adventure 1874-1911* (1961)
Moody, T.W., 'Michael Davitt and the British Labour Movement

1882-1906', *Transactions of the Royal Historical Society*, 5th ser. 3, 1953, 53-76

———— 'Parnell and the Galway Election of 1886', *Irish Historical Studies*, 9 (1954-5), 319-28

Mowat, C.L., *Britain between the Wars, 1918-1940* (1953)

Norman, E.R., *The Catholic Church and Ireland in the Age of Rebellion 1859-1873* (1965)

O'Brien, C.C., *Parnell and his Party, 1880-1890* (Oxford, 1957, rev.ed., 1964)

———— (ed), *The Shaping of modern Ireland* (1960)

O'Brien, J.V., *William O'Brien and the Course of Irish Politics 1881-1918* (Berkeley, Cal., 1976)

Ó Broin, Leon, *The Chief Secretary, Augustine Birrell in Ireland* (1969)

———— *The Prime Informer, a Suppressed Scandal* (1971)

O'Day, Alan, *The English Face of Irish Nationalism, Parnellite Involvement in British Politics 1880-86* (Dublin, 1977)

O'Farrell, Patrick, *Ireland's English Question, Anglo-Irish Relations 1534-1970* (New York, 1971)

———— *England and Ireland Since 1800* (Oxford, 1975)

O'Leary, Cornelius, *The Elimination of Corrupt Practices in British Elections, 1868-1911* (Oxford, 1962)

Owen, Frank, *Tempestuous Journey* (1954), biography of Lloyd George

Pakenham, F., *Peace by Ordeal, the Negotiation of the Anglo-Irish Treaty of 1921* (1935)

Pelling, Henry, *The Origins of the Labour Party* (1954)

———— *Social Geography of British Elections, 1885-1910* (1967)

Reynolds, J.A., *The Catholic Emancipation Crisis in Ireland* (New Haven, Conn., 1954)

Russell, A.K., *Liberal Landslide, the General Election of 1906* (1973)

Shannon, R.T., *Gladstone and the Bulgarian Agitation, 1876* (1963)

Stewart A.T.Q., *The Ulster Crisis* (Glasgow, 1967)

Strauss, E., *Irish Nationalism and British Democracy* (1951)

Thompson, Paul, *Socialists, Liberals and Labour, the Struggle for London, 1885-1914* (1963)

Thornley, D., 'The Irish Home Rule Party and Parliamentary Obstruction, 1847-1887', *Irish Historical Studies*, 12 (1960-1), 38-57

———— *Isaac Butt and Home Rule* (1964)

Vincent, J.R., *The Formation of the British Liberal Party 1857-68* (1966)

_____ *Pollbooks, How Victorians Voted* (Cambridge, 1967)

Walker, B., 'The Irish Electorate, 1868-1915', *Irish Historical Studies,* 18 (1973), 359-406

Ward, Alan, *Ireland and Anglo-American Relations* (1969)

Whitford, F.J., 'Joseph Devlin; Ulsterman and Irishman', M.A. thesis, University of London, 1959

Whyte, J.H., *The Independent Irish Party 1850-9* (Oxford, 1958)

_____ 'The Influence of the the Catholic Clergy on Elections in Nineteenth Century Ireland', *English Historical Review,* 75 (1960) 239-59

Wollaston, E.P.M., 'The Irish Nationalist Movement in Great Britain 1886-1918', M.A. thesis, University of London, 1958

F. Journalism, Letters, and Sociological Works

1. Contemporary Works and narrative histories

Older histories of journalism tend to be anecdotal and obsessed with personality. They are often so derivative as to be almost indistinguishable.

Andrews, Sir Linton, *Problems of an Editor* (1962)

Arnold, Matthew, 'Up to Easter', *Nineteenth Century,* 123, May (1877), 638-9

Blumenfeld, R.D., *The Press in my Time* (1933)

Burnham, Lord, *Peterborough Court* (1955)

Chisholm, H., 'Newspapers in Great Britain', *Encyclopaedia Britannica, xi ed., 1910-11*

Cook, Sir Edward, *Delane of 'The Times'* (1915)

Dilnot, G., *Romance of the Amalgamated Press* (1925)

Dilnot, F., *The Adventures of a Newspaperman* (1913)

Escott, T.H.S., *Masters of English Journalism* (1911)

Fox-Bourne, H.R., *English Newspapers* (2 vols., 1887)

Fyfe, Hamilton, *Sixty Years of Fleet Street* (1949)

Gibbs, Philip, *Adventures in Journalism* (1923)

_____ *The Journalist's London* (1952)

Greenwood, Frederick, 'Birth and Infancy of the 'Pall Mall Gazette', *Pall Mall Gazette,* 14 Apr. 1867

Hammond, J.L., *C.P. Scott* (1934)

Hatton, J., *Journalistic London* (1882)

Herd, H., *The Making of Modern Journalism* (1927)

_____ *The March of Journalism* (1952)

Hudson, Derek, *British Journalists and Newspapers* (1945)

Irvine, St. John, *Bernard Shaw, his Life, Work, and Friends* (1956)

Jones, Kennedy, *Fleet Street and Downing Street 1850-1880* (1920)

Mackenzie, F.A., *The Mystery of the 'Daily Mail' 1896-1921* (1921)

Massingham, H.W., *The London Daily Press* (1892)

Morrison, Stanley, *The English Newspaper* (Cambridge, 1932)

Northcliffe, Lord, *The Rise of the 'Daily Mail'* (1916)

Peabody, C., *English Journalism and the Men who Made it* (1882)

Pendleton, J., *Newspaper Reporting in Olden Time and Today* (1890)

Pope, Wilson, *The Story of the 'Star'* (1938)

Raymond, E.T., *Portraits of the Nineties* (1921)

Robertson-Scott, J.W., *The Life and Death of a Newspaper* (1932)

———— *"We" and Me* (London, 1956)

Shaw, G.B., *London Music in 1888-9* (1937)

———— *Sixteen Self Sketches* (1949)

Simonis, H., *The Street of Ink* (1917)

Spender, J.A., *Life, Journalism and Politics* (2 vols., 1927)

Stannard, Russell, *With the Dictators of Fleet Street* (1934)

Stead, H.W., *Through Thirty Years, 1892-1922* (1924)

Stead, W.T., 'The Future of Journalism', *Contemporary Review*, 50, Nov. 1886, 663-79

———— 'Government by Journalism', *Contemporary Review*, 49, May 1886, 53-74

———— *A Journalist in London* (1891)

Sullivan, Mark, *The Education of an American* (New York, 1938)

Straus, R., *Sala; Portrait of an Eminent Victorian* (1942)

White, William, *The Inner Life of the House of Commons* (1897, reprint ed., E.J. Feuchtwanger, 1973)

Whyte, F., *The Life of W.T. Stead* (1925)

2. Later works

Baylen, J.O., 'The New Journalism in Late Victorian Britain', *Australian Journal of Politics and History*, 18 (1972), 367-85

Brown, Malcolm, *The Politics of Irish Literature from Thomas Davis to W.B. Yeats* (1972)

Costello, Peter, *The Heart Grown Brutal, the Irish Revolution in Literature, from Parnell to the Death of Yeats* (Dublin, 1977)

Dwyer, J.J., 'The Catholic Press, 1850-1950' in G.A. Beck, (ed.), *The English Catholics 1850-1950* (1950), pp. 475-512

Ellmann, Richard, *James Joyce* (Oxford, 1966)

Fussell, Paul, *The Great War and Modern Memory* (Oxford, 1975)

Gollin, M.A., *'The Observer' and J.L. Garvin* (1960)

Green, Martin, *Children of the Sun, a Narrative of 'Decadence' in England After 1918* (1977)

Gross, John, *The Rise and Fall of the Man of Letters, English Literary Life Since 1800* (1969)

Hambro, C.J., *Newspaper Lords in British Politics* (1958)

Havighurst, A.F., *Radical Journalist; H.W. Massingham 1860-1924* (Cambridge, 1974)

History of 'The Times', vol. iii, 1884-1912 (1947), vol. iv, part i, 1912-1920 (1952)

Hudson, Derek, 'Reading' in Simon Nowell-Smith (ed.), *Edwardian England* (1964), pp. 303-26

Inglis, Brian, 'Moran of the *Leader* and Ryan of the *Irish Peasant*' in C.C. O'Brien (ed.), *The Shaping of Modern Ireland* (1960), pp. 108-23

Kenner, Hugh, *The Stoic Comedians, Flaubert, Joyce, and Beckett* (1964)

Koss, S.E., *Fleet Street Radical; A.G. Gardiner and the 'Daily News'* (1973)

Lancaster, M.J., *Brian Howard, Portrait of a Failure* (1968)

Laurence, Dan H., *The Unrepentant Pilgrim, a Study in the Development of Bernard Shaw* (1966)

Lee, A.J., *The Origins of the Popular Press 1855-1914* (1976)

O'Brien, C.C., 'Passion and Cunning, an Essay on the Politics of W.B. Yeats' in N. Jeffares and K.G.W. Cross (eds.), *'In Excited Reverie', a Centenary Tribute to W.B. Yeats, 1865-1939* (1965)

Orth, S.P., *The Boss and the Machine* (New Haven, Conn., 1919)

Ostrogorski, M.I., *Democracy and the Organization of Political Parties* (2 vols., trans., F. Clarke, 1902)

Pound, R. and G. Harmsworth, *Northcliffe* (1959)

Sennett, Richard, *The Fall of Public Man* (Cambridge, 1977)

Thompson, W.I., *The Imagination of an Insurrection, Dublin Easter 1916* (Oxford, 1966)

Watson, George, *The English Ideology, Studies in the Language of Victorian Politics* (1973)

Williams, Raymond, *The Long Revolution* (1961)

Yeats, W.B., *Memoirs* ed. D. Donoghue (1972)

G. Migrant and Liverpool History

The history of British cities and their politics has been neglected until relatively recently. Liverpool provides an interesting case study (though not always a typical one) because of the mobility of its population. Irish politics in the city make the story more unusual but the study of Irish migration to Britain has been more remarkable for mechanistic theories on migration and politics and it is occasionally difficult not to avoid the conclusion that the availability of detailed records has itself created the emphasis on this migration. All the following have been used in this study but sometimes as a yardstick against which to measure the particularities of O'Connor's life and the lives of his constituents.

Beck, G.A. (ed.), *The English Catholics 1850-1950* (1950)

Birrell, Augustine, *Some Early Recollections of Liverpool* (Liverpool, 1924)

Bower, F., *Rolling Stonemason* (1936)

Brady, E.M., *Ireland's Secret Service in England* (Dublin, 1928)

Burke, T., *A Catholic History of Liverpool* (1910)

Coleman, T., *The Railway Navvies* (1968)

Curtis, L.P., *Anglo-Saxons and Celts, a Study of Anti-Irish Prejudices in Victorian England* (Bridgeport, Conn., 1958)

———— *Apes and Angels, the Irishman in Victorian Caricature* (Newton Abbot, 1971)

Denvir, John, *The Irish in Great Britain from the Earliest Times to the Fall and Death of Parnell* (1892)

———— *The Life Story of an Old Rebel* (Dublin, 1910)

Fox, R.M., *Jim Larkin, the Rise of the Underdog* (1965)

Forde, Frank, 'The Liverpool Irish Volunteers', *Irish Sword*, 10, 39 (1971), 106-31

Forwood, A.B., 'Democratic Toryism', *Contemporary Review*, 43, 1883, 294-304

Forwood, Sir William, *Recollections of a Busy Life* (1910)

Foster, John, *Class Struggle and the Industrial Revolution, Early Industrial Capitalism in Three English Towns* (1974)

Fraser, Derek, *Urban Politics in Victorian England, the Structure of Politics in Victorian Cities* (Leicester, 1976)

Gilley, Sheridan, 'English Attitudes to the Irish in England, 1780-1900' in Colin Holmes (ed.), *Immigrants and Minorities in British Society* (1978)

Hamling, W., *A Short History of Liverpool Trades Council 1848-1948* (Liverpool, 1948)

Handley, J.E., *The Irish in Modern Scotland* (Cork, 1947)

Handlin, Oscar, *Boston's Immigrants 1790-1865* (Harvard, 1941)

Hansen, M.L., *Atlantic Migration* (Cambridge, 1940)

Hikins, H.R., 'The Liverpool General Transport Strike, 1911', *Transactions of the Historic Society of Lancashire and Cheshire*, 113, 1961, 169-95

Inglis, K.S., *Churches and the Working Classes in Victorian England* (1963)

Jackson, J.A., *The Irish in Britain* (1963)

Joyce, Patrick, 'The Factory Politics of Lancashire in the Later Nineteenth Century', *Historical Journal*, 18 (1975), 525-53

Kennedy, Robert E., *The Irish, Emigration, Marriage, and Fertility* (Berkeley, Cal., 1973)

Kerr, Barbara M., 'Irish Seasonal Migration to Great Britain, 1800-38', *Irish Historical Studies*, 3 (1942-3), 365-80

Larkin, E., *James Larkin, Irish Labour Leader 1876-1947* (1965)

Lawton, R., 'Irish Immigration to England and Wales in the Mid Nineteenth Century', *Irish Geography*, 4, (1959), 35-54

_____ 'The Population of Liverpool in the Mid Nineteenth Century', *Transactions of the Historic Society of Lancashire and Cheshire*, 108, 1955, 89-120

_____ and Pooley, C.G., 'The Social Geography of Merseyside in the Late Nineteenth Century', final report to S.S.R.C., July 1976

Lebow, R.N., *White Britain and Black Ireland, the Influence of Stereotypes on Colonial Policy* (Philadelphia, Penn., 1976)

Lees, Lynn Hollen, *Exiles of Erin, Irish Migrants in Victorian London* (Manchester, 1979)

Lowe, W.J., 'The Irish in Lancashire, 1846-71; a Social History', Ph.D. thesis, University of Dublin, Trinity College, 1974

_____ 'Lancashire Fenianism, 1864-71', *Transactions of the Historic Society of Lancashire and Cheshire*, 128 (1976), 156-85

Menzies, E.M., 'The Freeman Voter in Liverpool, 1802-1835', *Transactions of the Historic Society of Lancashire and Cheshire*, 124 (1973), 85-107

Midwinter, Eric, *Old Liverpool* (1971)

Muir, Ramsay, *A History of Liverpool* (1907)

Murphy, J.R., *The Religious Problem in English Education, the Crucial Experiment* (Liverpool, 1959)

Norman, E.R., *Anti-Catholicism in Victorian England* (1968)

O'Connell, Bernard, 'Irish Nationalism in Liverpool, 1873-1923', *Eire-Ireland*, 11, (1975), 24-37. Unfortunately, this journal did not print notes on sources at this juncture.

O'Connor, Kevin, *The Irish in Britain* (1972)

O'Farrell, Patrick, 'Emigrant Attitudes and Behaviour as a Source for Irish History', *Historical Studies, X, Papers Read Before the Eleventh Conference of Irish Historians*, May 1973, ed. G.A. Hayes McCoy, pp. 109-131

O'Mara, P., *The Autobiography of a Liverpool Irish Slummy* (1934, reprinted Bath, 1967)

Rathbone, Eleanor, *William Rathbone, a Memoir* (1905)

Redford, A., *Labour Migration in England 1800-1850* (Manchester,

1926, rev. ed., 1976)

Roberts, David, A., 'Religion and Politics in Liverpool Since 1900', M.Sc. thesis, University of London, 1965

Rossi, John Patrick, 'Home Rule and the Liverpool By-Election of 1880', *Irish Historical Studies*, 19 (1974), 156-69

Salvidge, S., *Salvidge of Liverpool, Behind the Political Scene 1890-1928* (1934)

Sellers, I., 'Non-Conformist Attitudes in Late Nineteenth Century Liverpool', *Transactions of the Historic Society of Lancashire and Cheshire*, 114 (1962), 215-239

Sexton, J., *Sir James Sexton; Agitator* (1934)

Simey, Margaret B., *Charitable Effort in Liverpool in the Nineteenth Century* (Liverpool, 1951)

Smith, Samuel, *My Life Work* (1903)

Smith, W., (ed.), *A Scientific Survey of Merseyside* (Liverpool, 1953)

Steele, E.D., 'The Irish Presence in the North of England, 1850-1914', *Northern History*, 12 (1976), 220-41

Taplin, E.L., *Liverpool Dockers and Seamen 1870-1890* (Hull, 1974)

Thompson, E.P., *The Making of the English Working Class* (1968)

Walker, W.M., 'Irish Immigrants in Scotland; their Priests, Politics and Parochial Life', *Historical Journal*, 15, (1972), 649-67

Walmsley, H.M., *The Life of Sir Joshua Walmsley* (1879)

Watkinson, C.D., 'The Liberal Party on Merseyside in the Nineteenth Century', Ph.D. thesis, University of Liverpool, 1968

White, B.D., *A History of the Corporation of Liverpool 1835-1914* (Liverpool, 1951)

Whittingham-Jones, Barbara, *Liverpool Politics; Pamphlet Collection* (Manchester, 1936)

INDEX

List of volumes in this series

Copies obtainable on order from
Swift Printers Ltd, 1-7 Albion Place, Britton Street, London EC1M 5RE